Svein Vigeland Rottem is Senior Research Fellow at the Fridtjof Nansen Institute, one of the world's leading Arctic research bodies. He received his PhD in Arctic Political Science from the Arctic University at Tromsø, Norway.

Ida Folkestad Soltvedt is a former Research Fellow at the Fridtjof Nansen Institute, focusing on Arctic affairs. She holds an MA in Political Science from the University of Oslo, Norway.

Geir Hønneland is former Director at the Fridtjof Nansen Institute and Professor of Political Science at Nord University in Bodø. He has published widely on territory disputes and environmental factors in the Polar North. He gained his PhD from the University of Oslo in 2000 and is one of the most respected commentators in the field of Arctic Studies.

ARCTIC GOVERNANCE

VOLUME III

Norway, Russia and Asia

EDITED BY
SVEIN VIGELAND ROTTEM
AND
IDA FOLKESTAD SOLTVEDT

SERIES EDITOR
GEIR HØNNELAND

I.B.TAURIS
LONDON • NEW YORK • OXFORD • NEW DELHI • SYDNEY

In association with the Fridtjof Nansen Institute

I.B. TAURIS
Bloomsbury Publishing Plc
50 Bedford Square, London, WC1B 3DP, UK
1385 Broadway, New York, NY 10018, USA
29 Earlsfort Terrace, Dublin 2, Ireland

First published in Great Britain 2020
This paperback edition published in 2021

Cover design: Liron Gilenberg

A catalogue record for this book is available from the British Library.

A catalogue record for this book is available from the Library of Congress.

ISBN: HB: 978-1-7845-3964-1
PB: 978-0-7556-3651-8
ePDF: 978-1-8386-0011-2
eBook: 978-1-8386-0010-5

Series: Arctic Governance

Typeset by Integra Software Services Pvt. Ltd.

CONTENTS

LIST OF ILLUSTRATIONS

Figures

Tables

LIST OF CONTRIBUTORS

Han Cheng is a PhD candidate in geography at the University of Cambridge. He is interested in the changing world of politics with a particular focus on the so-called rising powers. His current research project at Cambridge addresses the growing emergence of diverse global development ideas, actors and practices. Prior to this, he worked for four years on international policy for sustainable development with leading think tanks in the US, China, India and South Africa. He studied area studies and geography in Beijing and Cambridge, and has been a visiting fellow at the MacMillan Center for International and Area Studies at Yale University.

Daniel Buikema Fjærtoft is an energy sector economist with extensive experience of working in Russia, the FSU and the High North/Barents Region in particular. He has worked extensively on the petroleum and power sector of Norway and Russia as well as other FSU countries, and specializes in stakeholder consultation, coordination and collaboration.

Gørild Heggelund, PhD, is a senior research fellow at the Fridtjof Nansen Institute (FNI) and until recently was FNI China representative (2014–17). She has carried out research on China's environmental, energy and climate change policy for three decades, including the Arctic. Current research concerns China's efforts to implement the Minamata Convention on mercury; China's potential leadership role on energy and climate post-Paris; China's development of ETS as a GHG mitigating policy tool; and the role of cities in addressing climate change.

Leif Christian Jensen was a senior research fellow at the Fridtjof Nansen Institute until 2018. He gained his PhD from the University of Tromsø in 2013. Jensen has published widely on the geopolitics of the Arctic in international peer-reviewed journals and academic books, in both English and Norwegian.

Øystein Jensen is a senior research fellow at the Fridtjof Nansen Institute. He obtained his PhD in international law from the University of Oslo in 2013. Jensen has published several articles on law of the sea issues in the Arctic Ocean, and on the Commission on the Limits of the Continental Shelf.

Arild Moe is Research Professor at the Fridtjof Nansen Institute. His degree is from the University of Oslo where he studied political science, Russian language and public law. Most of his research has been devoted to Russia, especially the energy sector and energy politics. Moe has also been involved in analyses of broader Arctic policy issues and has recently published several articles on Arctic shipping.

Indra Øverland is Research Professor at the Norwegian Institute of International Affairs (NUPI). He currently heads NUPI's Energy Programme, and is also Professor at Nord University. Øverland did his PhD at the University of Cambridge and has since worked extensively on the post-Soviet energy sector, including oil, gas and renewables.

Iselin Stensdal is a research fellow at the Fridtjof Nansen Institute and a PhD candidate at the Department of Culture Studies and Oriental Languages, University of Oslo. In her research, she has covered extractive industries in the Arctic and Asian countries' Arctic research. Other fields of expertise include China's climate and energy policies.

Olav Schram Stokke is Professor at the Department of Political Science, University of Oslo, and Research Professor at the Fridtjof Nansen Institute, where he also served as research director for many years. Stokke is a leading scholar in Arctic affairs, and has published extensively on topics such as international relations, institutional analysis, resource and environmental management, and regional cooperation.

INTRODUCTION

Prompted by a changing climate, the Arctic has once again found its way onto the international agenda. Higher temperatures and diminishing ice cover are changing the perameters for stakeholders with interests in the region. Commercial activity is increasing and all the Arctic states want to have a say in determining the contours of the 'new' Arctic. An increasing number of non-Arctic states have aspirations in the region too, with agendas ranging from scientific research to geopolitics. What everyone acknowledges is that something is happening in the Arctic that requires constant vigilance. The Arctic is popular.

One important insight, however, is that there is no single Arctic. Despite many similarities, the differences are at least as numerous. Climate, geography and economic factors differ widely between the Arctic regions. Greenland's weak infrastructure, and the extensive but inaccessible ice-infested waters in northern Canada and the much more accessible Barents Sea, coupled with an array of commercial actors, all affect what states perceive as important when it comes to safeguarding their national interests in the region. States have different agendas and different ambitions along with different identity-related and cultural ties to the Arctic. Nevertheless, states are the most important stakeholders in the region. Researchers at the Fridtjof Nansen Institute (FNI) have devoted much of their time and resources to the study of the respective Arctic policies of Russia and Norway. Lately, however, the interests and activities of Asian states in the region have attracted analytical attention as well.

These factors taken together provide the starting point for the third volume in the series 'Arctic Governance'. As in the preceding books, we have assembled key studies from FNI researchers on Arctic issues. This is the last book in the series and has been given the title: *Arctic Governance: Norway, Russia and Asian States*. As its title indicates, it is divided into three parts: i) Norway; ii) Russia; and iii) Asian states. Each part consists of four chapters.

FNI is a research institute dedicated to the study of Norwegian foreign policy and international law. Its headquarters are located in what was once the home of polar explorer and Nobel Peace Prize laureate Fridtjof Nansen (1861–1930). Research on international law and political cooperation in the Arctic has deep roots at the FNI, where the emphasis is on the environment, energy, fisheries, marine transport, health, security and jurisdictional matters. In each of the last four years, the Norwegian Research Council has awarded the institute top place in the field of academic publishing in competition with all the other Norwegian research institutes, across all academic disciplines. Furthermore, FNI's position as a world-leading research institute was affirmed in the summer of 2017, 2018 and 2019 when it received the 'Best European Think Tank' award from *Prospect Magazine* for accomplishments in the fields of energy and the environment. Nomination criteria included a 'coherent selection of topics of importance, innovative and plausible policy prescription, rigour of analysis, influence on politics, influence on media and wider impact and convening power'.

The Arctic Governance series brings together contributions by FNI researchers to the debate on 'the New Arctic'. A distinguishing feature of the series is that it showcases research by a closely integrated group of people studying the same geographical area, albeit with different thematic fields of specialization and from different theoretical angles. In recent years, researchers at FNI have published several books, journal articles, book chapters and reports on: the political and legal architecture of the Arctic; the politics of energy, marine living resources and shipping in the region; and Arctic policies of different states, especially Norway, Russia and Asian states. As in the two first books in this series, contributions from FNI researchers to the debate on the future of the Arctic are gathered together in one place. The different chapters in the book series build on previously published research in academic journals, reports, and chapters in edited volumes and books. All of the contributions have been revised to fit the format of the new series. Some of the more 'classical' contributions have only been slightly updated and revised, while others have gone through extensive revisions and updates. The extent of these revisions is explained in every chapter. A key point is to showcase the breadth of FNI's contributions to the academic debate on the new Arctic, ranging from general surveys to detailed explorations of specific issues focusing on state activity (or lack of such activity) in the Arctic.

The first chapter in the first section is written by Professor Geir Hønneland, Director of FNI, and former senior research fellow at FNI, Leif Christian Jensen. They are both experts on Norwegian High North politics, and discuss the evolution of contemporary Norwegian High North policies, with particular emphasis on the first decade of the twenty-first century. What was it, they ask, that managed to transform the mounting sense of fatigue surrounding Norway's institutional collaboration with Russia in the early 2000s into an excess of euphoria towards the end of the decade?

The next chapter is also written by Jensen but this time in collaboration with senior research fellow Svein Vigeland Rottem. They set out to compare Norwegian Arctic and Antarctic strategies and policies. Although the laws regulating activity and resources in the Antarctic and Arctic differ in many ways, there is considerable overlap when it comes to national and scientific strategies, actors and networks. These differences and similarities have not been studied or properly understood from a comparative perspective before. This chapter represents a first attempt to fill this gap and a call to other political and social scientists to undertake similar research.

Ida Folkestad Soltvedt, a former research fellow at FNI, focuses her work on Arctic affairs and the science-policy interface. In Chapter 3 she analyzes Norwegian implementation of six Arctic Council recommendations. She discusses the criticism levelled at the Arctic Council regarding its lack of legal status and, consequently, low levels of implementation by member states. She asks: does the work of the Arctic Council make any difference?

Chapter 4 pursues this theme further. Rottem, who is an expert on the Arctic Council, explores the ways in which scientific knowledge on Persistent Organic Pollutants (POPs) in the Arctic has informed the design of international regulations, and how it can be used today. More specifically, he looks at Norway's nominations over the past decade of new POPs to the Stockholm Convention, nominations that need a scientific knowledge base, and where scientific knowledge of the Arctic and the work of the Arctic Council working groups have been a prerequisite for action.

The second section's empirical focus is on Russia. In the first chapter, Chapter 5, Hønneland first notes the upsurge in interest in the study of identity within international relations (IR) since the end of the Cold War, when it became untenable to view identity as a unitary, fixed and given substrate derived from an individual's nationality. In analysing the Russian Arctic discourse, he describes the Russian debate about the Arctic as consisting of at least two major metanarratives: 'Russia vs. the West', and 'Russia and the Arctic'.

Chapter 6 seeks to explain why the Barents Sea delimitation dispute between Norway and Russia reached a resolution in 2010, and not before. It is written by three researchers: Arild Moe, Research Professor at FNI, and a leading expert on Arctic energy, shipping and Russia for more than three decades; Daniel Buikema Fjærtoft an energy sector economist with extensive experience of working in Russia; and Indra Øverland, head of the Energy Programme at the Norwegian Institute of International Affairs (NUPI), and Professor at Nord University. Any explanation of the timing of the 2010 agreement resolving the marine delimitation dispute between Norway and Russia in the Barents Sea needs to be sought, they contend, mainly on the Russian side of the fence. Russia's willingness to offer concessions to resolve the spatial disagreements between the two countries at this specific juncture was not, as is sometimes assumed, driven by a thirst to get its hands on the energy resources in the formerly disputed area, but instead by broader Russian foreign policy considerations.

Chapter 7, written by Hønneland, approaches the delimitation agreement from a different angle. In this chapter, Hønneland analyzes the public debate in Russia on the merits of the delimitation agreement. The Russian government's defence of its agreement with Norway portrays it as a necessary step to secure Norwegian support in 'the global fight against Canada in the Arctic'. Critics claim, however, that Norway will use the agreement to further bolster its efforts to get the Russians thrown out of the Barents Sea altogether.

In Chapter 8, senior research fellow Øystein Jensen, an international lawyer at FNI specializing in the legal organization of the Arctic and especially the delimitation of the Arctic continental shelf, analyzes Russia's revised Arctic seabed submission to the International Seabed Authority. Focusing on procedural and substantive legal issues, including how seafloor highs are legally classified and how Russia used referenced 'sector lines' to determine the outer limits of its shelf, the chapter identifies the key aspects of the Partial Revised Submission of the Russian Federation with respect to continental shelf areas beyond 200 nautical miles in the Arctic Ocean.

In the final section of this book we take a closer look at the role of Asian states in general, and China in particular, in Arctic affairs. The first chapter, Chapter 9, is written by Olav Schram Stokke, Professor at the Department of Political Science, University of Oslo, and Research Professor at FNI. Stokke has been widely recognized for nearly three decades as one of the leading scholars on Arctic affairs. Building on stakeholder management theory, he examines the salience of Asian stakes in three key areas of Arctic governance: management and use of natural resources; shipping; and environmental protection. The Asian states that are now permanent observers on the Arctic Council have significant stakes in Arctic governance, even though, as Stokke argues, their salience varies considerably across the respective fields.

This relatively broad introduction is followed by two chapters by research fellow Iselin Stensdal. Stensdal's research mainly concerns China. Specifically, she works on two subject areas: Chinese interests in the Arctic; and Chinese climate, energy and environmental politics. In her first chapter, Chapter 10, she explores ten years of Asian involvement in Arctic research, from 2004 to 2013. The Asian countries have consolidated their Arctic-research efforts, with their publication output, funding and infrastructure showing a marked increase since 2008. As to the relationship between research and policy, however, Stensdal finds little evidence of Asian governments seeking to gain political influence through their Arctic research.

In Stensdal's second chapter, Chapter 11, she notes how several authors have failed to properly distinguish between Chinese private and state companies, or between Chinese companies and the Chinese government. There is a need to look for evidence and facts in order to understand the new Arctic actors. She takes the Isua iron-ore project as an example. Within a few years it went from generating glaring headlines to no activity at all. What happened exactly? To what extent was there any Chinese involvement in the Isua project?

The final chapter, Chapter 12, is written by FNI senior research fellow Gørild Heggelund, an expert on China's energy, environment and climate change policies, and Han Cheng, a PhD candidate in geography at the University of Cambridge where he focuses on the so-called rising powers. The chapter discusses whether and to what extent there is an Arctic dimension in Chinese climate policy, and whether there are links between China's engagement in the Arctic and its domestic climate policies. Although there is no direct connection to domestic climate policy, the chapter concludes that an Arctic dimension does exist, and in several areas. The chapter also gives a short introduction to China's first Arctic white paper from December 2017.

We would once again like to take this opportunity to thank all of the contributors to this book series. Their commitment and engagement throughout the project show why FNI is a world-leading Arctic-research institute. Thanks also to Tomasz Hoskins at I.B. Tauris for excellent cooperation during the project.

Svein Vigeland Rottem
Ida Folkestad Soltvedt
Lysaker, May 2019

PART I

NORWAY

CHAPTER 1

NORWAY'S APPROACH TO THE ARCTIC: POLICIES AND DISCOURSE

Geir Hønneland and Leif Christian Jensen

Introduction

Arctic affairs are an integral part of Norway's foreign policy. The strength of this component in Norwegian foreign policy has varied over time, as has its profile and formal designation. In general, the term 'Arctic' is rarely used in Norwegian foreign policy discourse, and then only in reference to something farther off in either time (like polar explorations before the Second World War) or space (outside Norway's immediate sphere of interest, such as the North Pole area or the American Arctic). 'The North' (in Norwegian: *nord*) or 'the northern regions' (in Norwegian: *nordområdene*) have been the preferred terms for describing practical foreign politics in the European Arctic. In practice, Norway's northern foreign policy is mainly about relations with other states in the Barents Sea region (see Figure 1.1). Of particular importance are relations with Russia.

This chapter discusses the evolvement of contemporary Norwegian High North policies, with particular emphasis on the first decade of the twenty-first century. In the first part of the chapter, we argue that these policies consist of layers from different time periods, ranging from the Cold War with its East–West tensions, to the immediate post-Cold War years when new institutional

---

The first part of this chapter (policy review) builds on Geir Hønneland, 'Norway's Arctic policy', in R. W. Murray and A. D. Nuttall (eds), *International Relations and the Arctic: Understanding Policy and Governance* (Amherst, Cambria Press, 2014), pp. 235–61. The second part (discourse analysis) builds on Leif Christian Jensen and Geir Hønneland, 'Framing the High North: Public discourses in Norway after 2000', *Acta Borelia* 8/1 (2011), pp. 37–54.

partnerships were established between Norway and Russia in the High North, and the years from around 2005, characterized by functional and geographical dispersion of Norwegian High North politics. In the second part of the chapter, we analyze Norwegian public discourse on the High North. We pay special attention to how the prevailing discourses reflected (and possibly spurred) the transition from one phase to another: why did the mounting fatigue that surrounded the institutional collaboration with Russia in the early 2000s transform into a new euphoria?

Norwegian High North Policies

With the end of the Cold War, reference to 'the north' in Norwegian foreign policy discourse almost disappeared, since it smacked of Cold War tensions or even of Norway's earlier reputation as an expansionist polar nation. Norway was now building up a reputation as a 'peace nation', heavily involved in mediating peace in various southern corners of the world. This did not mean that Norwegian foreign politics in the European Arctic no longer existed – only that the main focus was now on institutional cooperation with Russia, referred to as 'strategies towards Russia', or 'neighbourhood policies'. In the mid-2000s, 'the northern regions' (*nordområdene*, with 'the High North' as the official English translation) were again explicitly defined as the number one priority of Norwegian foreign policy. Although this happened to coincide with the international buzz about a 'rush for the Arctic', it can largely be explained, as will be shown later, by internal issues in Norwegian politics, and in the country's relationship with Russia. Above all, this new northern policy has seen the disappearance of the division between foreign and internal politics. While it encompasses both traditional security politics in the European Arctic and the 'softer' institutional collaboration with Russia initiated in the 1990s, many see Norway's 'new' northern policies as mainly an instrument for further developing business and science in the country's northern regions.

The Cold War legacy: Security, jurisdiction and fisheries management

The Northern Fleet, established on the Kola Peninsula in 1933, remained the smallest of the four Soviet naval fleets until the 1950s, when a period of expansion set in. By then, the Soviet Union had entered the nuclear age: the country's first nuclear submarine was stationed on the Kola Peninsula in 1958, at Zapadnaya Litsa, close to the border with Norway. Six new naval bases for nuclear submarines were built, as well as several smaller bases for other vessels. By the late 1960s, the Northern Fleet ranked as the largest of the Soviet fleets.

In this situation, Norway chose the combined strategy of deterrence and reassurance. Deterrence was secured through NATO membership and by maintaining the Norwegian armed forces at a level deemed necessary to hold back a possible Soviet attack until assistance could arrive from other NATO countries. So that the Soviets should not misinterpret activities on the Norwegian side as aggressive, Norway placed a number of self-imposed restrictions upon itself. Notably, other NATO countries were not allowed to participate in military exercises east of the 24th parallel, which runs slightly west of the middle of Norway's northernmost county, Finnmark. The border between Norway and the Soviet Union was peaceful, but strictly guarded; there was no conflict, but there was also little interaction.

Besides regular diplomatic contact, management of the abundant fish resources of the Barents Sea was an area of particular joint interest for Norway and the Soviet Union. From the late 1960s, the two countries had informally discussed the possibilities of bilateral management measures. A window of opportunity came with the drastic changes in the law of the sea that were implemented in the mid-1970s. The principle of 200-mile exclusive economic zones (EEZs) was adopted at the third UN Conference on the Law of the Sea in 1975. The right and responsibility to manage marine resources within 200 nautical miles of shore was thus transferred to the coastal states at this time. When Soviet Minister of Fisheries Aleksandr Ishkov visited Oslo in December 1974, the two countries agreed to establish a joint fisheries management arrangement for the Barents Sea.[1] The agreement established the Joint Norwegian–Soviet (now Norwegian–Russian) Fisheries Commission, to meet at least once every year, alternately on each party's territory. When the first session took place in January 1976, the parties had agreed to jointly manage the two most important fish stocks in the area, cod and haddock, sharing the quotas 50–50. In 1978, they agreed to treat capelin as a shared stock, and split the quota 60–40 in Norway's favour.

Both Norway and the Soviet Union established their EEZs in 1977 (see Figure 1.1). However, the two states could not agree on the principle for drawing the delimitation line between their respective zones. They had been negotiating the delimitation of the Barents Sea continental shelf since the early 1970s, and the division of the EEZs was brought into these discussions. The two parties had agreed to use the 1958 Convention on the Continental Shelf as a basis. According to this convention, continental shelves may be divided between states if so agreed. If agreement is not reached, the median line from the mainland border shall normally determine the delimitation line, but special circumstances may warrant adjustments. In the Barents Sea, Norway adhered to the median-line principle, whereas the Soviet Union claimed the sector-line principle, according to which the line of delimitation would run along the longitude line from the tip of the mainland border to the North Pole. The Soviets held out for the sector-line principle, having claimed sector-line limits to Soviet Arctic waters as early as 1928. Moreover, they argued that in the Barents Sea special circumstances – notably the size of the Soviet population in the area, and the strategic significance of this region – warranted deviation from the median line.

In 1978, a temporary Grey Zone agreement was reached, to avoid unregulated fishing in the disputed area.[2] This agreement required Norway and the Soviet

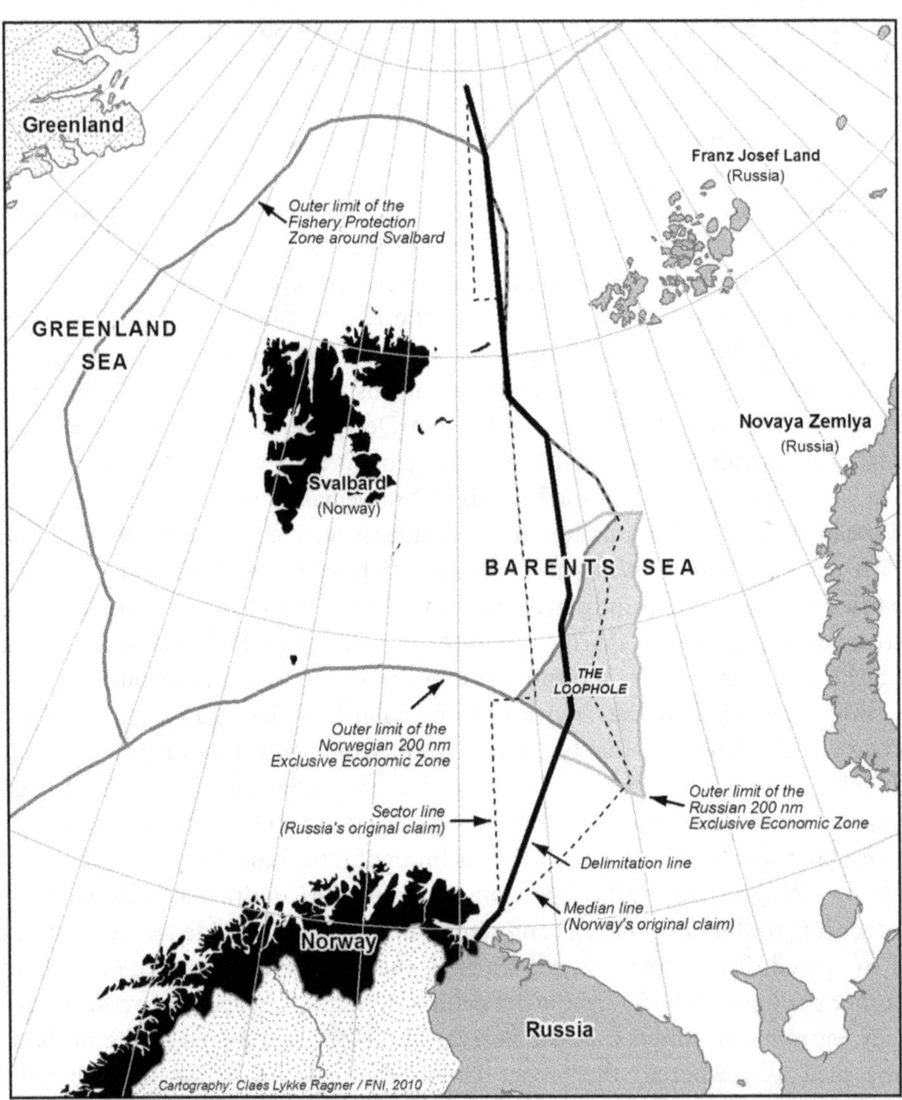

Figure 1.1 Jurisdiction of the Barents Sea.[4]

Union to regulate and control their own fishers and third-country fishers licensed by either of them, and to refrain from interfering with the activities of the other party's vessels, or vessels licensed by them. The arrangement was explicitly temporary and subject to annual renewal. The Grey Zone functioned well for the purposes of fisheries management, but the prospect of underground hydrocarbon resources in the area pressed the parties to a final delimitation agreement, which was reached in spring 2010.[3] The agreement is a compromise, with the delimitation line midway between the median line and the sector line.

Another area of contention is the Fishery Protection Zone around Svalbard. Norway claims the right to establish an EEZ around the archipelago, but has so far refrained from doing so because the other signatories to the 1920 Svalbard Treaty have signalled that they would not accept such a move.[5] The Svalbard Treaty gave Norway sovereignty over the archipelago, which had been a no man's land in the European Arctic. However, the treaty contains several limitations on Norway's right to exercise this jurisdiction. Most importantly, all signatory powers enjoy equal rights to let their citizens extract natural resources on Svalbard. Further, the archipelago is not to be used for military purposes, and there are restrictions on Norway's right to impose taxes on the residents of Svalbard. The original signatories were Denmark, France, Italy, Japan, the Netherlands, Norway, Sweden, the UK and the USA. The Soviet Union joined in 1935.

The other signatories (other than Norway) hold that the non-discriminatory code of the Svalbard Treaty must also apply to the ocean area around the archipelago,[6] whereas Norway refers to the treaty text, which deals only with the land and territorial waters of Svalbard. The waters around Svalbard are important feeding grounds for juvenile cod, and the Protection Zone, determined in 1977, represents a 'middle course' aimed at securing the young fish from unregulated fishing. However, the zone is not recognized by any of the other states that have had quotas in the area since the introduction of the EEZs. To avoid provoking other states, Norway refrained for many years from penalizing violators in the Svalbard Zone. Force was used for the first time in 1993, when Icelandic trawlers and Faroese vessels under flags of convenience – neither with a quota in the Barents Sea – started fishing there. The Norwegian Coast Guard fired warning shots at the ships, which then left the zone. The following year, an Icelandic fishing vessel was the first to be arrested for fishing in the Svalbard Zone without a quota.

Soviet/Russian vessels have been fishing in the Svalbard Zone regularly since its establishment – indeed, they represent the majority of fishing operations in the area. They do not report their catches in the area to Norwegian authorities, and Russian captains consistently refuse to sign inspection forms presented by the Norwegian Coast Guard. But they welcome Norwegian inspectors on board, and the same inspection procedures are pursued in the Svalbard Zone as in the Norwegian EEZ.

In 2009, the Commission on the Limits of the Continental Shelf approved the Norwegian submission, confirming the existence of a Norwegian shelf beyond 200 nautical miles in three places: the Western Nansen Basin north of Svalbard, in parts of the 'Loophole' in the east, and the 'Banana Hole' in the south-west (see Figure 1.2).[7]

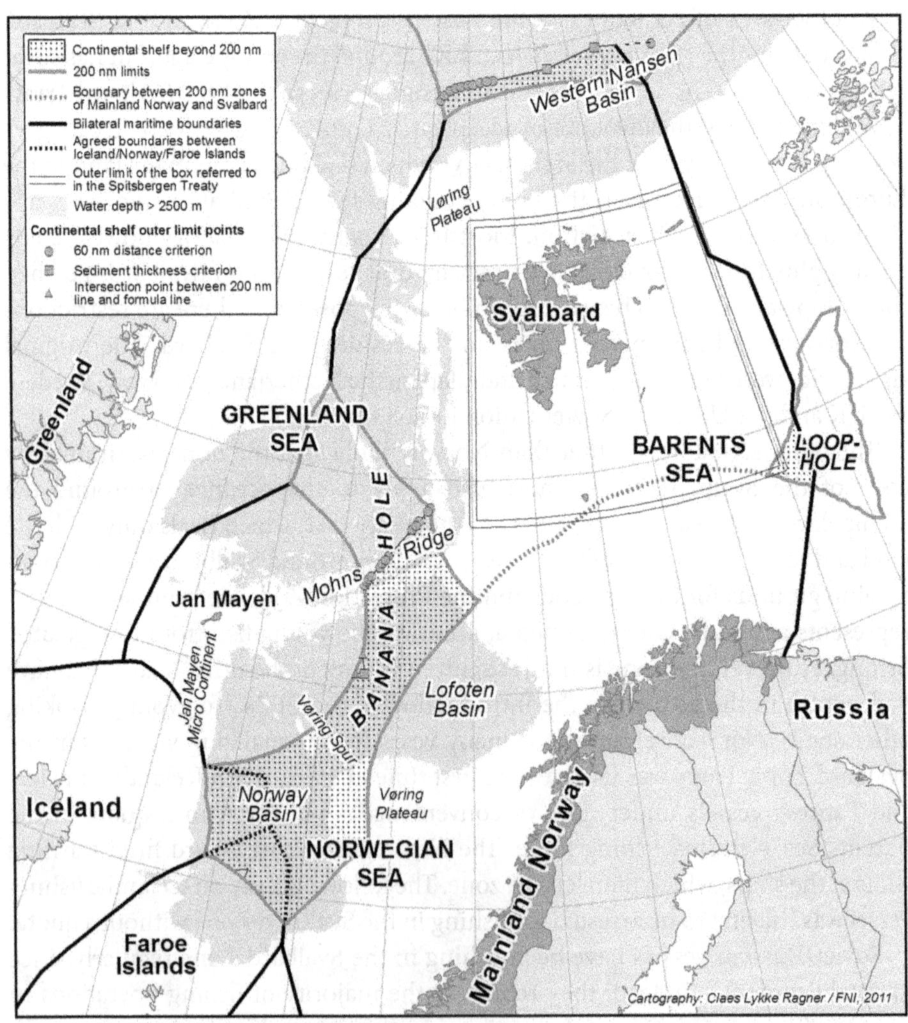

Figure 1.2 Barents Sea continental shelf.[8]

The legacy of the 1990s: Institutional collaboration with Russia

Norway's foreign policy in the European Arctic during the 1990s was mainly concerned with bringing Russia into collaborative networks. The idea of a 'Barents region' was first aired by Norwegian Minister of Foreign Affairs Thorvald Stoltenberg in April 1992. After consulting with Russia and the other Nordic states, the Barents Euro-Arctic Region (BEAR) was established by the Kirkenes Declaration of January 1993, whereby Norway, Sweden, Finland and Russia pledged to work together at both regional and national levels.[9] At the regional level, the BEAR initially included the three northernmost counties of Norway, together with Norrbotten in Sweden, Lapland in Finland, Murmansk and Arkhangelsk Oblasts and the Republic of Karelia in Russia (see Figure 1.3). They were joined in 1997 by Nenets Autonomous Okrug, located within Arkhangelsk Oblast, which became a member in its own right, and later by Västerbotten (Sweden), Oulu and Kainuu (Finland) and the Republic of Komi (Russia). All these regional entities are represented on the Regional Council of the BEAR, as are the indigenous peoples of the region.[10] The Barents Euro-Arctic Council (BEAC), on which Denmark, Iceland and the European Commission sit in addition to the four core states, was created to promote and facilitate intergovernmental cooperation. The following countries have observer status: Canada, France, Germany, Italy, Japan, the Netherlands, Poland, the UK and the USA.

The BEAR was designed to promote stability and prosperity in the area. Its purpose is enshrined in the concepts of normalization, stabilization and regionalization. It focuses on reducing the military tension, allaying environmental threats and narrowing the East–West gap in standards of living in the region. It is also part of the regionalization process underway in Europe as well as in the Arctic, turning previously peripheral border areas into places where governments can meet in a transnational forum serving a range of interests. Areas of particular concern are environmental protection, regional infrastructure, economic cooperation, science and technology, culture, tourism, healthcare, and the indigenous peoples of the region.

One of the most striking features of East–West relations in the European North since the end of the Cold War has been the massive flow of people in both directions across national borders, some of whom decide to settle for good in their new country. Annual crossings between Norway and Russia increased from 3,000 plus in the early 1990s to nearly 110,000 by the mid-2000s.[11] East–West tourism is thriving; political and business delegations frequently visit partners on the other side of the border; students visit for longer or shorter periods; and finally, most of the towns on the Nordic side of the border are home to Russian communities of varying sizes.

As a political project, the BEAR has had its ups and downs.[12] While ambitions were high during the formative years, creating viable cross-border business partnerships in the Barents region proved more difficult than anticipated. Ostensible successes ended in failure. In some notorious cases, the Russians simply forced out their Western counterparts once the joint company started to make a profit. As a result, the BEAR downgraded large-scale business cooperation as a priority in the late 1990s, devoting its energies instead to small-scale business and people-to-people cooperation: student exchanges, cultural projects and other ventures bringing Russians and nationals of the Nordic countries together. The BEAR set up a Barents Health Programme in 1999, focusing primarily on new and resurgent communicable diseases such as HIV/AIDS and tuberculosis.[13] Both people-to-people cooperation and the Barents Health Programme are generally judged to be successful, and cooperation between small businesses has also been growing.

A Joint Norwegian–Soviet Commission on Environmental Protection was established in 1988.[15] The previous year, Soviet leader Mikhail Gorbachev had made his famous 'Murmansk speech', in which he urged the 'civilisation' of the militarized European Arctic in general, and wider international cooperation on environmental protection in particular.[16] The Soviet Pechenganikel nickel smelter had already ravaged the countryside on the Kola Peninsula (with visible damage also on the Norwegian side); the Joint Norwegian–Soviet

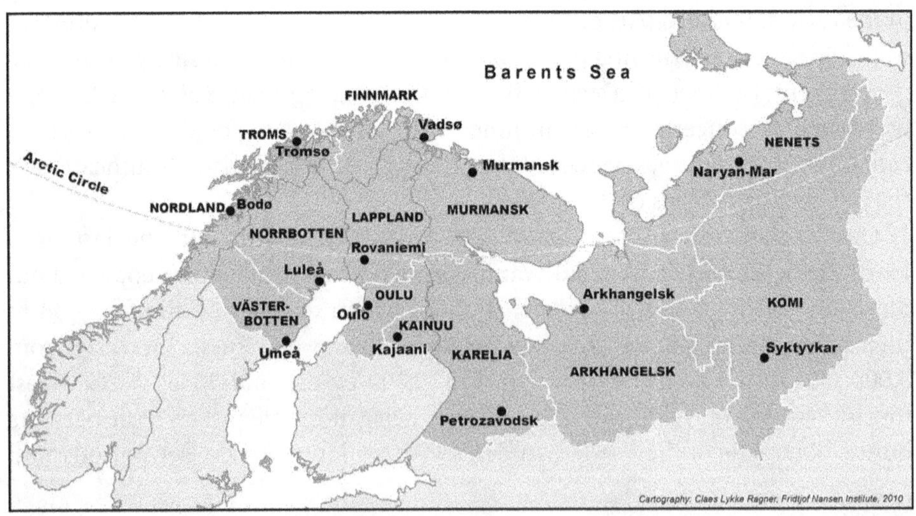

Figure 1.3 The Barents Euro-Arctic Region.[14]

Commission on Environmental Protection made it a top priority during the first few years of its existence to modernize Pechenganikel and reduce SO_2 emissions. By the early 1990s, nuclear safety had become the new priority. It was public knowledge that the Soviets had been dumping radioactive waste in the Barents and Kara Seas because they were overwhelmed by an ever-growing stockpile of spent nuclear fuel and radioactive waste on the Kola Peninsula. There was also mounting concern about safety at the Kola nuclear power plant, located in Polyarnye Zori in the southern part of the Kola Peninsula. Norway launched a Plan of Action on nuclear safety in north-western Russia in 1995, and three years later a separate Joint Norwegian–Russian Commission on Nuclear Safety was established. Over the next ten years, Norway spent around US$ 150 million on nuclear safety projects on the Kola Peninsula. The Plan of Action was aimed at protecting public health, the environment and business from radioactive contamination and pollution from chemical weapons. It addressed four defined areas: safety measures at nuclear facilities; management, storage and disposal of radioactive waste and spent nuclear fuel; research and monitoring of radioactive pollution; and arms-related environmental hazards. The immediate priority was to make the Kola nuclear power plant safe, to investigate and report on pollution in northern ocean areas and to hasten the construction of storage and effluent treatment facilities for radioactive waste and spent nuclear fuel. Since the turn of the millennium, the emphasis has been on preparing the removal of nuclear waste from the Northern Fleet's old storage facility in Andreeva Bay in western Kola Peninsula, replacing the old radioisotope thermoelectric generators used in navigation buoys with environmentally friendly solar cells, and finally on enabling the Russians to maintain progress in dismantling nuclear submarines at the naval shipyard on the Kola Peninsula.

While nuclear safety absorbed most of the funding earmarked for the environment under the bilateral environmental agreement between Norway and Russia, the Joint Norwegian–Russian Commission on Environmental Protection was promoting institutional cooperation between the two countries in areas such as pollution control, biodiversity and protection of cultural heritage. *Institutional* cooperation became the hallmark of the Commission around the mid-1990s. Emphasizing not only solutions to urgent environmental problems, the Commission also tried to build a workable system of cooperation between Norwegian and Russian environmental institutions, mainly aimed at helping Russia strengthen its environmental bureaucracy. Since 2002–03, protecting the marine environment of the Barents Sea has been the main objective of the Commission. Its initial main priority, the modernization of the Pechenganikel combine, has not materialized.

The legacy of the 2000s: The High North as national priority

The first years after the turn of the millennium saw little attention given to the north in Norwegian foreign policy discourse. The northern waters were still regarded partly as a scene of Cold War theatre. Moreover, the previous decade's institutional collaboration with Russia showed signs of wear. The BEAR had not produced the results many had hoped for in large-scale business cooperation between East and West. Norway's plan of action for nuclear safety in north-western Russia was heavily criticized by the Norwegian public for spending too much money too quickly, again with limited practical results. When Conservative Minister of Foreign Affairs Jan Petersen appointed a committee to evaluate opportunities and challenges in the north in early 2003, this received little media attention. The act was seen by many as a sop to Cold War romantics in the armed forces and the right-wing political establishment, who regretted that Norway's foreign policy was now mainly directed southwards – to mediation for peace and humanitarian aid in the Third World. The committee was headed by the director of the Norwegian Polar Institute, Olav Orheim, and had representatives from academia, the state bureaucracy, business, the environmental movement and indigenous peoples. Its report, published in December 2003, called for clarification of Norway's relationship with Russia through one overarching agreement that would solve all outstanding issues between the two countries – notably the delimitation line between their EEZs, and the status of the seas around Svalbard.[17] The committee also proposed removing the national tier of the BEAR collaboration, leaving only cooperation at the regional level, and instead strengthening bilateral collaboration with Russia and Norway's participation in the Arctic Council. It further recommended a steep increase in funding to develop north Norwegian science and businesses, and suggested that money should be taken from the plan of action for nuclear safety in north-western Russia. In sum, the Orheim Committee proposed a change of course away from the 1990s' institutionalized partnerships with Russia, towards greater attention to circumpolar issues and the development of north Norwegian science, trade and industry. The report was sharply criticized by political actors in Kirkenes, the town in Norway's north-eastern corner that had become the Norwegian 'Barents capital' since the early 1990s. They condemned the scientific emphasis of the Orheim report, obviously fearing that funding and the political capital would be transferred to Tromsø, home to the Norwegian Polar Institute and the world's northernmost university.

In April 2005, the Norwegian government responded to the Orheim report through a white paper on opportunities and challenges in the north, prepared by the Ministry of Foreign Affairs.[18] It did not follow up the proposals of the Orheim

Committee. There was no mention of abolishing the national tier of the BEAR, nor of downsizing assistance given to nuclear safety in north-western Russia. The white paper paid considerable attention to the challenges associated with the latter, as well as to jurisdictional issues in the Barents Sea. It briefly mentioned circumpolar collaboration and indigenous issues, without indicating any change of course.

In the time between the appointment of the Orheim Committee and the publication of the government white paper, a change had taken place in Norwegian public discourse (discussed later). The north became a major issue in the campaign leading up to Norway's general election in September 2005. While the northern waters had until then largely attracted the interest of right-wing politicians concerned with military security and economic interest (except the BEAR, which was the Labour Party's 'baby'), now even the leader of the Socialist Left Party declared that Norway's most important foreign policy challenges were those in the north. The elections were won by a 'Red-Green coalition' consisting of the Labour Party, the Socialist Left Party and the Centre Party, and rising star Jonas Gahr Støre (the preferred assistant of erstwhile prime minister Gro Harlem Brundtland) became minister of foreign affairs. When he took office, it had just become known that the two major Norwegian oil companies, Statoil and Hydro, were on the Russian gas company Gazprom's shortlist for the gigantic Shtokman project in the Russian part of the Barents Sea (in addition to American Chevron, ConocoPhillips and French Total). In what was arguably the most famous political speech in Norway since the turn of the millennium, Jonas Gahr Støre, speaking in Tromsø, convincingly declared the North to be the number one priority of Norwegian foreign policy.

In early autumn 2006, events took an unexpected turn. Gazprom suddenly declared that it would not have any foreign partners in the Shtokman development, but would go it alone instead. When the Norwegian government announced its Strategy on the High North in December 2006, the Shtokman issue was downplayed.[19] Now the northern areas – or the High North, which became the official English translation of the Norwegian term *nordområdene* – are declared a 'national priority'. The strategy lists all thinkable challenges in the region, ranging from environmental protection and indigenous issues to the business opportunities associated with future offshore petroleum extraction in the Barents Sea. Nevertheless, it erases the dividing line between foreign and national policies, and stresses the development of Norway's northern regions mainly in terms of science and business. This was followed up in the strategy's 'step two' in spring 2009, *New Building Blocks in the High North*, a purely domestic policy document.[20] The main topic in step two of the strategy was the establishment of a new scientific centre on climate change and the environment in Tromsø.

Fram – The High North Research Centre for Climate and the Environment (the Fram Centre) was opened in 2010, with the Norwegian Polar Institute as its main constituent body.

The Shtokman issue took yet another new turn in summer 2007, when Total was invited back in, and soon thereafter StatoilHydro (merged Statoil and Hydro, since 2009 operating under the name Statoil). Total and Statoil had no ownership of the resources; their role was limited to that of partners in the development project. A final decision on whether the Shtokman field would actually be developed was postponed several times, and changes in the international gas market eventually put the entire project on ice. In the Norwegian public debate, the 2010 delimitation line has largely ousted Shtokman as the big promise for the future. Although it will take some time for things to actually happen, there are expectations that the former disputed area contains extractable hydrocarbon resources.

Norwegian High North Discourse

How did the High North around 2005 again become a debatable subject in Norwegian foreign policy – and a politically opportune one at that? In this part of the chapter we will, based on a review of newspaper articles, tell a story of highs and lows in one of the broadest and most prominent Norwegian public debates on domestic and foreign politics and policies – a debate that has engaged a broad range of actors from the whole country. The High North is not only topping the foreign policy agenda, but has very much also become the 'people's business'.

Not unexpectedly, there was a sizeable increase in references to the High North in the years after the turn of the millennium. Our search in the Norwegian Atekst database for 'High North' (*nordområde*) had about 100 hits in the year 2000; 200 for the years 2001–04; followed by a steep rise to about 1,000 hits in 2005.[21] Like the politics, the debates of the early 2000s were rather low-key affairs, centred on the prominent themes of the 1990s, but discussed with less urgency than before. The expression 'High North' features notably and mainly in the foreign policy debate. Two issues dominate. The first was the combined plans to downscale the military presence in northern Norway and Russia's response to the establishment of the Globus II Radar Station at Vardø. The second issue was nuclear security and was also twofold. Russia was planning to transport nuclear waste by ship along the Norwegian coast, and Norway was putting together its own action plan to address the atomic waste situation in north-west Russia. In stories about the latter, the press blew alternately hot and cold, with positive stories about the long-awaited opening of the effluent treatment facility for liquid radioactive waste in Murmansk (which never became operational) and negative stories about the Russian mafia and disappearing Norwegian money.

In the following, our findings are presented through three overarching, interconnected narratives, which encapsulate and capture the essence of the Norwegian public discourses on the High North during the first decade of the twenty-first century, as they appeared through our readings of approximately 3,000 articles from four Norwegian newspapers. The narratives reflect how disappointment with the 1990s' collaboration with Russia was followed by new enthusiasm for northern affairs around 2005, and then a certain scepticism again towards the end of the decade.

Fragments from the 1990s

By the year 2000, a certain lethargy had crept into Norway's policy on Russia to use the government's preferred term at the time. The creation of the Barents cooperation had been a peace-promoting effort, aimed at accelerating economic growth in communities in northern Norway. The Iron Curtain had disappeared for good, and East and West were finding common cause in the north. The idea was to promote peace, expand infrastructure and, above all, encourage growth in commerce, business and trade between the peoples of Norway and Russia. It was a golden opportunity, a northern gold rush waiting to happen, so to speak, with no time to lose. Although some observers and critics were not convinced, their voices could hardly be heard above the din. This was a great period of excitement and anticipation about everything Barents and it held sway for several years in the public mind.

What comes in with a roar often goes out with a whimper. The post-Soviet economy was in critical shape, all the more critical given the wild optimism and spectacular feats Norway and Russia were to achieve together. As the 1990s drew to a close, press commentators were starting to question the viability of the large-scale projects Norway was managing in north-west Russia. Expectations, politicians and government officials quickly admitted, may have been too high. The condensed storyline went something like this: 'Norwegian businesses invest in north-west Russia (often with government support). Russian businesses were beginning to turn in a profit. Norwegians back out of their Russian partnerships.' Or when the subject was different forms of governmental support, such as Norway's contribution to nuclear security and other environmental programmes in north-west Russia: 'Norway gives Russia money. Russians refuse to say how they spend it. They're probably using it to line their own pockets. And the programmes will fail anyway.' There are many examples of this storyline in the press: 'Foreign Office blows NOK 1.1 billion in Russia – Wasted on pathetic schemes'[22]; 'Wing-clipped in Russia'[23]; 'Regrets Russian Adventure'[24]. The enthusiasm of the late 1990s morphed into a discourse of disaster. There were stories about the Russian mafia and general plight of the Russian population. The mainstay of the early 1990s 'misery narratives' was the perception of north-west Russia as a ticking environmental time bomb and radiation hotspot.[25] As the decade progressed, the press printed stories of social disintegration and poverty, and the threat to Norway posed by Russian depravity seeping over the border crossings, bringing high-octane criminals, prostitution and infectious diseases in its wake. The associated mafia narrative portrayed Russians as cunning, calculating and ready to exploit the good intentions of easily duped Norwegians.

> Speaking off the record, Norwegian officials deplore the state of affairs, and have done for some time. It is particularly irritating when corruption affects joint efforts to clear up the nuclear waste in the north of Russia. As a Norwegian observer talking to *Aftenposten*'s correspondent some time ago explained, 'If we launch a project and the funding is mainly Western money, you can bet your bottom dollar the Russians will dig up some business or other that's "ready and willing" to accept the assignment. If we turn that offer down, you can bet your second bottom dollar that the Russians will quietly let the project gather dust on a shelf. If you investigate who's behind the firm, you'll soon see it belongs to people inside the Russian atomic energy ministry.'[26]

The Barents cooperation was not a major item in the public debates of the early 2000s, at least not if we take as our point of comparison how enthusiastically the Barents project had been greeted just ten years before, or indeed the clamour of criticism when the partnership failed to 'deliver the goods' within what observers felt was a reasonable period of time. Heads were turned for a moment when the Orheim Committee presented its report, in which it recommended scaling back the national component of the cooperation and elevating instead the Arctic Council and bilateral cooperation with Russia. The head of the Norwegian Barents Secretariat said in that connection,:

> If this proves correct, I would say it was unbelievable. The Barents cooperation is to all intents and purposes a complete success. One has managed to establish important links between people. … And there's talk about eliminating popular involvement.[27]

The Governor of Finnmark, Norway's northernmost county, was also disappointed:

> I would say the report has all the signs of having been made by a panel of experts. It's all well and good counting polar bears and ice floes, and wanting resources to step up competence building. But it all has to happen from the bottom up, with a basis

> in our local situation. The Committee's perception of the issues is completely alien to us in Finnmark. We are discussing resources, and rights make up a key element in this discussion, but the Inquiry has not addressed this at all competently. … [On the Barents cooperation:] It's been done without the requisite respect. The Barents cooperation has been an overwhelming success with the public. But they want to turn it into a simple regional affair. One of the reasons is because the bureaucrats have lost their enthusiasm. Is the Barents cooperation there so that bureaucrats can enjoy themselves at work, or is it so that we who live here will get some benefit from it? No, it does get me down.[28]

Reports of the dismal failure of joint Norwegian–Russian projects continued to surface from time to time, and, surprisingly, faint reminders of that initial sense of enthusiasm towards the Barents cooperation. It sounds like an echo from the 1990s when a member of parliament wrote: 'Now's the time for a new push in Norwegian policy on the Barents. … If the Pomor trade could be resuscitated it would create completely new opportunities for the northernmost Norway.'[29] Comments made by the head of the Norwegian Barents Secretariat looked somewhat more to the future: 'The enormous deposits of oil and gas in the Barents region, especially in the Russian areas, will turn what we have today of Barents cooperation upside down.'[30]

While politicians had, up until the change in government in 2005, been wont to visit *northern Norway* or the *Barents region*, the new foreign minister Jonas Gahr Støre travelled to the *High North* whether the destination was Kirkenes, Murmansk or anywhere else (onshore or offshore) north of the Arctic Circle. High North policy was the new buzzword for Cold War security policy, policy towards Russia in the 1990s and the Barents cooperation. It was a timely designation signalling optimism and vitality, largely personified by the foreign minister himself, with his professional confidence and dynamic manner. The expression won a place in the debates on domestic policies as a 'cool' variant, with earlier times' northern Norway stimulus packages smacking of rural policy and provincial melancholia. The new High North policy is the story of where northern Norway fits into the wider world.

The great narrative of the High North

The white paper promised by the government following the Orheim Inquiry report had, as mentioned earlier, been postponed several times. It was scheduled first for the spring of 2004, but finally appeared a year later. In terms of concrete proposals it can hardly be described as anything but disappointing: steps should be taken to continue talking with our allies on matters relating to the High North (named *High North dialogues*) and strengthening collaborative mechanisms with Russia.

Nevertheless, something was beginning to happen. Influential players in the north, not least regional media, were beginning to tell a new story about the north, adding to the emerging narrative of 'it's happening in the north', with an 'it's happening *now*!'

> We at the newspaper [*Nordlys*] have long been urging the political parties – of all hues – to bestir themselves and look at the north. Because if they do, they'll see the Norway of the future, land of opportunities. It's along the coast and in the north this future can be created by adopting a pro-active coastal and High North policy. The next petroleum Klondike will unfold in the High North, and it is in the north we have an enormous potential for economic growth and value generation.[31]
>
> Our vital national interests lie in the north. This should be the target of Norwegian foreign policy over the foreseeable future. We stand on the brink of the greatest foreign policy challenge of the post-WWII era.[32]

There had already been an extensive debate over the prospect of commercially extracting the oil and gas reserves under the Barents Sea. Oil and gas deposits under the Russian Barents Sea were sporadically referred to as very significant. Around the mid-2000s, the potential reserves under the Russian shelf were increasingly mentioned by participants debating Norwegian commercial exploitation, and indeed, in connection with the wider discourse on the High North per se. The ensuing storyline was partly visionary, though based on a relatively conservative assessment of the interests of the different states: 'Shtokman will be one of the world's biggest gas fields when it finally comes online. The Russians will need foreign technology and capital to develop the field, and Norwegian companies stand a good chance. The ripple benefits will be highly significant for northern Norway.' If we include the interests of the great powers, the storyline is filled out as follows: 'The US is interested in Russian gas, and Norway will have to take care not to be marginalized by an international partnership in the High North.'

A more diffuse and nervous sounding storyline was mixed in: 'The Russians have already started. We haven't a second to lose.' And in the great power variant: 'The Americans are already involved. Them too.' The origin of these assumptions is unclear, but that many people do in fact believe that the Russians have been extracting oil and gas from the Barents Sea for some time – which is not the case as of 2010 – is in our view incontrovertible. Here are a couple of examples from the media: 'The Russians are already well under way with installing an oil industry in the High North'[33]; 'For every passing day, the pace of petroleum activity in the north is turned up a notch for Norway and Russia.'[34] An increase in the transportation of Russian oil (produced on land further east) down the Norwegian coast since 2002 may have created the 'well under way' impression. Whatever the reason, that the Russians were poised to begin work on production is viewed as a near certainty by many. What sort of response this storyline prescribes is not entirely clear. It was often used in connection with more general arguments concerning the High North; in attempts, for example, to underscore the importance of the High North and the necessity of some course of action or other, such as the appointment of 'a dedicated minister of High North affairs'. It became politically incorrect to express 'anti-High North' opinions. Simply talking about the High North without a sense of optimism and confidence was considered bad manners, a breach with the dominant discourse of the time.

In what follows we provide some quotes that we believe are representative of the great sense of urgency and euphoria to which the High North gave rise.

> The Russians are sailing up as the leading oil and gas suppliers in the north. Both the US and EU are negotiating with the Russians directly, over the head of Norway, to get the best possible terms. American companies are lining up and will certainly want to make use of Norwegian off-shore know-how, which without our usual penchant for self-aggrandisement can be called the best in the world. Hydro and Statoil are obviously interested in the Barents Sea.[35]

> In our opinion, that the foreign office and Jan Petersen [then foreign affairs minister] are incapable of finishing a white paper on the High North in light of the *Look North!* report is almost scandalous. It sits in the ministry gathering dust while the US, EU and Russia have already entered the oil and gas era here in the north.[36]

> The production of oil and gas, of which we only see the start, is in a totally different league from what Norway is used to dealing with. Just the disputed area between Norway and Russia is as big as the whole Norwegian North Sea shelf. In addition, we must remain acutely aware of the possibility of landing in the middle of a new geopolitical tug-of-war. In a situation where Russia needs capital, the EU needs easy access to cheap oil, and the US needs a reliable supplier with a population that doesn't hate the US, Norway could easily become a midget among giants. When oil's on the menu, old friendships can quickly turn sour.[37]

It is hard not to notice the inter-discursive connections between the sense of enthusiasm that swept the country in the early 1990s and this sense of euphoria on behalf of the High North in the mid-2000s. One noticeable similarity is the storyline they share regarding the urgency of the situation: 'we're running out of time'. In the early 1990s, according to those urging the establishment of business relations with north-west Russia, Norway was being left behind by everyone else: 'The Swedes are investing, the Finns are investing; even the Germans are investing, the Portuguese are investing – And us Norwegians, we're sitting on the fence with our hands in our pockets.' By the mid-2000s, Norway, ostensibly, was being overtaken by the major powers in the Barents Sea. Exxon and Halliburton were hard at work developing the Shtokman field, some professed. In both cases the warnings originated with northern Norwegian actors, whose patience was often sorely tried by the tardiness of an Oslo milieu unable or unwilling to take stock of the situation and grasp the opportunities to be had in the High North. If someone in the heat of the euphoric moment uttered anything but 'hooray!', they and their arguments were soon stripped of legitimacy. If southern Norwegians tried to pour cold water onto hot northern blood, they were ill informed. And if the offenders were themselves northerners, they were virtually traitors.[38] We shall not go so far as to question whether there was any substance at all in the wave of enthusiasm for the Barents project or euphoria for the High North project. The opening of the border between Russia and Norway in the north in the early 1990s is a fact. And the Barents Sea was being opened for oil and gas exploration a decade later. Admittedly, the Germans and Portuguese were investing in Murmansk, and the USA looked for some time as if it would be the main beneficiary of LNG gas from the Shtokman field if and when it started producing. Whether the Portuguese landed deals in Murmansk before Norway (which, by the way, they did not), or Shtokman gas ends up in the United States (which it obviously will not) is not our main concern here. The intriguing thing is that the discourses assumed this particular form, and in both cases unfolded in ways that were so similar. Is the story being told a familiar one – about hope, urgency and an arrogant capital city?

Mixing cold water with hot blood

During the slow simmer of the 1990s and early 2000s and ensuing euphoria over the High North, critical voices were few and far between. But there were some, and more have joined the fray since the end of the period under discussion in this chapter. What we mean by a 'critical voice' is not someone who criticizes the government for tardiness in the High North question, but someone who questions the measures and priorities put in place. We are not thinking so much about people who criticize failed projects, but rather the underlying project rationale. There are isolated instances in the Norwegian press of government projects being hauled over the coals, one such being the nuclear safety action plan. Some ask whether the High North euphoria has any basis in fact and whether it is prudent to make such 'a song and dance' about it anyway. By the end of the period, critical voices were calling for a fundamental overhaul of the principles of Norway's relations with Russia in the High North. These voices are united in questioning perceptions of reality in current Norwegian High North policy and in the policy debates. The storyline goes: 'What have we let ourselves in for? Isn't it time for a reality check?'

Criticism of the rationality of the grand undertakings of 1990s High North policy was, as mentioned, not particularly vociferous. Commentators criticized the lack of tangible and significant results of Norwegian–Russian economic collaboration, but no one condemned the entire project. The nuclear safety action plan was slammed for having put too much money into Russian hands a bit too quickly. Questions have been asked at irregular intervals since Norway started funding nuclear safety projects in north-west Russia in the early 1990s, but they have never really undermined the image of impending disaster, created in large part by the Norwegian environmental organization Bellona. And public opinion appears to consider the Kola Peninsula with some concern, as a radioactive wasteland. So it's a good thing we're addressing the problems, after all.

Some experts, on the other hand, can't see what the fuss is all about. According to them, the scrapped submarines and the atomic waste in the Kola Peninsula aren't endangering anyone or anything beyond those in the closest proximity. They attack environmentalists for playing on latent fears surrounding anything remotely connected with radiation – natural radiation is everywhere, after all. Politicians are too willing to throw money at a problem simply to placate a concerned public. These commentators point to the prevailing discourse's tacit assumptions, the things that usually elude critical discussion. In this instance, the assumption is that nuclear waste in the Kola Peninsula constitutes a risk to the life and health of Norwegians. The experts urge the government to take a reality check and ask themselves what they are really up to. It is all well and good to protect a few fjord inlets in the Kola Peninsula from pollution, but it is not a sensible idea to portray the discarded submarines as another Chernobyl waiting to go into critical meltdown:

> *Aftenposten* has had several reports on how the scrapped Russian submarines and atomic waste are being handled in the High North. Based on an idea of the probable consequences to the fishing industry and population of our northern counties of a hazardous leak, our authorities have now budgeted about NOK 1 billion to help the Russians clear up the mess. It is difficult to find sound scientific justification for this type of aid. Indeed, there are no scientific grounds whatsoever for the idea that radioactive pollution of a given area of the northern waters would adversely affect health or environment in Norway. … In terms of the media, radioactivity tends to create the big headlines, but it is meaningless not to mention natural radioactivity in assessments of radioactivity. Studies of the environment show that if the radioactivity of 200 scrapped submarines was to leak into the Barents Sea, total radioactivity in the same sea would rise by a thousandth. In terms of health, the decisive thing is the amount of radiation people could be exposed to by eating fish or other sea foods polluted by small levels or radioactivity from a 'leaking'

submarine core. As analyses demonstrate, these doses will always be small and virtually insignificant in relation to the doses from natural radiation. As far as I am aware, the political decision to give Russia financial aid to clear up northern areas was not based on these analyses. What, then, is the explanation for these decisions? There may be many laudable reasons to help a neighbouring country address its environmental problems when the assumptions are based on verifiable scientific evidence. But the evidence in this case is unclear, not to say completely absent.[39]

Another type of intervention denies that the Russians are already producing oil and gas in the Barents Sea, something many in Norway appear to believe. At the same time, more and more voices are stressing the reliance of Norwegian optimism regarding the High North on how much oil and gas is found in the Russian Barents Sea – not least because of the disappointing results as regards the Norwegian Barents Sea shelf.

Professor Olav Orheim pours cold water on [Prime Minister] Kjell Magne Bondevik's aspirations. The Russians may not start work on the Shtokman field for a long time yet, he says. … The plans Russians have for Asia are ambitious, he points out, and they will probably want to consider Chinese, Japanese and Indian wishes before starting on the Shtokman project.[40]

'[Consultancies in northern Norway] write glowing reports based on the discovery of significant oil deposits in the Barents Sea. According to studies done by the authorities themselves, there is little chance of finding much oil in the Barents Sea. [The consultancies] stoke up unrealistic expectations regarding exploration in the north and their attempts to convince the public are frankly disingenuous', says Bellona representative Guro Hauge. What upsets her in particular are the projects [the consultancies] conduct [ostensibly showing] the likely benefits of oil in the north. She condemns those she alleges are only seeking to make a profit from people's hopes and expectations. '[They] have been the leading advocates of oil exploration in the north. I have no confidence in their ability to give an unbiased picture of the benefits likely to flow from an oil and gas industry. These people have a direct economic interest in creating expectations to the High North.'[41]

It was only a year ago Jonas Gahr Støre was whipping up a frenzy in northern Norway with his 'Tromsø speech'. Today, the grand visions are gone, replaced by a sensible plan for the High North which few will find reason to celebrate. … The question is whether Støre hasn't fastened the High North project too firmly to the Shtokman mast. Støre, for example, prevailed upon former Statoil director Arve Johnsen to assess the feasibility of a 'Pomor zone' in the north. The Government will be moving to accelerate economic relations and collaboration, it says, and is proposing a dual economic and industrial zone linking areas in northern Norway and northwest

> Russia. With hindsight, the proposal will undeniably lose credibility if nothing comes of the planned gas field. So what do they intend to fill the economic zone with, that's the question. It would be a far more lucrative proposition if production started and Hydro and Statoil were partners. As it is, Shtokman is likely to stay on the back burner for a significant stretch. And according to some, the Kremlin and Gazprom appear to be more interested in Siberia. This is not good news for Norwegian manufacturers, subcontractors and others expecting the north to enjoy some of the fringe benefits. And it is a bellyflop for foreign minister Støre's plans for the High North.[42]

In this last example we see the start of what we can call a slight depression in the Norwegian debate on the High North. The Russian 'no' to a Shtokman partnership with Norway converted the febrile sense of elation over the ability of the almost unlimited potential of the High North to save the region and the nation into a sense of gloom. The turnaround was almost immediately evident with a sharp drop in the number of hits in the news databases and, in the wider media picture, a palpable change of heart. The penny, so to speak, had dropped at last. One now saw how far the Norwegian High North adventure depended on Norwegian participation on the Russian shelf. This sense of being locked out in the cold lasted only a year or two, however. Spirits quickened when word spread that StatoilHydro – the outcome of a merger between the two companies – would, after all, be a partner in this mammoth undertaking. Almost overnight, the old sense of optimism received a new lease of life; the grand visions for the High North were dusted down and shunted into service again in the Norwegian press.

Conclusion

Since the mid-2000s, Norway has had an explicit policy on the High Arctic, designated as the Strategy on the High North. The strategy contains elements from three layers of the country's northern policies:

- the High North as an arena for great-power politics (mainly a legacy from the Cold War);
- the High North as an arena for institutionalized collaboration with Russia (mainly a legacy from the 1990s);
- the High North as a national priority (mainly a legacy from the mid-2000s).

The relationship with Russia ranks above most other concerns in Norway's High North policy. During the Cold War, the Soviet Union represented the Russian bear, in whose company small-state Norway could never allow itself to feel secure. In the 1990s, Russia became the impoverished recipient of humanitarian aid from Norway. Now, after the turn of the millennium, the Russian bear has re-emerged with both financial and military clout. The internal debate in Norway towards the end of the first decade of the twenty-first century centred on the continuation of financial support for Russian institutions and civil society. Shouldn't a country that could manage to re-arm itself also be expected to take responsibility for its environment and health services? Moreover, Russia was assuming a new role as a potential market and business partner for Norway. Participation in the Shtokman development was arguably the main driving force behind Norway's 'new' northern policies. Thus, we see that Russia played the main role in Norway's High North policies during the Cold War, in the 1990s and after the turn of the millennium.

Actors concerned with Norway's security have found common ground with those mainly interested in investments and better possibilities for north Norwegian business. These actors focus on Norway's 'near abroad' in the Barents Sea region, generally seeing presence in the north – whether in the form of naval vessels or increased population – as a good thing in itself. Regional politicians, media and business representatives have found allies in top national politicians concerned about Statoil's access to new resources, preferably in the 'near abroad' so that regional trade and industry can also achieve ripple effects. While there is a cleavage between actors located close to the border with Russia (mainly in Kirkenes) and actors in the rest of northern Norway (mainly the academic regional capital of Tromsø), the emphasis of both groups is on relations with Russia and on the High North as a 'national project'.

An additional interest group that in part competes with these groups (only to a limited extent, as the common interest is also highly visible) consists of those arguing for a greater focus on circumpolar cooperation and indigenous issues. As noted, the 2003 Orheim Committee had proposed downplaying the BEAR collaboration and nuclear safety projects in Russia (though it, too, favoured a strong emphasis on relations with Russia and considerable new investments in northern Norway), and was criticized for being mainly concerned about 'counting polar bears and ice flakes, [and disregarding] those of us who live here [in the High North]' (see earlier discussion). The committee's report is often referred to – despite its explicit call for investment in northern Norway – as a document that places the focus of Norway's foreign policy off in the distance, if not on humanitarian action in the Third World (a hallmark of Norwegian foreign policy for decades), then on indigenous and environmental concerns somewhere in the far-off Arctic. It is seen as defending the narrow interests of researchers from the Norwegian Polar Institute, keen to participate in Arctic Council-initiated activities across the circumpolar north. The establishment of the Fram

Centre in Tromsø in 2010 also led many to conclude that science was the winner in the 'new' Norwegian politics of the High North. Whereas Russia (whether as regards delimitation line discussions, settlement of fish quotas or the opening of the Shtokman field) was definitely a moving target, scientific infrastructure in the north was safely within the control of Norwegian central authorities.

Norwegian High Arctic policy is indeed still primarily focused on the 'lower' Arctic of the near abroad – and on the domestic scene.

Notes

1 Norwegian Ministry of Foreign Affairs, 'Avtale mellom Regjeringen i Unionen av Sovjetiske Sosialistiske Republikker og Regjeringen i Kongeriket Norge om samarbeid innen fiskerinæringen', in *Overenskomster med fremmede stater* (Oslo, Norwegian Ministry of Foreign Affairs, 1975), pp. 546–9.

2 Norwegian Ministry of Foreign Affairs, 'Avtale mellom Norge og Sovjetunionen om en midlertidig praktisk ordning for fisket i et tilstøtende område i Barentshavet med tilhørende protokoll og erklæring', in *Overenskomster med fremmede stater* (Oslo, Norwegian Ministry of Foreign Affairs, 1978), p. 436.

3 Norwegian Ministry of Foreign Affairs, 'Treaty between Norway and the Russian Federation concerning Maritime Delimitation and Cooperation in the Barents Sea and the Arctic Ocean' (Oslo, Norwegian Ministry of Foreign Affairs, 2010).

4 Map created by Claes Lykke Ragner, Fridtjof Nansen Institute.

5 For a thorough examination of the legal aspects of the Fishery Protection Zone, see Geir Ulfstein, *The Svalbard Treaty: From Terra Nullius to Norwegian Sovereignty* (Oslo, Scandinavian University Press, 1995).

6 The strongest opposition to the Protection Zone has come from the UK. The USA, Germany and France have formally reserved their position, which implies that they are still considering their views. Finland declared its support for the Protection Zone in 1976, but has since not repeated it. Canada also expressed its support for the Norwegian position in a bilateral fisheries agreement in 1995, but this agreement has not entered into force. These other Western countries generally accept that the waters surrounding Svalbard are under Norwegian jurisdiction, but they claim that this jurisdiction must be carried out in accordance with the Svalbard Treaty. See Torbjørn Pedersen, 'The constrained politics of the Svalbard offshore area', *Marine Policy* 32 (2008), pp. 913–19; 'Norway's rule on Svalbard: Tightening the grip on the Arctic islands', *Polar Record* 45 (2009), pp. 147–52; 'Denmark's policies toward the Svalbard area', *Ocean Development and International Law* 40 (2009), pp. 319–32; 'International law and politics in US policy-making: The United States and the Svalbard dispute', *Ocean Development and International Law* 42 (2011), pp. 120–35, for discussions of other countries' stances on the Svalbard zone. Russia, on the other hand, formally considers the waters around Svalbard to be high seas. See A. N. Vylegzhanin and V. K. Zilanov, *Spitsbergen: Legal Regime of Adjacent Marine Areas* (Utrecht, Eleven International Publishing, 2007). In practice, however, Russia has accepted Norwegian enforcement of fisheries regulations in the Svalbard zone. See Geir Hønneland,

'Compliance in the Fishery Protection Zone around Svalbard', *Ocean Development and International Law* 29 (1998), pp. 339–60; *Coercive and Discursive Compliance Mechanisms in the Management of Natural Resources: A Case Study from the Barents Sea Fisheries* (Boston, Springer, 2000).

7 For details, see Øystein Jensen, *The Commission on the Limits of the Continental Shelf: Law and Legitimacy* (Leiden, Martinus Nijhoffs, 2014).

8 Map created by Claes Lykke Ragner, Fridtjof Nansen Institute.

9 See Barents Euro-Arctic Region, The Kirkenes Declaration from the Conference of Foreign Ministers on Co-operation in the Barents Euro-Arctic Region, Kirkenes, 11 January 1993.

10 The Saami are the only indigenous people found in all four countries in the region. On the Russian side, the Nenets in Nenets Autonomous Okrug and the Vesps in the Republic of Karelia also enjoy status as indigenous peoples.

11 Norwegian Ministry of Foreign Affairs, *Interesser, ansvar og muligheter: Hovedlinjer i norsk utenrikspolitikk*, St.meld. nr. 15 (2008–09) (Oslo, Norwegian Ministry of Foreign Affairs, 2009).

12 A discussion of the BEAR cooperation at the time it was established can be found in Olav S. Stokke and Ola Tunander, *The Barents Region: Cooperation in Arctic Europe* (London, Sage, 1994). The achievements of the collaboration a decade later are discussed in Olav S. Stokke and Geir Hønneland (eds), *International Cooperation and Arctic Governance: Regime Effectiveness and Northern Region Building* (London, Routledge, 2007).

13 See Geir Hønneland and Lars Rowe, 'Western vs. post-Soviet medicine: Fighting tuberculosis and HIV/AIDS in North-West Russia and the Baltic States', *Journal of Communist Studies and Transition Politics* 21 (2005), pp. 395–415.

14 Map created by Claes Lykke Ragner, Fridtjof Nansen Institute.

15 Norwegian Ministry of the Environment, 'Overenskomst mellom Kongeriket Norges Regjering og Unionen av Sovjetiske Sosialistiske Republikkers Regjering om samarbeid på miljøvernområdet' (Oslo, Norwegian Ministry of the Environment, 1988).

16 Gorbachev's Murmansk initiative is presented in Kristian Åtland, 'Mikhail Gorbachev, the Murmansk Initiative, and the desecuritization of interstate relations in the Arctic', *Cooperation and Conflict* 43 (2008), pp. 289–311.

17 Ekspertutvalg for nordområdene, *Mot nord! Utfordringer og muligheter i nordområdene: ekspertutvalg for nordområdene nedsatt av regjeringen 3. mars 2003: avgitt til Utenriksdepartementet 8. desember 2003, Norges offentlige utredninger; NOU 2003:32* (Oslo, Statens forvaltningstjeneste, Informasjonsforvaltning, 2003).

18 Norwegian Ministry of Foreign Affairs, *Muligheter og utfordringer i nord*, St.meld. nr. 30 (2004–05) (Oslo, Norwegian Ministry of Foreign Affairs, 2005).

19 Government of Norway and Ministry of Foreign Affairs, *Regjeringens nordområdestrategi* (Oslo, Government of Norway and Ministry of Foreign Affairs, 2006).

20 See Government of Norway, *Nye byggesteiner i nord: Neste trinn i Regjeringens nordområdestrategi* (Oslo, Government of Norway, 2009).

21 The data are drawn from a large corpus of texts that were obtained during searches in the press database Atekst for the period 1 January 2000–31 December 2006. Our study

is based on systematic, chronological and extensive qualitative readings of a total of 3,043 articles in the four selected Norwegian newspapers: *Aftenposten* (The Evening Mail), *Dagens Næringsliv* (Today's Business), *Klassekampen* (The Class Struggle) and *Nordlys* (Northern Light). The newspapers were chosen on the basis of their slightly different profiles and focus areas, which improves the quality and broadens the scope of the analysis. Although in danger of oversimplification, one could say that *Aftenposten* is the 'national and conservative newspaper', *Dagens Næringsliv* is the 'business and financial newspaper', *Nordlys* is the 'regional, northern newspaper', and lastly, *Klassekampen*, despite its uncompromising title, may be branded the 'slightly radical and leftist newspaper'. For more details on the methodology of the study, see Leif Christian Jensen, 'Seduced and surrounded by security: A post-structuralist take on Norwegian High North securitizing discourse', *Cooperation and Conflict* 48/1 (2013), pp. 80–99.

22 *Aftenposten*, 25 February 2000.

23 *Aftenposten*, 15 September 2000.

24 *Aftenposten*, 19 October 2000.

25 Geir Hønneland, *Russia and the West: Environmental Cooperation and Conflict* (New York, Routledge, 2003).

26 *Aftenposten*, 6 March 2001.

27 *Nordlys*, 6 December 2003.

28 *Nordlys*, 9 December 2003.

29 *Nordlys*, 17 July 2000.

30 *Nordlys*, 4 February 2002.

31 *Nordlys*, 4 February 2005.

32 Thorbjørn Jagland, Chair of the Standing Committee on Foreign Affairs, to *Nordlys*, 16 June 2005.

33 *Nordlys*, 14 March 2003.

34 *Nordlys*, 17 June 2005.

35 *Aftenposten*, 10 January 2005.

36 *Nordlys*, 12 January 2005.

37 *Nordlys*, 4 February 2005.

38 See for instance historians Einar-Arne Drivenes and Harald Dag Jølle from the University of Tromsø pointing to elements of megalomania in the High North rhetoric in *Nordlys*, 4 June 2005. See *Nordlys*, 23 June 2005 and 29 June 2005 for the responses they received after speaking against the dominant discourse.

39 *Aftenposten*, 10 November 2003.

40 *Dagens Næringsliv*, 23 June 2005.

41 *Nordlys*, 29 March 2006.

42 *Dagens Næringsliv*, 1 December 2006.

CHAPTER 2

ACTORS, STRATEGIES AND NETWORKS IN A NEW BIPOLAR GEOPOLITICAL RESEARCH AND POLICY AGENDA: THE CASE OF NORWAY

Leif Christian Jensen and Svein Vigeland Rottem

Introduction

On 12 June 2015 Norway released a white paper explaining the country's interest in and policy on Antarctica. As the first white paper on the Antarctic in nearly eighty years, it bears witness to the renewal and strengthening of the government's political ambitions in the region. Although the Antarctic has always been of significant interest to Norway, policy towards the region has never been reviewed in such depth and detail before. Indeed, while numerous governmental reports and strategies have addressed various aspects of Norway's Arctic policy, no white paper or other policy or strategy review has been undertaken to explain the foundations and framework of Norway's policy towards the Antarctic, which is all the more startling given the importance of the Antarctic to Norway's wider foreign policy, polar research and economy. This, however, is precisely what white paper No.32 2014–15 *Norwegian interests and policies in the Antarctic* (*Norske interesser og politikk i Antarktis*) does.

This chapter is the result of research undertaken in connection with the POLGOV project (no. 257664), funded by the Research Council of Norway. The chapter is also based on Leif Christian Jensen, *International Relations in the Arctic: Norway and the Struggle for Power in the New North* (London, I.B. Tauris, 2016), and 'From the High North to the Low South: bipolar Norway's Antarctic strategy', *The Polar Journal* 6/2 (2016), pp. 273–90.

The Arctic and the Antarctic share unique climatic extremes and biodiversity, and both have extensive histories of European and Asian exploration. The polar regions are hosts to different actors and political structures, but face the same environmental and economic challenges in the twenty-first century, including the need to ensure sustainable and wise development, to understand and respond to global climate and environmental change.[1] Based on a close reading and analysis of the white paper, this chapter will first present Norway's main interests and political priorities concerning the Antarctic. It should also be seen as a contribution to the international relations literature on the region. Second, this chapter seeks to make a case for a research agenda that can explain why so many of the same actors and networks are present and operating at both poles and why the justifications for doing so are so similar. Although the laws regulating activity and the resources in the Antarctic and Arctic differ in many ways, there is considerable overlap when it comes to national and scientific strategies, actors and networks. These differences and similarities have not been studied or properly understood from a comparative perspective before. This chapter is both a first attempt to fill this gap and a call for political and social scientists to undertake similar research.

Background

Norway is the only truly bipolar state, the only one with territorial claims to areas in both the Arctic and the Antarctic. The Antarctic areas – Dronning Maud Land,[2] Peter I Øy and Bouvetøya – amount to an area seven times the size of Norway itself. In addition to its territorial claims, Norway is the largest commercial actor in the region with its fisheries. The Norwegian Arctic is usually termed 'The High North' – a broad concept both geographically and politically. According to the Norwegian Ministry of Foreign Affairs (hereafter MFA), in geographical terms, the Arctic comprises the waters and land, including islands and archipelagos, stretching northwards from the southern boundary of Nordland County in Norway and eastwards from the Greenland Sea to the Barents Sea and the Pechora Sea.[3] In political terms, it includes the administrative entities of Norway, Sweden, Finland and Russia that are members of the Barents Euro-Arctic Cooperation arrangement.[4] Norway's High North policy has points in common with its policy on Nordic cooperation, its relations with the USA and Canada through the Arctic Council, and with the European Union under the so-called Northern dimension. Commercially, Norway's main interests in the Arctic are petroleum resources and fisheries, where the country controls some of the world's most productive fishing grounds.

Norway's traditions as both a northern and southern polar nation go as far back as the late 1890s, and tell a story of exploration, scientific curiosity, commercial and political interests and engagement. Norwegian Antarctic history is rooted in the pioneering efforts to explore the region, and in the commercial whaling activities from the 1890s. Whaling played a major role in the Norwegian economy, affecting growth, employment and foreign trade. Whaling was also the main reason Norway annexed parts of the Antarctic and Subantarctic during the interwar period – Bouvetøya (1928), Peter I Øy (1931) and Dronning Maud Land (1939), all of which received status as Norwegian dependencies. The Antarctic Treaty, which entered into force in 1961, created a new framework for Norway's Antarctic policy. Since then, policy has accentuated scientific research and protection of the unique environment. Norway has also made active contributions to facilitating international collaboration under the Antarctic Treaty.[5] But the history of Norway's presence in the Antarctic is not just about 'Norway being in the Antarctic'. It is a story of Norway as a key actor on the global stage with a hand in the drafting of the international regimes for the region. Norway is an active state-party to the Antarctic Treaty and its green credentials are evident in its participation in the Environmental Protocol to the treaty and membership of the Commission for the Conservation of Antarctic Marine Living Resources (CCAMLR).

However, in the absence of a comprehensive strategic review of Norwegian Antarctic policy, policy has been pieced together and implemented on the go in the offices of the Norwegian MFA, without the benefit of an overarching political strategy that looks beyond day-to-day management issues. Despite this somewhat haphazard approach, policy has remained relatively consistent down the years, mainly because it has followed the familiar Norwegian pattern of promoting international law, peace, scientific research, and protection of the environment through established regimes while avoiding unnecessary bilateral face-offs with stronger powers: very similar, in fact, to Norway's approach to the Arctic. It might be stretching things to say that Norway's Antarctic policy is based on the Arctic model, but it *is* safe to say – after having analyzed every Norwegian white paper and strategy document on the Arctic since 2005[6] – that Norway's Antarctic policy is strikingly similar to the well-thought-out approach Norway has pursued vis-à-vis the Arctic ever since former prime minister Jens Stoltenberg in 2005 called the Arctic 'Norway's most important strategic area'. So while it would be unfair to criticize Norway for lacking a general Antarctic strategy, it would not be unfair to say that Norway's relative success in developing a comprehensive approach for the Arctic, together with the synergies and best practices it has produced, has also informed the country's approach to the Antarctic. These similarities in Norwegian interests and synergies in the two polar areas will become even clearer in the years to come, as political and commercial interests in the two regions converge, especially when compared to Norway's policy towards both regions since the end of the Cold War. The number of states and other actors displaying an interest in the Antarctic is rising steadily.[7] New players and new issues are complicating and stretching the capabilities of the Antarctic treaty system. This is why Norway as a claimant state with multiple interests in the area felt the need to systemize, analyze and formulate these interests and priorities in a coherent policy document.

The compass and framework of its Antarctic policy allows Norway to safeguard its interests as a claimant state while fulfilling its international obligations, especially those related to the Antarctic Treaty, the treaty's Environment Protocol and the CAMLR Convention. These are also intended to enhance Norway's collaborative role as a state party to the Antarctic Treaty system by increasing relevant synergies between Antarctic and Arctic expertise on, for example, climate change. Norway is also intent on promoting sustainable Norwegian business interests. Although this hierarchy of goals set out in the white paper may seem somewhat arbitrary in light of the wider strategy, chapter two of the white paper, 'Primary Goals', adds flesh to the bones.[8] The primary objective of Norway's Antarctic policy is to serve the nation's interests 'across a diverse range of activities in an enormous geographical area'.[9] These interests must further be safeguarded and promoted 'within the bounds of an international regulatory framework and a dynamic set of international actors'.[10]

In the rest of this chapter we present the key components of the white paper with examples showing the connections between Norwegian Antarctic and Arctic policy: strategies, actors, networks, commercial activity, legal framework, science and research.

Legal Framework

In the Norwegian white paper on Antarctica[11] we find general information on international law of relevance to the Antarctic and specifically to Norway. Given that the geographical scope of the Antarctic Treaty, set out in Article VI, extends beyond 60 degrees south both offshore and onshore, it therefore applies to the Norwegian territories of Dronning Maud Land and Peter I Øy, but not Bouvetøya, which is located further north. Although the Dependencies Act applies to Bouvetøya as well, a separate white paper is devoted to matters relating to the island: *Norwegian interests and policy in relation to Bouvetøya*.[12]

The white paper contains an interesting textbox headed 'Dronning Maud Land – The question of its southward geographic extent'. This warrants scrutiny as it seems to mark a change from the way Norway used to demarcate its territorial boundaries to the south – or rather how boundaries grew increasingly indistinct the closer they got to the pole. As such, the change should perhaps be seen as a sign of a more assertive Antarctic Norway.

Norway laid claim to Dronning Maud Land in 1939. According to the Norwegian MFA the wording of this claim was very carefully thought out.[13] Halvdan Koht, Norway's foreign minister at the time, defined the annexed area as 'that portion of the Antarctic mainland coast which extends from the limits of the Falkland Islands Dependencies in the west (the limits of Coats Land) to the limits of the Australian Antarctic territory in the east (45° E long.) with the land lying inside this coast and the environing sea'.[14]

The principles on which Norway's polar policies are based apply, as the wording shows, to both the Arctic and the Antarctic. But as the document also makes clear, the Norwegian claim in the Antarctic does not constitute a sector. Norway has consistently refused to use the so-called sector principle – which several other states employ as a basis for their claims in both northern and southern polar areas – since the early 1900s, and it remains a cornerstone of Norwegian polar policy to this day.[15] Anyway, the wording was not meant to indicate any huge difference in reality, according to the ministry.

It followed from the 1939 white paper on Norwegian sovereignty in the Antarctic that the purpose of the annexation was to lay claim to 'the land which until now has no owner and which no others than the Norwegians have examined and mapped'. While the eastward and westward boundaries of Dronning Maud Land are clearly marked, they often dissolve into a rather diffuse curly line a few miles from the South Pole, or simply fade out altogether on the official Norwegian maps. This state of indetermination could be about to change according to the current white paper. The Norwegian MFA has for the first time concluded that the geographic extension to the south does indeed go all the way to the pole[16]: 'On this basis, Norwegian authorities have not opposed any interpretation of the Norwegian claim as extending all the way to, and including, the pole itself.'[17]

Norway is one of seven states with claims to territory in the Antarctic. How Norway deploys its powers of control is regulated by the Act of 27 February 1930 relating to the Bouvetøya, Peter I Øy and Dronning Maud Land etc., known as the Dependencies Act (which also includes Bouvetøya). According to section 1 of the Dependencies Act, Dronning Maud Land and Peter I Øy are both subject to Norwegian sovereignty as dependencies, meaning among other things that although they are Norwegian territory, they are not part of the 'Kingdom of Norway'.[18] In a constitutional context, no territory that is part of the Kingdom of Norway may be ceded. The opposite is true of dependencies, however. This follows from section 1 of the Norwegian Constitution, according to which 'the Kingdom of Norway is a free, independent, indivisible and independent realm'. Beyond this constitutional meaning, their *status* as dependencies has no bearing on Norwegian legislation affecting Dronning Maud Land and Peter I Øy. Norwegian laws must, as in all other areas, comply with Norway's international legal obligations.[19] Among these obligations, those deriving from the Antarctic Treaty system are of particular importance. In principle, Norway's treaty obligations apply to its dependencies, unless exceptions have been agreed. It will often follow from an interpretation of the relevant treaty and its context whether it applies in those places, making any such exemption therefore redundant.

Private law, criminal law and procedural law apply in full in the Antarctic dependencies.[20] On the other hand, Norwegian governments have traditionally been reluctant to pass laws and regulations applicable to the other dependencies. Legislative purpose and practical reasons such as geographic location (i.e., remoteness from Norway), activity levels and other local circumstances have also been used to justify a cautious approach.[21] Furthermore, there is nothing to suggest that Norway is about to change in this regard, although it cannot be ruled out, given Norway's current political engagement and commercial involvement in Antarctica. Norway's Gene Technology Act and Electronic Communications Act have both seen their scope of application widened to include these areas in recent years. Norwegian legislation in Antarctica is based on the principle of territorial and personal jurisdiction. Territoriality means that legislation applies geographically to the Norwegian territories of Dronning Maud Land and Peter I Øy and to any person in those territories at any time. Under the principle of personal jurisdiction, the law applies to all Norwegian nationals wherever they happen to be in the Antarctic.[22] In addition to territorial and personal jurisdiction, Norway has flag state jurisdiction over vessels registered in Norway. Flag state jurisdiction means, among other things, that Norway is entitled to regulate the activity of Norwegian vessels on the high seas.[23] The Act relating to the Norwegian territorial waters and the contiguous zone is also applicable in Dronning Maud Land and on Peter I Øy, but is still not in force in those areas. Norway has to date issued no special instructions or directives concerning baselines and territorial waters. Norway has not established a 200-mile economic zone in these areas either.[24]

The Dependencies Act is an essential piece of legislation for Norway's dependencies in Antarctica, both because section 1 of the Act establishes their constitutional status, and because section 2 provides the basis for the application of the law in those territories. Under section 2 of the Dependencies Act, Norwegian private and criminal law and Norwegian legislation on the administration of justice ('procedural law') apply in Norway's Antarctic dependencies. The Norwegian king determines the extent to which other laws shall apply. In other words, section 2 of the Dependencies Act spells out the methodological basis for the legal techniques to be used to ascertain whether a specific law and associated regulations apply in the dependencies. The provision must be understood such that if the provision in question is not regarded as a provision of private, criminal or procedural law, it will not apply in the dependencies unless the king has decided otherwise.[25]

Here it is interesting to note how Norway's long-standing and wide-ranging experience in the Arctic is put to use in the Antarctic. The idea of separating private, criminal and procedural law from other areas of legislation was also adopted in the Act of 17 July 1925 relating to Svalbard and the Act of 27 February 1930 relating to Jan Mayen. As Norwegian activity in the Antarctic increases, we can gain a good understanding of how Norway will approach different issues by looking at how Arctic questions have been addressed. Indeed, the government clearly states in this white paper that Norway should capitalize on synergies created in the Arctic to benefit activity in the Antarctic.

According to *Norway's Arctic Strategy – Between geopolitics and social development*,[26] a 'broad international awareness of, and compliance with, the UN Convention on the Law of the Sea, and that the Convention forms the legal basis for the management of the Arctic Sea areas' are both factors of importance. In 2015, the Arctic coastal states (Norway, Canada, Denmark/Greenland, Russia and the USA) signed what is known as the Oslo Declaration on research cooperation and on preventing unregulated fishing in the international part of the central Arctic Ocean. In December 2017, a legally binding agreement banning fishing in the central Arctic Ocean for sixteen years was signed by the EU, Iceland, Japan, China and South Korea. Norway has demonstrated its proactive stance and desire to act as a responsible steward of the Arctic Oceans. The ban received widespread international attention, and Norway and Russia have been urged to show the same commitment in the Southern Ocean.

It makes sense for both countries to actively seek measures to safeguard the waters in the Arctic, which is after all their backyard. But both are also critical actors internationally and should work more closely with other nation states to protect the world's seas. Antarctica's remote Southern Ocean contains some of the most pristine marine environments on Earth, providing scientists with a source of much needed data on how fully intact and healthy marine ecosystems respond to climate change, free of industrial fishing. Norway and Russia have active fishing interests in the Southern Ocean and both are parties to the regulatory body for Antarctic waters, the CCAMLR.[27]

It will be interesting to see whether Norway takes steps regarding the regulation of fishing and to compare its actions in the two polar regions given the current and future importance of the industry to the country. Returning to the Antarctic strategy, the wording expresses a clear intent on Norway's part to give significant priority to the Antarctic in its foreign policy. Insofar as the Paris Agreement in conjunction with Norway's self-proclaimed role as one of the first countries to reach its global climate goals have effectively delivered the coup de grâce to any lingering dreams of the Arctic as the next chapter in Norway's oil and gas fairy tale, it is our working hypothesis that the strategy marks merely the beginning of a much stronger policy towards the South, and of a small state with increasingly big-power interests and a desire for greater visibility in the Antarctic. Norway is a small country with wide-ranging interests and sizeable ambitions, and the Antarctic seems to fit the bill on both counts.

As a small country, political science theory would predict that Norway needs to make sure that changes in foreign policy are visible and relevant to the international community. It is hard to imagine two more relevant platforms in this sense than the Arctic and Antarctic, not least in light of Norway's history and interests in the regions. As a small state, Norway will always be wary of playing a high-stakes game with a much stronger power. The Antarctic regime functions as well as the Arctic regime in this respect, where peaceful international cooperation, law and order are the norm. This fits perfectly with Norway's self-interests.

Research and Knowledge

According to the Antarctic strategy, Norway is also one of the leading polar nations in the field of science and research. While the Arctic has attracted most of the scientific attention, Norway has also, as mentioned in the introduction, a long history of research, exploration and commercial activity in Antarctica. This tradition, along with Norway's logistical resources and scientific expertise, provides a solid platform for Norwegian research in Antarctica. The fact that Norway conducts polar research in both the Arctic and Antarctic is obviously useful,[28] but could be put to even better use. The experience and knowledge acquired through research in the former region represent a large, untapped potential that could be used to expand research in Antarctica. Studies of the environment and ecosystem, ice, oceans and atmosphere in both polar regions will ease the acquisition of more evidence-based knowledge of global phenomena such as climate change, transboundary pollution, ecosystem dynamics, atmospheric processes and ocean currents.[29] Arctic expertise could be used to an even greater extent to understand the evolution of the Antarctic. In this area of research, Norway is in a unique position. Antarctica – just like the Arctic – has been affected by and influences in turn global climate change.

Several research institutions are operating in both regions, and the actors and their networks are often the same as well. The Norwegian Polar Institute and the Norwegian Institute of Marine Research are two of the most prominent examples, each with research projects in the Arctic and Antarctic. The new state-of-the-art icebreaker, the research vessel *Kronprins Haakon*, operates in northern parts of the Barents Sea and Arctic Ocean – areas that are difficult to access for normal vessels. One of the ship's main missions is to monitor the environmental and climatic status and changes in both polar areas. It is also scheduled to study krill in the Southern Ocean during the northern winter of 2018/19. At a more overarching level, science itself is well known as a form of political currency in the Antarctic. It is important therefore to understand more about how science is used politically in the Arctic and Antarctic.

In terms of citation numbers, Norwegian polar research scores above the world average, but still lags behind the leading nations. The high numbers are, however, largely a reflection of Norwegian research in the Arctic: Norway was ranked third in Arctic studies but only twenty-first in Antarctic research in 2010. Norway has all the resources, according to the Norwegian MFA,[30] to become one of the top ten Antarctic nations, and could do so by expanding capacity, recruiting talented researchers and profiting from a high level of international cooperation. Norwegian polar research will experience a generational change in the near future. It is therefore vital, in the government's view, to give researchers the best opportunities to develop and utilize their expertise in Antarctica.[31] The government is therefore urging affected parties to redouble and streamline efforts to tailor Norwegian research initiatives for the Antarctic while building expertise and readiness over the longer term.

The Norwegian government intends to boost Norwegian research in Antarctica by capitalizing on Norway's advantages as a polar research nation while supporting and promoting Norwegian management and activity in the Antarctic. The government will work to gain a better insight into global climate and environmental change, in part by exploiting the synergies between polar research in the South and in the North. Finally, research-based knowledge will be acquired with a view to optimizing Norway's ability to fulfil its obligations as a treaty party.[32]

The list of tasks the country has set itself to support and strengthen research in the Antarctic includes promoting the development of knowledge in and of the Antarctic and facilitating the recruitment of new and established scientists, within current budgetary limits, to conduct research in the Antarctic. Norway will work to improve the exploitation of available infrastructure by setting priorities and expanding capacity. Steps will be taken, within established frameworks, to meet the requests of foreign institutions wishing to establish a presence at the Troll research station, as well as deploying the new research vessel *Kronprins Haakon* in international scientific projects on marine ecosystems and stocks.

Technology enabling automatic and remote measurements (by satellite, aircraft, drones and unmanned vessels) will be developed and implemented, and the use of fishing vessels for scientific purposes will be encouraged. Norway wants to play a central role in international efforts to establish multilateral cooperation on infrastructure and data sharing in the Antarctic while also encouraging

Norwegian Antarctic scientists to play a more active role in SCAR[33] working groups and to publish more often in international scientific journals. Research institutions will be motivated to work more closely with the private and public sectors on the training of polar researchers, and businesses and industry will be incentivized to learn more about the Antarctic and participate in international polar research. Norway wants to work with other countries to understand the role of the Antarctic in the global climate system, and how ice mass changes will affect sea level. The necessary level of monitoring and mapping activities will also be ensured in the Norwegian Antarctic dependencies, allowing Norway to protect its interests and fulfil its international obligations.[34]

Although the most striking feature of Norway's Antarctic-research strategy is the prominence of the natural sciences, some of the best Norwegian studies in the Arctic are in the field of international politics and international law, which helps explain why Norway ranks as number three in the world by number of research publications. That Antarctic research is mainly discussed in terms of the physical and life sciences rather than social sciences is not unique to Norway. But it is difficult to understand why so little social scientific research has been conducted internationally given how politicized and complicated Antarctica has become. This is not just a 'Norwegian' issue, of course; it is something that the international community, with the claimant countries in the lead, should take seriously and do something about. As Brady says:

> Although Antarctic affairs are highly politicised and frequently contentious, much of the debate and analysis of what goes on has been conducted by politicians, activists, lawyers, geographers, historians and scientists. In contrast, currently only a handful of political scientists worldwide are actively engaged in research on Antarctic politics. For an area of such strategic importance this is a surprising anomaly.[35]

Indeed, as she goes on to say: 'What work that has been done on Antarctic politics in the past is mostly scattered in papers in academic journals or gathered together in a few classic books', for instance by Stokke and Vidas,[36] and Joyner.[37] The lack of political research in the Antarctic is thus an international problem, but also one that Norway should see as its particular responsibility to rectify. Again, to put it in Brady's words:

> The post-Cold War challenges facing Antarctic governance require a much greater investment in new political science-based research, especially to understand the interests of the new and rising players in Antarctic affairs such as China, India, Korea, Pakistan, and Malaysia and how other key players such as Russia or claimant states … are coping in this new global order.[38]

The Norwegian white paper analyzed in this chapter is comprehensive and well written, but it lacks a concentrated focus on the political challenges – both old and emerging. This is a weakness but possibly telling of the predominance of the natural science discourse in Norway regarding the Antarctic. The difference from the Norwegian discourse on the Arctic is striking. Here, natural science – although central and important – always seems to be framed and contextualized politically. Nevertheless, there is still an urgent need for interdisciplinary and multidisciplinary research in both polar regions involving political scientists and legal scholars along with physical and life scientists. In the Norwegian government, many of the same people are responsible for formulating policy (and pursuing policy discourse) in both polar areas. It is therefore interesting to note the stark difference in the discourse between Arctic and Antarctic strategies. Whereas politics and political interests permeate the former, in the latter, politics and national interests are narrowly defined through the natural sciences and encoded in the language of cooperation, environmental protection and science. In order to gain a better understanding of how nation states are positioning themselves vis-à-vis the polar areas, we also need to understand more about the limited number of actors, networks and national governments operating in and formulating policies on both regions.

As a 'double' polar nation, Norway will be a driving force in efforts to preserve the Antarctic environment, as well as a reference area for scientific research on the region's crucial importance in global climate change.[39] There is little to indicate that Antarctica is as affected by long-range transboundary pollution as the Arctic, but even though scientists have found pollutants in animals, other substances are causing greater concern. For example, high levels of long-range transboundary insecticides and pesticides (Mirex and HCB) have been found in the south polar skua, which breeds in Dronning Maud Land. Few studies have so far been done on the effect of these substances on wildlife in the Antarctic, and it is important to learn more. Steps to map pollution in Antarctica were initiated as part of the ongoing Atmosphere Research Programme at the Troll station. The Norwegian Institute for Air Research (NILU) has recorded traces of long-range transboundary air pollutants from the burning (deforestation) of Amazonian forests.[40] The Norwegian government is also preoccupied with the protection of Antarctica's cultural heritage. Of the ninety cultural monuments on the Antarctic Treaty Consultative Meeting's (ATCM) 2014 list, nine are associated with Norwegian activity on the continent. As part of its cultural heritage policy, the government wants to see this heritage preserved and maintained. Active participation in international fora for the preservation of cultural heritage in Antarctica is seen as a natural adjunct to Norway's policy and role in the Antarctic Treaty regime.[41] Because most of the well-known cultural assets are found in areas claimed by other countries, international cooperation is important and will affect the type of measures that can and should be taken. While the government has implemented measures to protect and preserve objects and sites in line with the detailed priority list set out in white paper No.16 (2004–05) *Living with Our Cultural Heritage*,[42] further work will be done to position Norway at the forefront of efforts to address environmental issues in the Antarctic and ensure that local activity affects the unique natural and cultural environmental values in the Antarctic as little as possible. Adhering to strict environmental criteria, Norway is, according to its Antarctic strategy, taking steps to:

1. learn more about the Antarctic environment to improve management;
2. secure important Norwegian cultural heritage in the Antarctic;
3. continue working with other nations to protect and preserve particularly important historical artefacts;
4. secure the continent as a reference area for research on the effects of global environmental and climate change and on the role of the Antarctic in the global climate system;
5. adapt the management of the Antarctic environment in response to climate change;
6. promote a holistic, ecosystem-based approach to the management of the marine and terrestrial environment in the treaty area, with a particular focus on protecting vulnerable areas of special value.

Marine Protected Areas (MPAs)

The world's largest marine reserve was created in the Ross Sea off Antarctica in October 2016. The Ross Sea is particularly important because it is the last intact marine ecosystem on the planet and the Southern Ocean is estimated to produce about three-quarters of the nutrients on which all life in the rest of the world's oceans rely.

The MPA came into effect in December 2017 and will be protected from commercial fishing for 35 years. The original suggestion from the US and New Zealand was to protect the area for 50 years, a so-called sunset clause. China only wanted 20 years. This is actually shorter than the lifespan of most of the Antarctic's top predators, whose protection the MPA was in part created for. Russia also refused to countenance the 50-year suggestion. Many countries, on the other hand, wanted to follow the best scientific advice and protect the area indefinitely – a politically impossible vision, however. The 35 years around which consensus was achieved is obviously better than nothing, but it still flies in the face of the scientific advice to implement indefinite protection if we want to ensure a truly sustainable ecosystem. Another complication was the fear of some states that the MPA would be used as a precedent to create other MPAs in international waters such as in the Arctic. Given the talk of creating MPAs in the Arctic there is a lot we can learn from the process leading up to the Ross Sea MPA, not least the horse-trading that goes on against scientific advice and best practices simply to cater to states' interests to exploit commercial opportunities in the Arctic. Furthermore, while the link between the Antarctic and the Arctic is pretty obvious, it remains an under-researched topic from a political science point of view. Norway is good when it comes to talking protection, but as the Ross Sea MPA process revealed, other nations believe Norway is somewhat weighed down by its obvious commercial interests in the Southern Ocean. It will therefore be interesting to see if there are any spillover effects when the Arctic MPA comes up for discussion.

Commercial Activity and Resource Management

The Norwegian private sector has had a foot in the Antarctic for over a century. In recent times, there has been an increasing focus on areas in which Norwegians possess particular skills sometimes due to a similar natural environment. Sectors in which the Norwegian state and/or private companies are active, or where there appears to be a significant commercial potential include, but are not limited to, fisheries, tourism, space-related activities, shipping and bioprospecting.[43] These activities are of course identical to those pursued by Norwegians in the Arctic where oil and gas related operations are still a key activity. Norway's activity in Antarctica will almost certainly increase – especially because the oil and gas adventure in the North is set to decline in the medium term. Norway's business policy in Antarctica is the same as it is in the Arctic: activity should be undertaken in compliance with a policy of responsible management, sustainable resource use and conservation of the natural environment. Within this ambit, there should be space to pursue environmentally sound research, tourism and commercial activity. Norwegian authorities have developed a set of national rules and regulations in accordance with Norway's international obligations, while facilitating commercial activity and employment in the region.[44]

Norway's fishing industry is the largest commercial activity in the Antarctic. In 2013/14, the Norwegian fleet (Aker BioMarine and Olympic Seafood) caught approximately 160,000 tonnes of krill. Norway harvests more krill than any other nation in the Antarctic area, and the industry is subject to the same standards of responsible management as in the Arctic and everywhere else Norwegians extract natural resources. The Norwegian Antarctic krill fishery accounts for about 60 per cent of the total catch of krill in the Convention area. Compliance with

Norway's policy of responsible management is partly ensured by the presence of an international observer on each of the three Norwegian krill vessels at any one time to monitor fishing activity and collect research data for the CCAMLR. This arrangement far exceeds the CCAMLR's recommended standards: having an observer present on at least 50 per cent of the krill vessels of each flag state.[45] Aker BioMarine have clear commercial interests in both the Arctic and the Antarctic. The Arctic biomass potential is massive, but still largely unknown. According to media reports, the company is positioning itself for the advent of a krill fishery in the Arctic by expanding its fleet and acquiring other companies.

The growth in tourism in Antarctica is often cited as a challenge to both the natural environment and treaty regimes. At present, roughly 40,000 tourists visit Antarctica every year. By comparison, the figure for 1992/93 was around 7,000 according to the International Association of Antarctica Tour Operators (IAATO). Over half of all cruises to Antarctica allow for disembarkation. At present, only one Norwegian cruise line is operating in Antarctica, but that number is also expected to rise. From a bipolar business-actor-network perspective, it is interesting to note that this cruise line is the Norwegian Hurtigruten. Their vessel *MS Midnatsol* travels up and down the coast of Norway and into the Arctic from May to September every year. The rest of the year, the ship operates in the Antarctic. We believe we need to have a much better understanding of how businesses operate in both polar areas and how their networks and relations with the Norwegian and other countries' governments work, and whether there are synergies or spillovers between the regions in terms of policies and operating licenses etc.

Besides the fishery, the satellite station TrollSat is the internationally most visible Norwegian activity in the Antarctic. TrollSat is close to the Troll research station in Dronning Maud Land, and a leading provider of downlink and control services for satellites in polar orbits. TrollSat is the largest satellite information reception station in Antarctica, and provides access to key data in fields such as meteorology, environmental monitoring and navigation. TrollSat also has the capacity to deliver near-real-time services for environmental monitoring in Antarctica, such as oil spills, ship detection and surveillance at sea. TrollSat also ensures reliable navigation data in Antarctica.[46] The Antarctic Treaty established an overarching framework for activity in Antarctica, including space activities. TrollSat operates in compliance with the Antarctic Treaty and obligations arising from it. Unlike similar operations on Svalbard in the Arctic, satellite downlink operations at the Antarctic ground station are not subject to statutory regulations, as of writing. Norway's ground station regulations are currently being revised, and separate regulations for ground stations in Antarctica are being drafted.[47] Again, we see the link between the two poles. Scientists and their networks operate in both regions, and there are bound to be comparative insights to be drawn from such close-knit communities given their operational relations and networks.

The potential for bioprospecting in the Arctic and Antarctic is attracting attention both in Norway and internationally. In the view of the Norwegian government, it is important that rules governing bioprospecting in Antarctica respect the Antarctic Treaty system, encourage research and effective knowledge sharing, safeguard the environment and ensure that the different national authorities supervise activities responsibly. But there is a need to devise a mechanism for governing the allocation of living resources used for commercial purposes. These matters should be considered in conjunction with efforts to promote research and commercial use of resources. Norway has rejected a proposal to unilaterally establish a principle of free access to genetic resources in the Antarctic. In Norway's view, access to and distribution of resources are two sides of the same coin and need to be drafted and coordinated concurrently. Because of the opposition of some countries to the development of a regulatory bioprospecting framework, it will be a particularly challenging task. As the situation stands today, Norway emphasizes the implementation of the 2013 Resolution on reporting and information exchange to determine the extent of this type of activity, and on the implementation of the specific duties set out in the Antarctic Treaty.[48] But it is not only the international community that lacks an overview: Norwegian authorities also want to learn more about the extent of Norwegian research on genetic resources in Antarctica as well as in the Arctic.

Private businesses will be encouraged to learn more about the Antarctic, develop expertise and collaborate in international polar research. A good example of such collaboration is the partnership between the krill industry and the scientific community to improve the science, monitor systems and ensure sound management of the Antarctic krill. These partnerships should be strengthened so that Norway can work even more effectively to improve the CCAMLR's management of marine living resources in the Antarctic – and again, Norway will look to the North to see how things are done there.

Norwegian space activity in Antarctica will be pursued in accordance with the Antarctic Treaty.[49] Norway will expand TrollSat's ground station and data reception services for international earth observation satellites as a long-term contribution to international environmental and resource monitoring. Any new activities or infrastructure will conform to guidelines governing the infrastructure at Troll. Norway will support work under the Antarctic Treaty System to develop regulations governing the collection and use of genetic resources to facilitate extraction and utilization of genetic material within an environmentally defensible framework. Work will target the creation of an effective reporting system that can streamline information sharing on this type of Antarctic activity within the ATCM and the CCAMLR. Norwegian stakeholders will be asked to report on this type of activity in the Antarctic, thereby allowing Norway to expand its knowledge base and exchange information in the ATCM and the CCAMLR. Norway would prefer the CCAMLR to retain an ecosystem-based management approach in which the conservation and rational use of marine living resources are viewed in relation to each other and properly balanced. Work will be done to institute international five-year monitoring and research programmes for marine ecosystems in the CCAMLR area to enhance research and monitoring of marine living resources. The CCAMLR will be encouraged to create a representative network of marine protected areas while taking other effective area-based management steps within the convention area. Last but not least, Norway will pursue the introduction of a payment system where vessels are charged a registration fee to fish in the CCAMLR area.

The Madrid Protocol to the Antarctic Treaty clearly states in Article 7: 'Any activity related to mineral resources, other than scientific research shall be prohibited.' The point here is that the treaty will come up for renegotiation in 2048 and it seems clear that some states – such as China and Russia – are playing the long game in the Antarctic, and positioning themselves in order to exploit future commercial opportunities. We as scientists must therefore also take the long view when assessing the politics affecting these areas, since it can help us explain why certain states behave as they do in both the Arctic and Antarctic. If changes are made in 2048 regarding mining and resource extraction in the Antarctic, we will likely see many of the same businesses operating in both areas.

Conclusion

Norway has long traditions as a polar nation both in the Arctic and the Antarctic. The long lines of history speak of a small country with big ambitions, exemplified by pioneering explorers, scientific curiosity and business interests. The first Antarctic strategy in nearly eighty years should be read as a clear signal of intent by the Norwegian government. It is uncommonly comprehensive and detailed, and covers most if not all of Norway's key foreign policy interests. If we remove petroleum and security policy from the Arctic equation, it is almost uncanny to see how similar Norwegian core interests are in the northern and southern hemispheres. The similarities between Norway's Arctic and Antarctic approaches are striking; indeed the document looks almost like a dated white paper on the Arctic. The takeaway message is really that by examining Norway's previous Arctic policies and actions we can get a pretty good idea of what Norwegian foreign policy towards the Antarctic will look like.

An important reason for the lack of comparative political science research on the Arctic and Antarctic is, we believe, the traditional focus on the differences between the two regions. After all, the name Antarctic literally means 'anti-Arctic or 'opposite to the north': in many ways, the Antarctic is everything the Arctic is not. For example, it is a continent, and has a very different legal status. But it is a view, we believe, that can easily miss the forest for the trees. If we take a closer look at the actors and their networks, it makes a lot more sense to bear the one region in mind while studying the other. As this chapter has shown, we have only just begun to scratch the surface of possible research themes, and have more questions than answers at this point. But that is the motivation behind the exercise; to formulate novel research questions so that we can look at the two polar areas through a new scientific lens.

Instead of looking at the macro level, where there are mostly differences, we argue that following the money, the actors and their networks will produce new insights into the politics on both areas and how they are more closely connected through actors and networks than it appears at first glance. It is, for instance, surprising to us to learn that in many foreign ministries, the same small number of officials deal with both the Arctic and the Antarctic. When we contact the Norwegian ministry, we often talk to the same people whether our questions are about the Arctic or Antarctic. To us, as political scientists, this is highly interesting. The same goes for business; it would be rewarding to examine actors operating in both areas. Norway has, as mentioned, the world's largest krill fishery in the Southern Ocean. The Norwegian company Aker BioMarine is currently fishing there, while at the same time exploring opportunities to fish krill in the Arctic Ocean. Such bipolar activity and the possible networks it forms are surely worth investigating further. Research on both poles is also highly interesting from a political science point of view; there are several examples of research institutions operating in both areas. The Norwegian Polar Institute is one example. Furthermore, science itself is a well-known form of political currency in the Antarctic, and ties to the various governments are tight. We need to understand more about how science itself is used politically in the Arctic.

The government–business–science nexus is found in both the Arctic and Antarctic, with many of the same actors – often in small numbers – operating in both areas. We believe there is a need to understand more about the dynamics and possible spillovers from one area to the other. These are under-researched questions and part of what we believe should become a new research agenda for political scientists and legal scholars specializing in the Arctic and/or the Antarctic.

Indeed, a comparative agenda holds up even if we shift focus from actors to policy areas. The MPA in the Ross Sea can give us valuable insights into the dynamics involved in creating an MPA in Arctic waters. The complicated, highly politicized process leading up to the Ross Sea MPA can teach us a great deal. It will be especially valuable to remember the horse-trading that went against scientific advice and best practices due to states' interests in future commercial opportunities if and when an Arctic MPA comes up for discussion. Many of the same actors will be engaged in that process.

When it comes to mining and other resource extraction, there are also clear scholarly and political parallels. It seems clear that some states, such as Russia and China, are playing a long game both in the Arctic and Antarctic, while positioning themselves to exploit any future commercial opportunities. As scientists we must also take the long view when assessing the politics in these areas, because such views help explain why certain states act as they do in both the Arctic and Antarctic. Again, the actors are largely the same.

A fruitful future research agenda for researchers studying Arctic politics would be to look at both regions through a more comparative lens than we have done here. From a political science point of view, the Antarctic is not really 'opposed to the Arctic', or everything the Arctic is not. It is rather like the distorting mirrors found in funfairs, inviting us to take a closer look and see Arctic issues in a new light.

Notes

1 See http://arctic.ucalgary.ca/parallels-arctic-and-antarctic-governance-and-resource-management (accessed 17 April 2018).

2 We are using the official Norwegian names of the areas to which the country lays claim. The English names are Queen Maud Land, Peter I's Island and Bouvet Island.

3 Norwegian Ministry of Foreign Affairs, *Norwegian Government's High North Strategy* (Oslo, Norwegian Ministry of Foreign Affairs, 2006), p. 13.

4 Cooperation in the Barents Euro-Arctic Region was launched in 1993 on two levels: intergovernmental Barents Euro-Arctic Council (BEAC) and interregional Barents Regional Council (BRC). The overall objective of Barents cooperation has been sustainable development. During the Cold War the Barents region was an area of military confrontation. The underlying premise was that close cooperation secures political long-term stability and reduces possible tensions. This objective has already been successfully achieved. The Barents cooperation has fostered a new sense of unity and closer contact among the people of the region, which is an excellent basis for further progress. See www.barentscooperation.org/en/About (accessed 17 April 2018).

5 Norwegian Ministry of Foreign Affairs, *Norwegian interests and policy in the Antarctic*, St.meld.nr. 32 (2014–2015) (Oslo, Norwegian Ministry of Foreign Affairs, 2015), p. 10.

6 Leif Christian Jensen, *International Relations in the Arctic: Norway and the Struggle for Power in the New North* (London, I.B. Tauris, 2016).

7 Anne-Marie Brady (ed.), *The Emerging Politics of Antarctica* (London, Routledge, 2013).
8 Norwegian Ministry of Foreign Affairs, *Norwegian interests and policy in the Antarctic*, p. 8.
9 Ibid.
10 Ibid.
11 Ibid.
12 Norwegian Ministry of Justice and Public Security, *Norske interesser og politikk for Bouvetøya*, St.meld.nr. 33 (2014–2015) (Oslo, Norwegian Ministry of Justice and Public Security, 2015).
13 Norwegian Ministry of Foreign Affairs, *Norwegian interests and policy in the Antarctic*, p. 17.
14 William James Mills, *Exploring Polar Frontiers: A Historical Encyclopedia* (Santa Barbara, ABC CLIO, 2003), p. 540.
15 Norwegian Ministry of Justice and Public Security, *Norske interesser og politikk for Bouvetøya*, p. 17.
16 *Aftenposten*, 19 September 2015.
17 Norwegian Ministry of Foreign Affairs, *Norwegian interests and policy in the Antarctic*, p. 17.
18 Ibid., p. 29.
19 Ibid.
20 Ibid.
21 Ibid.
22 Ibid., p. 30.
23 Ibid.
24 Ibid., p. 32.
25 Ibid., p. 30.
26 Norwegian Ministries, *Norway's Arctic Strategy – between geopolitics and social development* (Oslo, Norwegian Ministries, 2017), p. 20–21.
27 Mark Epstein, 'Russia and Norway can be global leaders for polar protection' (n.d.). Available at https://www.asoc.org/component/content/article/9-blog/1407-russia-and-norway-can-be-global-leaders-for-polar-protections (accessed 17 April 2018).
28 Norwegian Ministry of Foreign Affairs, *Norwegian interests and policy in the Antarctic*, p. 34.
29 Ibid.
30 Ibid., p. 35.
31 Ibid.
32 Ibid., p. 37.
33 SCAR is a committee under the International Council for Science (ICSU) tasked with implementing, promoting and coordinating scientific research in Antarctica.
34 Norwegian Ministry of Foreign Affairs, *Norwegian interests and policy in the Antarctic*, p. 35–41.
35 Brady, *The Emerging Politics of Antarctica*, p. 3.
36 Olav S. Stokke, and Davor Vidas (eds), *Governing the Antarctic: The Effectiveness and Legitimacy of the Antarctic Treaty System* (Cambridge, Cambridge University Press, 1995).

37 Chris C. Joyner, *Governing the Frozen Commons: The Antarctic Regime and Environmental Protection* (South Carolina, University of South Carolina Press, 1998).
38 Brady, *The Emerging Politics of Antarctica*, p. 3.
39 Norwegian Ministry of Foreign Affairs, *Norwegian interests and policy in the Antarctic*, p. 42.
40 Ibid., p. 47.
41 Ibid., p. 44.
42 Norwegian Ministry of Environment, *Leve med kulturminner*, St.meld.nr. 16 (2004–05) (Oslo, Norwegian Ministry of Environment, 2005).
43 Norwegian Ministry of Foreign Affairs, *Norwegian interests and policy in the Antarctic*, p. 49.
44 Ibid., p. 49.
45 Ibid., pp. 56–7.
46 Ibid., p. 60.
47 Ibid.
48 Ibid., pp. 63–4.
49 Norwegian Ministry of Trade and Industry, *Between Heaven and Earth: Norwegian space policy for business and public benefit*, St.meld.nr. 32 (2012–2013) (Oslo, Norwegian Ministry of Trade and Industry, 2013).

CHAPTER 3

SOFT LAW, SOLID IMPLEMENTATION? NORWEGIAN FOLLOW-UP OF ARCTIC COUNCIL RECOMMENDATIONS

Ida Folkestad Soltvedt

Introduction

During recent debates concerning the Arctic Council, scholars have highlighted the Council's putative weakness as a soft-law body, and generally questioned its effectiveness.[1] This criticism is largely rooted in a lack of legal bindingness: the Arctic Council does not hold the power to contract or enforce legally binding agreements, nor to apply sanctions against its member states. Its recommendations are only politically binding, whereas domestic follow-up is voluntary. Accordingly, it has been claimed that few incentives for national implementation exist. However, only a few studies have examined how the Council's recommendations actually affect national processes,[2] or, more broadly, the positive effects of soft law on national implementation. This chapter explores the extent to which the Norwegian authorities have implemented the recommendations from two of the Council's foremost policy contributions: the 2004 *Arctic Climate Impact Assessment* (ACIA), which put climate change adaptation on the global agenda; and the 2009 *Arctic Marine Shipping Assessment* (AMSA), the first and only report to cover shipping throughout the Arctic region.[3]

I begin by assuming that international law is not binary, that soft law is not a uniform phenomenon, and that soft law recommendations may entail certain

---

This chapter is based on Ida F. Soltvedt, 'Soft law, solid implementation? The influence of precision, monitoring and stakeholder involvement on Norwegian implementation of Arctic Council recommendations', *Arctic Review on Law and Politics* 8 (2017), pp. 73–94.

characteristics that enhance their domestic implementation. In particular, I ask how precision, procedures for monitoring state behaviour, and the involvement of stakeholders in norm development, can act as drivers of national implementation. In addition, malignancy – an important barrier to national implementation – is taken into account.[4] Data from interviews and documents indicate that these first three characteristics are relevant to Norwegian implementation, i.e. translating recommendations into action at the national level. However, the absence of malignancy appears to be the most significant condition for achieving implementation. In the following, I clarify the concept of implementation, and then present my fundamental arguments and how the selected characteristics are expected to affect national implementation. Subsequently, I examine whether the recommendations – three derived from the ACIA and three from the AMSA[5] – have been implemented, and how their characteristics, as well as malignancy, alone and in interaction, have affected varying outcomes.

What Does National Implementation Entail?

International commitments usually require behavioural change at the domestic (national) level. National implementation concerns the steps taken to induce those changes.[6] In accordance with this understanding, national implementation is commonly defined as the process whereby international commitments are translated into action at the domestic level, attempting to steer actors towards specific behaviours.[7] The definition applied in this chapter rests on the same principles. Specifically, I take national implementation to include domestically conducted programmes or actions in response to the soft-law recommendations of the Arctic Council. Indicators of such programmes or actions are administrative measures and/or budget allocations. Furthermore, national programmes and actions may be initiated in order to influence other states' policies through international organizations and institutions. According to the definition applied here, in order to be considered as national implementation, this chain of events must result from the recommendation in question, and induce certain changes at the national level, before 'bouncing' back to the international one. At the international level, this should result in Norwegian initiatives and/or projects being carried out within the relevant organization.

This concept of implementation is closely linked to causality, implying that outputs (in this case, Arctic Council recommendations) affect the behaviour of relevant actors, and that it is possible to trace causal mechanisms to show an actual link between them. Precisely because of its inherent causality, I have chosen to focus on implementation – not compliance, as commonly studied within the academic literature. Compliance, as opposed to implementation, concerns whether the behaviour of states and their actors conforms to international provisions. Compliance may even be accidental, resulting from laws and regulations already initiated, whereas implementation is by definition instrumental in nature.[8]

Of course, the determination of causation is a highly complex issue, and the reader must be aware that only a part of the greater picture is presented here. Still, I believe that focusing on causation lowers the risk of ascribing too much credit to the Arctic Council and is therefore a useful exercise. Now, before moving on to the analysis, a closer look at the phenomenon of international law, and especially soft law, is in order.

The Dynamics of International Law: Different Forms of Soft Law?

International law has traditionally been considered a binary phenomenon.[9] Hard law is understood as obligations that are legally binding, whereas soft law refers to norms that are deliberately non-binding in character, located 'in the twilight between law and politics'.[10] When the two are pitted against each other, the former is often favoured over the latter. Scholars within strands of legal positivism, for instance, privilege hard law: they consider the legal obligation to be crucial – the one element that distinguishes law from mere norms. By definition, then, 'law' becomes binding, and the very concept of 'soft law' is rejected.[11] In line with this view, conventional wisdom holds that the most effective commitments are those that are legally binding.

Recent years have witnessed an upsurge in studies of international law and its effects on state behaviour. Through contemporary debates, new perspectives have appeared that challenge the 'binary divide'. Among its key opponents, Abbott and Snidal hold that the hard law/soft law distinction is incorrectly taken as dichotomous.[12] Instead, international law should be understood as dynamic and a matter of gradation. They portray the broader phenomenon of international law as consisting of three dimensions: obligation – that states or other actors are bound by a rule or commitment, making their behaviour subject to scrutiny under international law; precision – that rules unambiguously define the conduct that is required, authorized, or prescribed; and delegation – that third parties are granted authority to implement, interpret, and apply the rules.[13] According to this understanding, hard law refers to 'legally binding agreements that are precise … and that delegate authority for interpreting and implementing the law'.[14] The realm of soft law, then, begins once legal arrangements are weakened along these dimensions.

Abbott and Snidal's claims have been both applauded and criticized, but one particularly important lesson can be drawn from their work: softening may occur in varying degrees, which in turn will have distinct implications for how soft-law agreements are interpreted and implemented.[15] Hence, soft law is neither fixed nor uniform: it exists in differing forms (as is also the case with hard law). By extension, I argue that the *characteristics* of a certain soft-law commitment – here I focus on precision, monitoring of state behaviour, and stakeholder involvement – can affect national decisions about implementing it.

Characteristics of the commitment as drivers of national implementation

The characteristics a commitment holds has not been particularly central to soft-law studies, but is of great relevance to studies of hard law. The three characteristics included in this study – precision, monitoring and stakeholder involvement – have been strongly associated with such agreements, and their presence is considered highly important for national implementation.[16] In conducting the analysis later in this chapter, I thus understand them, in line with those earlier works, as involving the following.

Precision refers to 'rules that unambiguously establish the conduct they require, authorise, or prescribe'.[17] A precise recommendation should specify what is expected – stating the objective and the necessary measures to achieve it.[18] Precision is important for impact because it reduces the leeway available to states and actors with regard to interpretation and discretion. Hence, domestic implementation is best facilitated by a clear message with minimal possibility for misinterpretation.[19] In contrast, general rules have several drawbacks. Most importantly, they render meaningful assessment of implementation difficult, as much less work is demanded on the part of states expected to abide by them.

Monitoring of state behaviour concerns the obligations of states to report back on national measures to meet a certain recommendation.[20] Such mechanisms make parties more accountable, particularly if any failure to fulfil obligations is publicly revealed.[21] Where some sort of monitoring exists, states will usually seek to avoid potential shaming. Monitoring also serves to keep the issue on national and international agendas. The presence or absence of progress may entail scrutiny at both levels, also enabling NGOs and other actors to challenge governmental positions and exert pressure.[22]

Stakeholder involvement concerns 'those actors who are affected by the institution or who are capable of influencing its performance' and, further, who are invited to participate in norm-development processes.[23] Such involvement is held to be positive, not least because stakeholders may seek to persuade their national decision makers to implement the norms that they themselves helped create. They therefore contribute to the internalization of international norms, by linking them to domestic policies. Or, stakeholders involved in international norm-development processes – persons/organizations knowledgeable about the matter in question – may be invited into subsequent domestic processes by the national authorities. Then, there may also be room to influence relevant decision makers at the national level.

These three characteristics have been well studied in the academic literature, which lends leverage to expectations of their effect on national implementation. Importantly, the three characteristics are particularly relevant in the context of the Arctic Council. Since the ACIA project and especially after 2009, with the release of the 'second-generation' AMSA report, the Council has formulated increasingly specific policy recommendations and follow-up actions.[24] Moreover, after the 2009 AMSA release, one of the most articulated criticisms regarding the Council's effectiveness – the lack of a formal monitoring mechanism – was challenged. Current trends within the Council also seem to have a bearing on the composition and involvement of various stakeholders. Through the permanent participants, indigenous peoples' groups play an important role in the policy work of the Council,[25] although they are sometimes marginalized due to lack of resources. Council observers, by contrast, have much more limited rights.[26] Additionally, given the Council's expanding agenda, this group cannot be expected to include all relevant stakeholders. Whether other stakeholders have the opportunity to inform policy processes will vary, and is likely to depend on more informal ways of inclusion. Thus, based on these contextual settings, the question is: when present, what bearing do the three above-noted characteristics have on national implementation?

Malignancy as an obstacle to national implementation

But first, one final point on malignancy and its negative effect on national implementation. Essentially, 'malignancy' concerns the complex political nature of a given problem and, consequently, the incentive to avoid following commitments.[27] In terms of national implementation one may thus ask: 'what accounts for such an incentive?' Here, I make use of two explanatory dimensions – political costs and economic costs.

'Political costs' refers to the divergent preferences among relevant actors that may obstruct implementation. However, within Norwegian High North politics, congruity between the parties in the parliament has become the norm. This is illustrated, inter alia, by the white paper *Opportunities and Challenges in the High North*, which sought to develop a new and comprehensive policy for the area's rich resources, and the firm support accorded to this policy by the Norwegian parliament. The same held true when the government presented *Nordkloden* (Norway's arctic policy) in 2014. As such, opposition or 'divergent preferences' tend to stem from groupings outside the political sphere. 'Economic costs', on the other hand, refers to the strain that implementation places on financial resources. Here, a rule of thumb is that economic costs exceed potential gains from implementation. Put briefly, then, and in simple terms: recommendations that do not invoke political or economic costs are non-malignant; while recommendations that invoke political *and/or* economic costs are malignant, thus considerably lowering the likelihood of implementation.

Implementing the Arctic Climate Impact Assessment

When it was presented in 2004, the ACIA represented a milestone in the Council's history. As the first regional climate change assessment, the ACIA dramatically challenged the global understanding of the Arctic as a 'frozen desert', and shed light on the vast and complex transformations underway in the region.[28] To combat the ongoing climate changes revealed through the ACIA project, recommendations based on two sets of actions were put forth: *mitigation*, to reduce greenhouse gas (GHG) emissions; and *adaptation*, to limit the adverse impacts of climate change by developing greater resilience.[29]

National context and selected recommendations

At the beginning of the ACIA project in 2000, mitigation already featured on national and international agendas. Through global regimes like the United Nations Framework Convention on Climate Change (UNFCCC), and the Kyoto Protocol in particular, Norway was legally committed to reducing its GHG emissions. Therefore, any change in state behaviour concerning mitigation must be viewed within the established context of these frameworks, not the Arctic Council.[30] However, serious discussion on adaptation had yet to emerge. In fact, adaptation was viewed by some as a highly problematic measure that would compromise efforts to reduce emissions.[31] Yet, a shift in priorities within the climate regime and the media discourse can be traced, drawing largely on the new knowledge produced by the ACIA.[32] The ACIA revealed how climate change had already caused severe problems for ecosystems and human communities in the Arctic. Moreover, it recognized that climate change had become inevitable, making adaptation vital. With its unique focus on the Arctic region, the ACIA succeeded in putting adaptation on the global agenda as well as on the national agenda of Norway.

The first Norwegian white paper on climate change, released in 1995, focused on GHG emissions, accompanied by mitigation measures aimed at reducing them.[33] It was only after a new white paper appeared in 2001 that adaptation gained momentum.[34] With regard to the Arctic, adaptation was viewed in the context of the ongoing ACIA process, where Norway occupied a central role. That same year, the Norwegian Ministry of the Environment established a steering committee responsible for the country's ACIA work. In the course of 2001 and 2002, four meetings were held on climate change and its consequences for the Norwegian North. The conclusions of these meetings were forwarded to the international process and the Norwegian state authorities.[35] As Arctic climate adaptation had received limited attention until the turn of the century, it may be that the ACIA, even before it was finalized, made the topic more central in Norwegian politics. Hence, the focus on adaptation and national measures to implement the ACIA recommendations (see Table 3.1).

National implementation

Recommendation: Help Arctic residents adapt

The first recommendation, 'help Arctic residents adapt', focused on the need for adaptation in the North through better access to information, decision makers, and institutional capacity for those living in the Arctic.[37] Of the various Norwegian initiatives related to this recommendation, one national programme – NorACIA – stands out as an important implementation measure. NorACIA was introduced in 2005, with responsibility for domestic follow-up of ACIA.[38] Its mandate was to generate and disseminate knowledge, and to provide the Ministry of the Environment with advice concerning relevant national processes.[39] Thus, a central

Table 3.1 The ACIA recommendations.[36]

Help Arctic residents adapt: Work closely with Arctic residents, including indigenous and local communities, to help them to adapt and manage the environmental, economic and social impacts of climate change and ultraviolet radiation change. Adaptation needs will vary. Arctic residents may need inter alia enhanced access to information, decision makers, and institutional capacity building to safeguard their health, culture and well-being.
Adaptive management, nature conservation, and reduction of risks: Implement as appropriate, adaptive management strategies for Arctic ecosystems, making use of local and indigenous knowledge and participation, review nature conservation and land and resource use policies and programmes, and to the extent possible reduce risks related to infrastructure damage, permafrost degradation, floods and costal erosion, taking into account costs and benefits.
Develop the Arctic in a sustainable manner: Recognize that opportunities related to climate change, such as increased navigability of sea routes and access to resources, should be developed and managed in a sustainable manner, including through the consideration of environmental and social impacts and taking appropriate measures to protect the environment, local residents and communities.

information platform was created for Arctic residents and for decision makers. Several seminars focused on the consequences of climate change related to infrastructure, shipping, Saami industries and societal aspects.[40] Involved in these meetings were actors from research communities, Saami institutions, and the government administration at both the national and regional levels.[41] Yet, the most striking feature of Norwegian implementation measures during this period was the focus on indigenous peoples in the design of adaptation policies. For instance, the 2006 High North Strategy stated: 'The Arctic Climate Impact Assessment (ACIA) documents how indigenous peoples have adapted to earlier climate change' and that 'the climate change currently taking place may have major impacts on the way of life of indigenous peoples'.[42] The indigenous dimension of the High North Strategy was further elaborated in the 2007 white paper, *Norwegian Saami Policy*, where indigenous knowledge and observation of climate change adaptation were mentioned as central to following up the ACIA.[43] How can we explain this positive outcome? In the following discussion (and in the discussion of the other ACIA recommendations), I omit the characteristic of 'monitoring', as a reporting system was not established for the ACIA. The focus is therefore on *precision, stakeholder involvement* and potentially the *malignant* nature of the issue.

First of all, we see that the recommendation is *precise*. It states the objective – 'to help Arctic residents adapt', with possible measures for achieving this – 'enhance access to information, decision makers, and institutional capacity building'. As precision is thought to reduce states' use of interpretation and discretion, it may well be that these aspects helped identify the necessary measures to be taken.

Regarding *malignancy*, the recommendation does not entail significant political cost. There was already widespread agreement in Norway on the importance of the ACIA and its findings. Moreover, access to information and decision makers are not measures that require great financial resources. The absence of malignancy *may* thus have facilitated follow-up actions.

Thirdly, the Arctic Council processes in which the recommendation was developed had *involved stakeholders*. In particular indigenous peoples' groups, as permanent participants, were involved in all aspects of the ACIA process, including policy work.[44] From the start, the focus was therefore directed towards the human dimension of climate change, framed largely as the impacts of climate change on indigenous peoples, their lives and livelihoods.[45] In the implementation of this specific recommendation, the Saami Council, a permanent participant representing the Saami population, played a role at the national level. Together with the other permanent participants, the Saami Council issued statements urging national governments to act.[46] Moreover, during initial NorACIA meetings, Saami Council representatives stressed the need for the participation and inclusion of

Saami interests.[47] The Saami Council, thereby, affected the national process by lobbying the national authorities and identifying potential representatives and experts from Saami communities.[48] Similarly, environmental organizations were included as stakeholders in the Arctic Council norm-development processes. The World Wide Fund for Nature (WWF) participated in several ACIA meetings at the international level and, subsequently in certain lobbying activities nationally. Shortly after the release of the ACIA report, a letter was sent to the Norwegian Minister of Foreign Affairs, encouraging national decision makers to develop and implement adaptation strategies.[49] Later, the WWF received funding from NorACIA for a factsheet series on the impacts of climate change. Thus, we see that the WWF was also involved in implementing the recommendation. In total, whereas the exact effect of *precision* is difficult to determine, both *stakeholder involvement* and the *absence of malignancy* would appear to have had positive impacts on implementation.

Recommendation: Adaptive management, nature conservation, and reduction of risks

The second ACIA recommendation, 'adaptive management, nature conservation, and reduction of risks', involved the following objectives: implementation of adaptive management strategies in cooperation with indigenous peoples; review of nature conservation and land use policies and programmes; and reduction of risks related to infrastructure damage, permafrost degradation, floods and coastal erosion.[50] National measures were also implemented in this case, but principally under NorACIA. As regards nature conservation and the review of such policies, an evaluation of key habitats in Northern Norway and on Svalbard was conducted in 2009, assessing whether current conservation practices were sufficient, or whether greater efforts were necessary to safeguard biodiversity.[51] These assessment reports have continued to provide an important framework for the management of protected areas on Svalbard.[52] In addition, several reports on infrastructure damage, as well as the vulnerability of Norway's northern counties and municipalities to floods and coastal erosion were prepared under the umbrella of NorACIA.[53]

What then can be said of the effects of the three chosen characteristics, plus malignancy, on the outcomes? As the recommendation merely states the objectives of adaptive management, nature conservation and risk reduction, without specifying any measures for achieving them, it is *imprecise*. However, this imprecision need not have a negative bearing on national implementation – indeed, the vague formulation may have made implementation less challenging.

The positive effect that imprecision may have on implementation is closely linked to the concept of *malignancy.* By being imprecise, the recommendation does not impose economic costs; likewise, formulations like 'review' and 'reduction of risks' do not invite significant political disagreement. Therefore, it is possible that the lack of precision served to reduce malignancy, in turn easing the implementation process.

Stakeholder involvement, on the other hand, seems to have had a limited effect on the positive implementation outcome here. Although the Saami Council and the WWF were actively involved in Arctic Council processes, we find no indication of their involvement in subsequent national processes. One explanation, especially regarding the Saami Council, may be that the assessment reports were scientific in nature and prepared exclusively by specialists.

Briefly, then: the *imprecision* of this recommendation seems to have had a positive bearing on the implementation outcome, by lowering the political and economic costs, and thereby *malignancy*. Lastly, we find nothing to indicate that *stakeholder involvement* affected the outcome.

Recommendation: Develop the Arctic in a sustainable manner

The third recommendation, 'develop the Arctic in a sustainable manner', encouraged member states to develop the Arctic sustainably, particularly in relation to the increased navigability of sea routes and access to resources, by protecting the environment, local residents and communities.[54] However, it did not result in any additional implementation measures nationally. To some extent, this can be explained by previously initiated measures that were consistent with the recommendation, in particular the *Management Plan for the Barents Sea and Lofoten Area*. Still, that plan came to exclude the human dimension of ecosystem-based management, an important deviation from what was stated in the recommendation.[55] By extension, the interests of the coastal Saami, who are heavily dependent on productive marine ecosystems and their resources, were not taken into account. This is an important point, as it indicates that further action could have been taken in order to accommodate the recommendation. *Why* then was nothing done?

Firstly, the recommendation is *imprecise*. It only states objectives, not measures for achieving them. Of course, when it comes to precision, or lack thereof, the findings have already proven ambiguous, and it is therefore difficult to determine any specific effect. With regard to *malignancy*, however, we see a more distinct pattern. Although the recommendation would have entailed few specific economic costs, resource exploitation does involve conflicting interests, especially among industrial and environmental groups. In the Arctic, indigenous peoples add a further dimension. Political costs are thus present and, subsequently a certain degree of malignancy.

Regarding *stakeholder involvement*, the same applies as with the first two recommendations. Indigenous peoples as well as environmental organizations were involved in the Arctic Council norm-development process, but we find no trace of their attempting to influence national processes in relation to this recommendation.

Therefore, it is possible that these aspects combined – the *lack of precision*, the *presence of malignancy*, and *no indications of stakeholders* attempting to affect national processes – had an obstructive effect on implementation.

Summary

For a long time, Arctic adaptation did not feature on international or national agendas. Scant attention was paid to the issue in Norway before the ACIA report. Taking into account this contextual setting and the upsurge in national adaptation measures from 2005, ACIA appears to have served as a key driver and as an agenda-setter in Norwegian politics. As for implementation, the Norwegian authorities did initiate measures related to two ACIA recommendations: 'help Arctic residents adapt' and 'adaptive management, nature conservation, and reduction of risks'. However, no additional measures were taken to implement the recommendation 'develop the Arctic in a sustainable manner'.

The picture is more nuanced when it comes to the impact of the three characteristics chosen for this study, plus malignancy, on implementation outcomes. No clear-cut implications of precision and its effect on implementation were identified. In fact, we can note potential positive influences from *both* precision *and* lack of precision: the former, by clarifying necessary measures to fulfil implementation; the latter, by lessening political and economic costs and, thereby, malignancy. In contrast, a consistent pattern was detected in connection with malignancy and its effect on implementation: the presence of malignancy appeared to hinder implementation, whereas the absence of malignancy facilitated positive implementation outcomes. As for the stakeholders involved in the Arctic Council processes, they participated in subsequent national implementation processes only in relation to the first recommendation, 'help Arctic residents adapt'. However, although this was not evident in connection with the other recommendations, we should not rule out the possible effects on implementation yet.

Implementing the Arctic Marine Shipping Assessment

A main finding of the ACIA report was in relation to the opening of the Arctic Ocean and a possible increase in Arctic marine activity.[56] To follow up this finding, the AMSA project was launched in 2004, aimed at mapping out shipping volumes in the Arctic marine regions.[57] When this work was finalized in 2009, the need for uniform international standards matching the Arctic conditions and greater coordination between member states had been identified.[58] To meet these challenges, member states were given recommendations centering on three themes: enhancing Arctic marine safety, protecting the Arctic peoples and the environment; and building Arctic marine infrastructure.[59]

National context and selected recommendations

As a leading maritime nation, Norway had already paid great attention to these issues, and the AMSA can hardly be seen as an agenda-setter at the domestic level. With close to 110,000 people working in the maritime sector, and with a value creation equalling 8.4 per cent of Norway's GDP,[60] Norwegian objectives and measures at the time were in line with the AMSA recommendations, focusing on safety, emergency preparedness, and environmental protection. In spite of this, the AMSA findings quickly gained momentum.[61] In Arctic shipping, however, Norway was ahead of other member states. Therefore, promoting Norwegian standards and greater cooperation within the Arctic Council became an important objective in national implementation.[62] It is these aspects – the promotion of Norwegian standards and cooperation – that are the focus of the AMSA analysis that follows. Here we can note a slight difference: while the ACIA generated national implementation measures were aimed at national actors, Norway's objectives related to the AMSA recommendations centred on influencing the policies of other member states. The three particular AMSA recommendations under scrutiny (see Table 3.2) are included because member states were specifically requested to initiate appropriate follow-up measures within their national implementation processes.[63]

Table 3.2 The AMSA recommendations.[64]

Reduce air emissions: That the Arctic states decide to support the development of improved practices and innovative technologies for ships in port and sea to help reduce current and future emissions of greenhouse gases (GHGs), nitrogen oxides (NOx), sulfur oxides (SOx) and particulate matter (PM), taking into account the relevant IMO regulations.

Arctic Marine Traffic System: That the Arctic states should support continued development of a comprehensive Arctic marine traffic awareness system to improve monitoring and tracking of marine activity, to enhance data sharing in near real-time, and to augment vessel management service in order to reduce the risk of incidents, facilitate response and provide awareness of potential user conflict. The Arctic states should encourage shipping companies to cooperate in the improvement and development of national monitoring systems.

Survey of Arctic Indigenous Marine Use: That the Arctic states should consider conducting surveys on Arctic marine use by indigenous communities where gaps are identified, to collect information for establishing up-to-date baseline data to assess the impacts from Arctic shipping activities.

National implementation

Recommendation: Reduce air emissions

'Reduce air emissions' requested member states to reduce their current and future emissions of greenhouse gases (GHGs), nitrogen oxides (NOx), sulfur oxides (SOx), and particulate matter (PM) from ships.[65] However, reduction of ship emissions to the atmosphere had already been on the Norwegian agenda for quite some time. The 2007 heavy fuel oil (HFO) ban is an illustrative example.[66] As regards implementing the AMSA recommendation, an important national measure appears to be the promotion of this ban to other member states.

In 2010, the Norwegian Maritime Authority (NMA) was requested to assist the Norwegian delegation to the Protection of the Arctic Marine Environment Working Group (PAME) and the Ministry of the Environment in following up the AMSA report. The NMA was specifically instructed to participate in PAME's workings, and to promote the Norwegian standpoint regarding an early ban on the use and carriage of HFO in Arctic waters. The final objective was to promote a joint proposal to the International Maritime Organization.[67] The same message was repeated in subsequent years and appears to have set the stage for a Norwegian initiative within the Arctic Council[68]: before the end of 2010, the Norwegian delegation to PAME had proposed a project to compile existing knowledge on the use and carriage of HFO in the Arctic.[69] The project would investigate the consequences of HFO in terms of potential spills and air pollution, including the formation of black carbon.[70] It resulted in three reports, the final one being issued in 2013.

Considering the implementation measure just reviewed, how can the characteristics and malignancy of this AMSA recommendation help explain the outcome? Firstly, the recommendation is not *precise* – it does not specify any measures for achieving the objective of reducing emissions. By allowing for interpretation and leeway, such lack of precision could be expected to hamper national implementation. In this case, however, imprecision appears to have worked in favour of Norwegian preferences. Given the disagreement among member states, specifying a ban on HFO within the recommendation would have been impossible,[71] whereas vagueness may have facilitated the promotion of a ban regardless of divergent member-state preferences.

Moreover, the recommendation was *non-malignant*, at least within the national context of Norway. An HFO ban, characterized by broad consensus, had already been established. Norway had also played an important role in the establishment of such a ban in the Antarctic,[72] which suggests that arriving at the subsequent decision to promote a similar ban within the Arctic Council was relatively easy.

Concerning *stakeholder involvement*, the norm-development process within the Arctic Council was marked by broad participation, including indigenous peoples' groups through the permanent participants, environmental organizations, and actors from the industrial sector. Some of these stakeholders also played a role in subsequent processes initiated by Norway. By evaluating cargo flows, risks and the environmental impacts of shipping, Det Norske Veritas GL (DNV GL), an international classification body, helped define the initial problem of atmospheric emissions during the AMSA process.[73] When the Norwegian HFO project was accepted by member states in 2010, DNV GL was approached as a consultant and tasked to carry out the assessment reports.[74] This shows how DNV GL, which was involved in the AMSA process, was accorded a role in Norwegian follow-up activities; thus, DNV GL may be seen as a contributor in implementing the recommendation.

The WWF was also involved in developing the AMSA recommendations, and emphasized the need to identify vulnerable areas.[75] After the AMSA process, the WWF stressed how HFO could damage sensitive areas within the Arctic.[76] Moreover, the WWF directly criticized the Norwegian government for inadequately promoting such a ban among the Arctic Council member states.[77]

Finally, *monitoring* was influential in terms of implementation, but not in line with the 'naming and shaming' paradigm. Rather, the AMSA reporting system helped keep the issue on the agendas of Norway and the Arctic Council. By extension, it became easier to propose solutions on how best to deal with the recommendation.[78]

In summation: the positive implementation outcome seems to have been facilitated by the involvement of stakeholders, the reporting system, and the absence of malignancy. Moreover, the very imprecision of the recommendation appears to have had a positive effect on implementation.

Recommendation: Arctic marine traffic system

As with the recommendation just discussed, the recommendation 'Arctic marine traffic system' did not introduce policies that were new to Norway. Although member states were requested to support the development of an Arctic marine traffic system, the Norwegian framework was already extensive. In particular, Norway's use of AIS and its security measures was superior to the situation in the other Arctic states.[79] Yet, the recommendation does appear to have launched the idea of developing a common system, where member states could share information and obtain a more holistic picture of Arctic shipping. In 2013, the Ministry of Foreign Affairs published a report on the consequences for Norway of increased Arctic shipping. The report pointed out that data on Arctic ship traffic was not collected systematically, nor regularly shared among the Arctic states.[80] The government was therefore advised to develop a joint monitoring and warning satellite-based system for the Arctic Ocean. Barents Watch, a monitoring and information system placed in the Arctic, was proposed as one platform for developing such Arctic cooperation.[81] In 2014, this advice was presented to the Arctic Council: during a PAME meeting, Norway offered to provide raw and processed satellite AIS data to the Council.[82] That same year, PAME initiated a new project, Arctic Shipping Data Service (ASDS), aimed at updating Arctic ship traffic data for use in assessments and trend analysis.[83] Norway and the USA were appointed lead countries. Under the ASDS project, Norway informed the member states of its own political measures, including extensive presentations on Barents Watch and Havbase – another system based on AIS data.[84] Norway also presented an update on ship traffic in the high seas areas of the Central Arctic Ocean, in line with its 2014 proposal.[85] Then in 2016, ASDS was reframed; the USA took charge, with project completion in 2017.[86]

We may now ask: how did the three characteristics of precision, stakeholder involvement and monitoring, plus malignancy, affect the outcome? This AMSA recommendation was precise. Its precision, however, did not have any effect on implementation activities: it specified measures for achieving the objective of a ship-traffic system, but such measures had already been implemented by Norway. On the other hand, the absence of malignancy may have helped national implementation. As Norway had basically fulfilled the recommendation already, there must have been broad national consensus on the importance of traffic monitoring. Moreover, the recommendation would entail few additional expenses. Such a situation is likely to have eased the role that Norway assumed within the Arctic Council.

Furthermore, the involvement of stakeholders – indigenous peoples, environmental organizations and industry – in the AMSA norm-development process does not seem to have affected the outcomes of national implementation. At least no trace of their participation in the national processes has been found.

However, monitoring did facilitate national implementation. By 2014, all AMSA recommendations had gained momentum within the Arctic Council, and the PAME agenda was governed and structured by the Council.[87] This made it easier to provide suggestions on how to implement the recommendation. In summary, then, the positive implementation outcome of this recommendation appears only to have been influenced by the reporting system and the absence of malignancy.

Recommendation: Survey of Arctic indigenous marine use

Unlike the two foregoing AMSA recommendations, the third one, 'survey of Arctic indigenous marine use', did not result in any national implementation measures. Here it was argued that a survey had been conducted in 2008, when the Coastal Fishing Committee investigated the rights of the Saami people and Arctic residents to fish in the coastal areas of Finnmark county.[88] This argument, however, is a source of disagreement. Although the Coastal Fishing Committee concluded that Saami and other residents had such rights, little was done by the government to ensure proper follow-up,[89] and the Coastal Fishing Committee did not conduct an actual survey on the Saami's traditional marine use of the area. Despite the absence of implementation measures, this case, like the recommendations discussed earlier, still shows that our three characteristics and malignancy have explanatory power.

First of all, this third recommendation was not *precise*: it merely stated the objective of conducting surveys on Arctic indigenous marine use, without specifying the measures necessary to achieve it. Imprecise recommendations allow for leeway and discretion and, therefore, run the risk of not being implemented. Norwegian authorities apparently took advantage of the recommendation's imprecise formulation, using it to justify the Coastal Fishing Committee's activities as implementation, thereby obviating the need to initiate other additional measures.

Moreover, the recommendation touched on a rather sensitive issue: whereas the national authorities claimed that a survey had been conducted, the Saami Council – a permanent participant of the Arctic Council – argued against this. According to the Saami Council, the lack of additional implementation measures was rooted in the question of indigenous peoples' rights, an issue the government was unwilling to address.[90] Although it is difficult to determine the economic costs such a survey would entail, this disagreement shows that political costs were present. Thus a certain level of *malignancy* existed, serving to obstruct the national implementation process.

As for *stakeholder involvement*, the Saami Council contributed actively to the AMSA project, resulting in recommendations that reflected the views of the Council.[91] Moreover, the Saami Council played an active role in promoting this recommendation to the national authorities. When attempts to persuade national decision makers failed, the Saami Council pursued an alternative direction. Together with the Aleut International Association (AIA),[92] the report 'Development of an Arctic Marine Use Survey Process' was submitted to PAME.[93] The report was intended as a study on which later measures could be based and as a way of approaching the topic without inflicting an unfavourable political situation on Norway.[94] However, due to lack of resources, the Saami Council was unable to continue participating in the project.[95] All the same, the course of events shows how stakeholders involved in Arctic Council processes may attempt to influence national implementation processes.

As regards the implementation measures pursued by the Saami Council, monitoring – the reporting system – was important. The recommendation was already part of the PAME agenda and was therefore difficult to overlook.[96] Thus, we find that both *stakeholder involvement* and *monitoring* were of importance in this case, even though implementation did not come about. Both the *imprecision* of the recommendation and its *malignancy* are likely to have hindered such implementation processes in unfolding nationally.

Summary

Due to its position as a leading maritime power, Norway had already implemented much of what AMSA came to recommend, before the report was released. However, the shipping sector is international in scope, and how other Arctic states operate affects Norwegian industry, climate and environment. Norway therefore followed up the AMSA recommendations by promoting its own national standards and greater member-state cooperation. The recommendations 'reduce air emissions' and 'Arctic marine traffic system' were implemented, whereas 'survey of Arctic indigenous marine use' did not result in any such measures.

As for the characteristics and malignancy of the AMSA recommendations, precision did not have any conclusive effect on implementation outcomes. Because Norway had already fulfilled most of the requirements, any clarification of measures to be taken had little significance. In fact, the absence of precision may have had a positive impact on the implementation of the recommendation 'reduce air emissions': since the recommendation was formulated in a way that provided leeway, Norway was able to pursue a solution that was not part of the recommendation, despite divergent member-state preferences. The effect of malignancy, on the other hand, was consistent across the recommendations. When present, malignancy had a hampering effect on implementation, whereas absence of malignancy favoured positive implementation outcomes. In addition, stakeholder involvement emerged as an important factor in connection with the recommendations 'reduce air emissions' and 'survey of Arctic indigenous marine use'. Finally, we note the importance of monitoring, which served as an agenda-setter both within the Arctic Council and at the national level.

Conclusion

Starting from the assumptions that international law is not binary, that soft law is not a uniform phenomenon, and that certain characteristics of the recommendations – precision, monitoring and stakeholder involvement – may enhance implementation, what conclusions can be drawn? First and foremost, Norway as a member state of the Arctic Council devoted considerable effort to implementing several of the Council's recommendations. Implementation, however, was pursued in two very distinct ways. The ACIA put adaptation on the national agenda, while the AMSA came into play in a different domestic context. Consequently, the ACIA process led to national measures conducted within national borders and directed at national actors. As to the AMSA process, Norway constituted a maritime power and had already implemented most of the measures proposed in the AMSA's recommendations. Therefore, an important implementation objective for Norway became the promotion of national standards and greater cooperation within the Arctic Council.

Of the six recommendations examined here, four – two from ACIA, and two from AMSA – generated implementation measures in Norway. This study indicates that three specific characteristics of the recommendations, along with the presence or absence of malignancy, did influence some of the outcomes. Although the effects of precision proved ambiguous, both monitoring of state behaviour and stakeholder involvement appear to have affected implementation positively, if the issues were non-malignant. When malignancy was present, there was no implementation.

While these findings are interesting in their own right, they also speak to the debate on the effectiveness of the Arctic Council and to the scholarly literature on effectiveness more generally. In contrast to assumptions that the Arctic Council, as a soft-law body, cannot be effective, this study has shown how recommendations from two significant reports were implemented in Norway. Although other aspects are also relevant, the structural and organizational characteristics of the Arctic Council's recommendations emerge as important explanatory factors, as long as the issue is not overly demanding. With regard to the literature on effectiveness more generally, this study has shown that characteristics often associated with hard-law agreements may be equally relevant in the application of soft-law commitments. Ultimately, then, the differences between the two may not be as great as often claimed. By extension, it is not necessarily the case that hard law is more effective for ensuring implementation than is soft law.

Notes

1 Paula Kankaanpää and Oran R. Young, 'The effectiveness of the Arctic Council', *Polar Research* 31 (2012), pp. 1–14; Timo Koivurova and Erik J. Molenaar, *International Governance and Regulation of the Marine Arctic: Overview and Gap Analysis* (Oslo, WWF International Arctic Programe, 2009), pp. 1–43; Timo Koivuriva and David Vanderzwaag, 'The Arctic Council at 10 years: Retrospect and prospect', *University of British Columbia Law Review* 40/1 (2007), pp. 121–94.

2 The few exceptions include Timo Koivurova, 'Implementing guidelines for environmental impact assessment in the Arctic', in C. J, Basmeijer and T. Koivurova (eds), *The Theory and Practice of Transboundary Environmental Impact Assessment* (Leiden, Nijhoff, 2008), pp. 151–74; Kristine Offerdal, 'Oil gas and the environment', in O. S. Stokke and G. Hønneland (eds), *International Cooperation and Arctic Governance: Regime Effectiveness and Northern Region Building* (Abingdon, Routledge, 2007), pp. 138–64; Nathaniel P. Valk, *Arctic Council Soft Law: An Effective Analysis* (2012); and Jessica F. McGrath, 'Evaluating Arctic State Implementation of Ecosystem-Based Management Recommendations Supported by the Arctic Council: Canada Norway, and the US', MA diss., University of Washington (2014).

3 The ACIA and the AMSA were selected according to a set of criteria: they both include policy recommendations (something which has become more common in recent years), a significant amount of time has passed since their release, and they allow for variation among the independent variables studied in this chapter.

4 Arild Underdal, 'Meeting common environmental challenges: The co-evolution of policies and practices', *International Environmental Agreements: Politics, Law and Economics* 13/1 2013, pp. 15–30.

5 An elaboration on this point will be given later in this chapter.

6 Geir Hønneland and Anne-Kristin Jørgensen, *Implementing International Environmental Agreements in Russia* (Manchester, Manchester University Press, 2003), p. 29.

7 Steinar Andresen, Jon Birger Skjærseth and Jørgen Wettestad, *Regime, the State and Society: Analyzing the Implementation of International Environmental Commitments*, IIASA Working Paper (1995), p. 3; Kenneth Hanf, 'The domestic basis of international environmental agreements', in A. Underdal and K. Hanf (eds), *International Environmental Agreements and Domestic Politics - The case of acid rain* (Aldershot, Ashgate, 2000), pp. 13–14; David Victor, Kal Raustiala and Eugene B. Skolnikoff, *The Implementation and Effectiveness of International Environmental Commitments: Theory and Practice* (Cambridge, MIT Press, 1998), p. 15.

8 Victor, Raustiala and Skolnikoff, *The Implementation and Effectiveness of International Environmental Commitments: Theory and Practice*, p. 7.

9 One alternative understanding is that of Michael W. Reisman (1988), who recognizes the 'sliding scale of hardness or softness in all norms', largely (as will be shown) paralleling the point of view tabled in this chapter. However, although Reisman views soft law as 'performing certain positive functions' he, like many others, concludes that most of the law made this way 'cannot be fulfilled in any effective fashion'. I, on the other hand, am of the opinion that the characteristics a soft law norm holds, the degree of hardness or softness if you will, is essential in determining exactly how effectively norms can and will be fulfilled.

10 Daniel Thürer, 'Soft law', in R. Bernhardt (ed.), *Encyclopedia of Public International Law* (Amsterdam, Elsevier, 2000), pp. 452–60, pp. 452–4.

11 Gregory C. Shaffer and Mark A. Pollack, 'Hard vs. soft law: Alternatives, complements and antagonists in international governance', *Minnesota Law Review* 94/3 (2009), pp. 706–99, p.707, p. 713.

12 Kenneth Abbott and Duncan Snidal, 'Hard and soft law in international governance', *International Organization* 54/3 (2000), pp. 421–56, p. 424.

13 Kenneth Abbott, Robert Keohane, Andrew Moravcsik, Anne-Marie Slaughter and Duncan Snidal, 'The concept of legalization', *International Organization* 54/3 (2000), pp. 401–19, p. 401.

14 Abbott and Snidal, 'Hard and soft law in international governance', p. 421.

15 Ibid., p. 422.

16 Edith B. Weiss and Harold Jacobson, *Engaging Countries: Strengthening Compliance with International Environmental Accords* (Cambridge, MIT Press, 1998); Victor, Raustiala, Skolnikoff, *The Implementation and Effectiveness of International Environmental Commitments: Theory and Practice*; Dinah Shelton, 'Introduction: Law, non-law and the problem of "soft law"', in D. Shelton (ed.), *Commitment and Compliance: The Role of Non-Binding Norms in the International Legal System* (Oxford, Oxford University Press, 2003), pp. 1–18; Jürgen Friedrich, *International Environmental 'Soft Law': The Functions and Limits of Nonbinding Instruments in International Environmental Governance and Law* (Berlin, Springer, 2013).

17 Abbott, Keohane, Moravcsik, Slaughter and Snidal, 'The concept of legalization', p. 401.

18 Ibid., p. 412.

19 Thomas M. Franck, *The Power of Legitimacy Among Nations* (Oxford, Oxford University Press,1990), p. 52

20 Ronald B. Mitchell, 'Sources of transparency: Information systems in international regimes', *International Studies Quarterly* 42/1 (1998), pp.109–30, p. 109.

21 Dinah Shelton (ed.), *Commitment and Compliance: The Role of Non-Binding Norms in the International Legal System* (Oxford, Oxford University Press, 2003), p. 15.

22 Friedrich, *International Environmental 'Soft Law': The Functions and Limits of Nonbinding Instruments in International Environmental Governance and Law*, p. 269.

23 Olav S. Stokke, 'Asian stakes and arctic governance', *Strategic Analysis* 38/6 (2014), pp. 770–78, p. 770; R. Edward Freeman, *Strategic Management: A stakeholder approach* (Boston, Pitman, 1984), p. 46.

24 Piotr Graczyk and Timo Koivurova, 'The Arctic Council', in L. C. Jensen and G. Hønneland (eds), *Handbook of the Politics of the Arctic* (Cheltenham, Edward Elgar, 2015), pp. 298–327, p. 313.

25 Except for voting rights, permanent participants have the same privileges as member states in political processes, including full consultation in connection with negotiations and decisions.

26 Observers are invited to attend meetings, but may make statements only at the discretion of the chair.

27 Arild Underdal, 'Meeting common environmental challenges: The co-evolution of policies and practices'; Olav S. Stokke, *Disaggregating International Regimes: A New Approach to Evaluation and Comparison* (London, MIT Press, 2012), p. 52.

28 Timo Koivurova, 'Limits and possibilities of the Arctic Council in a rapidly changing scene of governance', *Polar Record* 46/2 (2010), pp. 149–56, p. 149.

29 Arctic Council, 'ACIA Policy Document' (2004). Available at http://www.acia.uaf.edu/PDFs/ACIA_Policy_Document.pdf (accessed 14 May 2016).

30 E. Carina, H. Keskitalo, Timo Koivurova and Nigel Bankes, 'Climate governance in the Arctic: Introduction and theoretical framework', in T. Koivurova, E. C. H. Keskitalo and N. Bankes (eds), *Climate Governance in the Arctic* (Dordrecht, Springer, 2009),

pp. 1–26, p. 10; Alf Håkon Hoel, 'Climate change', in O. S. Stokke and G. Hønneland (eds), *International Cooperation and Arctic Governance: Regime Effectiveness and Northern Region Building* (Abingdon, Routledge, 2007), pp. 112–37, p. 114, p. 132.

31 Roger Pielke, Gwyn Prins, Steve Rayner and Daniel Sarewitz, 'Lifting the taboo on adaptation', *Nature* 445/8 (2007), pp. 597–8, p. 597; Koivurova, 'Limits and possibilities of the Arctic Council in a rapidly changing scene of governance', p. 149. As an additional note: although the existing climate regime, including the UNFCCC, did address both mitigation and (to a lesser extent) adaptation, the latter was largely perceived as something necessary only for developing countries and, therefore, as less relevant to developed states.

32 Koivurova, 'Limits and possibilities of the Arctic Councilin a rapidly changing scene of governance', p. 149.

33 Norwegian Ministry of Environment, *Om norsk politikk mot klimaendringer og utslipp av nitrogenoksider*, St. meld. nr. 41 (1994–95) (Oslo, Norwegian Ministry of Environment, 1995). Available at https://www.stortinget.no/no/Saker-og-publikasjoner/Stortingsforhandlinger/Lesevisning/?p=1994-95&paid=3&wid=d&psid=DIVL516 (accessed 20 May 2016).

34 Norwegian Ministry of Environment, *Tilleggsmelding til St.meld. nr. 54 (2000–01) Norsk klimapolitikk*, St. meld. nr. 15 (2001–02) (Oslo, Norwegian Ministry of Environment, 2002), p. 62. Available at https://www.regjeringen.no/contentassets/471533eed2ff47f987699d32b8207043/no/pdfa/stm200120020015000dddpdfa.pdf (accessed 20 May 16).

35 Norwegian Polar Institute, *Arctic Climate Impact Assessment. Presentasjoner og oppsummeringer fra fagmøtet Effekter av marine klimaendringer med spesielt fokus på Barentshavet* (2003), p. 13. Available at https://brage.bibsys.no/xmlui//bitstream/handle/11250/172936/Internrapport14.pdf?sequence=1 (accessed 9 May 2016).

36 Arctic Council, 'ACIA policy document'.

37 Ibid., pp. 5–6.

38 Norwegian Polar Institute, *NorACIA. Norsk Oppfølging av Arktisk Råd-Prosjektet 'Arctic Climate Impact Assessment': Handlingsplan 2006* (2006). Available at http://docplayer.no/6253871-Noracia-norsk-oppfolging-av-arktisk-rad-prosjektet-arctic-climate-impact-assessment-handlingsplan-2006-2009.html (accessed 14 May 2016).

39 Ibid., p. 4.

40 Norwegian Polar Institute, *Klimaendringer i norsk Arktis: Kunnskapsbehov og tilpasningsstrategier for infrastruktur* (2005); *Klimaendringer og tilpasningsstrategier for samiske næringer* (2005). Available at http://noracia.npolar.no/litteratur/rapport-fagmote-samisk-2005.pdf (accessed 9 May 2016); *Klimascenarier for norsk Arktis* (2006); *Klimaendringer i norsk Arktis – ekstremvær og konsekvenser for samfunnet* (2007). Available at http://noracia.npolar.no/fagmoter/foredragene-fra-ekstremverseminaret.html (accessed 9 May 2016).

41 Ibid.

42 Norwegian Ministry of Foreign Affairs, *The Norwegian Government's High North Strategy* (Oslo, Norwegian Ministry of Foreign Affairs, 2006), p. 37. Available at https://www.regjeringen.no/globalassets/upload/UD/Vedlegg/strategien.pdf (accessed 9 May 2016).

43 Norwegian Ministry of Labour and Social Inclusion, *Sami Policy*, St. meld. nr. 28 (2007–08) (Oslo, Norwegian Ministry of Labour and Social Inclusion, 2008), p. 41. Available at https://www.regjeringen.no/contentassets/8e1e26b083304fa394b6495db574a060/no/pdfs/stm200720080028000dddpdfs.pdf (accessed 20 May 2016).

44 Interview, Permanent Participant, 2016.

45 Annika E. Nilsson, 'A changing Arctic climate: Science and policy in the Arctic Climate Impact Assessment', in Koivurova, Keskitalo and Bankes (eds), *Climate Governance in the Arctic*, pp. 77–95, p. 87; Interview, 2016.

46 Arctic Athabaskan Council, Gwich'in Council International, Saami Council, Russian Association of Indigenous Peoples of the North, Inuit Circumpolar Conference, Aleut International Association, 'Time for Action on Climate Change: A Statement by Arctic Indigenous Peoples' (2004) (unpublished); 'Indigenous Peoples Urge Arctic States to Take Steps in Addressing Climate Change, Following Policy Release' (2004) (unpublished).

47 Interview, Permanent Participant, 2016.

48 Interview, Permanent Participant, 2016.

49 WWF, 'Arktisk Råd og den politiske oppfølgingen av ACIA-rapporten' (2004) (unpublished).

50 Arctic Council, 'ACIA Policy Document', p. 6.

51 Signe Nybø, Karl-Birger Strann, Jarle W. Bjerke, Hans Tømmervik, Dagmar Hagen and Annika Hofgaard, *Tilpasninger til klimaendringer i Nord-Norge og på Svalbard. Vurdering av vernebehovet og terrestriske økosystemers evne til å binde karbon* (2009), pp. 3–4. Available at http://www.nina.no/archive/nina/PppBasePdf/rapport/2009/436.pdf (accessed 14 May 2016).

52 Interview, Government Official, 2016.

53 Kyrre Groven, Hogne Satøen and Carlo Aall, *Regional klimasårbarheitsanalyse for Nord-Norge. Norsk oppfølging av Arctic Climate Impact Assessment (NorACIA)* (2009). Available at https://www.vestforsk.no/sites/default/files/migrate_files/vf-rapport-4-06-noracia.pdf (accessed 14 May 2016).

54 Arctic Council, 'ACIA Policy Document', p. 6.

55 Interview, Permanent Participant and Government Officials, 2016.

56 Susan J. Hassol, *Impacts of a Warming Arctic. Arctic Climate Impact Assessment* (Cambridge, Cambridge University Press, 2004), p. 8.

57 Timo Koivurova, 'Governing Arctic shipping: Finding a role for the Arctic Council', *The Yearbook of Polar Law* 2/1 (2010), pp. 115–38, p. 128.

58 PAME (Protection of the Arctic Marine Environment), *Arctic Marine Shipping Assessment 2009 Report* (2009), p. 4.

59 Ibid., pp. 6–7.

60 For more information, see https://www.regjeringen.no/en/id4/or https://www.rederi.no/en/.

61 Norwegian Ministry of Foreign Affairs, *New Building Blocks in the North: The Next Step in the Government's High North Strategy* (Oslo, Norwegian Ministry of Foreign Affairs, 2009). Available at https://www.regjeringen.no/globalassets/upload/ud/vedlegg/nordomradene/new_building_blocks_in_the_north.pdf (accessed 9 May 2016); *The High North: Visions and Strategies* (Oslo, Norwegian Ministry of Foreign Affairs, 2011). Available at https://www.regjeringen.no/globalassets/upload/ud/

vedlegg/nordomradene/ud_nordomrodene_en_web.pdf (accessed 9 May 2016); Norwegian Ministry of Transportation, *National Transport Plan (2014–23)*, St. meld. nr. 26 (2012–13) (Oslo, Norwegian Ministry of Transportation, 2013). Available at https://www.regjeringen.no/contentassets/e6e7684b5d54473dadeeb7c599ff68b8/en-gb/pdfs/stm201220130026000engpdfs.pdf (accessed 20 May 2016); Norwegian Ministry of Trade and Industry, *Regjeringens Maritime Strategi. Stø Kurs 2020* (Oslo, Norwegian Ministry of Trade and Industry, 2013); Norwegian Ministry of Foreign Affairs, *Økt skipsfart i Polhavet – muligheter og utfordringer for Norge* (Oslo, Norwegian Ministry of Foreign Affairs, 2013). Available at https://www.regjeringen.no/globalassets/upload/ud/vedlegg/nordomrc3a5dene/oekt_skipsfart_i_polhavet_rapport.pdf (accessed 29 April 2016).

62 Interview, Government Officials, 2016.

63 PAME (Protection of the Arctic Marine Environment), *PAME Working Group Meeting Report No: PAME I-2009* (2009). Available at https://pame.is/images/02_Document_Library/Meeting_Reports/PAME_I-2009Report._samsett.pdf (accessed 18 May 2016), p. 5. A short elaboration is at this point needed. The category did initially include seven recommendations. However, several of these recommendations were excluded from the analysis: three of them – 'engagement with Arctic communities', 'protection from invasive species' and 'addressing the infrastructure deficit' – due to space limitations and to their being of less relevance to Norway. The last one, 'investing in hydrographic, meteorological and oceanographic data', was also excluded due to space limitations. Yet, it was included in the larger study on which this chapter is based. In that respect, the findings indicated that implementation measures had been initiated, but that the characteristics had few bearings on the outcome.

64 PAME, *Arctic Marine Shipping Assessment 2009 Report.*

65 Ibid., p. 6.

66 The ban introduced in 2007 covered the nature reserves on the eastern side of Svalbard. In 2009 the ban was expanded to the reserves on the western side of Svalbard.

67 Norwegian Ministry of Environment, 'Tildelingsbrev 2010 til Sjøfartsdirektoratet' (2010), p. 9. Available at https://www.sjofartsdir.no/Global/Om%20Sdir/Presentasjon%20av%20direktoratet/TIldelingsbrev%20fra%20NHD%20og%20MD/Endelig%20tildelingsbrev%20MD%202010.pdf (accessed 20 April 2016).

68 Norwegian Ministry of Environment, 'Tildelingsbrev 2011 til Sjøfartsdirektoratet' (2011). Available at https://www.regjeringen.no/globalassets/upload/md/2011/vedlegg/brev/tildelingsbrev_2011/tildelingsbrev_sjofartdir.pdf (accessed 20 April 2016); 'Endelig tildelingsbrev 2012 for Sjøfartsdirektoratet' (2012). Available at https://www.regjeringen.no/contentassets/7999c83ccc2a4fc39121d776172b7257/sjofartsdirektoratet_2012.pdf (accessed 20 April 2016); 'Endelig tildelingsbrev 2013 for Sjøfartsdirektoratet' (2013). Available at https://www.regjeringen.no/contentassets/eac76c5b603a4ceebfdd7153b5cf5d2f/sjofartsdirekoratet_tildelingsbrev_2013.pdf (accessed 20 April 2016); 'Tildelingsbrev 2014 for Sjøfartsdirektoratet' (2014). Available at https://www.regjeringen.no/globalassets/upload/kld/tildelingsbrev/sjofartsdir_tildelingsbrev_2014.pdf (accessed 20 April 2016).

69 PAME (Protection of the Arctic Marine Environment), *PAME Working Group Meeting Report No: PAME I-2009* (2010), annex II. Available at http://www.pame.is/images/02_Document_Library/Meeting_Reports/PAME_I-2009Report._samsett.pdf (accessed 18 May 2016).

70 Ibid.
71 Interview, Government Officials, 2016.
72 Following a proposal by Norway, a chapter banning the use and carriage of HFO in the Antarctica was added to MARPOL in 2010.
73 PAME (Protection of the Arctic Marine Environment), *Program for the Protection of the Arctic Marine Environment PAME* (2006), appendix V–1. Available at http://www.pame.is/images/02_Document_Library/Meeting_Reports/PAME%20report%20I-2006.pdf (accessed 18 May 2016).
74 PAME (Protection of the Arctic Marine Environment), *PAME I-2016 Meeting Report* (2016). Available at http://www.pame.is/images/02_Document_Library/Meeting_Reports/2016/PAME_I_2016_Meeting_Report.pdf (accessed 21 May 2016).
75 PAME (Protection of the Arctic Marine Environment), *Program for the Protection of the Arctic Marine Environment PAME* (2005), p. 18. Available at http://www.pame.is/images/02_Document_Library/Meeting_Reports/PAME%20report%20II-2005.pdf (accessed 18 May 2016); *Program for the Protection of the Arctic Marine Environment PAME* (2006), p. 8.
76 WWF, 'Beskyttelse av Arktis lagt på is' (2012). Available at http://www.wwf.no/?35505/Beskyttelse-av-Arktis-lagt-p-is (accessed 19 May 2016); 'WWF ber om tungoljeforbud i Arktis' (2013). Available at http://www.wwf.no/?39268/WWF-ber-om-tungoljeforbud-i-Arktis (accessed 21 April 2016); 'WWFs løsninger for Arktis' (n.d.). Available at http://www.wwf.no/dette_jobber_med/hav_og_kyst/arktis/wwfs_losninger_for_arktis/(accessed 15 April 2016).
77 WWF, 'WWF ber om tungoljeforbud i Arktis'.
78 Interview, Government Officials, Arctic Council Working Group, 2016.
79 Interview, Government Officials, Arctic Council Working Group, 2016.
80 Norwegian Ministry of Foreign Affairs, *Økt skipsfart i Polhavet – muligheter og utfordringer for Norge*, p. 8.
81 Ibid.
82 PAME (Protection of the Arctic Marine Environment), *Working Group Meeting Report* (2014). Available at http://www.pame.is/images/02_Document_Library/Meeting_Reports/Meeting_Reports/PAME_II_2014_Meeting_Report.pdf (accessed 1 May 2016), p. 5.
83 PAME (Protection of the Arctic Marine Environment), *Final draft PAME Work Plan for the SAO Report to Ministers* (2015), p. 2. Available at https://oaarchive.arctic-council.org/bitstream/handle/11374/1472/PAME_WORKPLAN_Doc2_Final_work_plan_2015-2017_AC_SAO_CA04.pdf?sequence=2&isAllowed=y (accessed19 May 2016).
84 Jon-Arve Røyset and Bjørnar Kleppe, 'Historical AIS data – "Havbase"' (2015). Available at http://pame.is/images/05_Protectec_Area/2015/PAME_2/Presentations/AMSA_4.1_-_Havbase.pdf (accessed 19 May 2016); Kjell Knudsen, *Barents Watch* (2015). Available at http://pame.is/images/05_Protectec_Area/2015/PAME_2/Presentations/AMSA_4.1_-_BarentsWatch_presentation.pdf (accessed 19 May 2016).
85 Geir Høvik Hansen, 'Update on ship traffic in the high seas area of the Central Arctic Ocean' (2015). Available at http://pame.is/images/05_Protectec_Area/2015/

PAME_2/Presentations/AMSA_IID_-_Update_on_Ship_Traffic_in_the_High_Seas.pdf (accessed 19 May 2016).

86 PAME (Protection of the Arctic Marine Environment), *Arctic Ship Traffic Data (ASTD) Project Plan* (2016), pp. 2–3. Available at http://www.pame.is/index.php/projects/arctic-marine-shipping/heavy-fuel-in-the-arctic-phase-i (accessed 1 May 2016).

87 Interview, Government Official, 2016.

88 Interview, Government Official, 2016.

89 Interview, Permanent Participant, 2016; Øyvind Ravna, 'Samerett og samiske rettigheter i Norge', in Ø. Ravna and T. Henriksen (eds), *Juss i nord: hav, fiske og urfolk: En hyllest til det juridiske fakultet ved Universitetet i Tromsøs 25-årjubileum* (Oslo, Gyldendal juridisk, 2012), p. 162.

90 Interview, Permanent Participant, 2016.

91 Interview, Permanent Participant, 2016.

92 The Aleut International Association is a permanent participant of the Arctic Council.

93 Victoria Gofman and Gunn-Britt Retter, *Development of an Arctic Indigenous Marine Use Survey Process* (2011). Available at http://www.pame.is/images/03_Projects/AMSA/Arctic%20Indigenous%20Marine_Use_Survey_Process/Agenda_item_4_AMSA_IIA-Scoping_Paper_Draft_Version_01_15_11.pdf (accessed 6 May 2016).

94 Interview, Permanent Participant, 2016.

95 Interview, Permanent Participant, 2016.

96 Interview, Permanent Participant, 2016.

CHAPTER 4

HOW ARCTIC SCIENCE TRAVELS: POPS, NORWAY AND THE STOCKHOLM CONVENTION

Svein Vigeland Rottem

Introduction

Climatic change and environmental challenges in the Arctic have been high on the international research agenda for some years. Wide-ranging studies on Arctic climate change and painstaking research on pollutants have informed numerous attempts by the international community to regulate emissions.[1] There are also studies that say something about whether and how this scientific knowledge has affected international environmental and climate policy.[2] The evidence indicates that this repository of 'Arctic knowledge' has indeed made a difference. Nevertheless, what has often been lacking in the scholarly literature is a fine-grained examination addressing what determines the influence of scientific knowledge on environmental regulations of relevance to the Arctic.

I want to examine how scientific knowledge of environmental challenges in the Arctic has been used in international regulations, and can be used today. I will describe the emergence of a specific environmental regime of relevance to the Arctic, i.e. the regulation of Persistent Organic Pollutants (POPs). The story behind the international POPs regime is, however, so complex and involves so many players that it is difficult to provide more than an overview of the various causes of success and failure here. This story has, moreover, been the subject of in-depth analyses by others.[3] The focus in this chapter is therefore narrower. I

This chapter is based on Svein Vigeland Rottem, 'The use of Arctic science: POPs, Norway and the Stockholm Convention', *Arctic Review on Law and Politics* 8 (2017), pp. 246–69.

will discuss the Stockholm Convention's relations with other legal instruments and provide an introduction to how the Convention works. Secondly, I will examine Norway's place in this regime. The account of the emerging POPs regime (with a specific focus on the Stockholm Convention) and Norway's role in it will prepare the ground for an analysis of how and why scientific knowledge of environmental challenges in the Arctic succeed or fail. More specifically, I explore Norway's active (and successful) nominations over the past decade of new POPs for the Stockholm Convention, nominations that need a scientific knowledge basis, and where Arctic scientific knowledge has been a prerequisite for action.

Framing the Research Question

POPs are chemical substances that persist in the environment and are transportable over long distances. Most POPs are created by humans in industrial processes (intentionally or as byproducts). They are bio-accumulated in the food web and pose a risk to the environment and human health. Exposure to POPs can, among other things, disrupt reproductive and immune systems.[4] One consequence of their transportability is their accumulation in environments where they were never used or emitted, e.g. the Arctic. And once in the Arctic, they tend to be 'trapped' there, as cold temperatures favour their persistence.[5] This is why international mechanisms are needed that are capable of addressing these environmental challenges. National measures and regulations alone are not enough.

The global community has taken a number of steps to tackle the transboundary movement of POPs and their management, including negotiating multilateral environmental agreements. This chapter focuses on the Stockholm Convention on Persistent Organic Pollutants, and one important property of the convention in particular: the opportunity to propose or nominate new candidates to the list of already regulated POPs. Adopted and opened for signature on 22 May 2001, the agreement called for international action on twelve POPs (the 'Dirty Dozen') but recognizes that regulating the Dirty Dozen is only the initial step. After the signing of the Stockholm Convention, fourteen new substances have been added to the list.[6] The nomination procedure takes place in the interface between science and policy. Norway, together with the European Union, has been at the forefront of this work. The question guiding the second part of this chapter is what determined the use of scientific knowledge in the Norwegian efforts leading up to a nomination of new POPs to the Stockholm Convention. Thus, Norway is used as a case study on the use of scientific knowledge, complementing the analysis at the international level. The focus is on environmental management design, state of knowledge, degree of political and economic controversy in the issue area, and the importance of the matter in public opinion and among policymakers.

There are several reasons why such a research focus is interesting. We find numerous studies on international negotiations leading up to the Stockholm Convention,[7] and Arctic knowledge transfer,[8] but fewer at the national level and none at all on the impact of science in Norway's efforts to nominate new POPs.[9] In international environmental politics, national initiatives and resources are key: no national action, no change. The processes under the Stockholm Convention are all country-driven.[10] This is most evident in the process under scrutiny here. The scientific committee of the Stockholm Convention (POPRC) does not nominate new substances: that is the role of states. While international structures, discourses, and negotiations clearly frame national actions and negotiations,[11] in this case, attention is directed at the role of domestic actors (i.e., the Norwegian environmental management system), the point being that without insight into the preconditions of state action, an important piece of the picture informing efforts to strengthen the Stockholm Convention (or any international environmental agreement), is missing.

Norway has a long history of establishing regulations to control environmental contaminants such as POPs, and Norwegian environmental authorities have also supported the work on a global convention (the Stockholm Convention). Norway's more proactive engagement is more recent, however. It is evident in efforts to improve knowledge of possible new POPs and propose new candidates when available information indicates the criteria (in Annex D of the Stockholm Convention) are met. In 2005, Norway initiated the process of nominating pentabromodiphenyl ether (PentaBDE).[12] The substance was added to the list in 2009. In 2008 Norway nominated hexabromocyclododecane (HBCD),[13] which appeared on the list in 2013. Norway also started work on decabromodiphenyl ether (DecaBDE)[14] in 2013 (still not on the list at the time of writing). Scientific findings in the Arctic region have been essential in this endeavour.

I analyze here the behaviour of domestic actors, or more precisely how and why Arctic science is used. My main question is thus not whether Norway influenced the work of the Stockholm Convention. The fact that Norway has succeeded in its efforts to nominate new POPs for inclusion on the list shows that Norway has influence. On the other hand, the behaviour of domestic actors cannot easily be separated from that of international actors. Influence motivates action and Norwegian environmental authorities will consider whether they can make a difference before choosing their mode of response, here providing the given scientific knowledge needed to proceed with a nomination. My ambition is, therefore, to look at the process of selecting a pollutant for nomination (and introducing it into formal negotiations at the international level). I shall only indirectly explain what it is that motivates Norway,[15] but rather analyze the room for manoeuvre in this field of environmental management. An analysis of the domestic scientific use can also tell us something about how and why scientific knowledge of the Arctic can make a difference, thus improving our understanding of how Arctic science 'travels' to global governance.

In the first section I outline the analytical framework. I then provide a brief history of the regulation of POPs, the Stockholm Convention, and the nomination of new substances, emphasizing the role of Norway and Arctic science production. In this section I will also discuss the Stockholm Convention's relations with other legal instruments and provide an introduction to how the Convention works. In the last section of the chapter, I discuss how Norway goes about nominating new POPs and ask how and why scientific knowledge is used in Norway's efforts to nominate new POPs to the Stockholm Convention. The analysis is based on interviews with senior officials at the Norwegian Environment Agency, Ministry of Climate and Environment (KLD), and several scientists.[16] The empirical data also consist of primary (budgets, statistics, white papers, etc.) and secondary sources (scientific reports and articles, etc.).

Scientific Use

Which analytical tools can we use to discuss the use of science in environmental management?[17] A basic assumption is that the extent to which scientific knowledge is used in environmental policy depends on organization, the state of the knowledge, degree of political and economic controversies in the issue area, and public and political attention.

Management systems rely on research institutions.[18] Decision makers are exposed to complex scientific findings produced by a variety of knowledge producers in different issue areas.[19] In the present case, it is important to ascertain how knowledge produced at different levels and in different sectors is integrated as part of the knowledge base of the environmental management system. It is therefore important to look at how the Stockholm Convention and the Norwegian environmental management system in relation to POPs is set up. Organizational structure can either limit or enable the integration of science in regulation. Different types of organizational structure – hierarchic, specialized, and loosely structured – are known to affect the integration of science in regulation.[20] A basic assumption in our case is that a mature (long history of research and regulation) and a specialized management system have increased the influence of science in the regulation of POPs and the nomination of new ones.

A second variable is state of knowledge. A well-established hypothesis is that the more conclusive and consensual the state of knowledge, the more likely it will be used as a basis in decision making. That is, scientific advice is more easily followed when it rests on scientific consensus. Developments in the ozone and acid rain regimes illustrate this point in that the emergence of consensual scientific knowledge was an important factor behind the increased effectiveness of these two environmental regimes.[21] A vital question, therefore, is whether it is possible to trace such a consensus on the state of knowledge as to the POPs in general and Norway's nominations in particular.

Furthermore, there is general agreement in the literature that the nature of the problem affects the influence of science.[22] The more politically controversial the problem/issue area, the less likely it is that scientific evidence will be used to inform important decisions. Two dimensions are helpful in this regard: political cost and economic cost. Political cost refers to the divergent preferences of relevant actors, differences that in turn are likely to hamper the work of nominating a new substance. Economic cost refers to the strain a nomination (and nomination process) puts on financial resources (and commercial actors). To illustrate, science has been met with less resistance in the low-conflict ozone regime than in the far more politically contentious issue of climate change and biodiversity regimes.[23] It is therefore pertinent to ask whether international and national work on POPs in general and in selecting new substances for nomination has been politically and commercially/economically controversial and if it has increased or lessened the use of scientific knowledge.

A fourth contextual variable is the issue-area's position on the political and public agenda. For low-conflict problem areas, public and political attention will tend to increase scientific influence, but for problems involving high levels of conflict, it may increase polarization and create difficulties for rational scientific input. The International Whaling Commission (IWC) is a typical case in point. In this case one could also argue that science does not get to the (ethical) heart of the differences in opinion. Due to the high level of political conflict in this area in recent decades, together with a good deal of public attention, the use of scientific advice, although advanced and highly consensual, has been very modest.[24] Does the level of public and political attention determine the use of scientific knowledge in our case?

Bringing these variables together, the proposal is that a mature and specialized environmental management system, consensual knowledge and high public and political attention in a low-conflict area have made it easier for Arctic scientific knowledge to end up in an international convention. First, it is necessary to look at international and regional cooperation mechanisms and initiatives, by briefly reviewing the history of the regulation of POPs and the Stockholm Convention and discussing the Convention's position in the legal landscape on POPs. This will also show that Norway and the Norwegian scientific community have played an important role in the regulation of POPs and science production, providing us with a historical background to Norway's proactive engagement over the past decade in nominating new pollutants. It will also show the importance of Arctic science.

A Short History of the Regulation of POPs

When and how did POPs emerge as a scientific and political concern?[25] The use of certain chemicals in industry and in pesticides increased dramatically during the 1960s and 1970s. Rachel Carson's *Silent Spring*, published in the United States in 1962, helped make the public aware of the dangers of DDT and other pesticides.[26] According to Selin,[27] the discovery of a wide range of hazardous chemicals in (northern) areas far removed from large-scale industrial and agricultural activities dates back to the 1960s and 1970s. One important contribution was the Swedish scientist Sören Jensen's discovery of PCBs in Baltic Sea fish in the mid-1960s. So, by the 1970s, there was growing awareness of increasing concentrations of contaminants entering the air, soil and water. In response, the USA banned DDT in 1972 except for uses critical to public health, and in 1973 the OECD Council called for restrictions on the production and use of specific chemicals, including PCBs. The pattern was repeated in Norway. DDT was prohibited as a pesticide in 1970 and PCB production and new uses were prohibited altogether in 1980.[28] Moreover, the discovery of surprisingly high contamination levels in the mid- and late 1980s sparked new concern. In 1985, Canadian scientists Kinloch and Kuhnlein, in separate studies, found high concentrations of PCBs and other POPs and metals in food species consumed by indigenous peoples in northern Canada and high PCB blood concentrations in parts of the population.[29] Norway also has a long history of research on POPs,[30] with the Norwegian Institute for Air Research (NILU) playing an especially prominent role by providing data on how pollutants travel by air.[31] Thus, POPs were on the scientific, political, and public agendas in the Nordic countries and in Canada, above all thanks to scientific findings from the Arctic.[32]

In 1989, the Working Group on Effects under the Convention on Long-range Transboundary Air Pollution (CLRTAP) was persuaded to include hazardous organic substances in its work plan, and in 1990, the Executive Body of CLRTAP decided to initiate POPs assessments. Relevant work was at the same time progressing under the Arctic Environmental Protection Strategy (AEPS).[33] The AEPS, established in 1991, was the forerunner of the Arctic Council. In fact, one of the main reasons for its establishment was scientific discoveries of high levels of POPs and heavy metals in the Arctic. Furthermore, cooperation between Canada and Sweden led to the establishment of a CLRTAP POPs Task Force in 1990, followed by a series of scientific assessments and political meetings, leading to more formal discussions on regional regulations.[34] In CLRTAP, the final meeting of the preparatory working group was held in October 1996 and protocol negotiations started in January 1997. The final negotiation session took place in February 1998. The CLRTAP POPs Protocol was then adopted in Aarhus in June

1998. Annex I contained ten pesticides and three industrial chemicals. Norway was not a key player here, but Arctic scientific knowledge was instrumental in setting the agenda.

At the same time, acknowledging that POPs not only were a European and North American concern, UNEP began investigating POPs and produced a short list of substances. UNEP's Governing Council adopted Decision 18/32 in 1995 in which it called on the International Forum on Chemical Safety (IFCS), the Inter-Organization Programme for the Sound Management of Chemicals (IOMC), and the International Programme on Chemical Safety (IPCS) to conduct an international assessment of twelve POPs and develop recommendations on international action. In November 1995, the Intergovernmental Conference to Adopt a Global Programme of Action for Protection of the Marine Environment from Land-based Activities (GPA) put POPs on their agenda, and called for negotiations on a legally binding treaty on POPs. In 1996, an IFCS ad hoc working group recommended beginning negotiations on a legally binding instrument, giving UNEP the basis to develop a mandate for global negotiations.[35] At the same time, the Arctic Council was established and the Arctic Monitoring and Assessment Programme (AMAP) (an Arctic Council working group) provided further scientific input on global processes.[36] In this respect it is worth noting that Norway has been one of the most important financial and political contributors to AMAP's work on POPs, and AMAP's secretariat is located in Norway.[37] Norway played an important role, albeit more as a financial contributor than a political driving force.

In addition, the UNEP Governing Council called on UNEP to prepare a legally binding international instrument on POPs. Negotiations for a global POPs treaty began in Montreal in July 1998[38] and The Stockholm Convention was signed in 2001, with 150 signatories agreeing to take action to reduce or eliminate the production and release of the 'Dirty Dozen'. Norway ratified in July 2002 and the Convention entered into force in May 2004. This short story on the regulation of POPs tells us that Arctic science was setting the agenda and that Norway and Norwegian researchers played an important role in this area of environmental management.

The Stockholm Convention and its Relations with other Legal Instruments

As set out in Article 1, the objective of the Stockholm Convention is to protect human health and the environment from persistent organic pollutants. One of the main provisions is that the Convention requires each party to prohibit and/or eliminate the production and use, as well as the import and export, of the intentionally produced POPs that are listed in Annex A to the Convention. Annex A allows for the registration of specific exemptions for the production or use of listed POPs. The import and export of chemicals listed in Annex A can take place under specific restrictive conditions. Furthermore, the Convention restricts the production and use, as well as the import and export, of the intentionally produced POPs that are listed in Annex B to the Convention. Annex B allows for the registration of acceptable purposes for the production and use of the listed POPs, and for the registration of specific exemptions for the production and use of the listed POPs. The import and export of chemicals listed in Annex B can take place under specific restrictive conditions, as set out in paragraph 2 of Article 3. Moreover, there is a provision aimed at reducing or eliminating releases from the unintentionally produced POPs that are listed in Annex C.

The Convention promotes the use of the best available techniques and best environmental practices for preventing the release of POPs into the environment and ensuring that stockpiles and wastes consisting of, containing or contaminated with POPs are managed safely and in an environmentally sound manner. Other provisions of the Convention relate to the development of, e.g., implementation plans, information exchange, public information, awareness and education, and research.

Of particular interest here, the Convention provides for procedures for the listing of new POPs. A committee composed of experts – the Persistent Organic Pollutants Review Committee (POPRC) – examines proposals for the listing of chemicals in accordance with the procedure set out in Article 8 and the information requirements specified in Annexes D, E, and F of the Convention. These scientific review processes have increased the number of listed POPs. When a POP is proposed for listing under the Stockholm Convention, a party must first submit a proposal and provide a scientific justification for the need for global control. A scientific evaluation is thereafter carried out in the respective technical subsidiary bodies under the Convention by experts from various countries. Since the signing of the Stockholm Convention, fourteen new substances have been added to the list, including certain polycyclic aromatic hydrocarbons (PAHs), brominated flame retardants, and other compounds. Thus, at the international level, the process of adding new POPs goes through four stages. In the first stage, the Expert Committee of the Stockholm Convention considers whether the substance proposed for listing meets Convention criteria and whether there is reason to believe the substance may be a POP. The background information is collected and submitted by the nominating party. In the second stage, the Expert Committee creates a global risk profile and assesses whether the substance is a POP. Health and environmental effects are considered, and whether the substance should be banned or strictly regulated globally is discussed. In the third stage, a global assessment of remedial measures looks at socio-economic consequences of regulating the production and use of the substance, the availability of substitutes, and the costs of phasing out the nominated substance. Finally, the Assembly, the supreme decision-making body under the Convention, adopts a final decision on whether to have the substance listed and how it should be listed. This is a scientifically demanding and time-consuming process.

In 2005, five chemicals were proposed for review (nominated); two by the EU, one by Mexico, one by Norway (PentaBDE), and one by Sweden. In 2006, five more substances were nominated; two by Mexico and three by the EU. At its fourth meeting, in May 2009, the Conference of the Parties listed nine of these substances.[39] At its fifth meeting in May 2011, the Conference of the Parties listed technical endosulfan and its related isomers with a specific exemption. Endosulfan was nominated by the EU. At its sixth meeting, from 28 April to 10 May 2013, the Conference of the Parties listed HBCD with specific exemptions. This substance was nominated by Norway in 2008. At its seventh meeting, 4–15 May 2015, three new substances were listed. As previously mentioned, Norway nominated DecaBDE in 2013.

To understand the Stockholm Convention's special position, we also need to see how it relates to other international regulations. The Convention covers a particular group of substances, POPs, and therefore only coincides directly with the POPs Protocol to the LRTAP.[40] The LRTAP is similar to the Stockholm Convention in having a mechanism for including new substances. The inclusion criteria and the regulations are also similar. The major differences between the two conventions lies first in the fact that the one is global and the other regional, and second in the reporting (i.e., how efficiency and performance are measured). In the POPs Protocol to LRTAP, there is currently an agreement to await the processes in Stockholm. In practice, no substances are being considered under the POPs Protocol to the LRTAP, while awaiting the process in Stockholm and, if necessary, setting forth regulations under the LRTAP – in order to save resources and not have parallel processes. This has been an important point for Norway,[41] and it shows how the Stockholm Convention takes precedence.

Stockholm also overlaps the Basel Convention,[42] but only with regard to the POPs waste regulations. The division of labour between the Stockholm Convention and the Basel Convention is set out in Article 6 of the Stockholm Convention. In practice, Stockholm mandates Basel to determine limit values and what is considered the suitable treatment of the waste etc., in line with Article 6 paragraph 2. The decision of the Stockholm Conference of Parties (COP) is reflected in a separate decision by the Basel COP and on that basis Basel then proceeds to formulate recommendations on the treatment of POPs containing waste. However, these guidelines are not legally binding in the same way as the requirements of the Stockholm Convention. Basel recently appointed its own working group on POPs waste: the Small Intersessional Working Group (SIWG) on POPs. This specialist forum was established as part of the synergies between the Stockholm, Rotterdam, and Basel conventions with a view to enhancing inter-convention collaboration while avoiding duplication/omissions and promoting a more comprehensive understanding and unified communication procedures across the conventions.[43]

There is also some overlap between the Rotterdam and Stockholm conventions in that both cover some of the same substances, such as the brominated flame retardants penta- and octaBDE, for example, and in that substances that are banned or strictly regulated in a country as a result of global regulations by the Stockholm Convention must be notified to Rotterdam. However, as a convention, Rotterdam differs clearly from Stockholm in being merely a means of notifying the export of certain hazardous chemicals. This means that, unlike Stockholm, it contains no bans/regulations, which makes it more akin to Basel, which is also a notification system for the export of waste.

While substances are not nominated under the Rotterdam Convention, states are nevertheless required to report/notify the Convention if a national ban is introduced. All notifications are evaluated on the basis of a set of criteria specified by the Convention (Annexes I and II).[44] When two notifications from two regions meet the criteria, the Chemical Review Committee (CRC) compiles the information submitted by the countries in a Decision Guiding Document (DGD) and a proposal is issued to include the substance on the Convention's Annex III list of substances subject to export/import notification obligations. The Rotterdam Convention undertakes no scientific assessment of the hazardousness of substances at the global level, unlike the Stockholm Convention where substances are assessed and listed subject to certain criteria based on the threat to health and the environment of properties of the substance in question. Under Rotterdam, judgements are based solely on the hazard assessment undertaken by the countries themselves when introducing the ban. Norway has recently contributed most to the work of the Stockholm Convention, but is also a participant in the efforts of both the LRTAP and Rotterdam. The achievement of a global regulation of new POPs has been the most important area of work.[45]

To sum up this first part of the chapter: John Anthony Buccini, who led the negotiations under the Stockholm Convention, describes the process towards a global agreement as 'long and winding'. This notwithstanding, he describes a process that at the time functioned reasonably well and without major controversy, unlike the development of a climate regime. One of the reasons, as he sees it, was the consensus on the scientific basis. Rather than a question of whether one should do something, it was when and how.[46] The impact of consensual science can therefore not be overestimated. Scientific consensus is a prerequisite of success. A similar point is made by members of the Norwegian delegation to the Stockholm Convention negotiations.[47] Furthermore, the human health nexus is clearer; and banning POPs does not require transformation of energy systems.

The Convention is an important agreement for Norway and even though Norway was not a lead state in these negotiations, it was very supportive.[48] Where Norway has taken a leading role is in the nomination of new substances, where it has been active since 2005. Only the EU and Mexico can demonstrate a similar level of activity. What this short presentation tells us is that Norway was very supportive of legal regulations from the beginning and started playing a proactive role after the signing of the Stockholm Convention, and that scientific knowledge has been influential. If we look at the international regulation of POPs (including the Basel and Rotterdam conventions), the Stockholm Convention occupies a special position: this is where new POPs are nominated and evaluated globally and, if decided, regulated. It is a process where the involvement of science and individual states is of paramount importance. The question begging to be answered is what has determined the use of scientific knowledge in the Norwegian efforts to nominate new POPs to the Stockholm Convention?

A Mature and Specialized Management System?

Three national bodies are essential to the work of initiating nomination procedures, thus linking science and policy. First, there is the KLD, which formally has the last word and lays out the general political guidelines for work on hazardous substances (including POPs). These guidelines are disseminated through legislation, white papers, and annual letters of allocation. The main body in our case is the Norwegian Environment Agency. The Environment Agency is a governmental body under the KLD. The agency is professionally independent in the sense of having a free hand to examine different cases and make decisions. The dissemination of knowledge and provision of advice on climate and environmental matters are other critical tasks. In the area of pollutants, the agency works to acquire and disseminate information, provide expert advice, and participate in international environmental activities and negotiations. In recent years the agency has been hiring highly qualified employees with professional experience in their respective fields, including POPs.[49] Nevertheless, the agency employs no scientists as such on its staff and therefore has to rely on formal and informal contacts with national and international scientific communities to acquire information on the latest developments, in this case POPs. The list of such establishments is long. Two of the most important are the Norwegian Institute for Air Research (NILU) and the Norwegian Polar Institute (NPI). Air pollution information has been of critical importance in Norway's nominations, and NILU is therefore often cited as one of the most important scientific institutes in this particular policy area.[50] The clear associations between these efforts and the Arctic environment have also given the NPI an important role. AMAP has been crucial as well.[51] Although AMAP is not a national research institute, its secretariat is based in Oslo, as mentioned earlier, and it is largely funded by Norway. The continuous work of AMAP since the beginning of the 1990s has been of great importance in informing environmental authorities on new scientific findings. Furthermore, in the last decade, numerous research programmes under the auspices of the Norwegian Research Council (e.g., PROFO, FORURENS, MILJØ 2015, MILJØFORSK 2015)[52] have funded projects in the scientific community investigating the consequences and persistence of POPs in the environment. What these scientific actors have in common is that the lion's share of recent research has been conducted in the Arctic.

The interaction between these three players is important. The basis for initiating a nomination process is the expertise of the Climate and Environment Ministry in dealing with environmental pollutants. The Environment Agency is given an 'order' to initiate a nomination by the ministry in a letter of allocation.[53] At this stage, however, the ministry does not compile a list of possible substances. On receiving the 'order', the agency seeks first to identify appropriate substances in close collaboration with the scientific community.

It has been hard to obtain information on the procedure in the case of PentaBDE in 2005, but it appears to have been rather arbitrary.[54] This is not really surprising since this was the first time Norway initiated a nomination. However, Norway had acquired broad competence in international environmental negotiations during the 1990s, and was considered an important player on the international scene.[55] Moreover, extensive research had been conducted. With regard to HBCD, the assessment was conducted by the agency (then known as the Norwegian Pollution Control Authority).[56] HBCD is also a brominated flame retardant, and the agency had acquired more competence in selecting pollutants for nomination. The agency was maturing and becoming more specialized.

The initial work on the latest nomination (DecaBDE in 2013) was outsourced to Bergfald, a private sector environmental consultancy.[57] Their mandate was to create a general list of substances for possible nomination (to see whether they passed the Annex D criteria, aka the screening criteria). They came up with a shortlist of fifteen. The agency evaluated the results and ended up with two pollutants.[58] It was then up to the ministry to decide which of the substances Norway wanted to nominate. My respondents underlined the scientific justification as the basis for each nomination (discussed shortly).[59] Regarding DecaBDE, the decision to proceed with a nomination to the Stockholm Convention was, however, also partly influenced by the fact that Norway had worked on regulations at EU-level.[60] It is also important to note that because the nomination process is so expensive (in terms of personnel and resources), the agency can only nominate one substance at a time.[61]

With regard to relations between the scientific community and the agency, the picture is very complex indeed; the research community is fragmented, including public health studies, studies of contaminant levels in Arctic species, chemical and oceanographic studies, etc. There are several formal and informal channels of communication. My respondents did not paint a clear picture. In general, however, evidence of the professionalization of management in this field was something several scientists highlighted, while also noting that employees at the Environment Agency are generally well abreast of scientific progress and have acquired specialized expertise in the 'use' of scientific knowledge. An interesting example is the Norwegian Environment Agency's direct use of AMAP expertise in the nomination process. AMAP has provided the Norwegian delegations with slides to be presented to the scientific committee under the Stockholm Convention (POPRC). What we have seen in Norway since 2005 is a prolonged joint effort and a more mature and specialized process involving scientific communities, government bodies, politicians and policymakers to nominate new substances. This has also made it easier to prolong the lifetime of this policy. Furthermore, the previous short story on the regulation of POPs also tells us that Norway has been involved in regional and global regulations of POPs for a long time (especially AMAP), and has developed in-depth and specialized competence in this issue area. However, a well-functioning environmental management system can only explain some of the influence of scientific knowledge.

Scientific Consensus?

As mentioned earlier, it is easier to gain acceptance for an environmental regulation if the scientific community describing the problem and how to address it is united. Unequivocal and frequently confirmed scientific studies revealed the damage caused by chlorofluorocarbon gases to the ozone layer.[62] Another example is the work on acid rain, where it was clear that precipitation tainted by sulfur and nitrogen led to acidification of water and soil.[63] In both cases, scientific consensus was essential in getting the international community to adopt regulations. If we consider the twelve substances that were initially governed by the Stockholm Convention, there was generally broad scientific consensus. As one of my respondents put it, 'the question wasn't whether there should be twelve; the focus was on exemptions, criteria, and financing'.[64] The head of the Stockholm Convention negotiations, John Anthony Buccini, also underlines this point in his detailed account of the road towards a global agreement.[65] But scientific consensus is still not a statistical quantity. Some of my respondents mentioned the increase in research activity in the international chemical industry. Industry scientists publish their research in the international scientific literature and, further, are questioning accepted truths.[66] At the national level, the effect is mostly indirect, but in the international processes that eventually lead to the listing of a new substance, the presence of the international chemical industry also becomes more pronounced when it comes to scientific status.[67] However, it is not univocal and a broader analysis of their role would be interesting, but I will not follow up on this discussion in this chapter. Another recurring question in the global environmental debate concerns the precautionary principle. What does it mean to say there is sufficient knowledge of the effects of something on the environment?

However, if we look at Norway's work on new substances, there was general agreement in the scientific community that the nominated substances (PentaBDE, HBCD and DecaBDE) displayed properties of POPs and posed a danger to the environment and health.[68] There is also broad scientific consensus that substances such as these (brominated flame retardants) should be regulated. This is evident in work done by AMAP. In what might be one of the most comprehensive assessments on Arctic pollution from 2002, a key recommendation is to regulate PentaBDE. Out of three substances that 'may be at or approaching levels in the Arctic that could justify regional and global action'[69] PentaBDE is listed first.[70] In the Arctic Pollution report from 2009 increased levels of HBCD is highlighted.[71] HBCD is ubiquitous in the Arctic and there is a need for global regulation. The same pattern is evident regarding DecaBDE.[72] It is also worth noting that all the substances are brominated flame retardants. They have common characteristics, and research has provided strong scientific evidence for urging their regulation. Furthermore, focusing on one category of POPs has provided the Norwegian environmental management system with wide-ranging and specialist expertise on a specific category of POPs. Internationally, the picture is more complex, despite the relatively high degree of consensus here too.[73] A key point in our case is that the Norwegian environmental authorities would hardly nominate a new substance if they were not more or less sure that they would succeed in their efforts or that a nomination had a justifiable basis in broad scientific consensus.[74] Consensual knowledge is, thus, a prerequisite for success. The influence of scientific knowledge is, therefore, in our case dependent on the state of knowledge. But this is still only part of the story. We need to take another step to get a more complete picture of the use of Arctic science.

Political and Economic Controversy?

The fact that the scientific community agrees that a given substance displays the properties of a POP and should be regulated does not mean that environmental agencies inevitably will take steps to nominate them. A recurring example is climate negotiations and the unwillingness of governments to commit to internationally agreed solutions. In this connection, a distinction is often drawn between political and economic cost. Will it be politically costly to start a nomination process and will this process and eventual nomination lead to commercial and economic challenges at the national level? In what follows, the three substances Norway has nominated will be treated as one. Although there are differences between them, they are not decisive with regard to economic and political controversy. It is nevertheless important here to distinguish what is perceived as controversial at the international level, and by other states, from what is potentially controversial in a national context. My analysis is limited mainly to the latter level.

Looking at the national political debate, the international regulation of hazardous substances with POPs properties has been uncontroversial. The debate over the storage of environmental waste has tended to be relatively lively (i.e., between local and national politicians), not surprisingly. With regard to POPs, the picture is less complex. Norway had already regulated virtually all of the original twelve substances on the Stockholm Convention list, and the same goes for those nominated by Norway.[75] One of my respondents put it as follows: 'In relation to the ministry and political leadership, there isn't much we need to explain.'[76] Neither has the expressed desire for further international regulation of pollutants been affected by the political colour of changing governments.[77] In allocation letters from the KLD to the Norwegian Environment Agency, the importance of pressing ahead to nominate new POPs is underlined.[78] So it has not been politically controversial to support steps to strengthen the Stockholm Convention. Indeed, there has been very little political interference: 'politicians have been really pleased to see good and important causes getting through without controversy'.[79]

The economic dimension is, of course, closely linked to the political. But here too the picture is relatively clear: none of the substances Norway has nominated is produced in Norway and there have been few if any protests from Norwegian commercial actors over their nomination. On the contrary: a tightening of the rules on substances has been seen as a means of levelling the playing field with competitors, and has therefore been welcomed at the national level.[80] Another point in this connection is that it is costly just to set a nomination process in motion. The Norwegian Environment Agency, for example, has three experts working on these processes almost constantly.[81] The agency also funds positions and projects in various research communities. So in that sense, active participation is demanding both in terms of personnel and money. However, looking at the wider picture, the issues are neither politically nor commercially controversial.

The international scene is certainly more complex. When deciding which substance to nominate (or which scientific knowledge to use), Norway has assessed what is politically possible and prudent at the international level. One example is the decision of the KLD regarding DecaBDE. The European Union (with Norwegian support) had unsuccessfully attempted to pass regulations for the EU area. It was therefore logical for Norway to bring the issue to the attention of the international community.[82] The agency also explores whether other states are considering nominating substances.[83] It would not make much sense if Norway initiated a nomination process for a substance on which the EU was already working, for example. The influence of scientific knowledge is therefore obviously affected by international and regional initiatives. Nominating a substance is scientifically demanding and costly, so parallel processes need to be avoided.

We can therefore say that in this case science has made a difference insofar as the policy is neither economically nor politically controversial. Processing a nomination, on the other hand, is resource intensive, and – presumably – dependent on direct or indirect political support if the country is to take a leading role in the nomination of new substances or bringing scientific knowledge to the attention of the domestic environmental authorities and from there to the global level. Therefore, more flesh needs to be attached to the bone when explaining the influence of scientific knowledge.

On the Political and Public Agenda?

An overriding characteristic of POPs is their complexity. POPs represent a subset of thousands of chemicals on the market, each of which has unique properties and usually a dedicated scientific designation most people find hard to understand. This could possibly dissuade the public from showing any interest in the issues. The nomination of new POPs can serve as an illustration. In the Norwegian public sphere, the question of contaminants attracts a great deal of interest and attention. This is not true of the individual substances Norway has nominated, as a search of Norway's largest newspaper (*Aftenposten*) makes clear. If we search for the individual pollutants Norway has nominated (using their specific designations), the number of hits is no more than four for the past decade. A collective search for brominated flame retardants has a higher ten-year score of thirty, just three per year, with widely varying annual figures. However, if we search using the broader category of *miljøgifter* (pollutants) the number of hits exceeds 500. We see the same tendency in official documents from the Climate and Environment Ministry; specific designations show wide annual variations but few hits.[84]

Discussions concerning the individual substances have attracted neither public nor political interest. The nomination of new POPs in general is, however, still inextricably linked to the notion of Norway as an environmental champion,[85] and we can therefore say that pollutants generally receive a great deal of political and public attention, even though the individual pollutants fall beneath the radar. One could argue that what we now have is a scientifically driven environmental foreign policy. The processes are so demanding, they simply do not get to feature in the political and public debates. One could also argue that science travels more easily if unnecessary 'noise' surrounding the scientific findings can be filtered out. This is linked to Underdal's argument that high salience may increase polarization and create difficulties for scientific input.[86]

Another important dimension in this context is the intense public interest in the Arctic in Norway. The public agenda is highly attuned to research on Arctic-related issues (including environmental contaminants). Documents published by Norwegian authorities (whatever the government's partisan composition) over the past decade confirm this massive interest.[87] The Arctic is a popular topic with the Norwegian public and Norwegian politicians, and environmental and climate research in the region is an important part of this picture.

What does all of this tell us? Basically, that pollutants are on the political and public agenda, and at times at the forefront of the public mind. This impression is reinforced by the amount of attention the Arctic has attracted in recent years. Conversely, the processes leading up to a nomination of individual substances do not figure in the public debate. Despite the fact that the Norwegian Environment Agency tries to make information as readily available as possible (as one of its main tasks),[88] work on new nominations has become depoliticized. We can say that while Norway's efforts to nominate new substances have cost little politically, the political rewards have been slight as well. As one of my respondents said: 'It's not hard to get politicians onboard. It's a popular issue. But attracting the interest of the media, that's a different matter.'[89] There are echoes here of Mitchell and colleagues,[90] who link scientific influence to whether a topic is useful and exploitable.[91] It seems that policymakers consider new nominations as something to brag about. Putting it bluntly, however, the public does not really care. Norway's 'victories' in terms of international regulation have rarely received media attention.[92] However, what is essential is that the nomination procedure has been perceived as politically important and useful to decision makers. To conclude, the interest of the public and politicians in pollutants is high in general, especially if the Arctic is involved, but low for the individually nominated substances. One could thus argue that scientific knowledge has travelled relatively easily without much public and political 'interference'.

The four variables discussed here, which are largely interdependent, need to be seen in context. Broad scientific consensus is not enough if the regulations are seen to be politically and economically controversial, and a well-functioning environmental management system is lacking. Again, the challenges arising from climate change are an obvious example. Furthermore, as previous studies have shown, high public interest can have a beneficial effect on future regulations.[93] As described in this chapter, the picture regarding POPs is more complicated. There is great interest in environmental issues in the Arctic in general, but little in the actual scientific work of nominating new POPs. The introductory proposition, 'that a mature and specialized environmental management system, consensual knowledge and high public and political attention in a low-conflict area have made it easier for Arctic scientific knowledge to travel through the national environmental management system and end up in an international convention' is strengthened nonetheless. As a finding it confirms earlier analyses of the environmental field. But it is still difficult to corroborate Underdal's hypothesis whereby 'high salience increases the demand for information'.[94] Pollutants may be high on the public agenda, but the specific nominations do not attract much public attention, and are also largely depoliticized. The demand for information, however, does not necessarily decrease. There are indications that Norway's management of the environment in this field is largely based on trust. The politicians and the KLD rely on the Norwegian Environment Agency to do a good job and the Environment Agency trusts the researcher's integrity.

A related question in this context is why more states are not taking an active role in these processes. Canada has historically been at the forefront in terms of political awareness and research into POPs. Canada was also active in the negotiations to formulate the Stockholm Convention.[95] For Canada's part, lack of resources cannot explain their wait-and-see attitude to international POPs regulations. Canada has devoted, and continues to devote, a great deal of resources to research on POPs, Arctic environmental monitoring, etc. Canada's Arctic policy is very industry-friendly as well.[96] This may be a significant reason why they have not nominated any substances. To illustrate Canada's approach, the country blocked the listing of chrysotile asbestos under the 2011 Rotterdam Convention negotiations,[97] something that has been linked to the mining industry in Quebec and that played an important role nationally. Another example is Canada's wish to be granted exemptions enabling the continued use of the flame retardant decaBDE in its automotive industry and in the recycling of the same substance.[98] What we see is that it will probably be more economically and politically controversial for Canada to nominate new POPs.

For developing countries, and countries with economies in transition (such as former Eastern European states), resources and capacity are the main challenges. Considerable resources are needed to nominate a substance and the process can also take several (three to four) years. There is also the question of scientific expertise, which few states have. The Arctic states are in a special position in this respect, and again the work under AMAP is often used as an illustration, especially regarding surveillance data from polar areas. Developing countries and countries with transitional economies are often focusing on other environmental challenges/types of substance than those regulated by the Stockholm Convention. Acute environmental challenges and recognized environmental hazards are higher on the agenda. In terms of chemicals, developing countries tend to have better expertise on pesticides than POPs (although pesticides can also be POPs). Of the more general challenges, more states are struggling with frequent changes at the political level and turnover in their civil services (contributing to a lack of stability), and face enough challenges simply to implement the Convention as it is today. A related example is the effectiveness evaluation presented at the Stockholm COP in 2017, according to which many countries are highly unlikely to achieve the goal of phasing out PCBs by 2025.[99]

Conclusion

There was broad scientific consensus that the twelve original substances on the Stockholm Convention list displayed POP properties and ought to be regulated globally. Arctic studies have played an important role in creating both awareness about these contaminants and providing scientific input. There were obviously discussions on exemptions, transitional arrangements, and financial contributions, but few disagreed that something had to be done given the properties of these substances.[100] Several of them had already been banned or severely restricted by many of the signatory countries. Norway was one of them and was also a supporter of a global convention, albeit not a driving force. One of the dynamic aspects of the Stockholm Convention in its relations with other legal instruments is the opportunity it gives to governments to nominate new substances for global regulation. This process is unique to the Stockholm Convention. The Basel and Rotterdam Conventions are key instruments in the POP regime, but do not have the same properties. The nomination process is demanding – scientifically, technically and financially. Since 2001, fourteen new substances have entered the list. Norway has been one of the main contributors to these processes. Success in these efforts is very much down to scientific knowledge. In this chapter I have attempted to identify what determines the use of scientific knowledge in the nominations by the Norwegian government of new POPs to the Stockholm Convention. An analysis of the question is timely given that the Stockholm Convention is driven by government involvement. Analyses of international cooperation should be complemented by national analyses explaining why some states are more 'environmentally friendly' than others or, more precisely, why and how scientific knowledge influences decision making. One of the main reasons may be that Norway is a 'downstream country' and dependent on a global deal to achieve a toxin-free environment. The sharper focus on the Arctic has also given the topic more urgency in political and media circles. The key policy documents on Norway's High North policy show how much attention is devoted to protection of the Arctic environment.[101] However, I did not want primarily to discover Norway's motivation but rather the conditions that made it possible for Arctic science to 'travel' through the domestic level to affect regulations at the global level. At a general level, there has been little controversy over tackling pollutants in the north. Regarding the more specific nominations of new POPs, the conditions have allowed Norway to act as a green ambassador. Norwegian environmental authorities have largely welcomed the science on POPs in general and the three substances Norway has nominated in particular. The laborious work on specific POPs is largely depoliticized and there have been few if any political and economic costs to extending the lifetime of this policy. But that does not mean the nomination process (national and international) is not resource-intensive for the agency concerned, requiring a significant financial commitment. But at a wider economic level, since there are no national commercial firms manufacturing any of the substances nominated by Norway, no negative sentiments have been expressed by the private sector about their regulation. Regulation has rather been seen as a competitive advantage insofar as most national regulations were already stricter than the international ones.

Lastly, one may ask why Norway got involved in the Stockholm Convention and new nominations from the start. Such an analysis must, however, be anchored in an in-depth historical description of Norway's international environmental efforts.[102] Whether individuals (scientists and officials) or coincidence made the nomination of new POPs seem important, I shall not attempt to answer. What I can say is that the conditions have generally been right, allowing Arctic scientific knowledge an 'easy' passage to international negotiations.

So what does this case study tell us? It tells us that to obtain a more complete picture of how science travels into global governance we need to bring the state in. We need to know how scientific knowledge is used (or not used) at the state level. It is therefore pertinent to ask what determined the influence of scientific knowledge in Norwegian efforts to nominate new POPs to the Stockholm Convention. As for Norway, the case study tells us that scientific knowledge has an easy path when conditions are right. It can of course be noted that such a conclusion is not particularly startling. However, what is more noteworthy is the degree of depoliticization of the field. Norway's involvement in the nomination of new POPs is not dependent on high public and political interest or on whether the subject moves up or down the popularity scale. It requires so much continuous work that processes must be independent of attention levels, otherwise the environmental authorities would fail. This speaks to the design of the environmental management system that has to be based on trust and continuity to succeed.

When analysing how Arctic knowledge 'travels' we need to understand what determines the influence of scientific knowledge. The thesis that science has an impact when the environmental management system is mature and specialized; when scientists agree; when the use of scientific knowledge is neither politically nor economically controversial; and when the issue is simultaneously part of a positive discourse (the North as a toxin-free zone), is – not surprisingly – confirmed. Norway has had little to lose by initiating work on regulating new POPs and being active in the nomination of new POPs. Being environmentally friendly (or using scientific knowledge) in this case has been scientifically demanding, but politically easy.

Notes

1 Of which the most important and prominent is the Arctic Climate Impact Assessment; see Arctic Council, 'ACIA Policy Document' (2004). Available at http://www.acia.uaf.edu/PDFs/ACIA_Policy_Document.pdf (accessed 23 April 2018).

2 For example David Leonard Downie and Terry Fenge (eds), *Northern Lights Against POPs: Combatting Toxic Threats in the Arctic* (Montreal, McGill-Queen's University Press, 2003); Sébastien Duyck, 'Which canary in the coalmine? The Arctic in the international climate change regime', in Timo Koivurova, Gundmundur Alfredsson and Waliul Hasanat (eds), *The Yearbook of Polar Law* (2012). Available at https://papers.ssrn.com/sol3/papers.cfm?abstract_id=2331137 (accessed 29 March 2017); Paula Kankaanpää and Oran R. Young, 'The effectiveness of the Arctic Council', *Polar Research* 31 (2012), pp. 1–14. Available at http://www.polarresearch.net/index.php/polar/article/view/17176 (accessed 16 March 2017); David P. Stone, *The Changing Arctic Environment: The Arctic Messenger* (New York, Cambridge University Press, 2015).

3 Downie and Fenge (eds), *Northern Lights Against POPs: Combatting Toxic Threats in the Arctic*; Stone, *The Changing Arctic Environment: The Arctic Messenger*.

4 For an accessible introduction see Stone, *The Changing Arctic Environment: The Arctic Messenger*.

5 Hayley Hung, Athanasios A. Katsoyiannis, Eva Brorström-Lundén, Kristin Olafsdottir, Wenche Aas, Knut Breivik, Pernilla Bohlin-Nizzetto, Arni Sigurdsson,

Hannele Hakola, Rossana Bossi, Henrik Skov, Ed Sverko, Enzo Barresi, Phil Fellin and Simon Wilson, 'Temporal trends of Persistent Organic Pollutants (POPs) in Arctic air: 20 years of monitoring under the Arctic Monitoring and Assessment Programme (AMAP)', *Environmental Pollution* 217 (2016), pp. 52–61.

6 For an overview see, the Stockholm Convention, 'The New POPs' (2016). Available at http://chm.pops.int/TheConvention/ThePOPs/TheNewPOPs/tabid/2511/Default.aspx (accessed 22 August 2017).

7 Downie and Fenge (eds), *Northern Lights Against POPs: Combatting Toxic Threats in the Arctic*; Henrik Selin, *Global Governance of Hazardous Chemicals: Challenges of Multilevel Management* (Cambridge, MIT Press, 2010); Margaret Morales, *The Stockholm Convention* (Durham, Duke University, 2014).

8 Downie and Fenge (eds), *Northern Lights Against POPs: Combatting Toxic Threats in the Arctic*; Selin, *Global Governance of Hazardous Chemicals: Challenges of Multilevel Management*.

9 Henry P. Huntington and Michelle Sparck, 'POPs in Alaska: Engaging the United States', in Downie and Fenge (eds), *Northern Lights Against POPs: Combatting Toxic Threats in the Arctic*, pp. 214–24, and Russel Shearer and Siu-Ling Han, 'Canadian research and POPs: The Northern Containments Program', in Downie and Fenge (eds), *Northern Lights Against POPs: Combatting Toxic Threats in the Arctic*, pp. 41–60, are, however, exceptions.

10 Pamela S. Chasek, David Leonard Downie and Janet Welsh Brown, *Global Environmental Politics* (Boulder, Westview Press, 2017), pp. 51–61.

11 Robert D. Putnam, 'Diplomacy and domestic politics: The logic of two-level game', *International Organization* 42/3 (1988), pp. 427–60.

12 PentaBDE (also known as pentabromodiphenyl oxide) is a brominated flame retardant. Commercial PentaBDE is most commonly used as a flame retardant in flexible polyurethane foam; it was also used in printed circuit boards in Asia, and in other applications. For an in-depth description see: http://chm.pops.int/Default.aspx?tabid=2301.

13 HBCD is a brominated flame retardant. Its primary application is in extruded (XPS) and expanded (EPS) polystyrene foam that is used as thermal insulation in the building industry. Other uses are upholstered furniture, automobile interior textiles, car cushions, and insulation blocks in trucks, packaging material, video cassette recorder housing, and electric and electronic equipment. For an in-depth description see: http://chm.pops.int/Default.aspx?tabid=2301.

14 DecaBDE is a brominated flame retardant. The chemical is used in conjunction with antimony trioxide in polymers, mainly in high impact polystyrene (HIPS) which is used in the television industry for cabinet backs. DecaBDE is also used for polypropylene drapery and upholstery fabric by means of back coating and may also be used in some synthetic carpets. For an in-depth description see: http://chm.pops.int/Default.aspx?tabid=2301.

15 One could argue that being a downstream Arctic state is motivation enough. But that doesn't explain the work on brominated flame retardants as such. Other substances have some of the same characteristics. Furthermore, it is often claimed that Norway 'considers' itself to be an environmentally friendly actor, and that this socially constructed notion of itself as an environmental champion is a motivation factor and

makes scientific knowledge travel 'easier'. The assumption that being active at the international level might create openings in other areas could also explain Norway's behaviour. I will not, however, pursue these arguments in this chapter.

16 There is little secondary literature on the subject and despite the fact that one finds more general political descriptions of Norway's engagement on environmental toxins in policy documents, it is impossible to analyze the more specific problems encountered in the selection of a new substance for nominations without interviewing the actors involved. Interview data are therefore essential in my analysis.

17 This part of the chapter is based on Steinar Andresen, Kristin Rosendal and Jon B. Skjærseth, 'Designing knowledge-based, integrated management systems for environmental governance', in A. Dinar (ed.), *Natural Resources and Environmental Policy in the Era of Global Change* (Singapore, World Scientific, 2017), pp. 439–56, building upon a framework developed by Arild Underdal, 'Science and politics: The anatomy of an uneasy partnership', in S. Andresen, T. Skodvin, A. Underdal and J. Wettestad (eds), *Science and Politics in International Environmental Regimes* (Manchester, Manchester University Press, 2000). Underdal's framework is developed for studies at the international level. I will, however, claim that it is just as relevant at the national level.

18 By 'management systems', I mean the policy decisions, measures, rules of procedure, norms and regulations that apply to specific policy areas.

19 Jon B. Skjærseth (ed.), *International Regimes and Norway's Environmental Policy – Crossfire and Coherence* (Farnham, Ashgate, 2004); Steinar Andresen, 'The role of scientific expertise in multilateral environmental agreements: Influence and effectiveness', in M. Ambrus, K. Arts, E. Hey and H. Raulus, *The Role of 'Experts' in International and European Decision-Making Processes: Advisor, Decision-maker or Irrelevant Actors* (Cambridge, Cambridge University Press, 2014), pp. 105–25.

20 James G. March and Johan P. Olsen, *Rediscovering Institutions: The Organizational Basis of Politics* (New York, Macmillan, 1989); Peter M. Haas, *Saving the Mediterranean: The Politics of International Environmental Cooperation* (New York, Columbia University Press, 1990); Roger N. Clark, Errol E. Meidinger and others, *Integrating Science and Policy in Natural Resource Management: Lessons and Opportunities from North America*, USDA Forest Service, General Technical Report (1998). Available at https://www.fs.fed.us/pnw/pubs/gtr_441.pdf (accessed 23 April 2018).

21 Jørgen Wettestad, *Clearing the Air – European Advances in Tackling Acid Rain and Atmospheric Pollution* (Farnham, Ashgate, 2002); Jon B. Skjærseth, 'International ozone policies: Effective international cooperation', in S. Andresen, E. L. Boasson and G. Hønneland (eds), *International Environmental Agreements: An Introduction* (New York, Routledge, 2012), pp. 38–48.

22 Edward L. Miles, Steinar Andresen, Elaine M. Carlin, Jon B. Skjærseth, Arild Underdal and Jørgen Wettestad, *Environmental Regime Effectiveness: Confronting Theory with Evidence* (Cambridge, MIT Press, 2002); Underdal, 'Science and politics: The anatomy of an uneasy partnership'.

23 Andresen, Rosendal, Skjærseth, 'Designing knowledge-based, integrated management systems for environmental governance'; Kristin Rosendal and Peter J. Schei, 'Convention on Biological Diversity: From national conservation to global responsibility', in Andresen, Boasson and Hønneland (eds), *International Environmental Agreements: An Introduction*.

24 Andresen, Rosendal and Skjærseth, 'Designing knowledge-based, integrated management systems for environmental governance'.

25 For an in-depth presentation of this history see Downie and Fenge (eds), *Northern Lights Against POPs: Combatting Toxic Threats in the Arctic*, and Selin, *Global Governance of Hazardous Chemicals: Challenges of Multilevel Management*. My short presentation is to a large extent based on their findings.

26 Rachel Carson, *Silent Spring* (Boston, Houghton Mifflin, 1962).

27 Selin, *Global Governance of Hazardous Chemicals: Challenges of Multilevel Management*.

28 Both DDT and PCB belong to the Dirty Dozen. For a list of national regulations (with exemptions) of pesticides covered by the Stockholm Convention see: Norwegian Ministry of Environment, 'Norwegian implementation plan for the Stockholm Convention on POPs' (Oslo, Norwegian Ministry of Environment, 2010). Available at http://www.pops.int/documents/implementation/nips/submissions/Norway.pdf (accessed 9 March 2017).

29 Downie and Fenge (eds), *Northern Lights Against POPs: Combatting Toxic Threats in the Arctic*, p. 277.

30 Bredo Berntsen, *Grønne linjer: Natur- og miljøvernets historie i Norge* (Otta, Unipub, 2011).

31 Interview with Ministry of Climate and Environment (KLD), 6 April 2016.

32 It is important to note the international breadth of the research community. However, my respondents and the secondary literature tend to emphasize in particular the role of North American, Swedish and Norwegian researchers.

33 Selin, *Global Governance of Hazardous Chemicals. Challenges of Multilevel Management*, p. 115.

34 Downie and Fenge, *Northern Lights Against POPs. Combatting Toxic Threats in the Arctic.*

35 Ibid.

36 AMAP (Arctic Monitoring and Assessment Programme), *Arctic Pollution Issues: A State of the Arctic Environment Report* (1998). Available at https://www.amap.no/documents/doc/arctic-pollution-issues-a-state-of-the-arctic-environment-report/67 (accessed 23 April 2018).

37 AMAP is still an important scientific actor in the field of POPs, see AMAP (Arctic Monitoring and Assessment Report Programme), *AMAP Assessment 2015: Temporal Trends in Persistent Organic Pollutants in the Arctic* (2015). Available at https://www.amap.no/documents/doc/AMAP-Assessment-2015-Temporal-Trends-in-Persistent-Organic-Pollutants-in-the-Arctic/1521 (accessed 23 April 2018).

38 Subsequent meetings of the INC were held in Nairobi, Kenya, in January 1999; in Geneva, Switzerland, in September 1999; in Bonn, Germany, in March 2000; and in Johannesburg, South Africa, in December 2000 where the negotiations were successfully completed.

39 Of ten substances nominated, nine were listed. The only exception was SCCP. See Selin, *Global Governance of Hazardous Chemicals. Challenges of Multilevel Management*, p. 158.

40 LRTAP, Protocol to the 1979 Convention on Long-range Transboundary Air Pollution on Persistent Organic Pollutants. Available at http://www.unece.org/fileadmin/DAM/env/lrtap/full%20text/1998.POPs.e.pdf (accessed 23 April 2018).

41 Interview with KLD, 19 February 2016.
42 The Basel Convention on the Control of Transboundary Movements of Hazardous Wastes and their Disposal. Available at http://www.basel.int/Portals/4/Basel%20 Convention/docs/text/BaselConventionText-e.pdf (accessed 23 April 2018).
43 Synergies among the Basel, Rotterdam and Stockholm conventions. Available at http://www.brsmeas.org/2017COPs/MeetingDocuments/tabid/5385/language/en-US/Default.aspx (accessed 23 April 2018).
44 Rotterdam Convention on the Prior Informed Consent Procedure for Certain Hazardous Chemicals and Pesticides in International Trade. Available at http://www.pic.int/TheConvention/Overview/TextoftheConvention/tabid/1048/language/en-US/Default.aspx (accessed 23 April 2018).
45 Interview with KLD, 19 February 2016.
46 John Anthony Buccini, 'The long and winding road to Stockholm: The view from the chair', in Downie and Fenge (eds), *Northern Lights Against POPs. Combatting Toxic Threats in the Arctic*, p. 253.
47 Interview with KLD, 6 April 2016; interview with Norwegian Institute for Air Research (NILU), 12 May 2016.
48 Interview with KLD, 6 April 2016.
49 Interview with Norwegian Environment Agency, 15 December 2015; interview with NILU, 12 May 2016.
50 Interview with Norwegian Environment Agency, 15 December 2015.
51 Interview with Norwegian Environment Agency, 15 December 2015; interview with Akvaplan-niva AS, 24 May 2016; interview with Norwegian Polar Institute (NPI), 28 June 2016.
52 For statistics and projects see Norwegian Research Council, available at https://www.forskningsradet.no/prosjektbanken (accessed 9 March 2017).
53 Norwegian Ministry of Climate and Environment, 'Letter of allocation, the Norwegian Environmental Agency' (2009). Available at https://www.regjeringen.no/globalassets/upload/md/vedlegg/brev/tildelingsbrev_2009/sft_etb_2009.pdf (accessed 23 April 2018); 'Letter of allocation, the Norwegian Environmental Agency' (2016). Available at https://www.regjeringen.no/contentassets/ab73dcc339ba4a498f8e17df76305bed/miljodirektoratet_tildelingsbrev_2016.pdf (accessed 23 April 2018).
54 Interview with KLD, 19 February 2016; interview with Norwegian Environment Agency, 15 December 2015.
55 Kristin Rosendal, 'Norway in UN environmental politics: Ambitions and influence', *International Environmental Agreements: Politics, Law and Economics* 7/4 (2007), pp. 439–55.
56 Interview with Norwegian Environment Agency, 15 December 2015.
57 N. Lambert, C. Rostock, B. Bergfald and L. M. Bjorvik, *Identifying POP candidates for the Stockholm Convention* (2011). Available at http://www.miljodirektoratet.no/old/klif/publikasjoner/2871/ta2871.pdf (accessed 23 April 2018).
58 Interview with Norwegian Environment Agency, 15 December 2015.
59 Interview with AMAP, 27 March 2017; interview with NPI, 28 June 2016; interview with KLD, 6 April 2016.
60 Interview with KLD, 19 February 2016.
61 Interview with KLD, 19 February 2016.

62 Skjærseth, 'International ozone policies: Effective international cooperation'.
63 Wettestad, *Clearing the Air – European Advances in Tackling Acid Rain and Atmospheric Pollution*.
64 Interview with KLD, 6 April 2016.
65 Buccini, 'The long and winding road to Stockholm: The view form the chair'.
66 Interview with NPI, 28 June 2016; interview with Norwegian Environment Agency, 15 December 2015.
67 Interview with Norwegian Environment Agency, 15 December 2015.
68 Interview with AMAP, 27 March 2017; interview with NPI, 28 June 2016; interview with NILU, 12 December 2016.
69 AMAP (Arctic Monitoring and Assessment Programme), *Arctic Pollution* (2002), p. 3. Available at https://www.amap.no/documents/doc/arctic-pollution-2002/69 (accessed 23 April 2018).
70 The two other substances are polychlorinated naphthalenes (PCNs), which are not in production, and endosulfan, which were later nominated by the EU.
71 AMAP (Arctic Monitoring and Assessment Programme), *Arctic Pollution* (2009). Available at https://www.amap.no/documents/doc/arctic-pollution-2009/88 (accessed 23 April 2018).
72 AMAP, *AMAP Assessment 2015: Temporal Trends in Persistent Organic Pollutants in the Arctic*.
73 Buccini, 'The long and winding road to Stockholm: The view from the chair'.
74 Interview with Norwegian Environment Agency, 15 December 2015.
75 HBCD is however an exception. The non-use of this substance in national production can explain the lack of regulations; interview with Norwegian Environment Agency, 15 December 2015.
76 Ibid.
77 Norwegian Ministry of Foreign Affairs, *The Norwegian Government's High North Strategy* (Oslo, Norwegian Ministry of Foreign Affairs, 2006). Available at https://www.regjeringen.no/globalassets/upload/ud/vedlegg/strategien.pdf (accessed 23 April 2018); and Norwegian Government, *Nordkloden. Verdiskaping og ressurser. Klimaendinger og kunnskap. Utviklingen nord på kloden angår oss alle* (Oslo, Norwegian Ministry of Foreign Affairs, 2014). Available at https://www.regjeringen.no/contentassets/23843eabac77454283b0769876148950/nordkloden_rapport-red.pdf (accessed 23 April 2018).
78 Norwegian Ministry Environment, 'Letter of allocation, the Norwegian Environmental Agency' (2009); 'Letter of allocation, the Norwegian Environment Agency' (2016).
79 Interview with KLD, 19 February 2016.
80 Interview with Norwegian Environment Agency, 15 December 2015.
81 Ibid.
82 Interview with KLD, 19 February 2016.
83 Ibid.
84 See KLD homepage for overview: https://www.regjeringen.no/no/dep/kld/id668/ (accessed 29 March 2017).
85 Berntsen, *Grønne linjer: Natur- og miljøvernets historie i Norge*.
86 Underdal, 'Science and politics: The anatomy of an uneasy partnership'.
87 Norwegian Ministry of Foreign Affairs, *The Norwegian Government's High North Strategy*; and *The High North. Visions and Strategies* (Oslo, Norwegian Ministry

of Foreign Affairs, 2011). Available at https://www.regjeringen.no/globalassets/upload/ud/vedlegg/nordomradene/ud_nordomrodene_en_web.pdf (accessed 23 April 2018); Norwegian Government, *Nordkloden. Verdiskaping og ressurser. Klimaendringer og kunnskap. Utviklingen nord på kloden angår oss alle.* For an exploration of the Norwegian Arctic discourse, see, for example, Leif Christian Jensen, *International Relations in the Arctic: Norway and the Struggle for Power in the New North* (London, I.B. Tauris, 2016).

88 Norwegian Environment Agency, *Strategy 2015–2020* (2014). Available at http://www.miljodirektoratet.no/no/Publikasjoner/2014/Desember-2014/Miljodirektoratets-strategi-for-2015-2020/ (accessed 23 April 2018).

89 Interview with KLD, 6 June 2016.

90 Ronald B. Mitchell, William C. Clark, David W. Cash and Nancy M. Dickson (eds), *Global Environmental Assessments: Information and Influence* (Cambridge, MIT Press, 2006).

91 For an in-depth theoretical discussion see ibid. They do not treat interests as given exogenously, but assume that interests are constructed through the process of knowledge production and policy formulation.

92 Ibid.

93 Underdal, 'Science and politics: The anatomy of an uneasy partnership'.

94 Ibid.

95 Buccini, 'The long and winding road to Stockholm: The view from the chair'.

96 Canadian Government, *Statement on Canada's Arctic Foreign Policy: Exercising Sovereignty and Promoting Canada's Northern Strategy Abroad* (2010). Available at http://www.international.gc.ca/arctic-arctique/assets/pdfs/canada_arctic_foreign_policy-eng.pdf (accessed 23 April 2018).

97 Steve Rennie, 'Canada blocks inclusion of chrysotile asbestos in UN convention', *Globe and Mail*, 22 June 2011. Available at http://web4.uwindsor.ca/users/w/winter/Winters.nsf/831fc2c71873e46285256d6e006c367a/b98c7c39d61ad93485257068006c4501/$FILE/asbestos_Canada_blocks_ban.pdf (accessed 18 August 2017).

98 IPEN, IPEN Press Release, 26 April 2017. Available at https://zerowasteeurope.eu/2017/04/ipen-press-release-at-un-meeting-canada-and-chile-stand-alone-trying-to-legitimize-e-waste-dumping-and-promote-recycling-of-toxic-chemical-into-childrens-products/ (accessed 18 August 2017).

99 The Stockholm Convention, 'Effectiveness evaluation of the Stockholm Convention on Persistent Organic Pollutants pursuant to Article 16' (2017). Available at https://www.informea.org/sites/default/files/imported-documents/UNEP-POPS-COP.8-22.English.pdf (accessed 18 August 2017).

100 Interview with KLD, 6 April 2016.

101 One could of course argue that in the case of oil and gas development in northern regions we see a completely different picture. That is, however, another story not to be told here.

102 For a historical introduction to Norway's environmental policy and engagement see Berntsen, *Grønne linjer: Natur- og miljøvernets historie i Norge.*

PART II

RUSSIA

CHAPTER 5

THE RUSSIAN ARCTIC DEBATE: THE RUSH FOR THE NORTH POLE

Geir Hønneland

Introduction

The international relations (IR) discipline has seen an upsurge in interest in identity since the end of the Cold War.[1] The maps of Eastern Europe and Central Asia were being redrawn, the European Union was effectively dismantling national borders in Western Europe, and globalization was picking up speed; it was no longer feasible to view identity as a unitary, fixed and given substrate derived from an individual's nationality. Identity came to be viewed as a relation rather than a possession, a quality conditioned by changeable, fluid situations rather than rock-solid categories. Identities, wrote Lapid in 1996, had become 'emergent and constructed (rather than fixed and natural), contested and polymorphic (rather than unitary and singular), and interactive and process-like (rather than static and essence-like)'.[2]

This chapter is an extended version of Geir Hønneland, 'The rush for the North Pole', in *Russia and the Arctic: Environment, Identity and Foreign Policy* (London, I.B. Tauris, 2016), pp. 43–70. Former student Torstein Vik Århus collected the media material used in this chapter through the search engine Meltwater News and the websites of selected national and regional media. Regional media in Northwest Russia included the regional editions of *Argumenty i fakty*, the digital news agencies *Nord News, Murmanskie Biznes-Novosti* and the regional radio and TV station *GTRK Murman*. At national level, the newspapers *Izvestia, Kommersant, Moskovski Komsomolets, Nezavisimaya gazeta, Novaya gazeta* and *Rossiyskaya gazeta*, as well as the news agencies *Lenta.ru, Gazeta.ru, Regnum.ru* and *Vzglyad*, were chosen. This covers a mix of official, business, independent and openly critical media. The systematic search included the words 'Arctic' and 'Norway' (as much of Russian Arctic politics has been directed at this country) and covered the period 2005–10. More occasional searches were made from 2011 to 2014.

Jørgensen categorizes the study of identity, which he considers a generic term rather than a specific theory, within the post-positivist tradition.[3] Post-positivists have primarily used identity, he notes, to explain where interests come from. Instead of assuming the existence of an externally given or geographically determined national interest (such as realists and geopolitically oriented theorists do), post-positivists search for the *origins* of interest. In this perspective, the question is not whether interests *or* identity determine politics, but how specific identities cause specific interests and, in turn, how these interests translate into policymaking. As a prominent example, Wendt claims that the international system is created and recreated in processes of interaction, where identities are not given (although relatively stable), but continuously developed, sustained and transformed by inter-subjectively grounded practice.[4] The behaviour of states is not reducible to where they stand in the distribution of power in the international system,[5] or to the maximization of their material interest. States have selves that colour their interaction with other states, and are themselves shaped, maintained or modified in this very interaction. There is an ongoing struggle within the state about which of the many stories of the self should be activated at any specific time.

Browning elaborates a theory of foreign policy analysis in which action is explained as the result of state interest determined by narratively constructed identities.[6] In his view, action only becomes meaningful in the process of narrating a constitutive story of the self: 'By establishing a linear story from whom we were in the past up until the present a narrative framework is created within which experiences become intelligible to ourselves and to others, and future action becomes meaningful.'[7] It is only by telling stories about who we are that it becomes possible to say what we want. Interestingly, Browning claims, although advocates of the narrative approach have criticized rational, materialist accounts for assuming implicitly that identities are pre-given, this is probably how identities must be presented by state authorities to resonate with the population.[8]

Ringmar proposes a narrative theory of action that, he argues, under certain circumstances explains states' behaviour towards other states as a defence not of their interests, but of their identity[9]: 'It is through the stories that we tell that we make sense of ourselves and our world, and it is on the basis of these stories that we act'.[10] The stories we tell define not only what we want, but also who or what *we are like*. The narratives through which our selves are constituted are always the more fundamental; stories of selves are preconditions for stories told about interests.

> 'Interests' can only be *someone's* interests and the establishing of this 'someone' is of course precisely what the action in question is designed to accomplish. The action does not seek to maximise utility or minimise loss, but instead to establish

> a standard – a self – by which utilities and losses can be measured. These are consequently not 'rational actions', but instead actions undertaken in order to make rational actions possible. We act, as it were, in 'self-defence' in the most basic sense of the word – in defence of the applicability of our descriptions of our selves.[11]

Ringmar emphasizes the importance of *recognition* for persons' and communities' identity, including that of states. It is through our quest for recognition that our identity is established. Identity is a precondition for interest, and in certain situations identity-driven explanations of foreign policy can substitute for interest-driven explanations altogether. This can happen when a state has experienced a loss of recognition under humiliating circumstances ('lost face'), or at 'formative moments' when new metaphors are launched and individuals tell new stories about themselves, and new sets of rules emerge through which identities are classified – in short, 'when the very definition of the meaningful is up for grabs'.[12] Meanings are contested and fought over, through, for instance, propaganda and other forms of rhetoric. Old identities can prevail, be defeated or revised: 'Formative moments, we could say, are characteristically periods of symbolic hyper-inflation – times when new emblems, flags, dress codes, songs, *fêtes* and rituals are continuously invented.'[13] At these moments, there is an urgent need to have one's constitutive stories recognized. In a later work, Ringmar shows how Soviet policy towards the West was a constant quest for recognition, first of Soviet Russia as a legitimate state, then as a great power, subsequently as a superpower and finally under Gorbachev as a legitimate inhabitant of the 'Common European Home/House'.[14] Studying Soviet foreign policy as the outcome of given material interests would equal the assumption that 'world politics is a game played by players without faces'; the fact that Russia is *Russia* and not any other state 'makes all the difference in the world'.[15]

Most IR studies of identity presuppose some form of 'othering', either externally (towards other states), internally (within the state) or historically (in relation to previous and future selves). While the role of external othering clearly dominates the IR debate on identity, ontological security theory focuses instead on internal othering through the construction of autobiographical narratives that draw on national histories and experience in order to create continuity in a state's identity.[16] Wæver likewise argues that the Other may also be a former incarnation of the self – he mentions the EU as an example, the primary ambition of which has been the 'never again' of European wars. And the Other need not, according to Berenskoetter, be the 'foreigner', an 'enemy'; recognition can also be sought from 'friends'.[17]

Narratives may be distinguished by the presence of a plot, the means by which events are brought together into a meaningful whole. Indeed, as Nishimura notes, in IR, '[p]lotting is political action *sui generis*'. Only after being plotted in a meaningful order, can experience make sense to the state's self (and make the state ready for action).[18] Ringmar contributes a particularly refreshing addition to his earlier work through his study of conflicting stories of the Iraq War, using literary theory to categorize decision-makers into different types of storytellers.[19] *Romances* usually involve a hero whose task is to save the world. They are recounted by people who 'believe that evil can be defeated, that the world can be made into a better place, and usually also that they are the very instruments chosen by God, Providence or History to carry out this task'.[20] *Tragedy* provides a completely different plot structure. Here the hero rebels against the established order but is destroyed in the process. They follow their own mind, 'proud, passionate or obsessed with some fanciful idea'.[21] The *comedy* is 'an account of oppositions and misunderstandings which in the course of the narrative are resolved thanks to some fortuitous intervention'.[22] The comic element lies in the twists and turns taken by the plot as the narrative gradually comes to a happy end. Finally, there is *satire*, which assumes an ironic distance from the world. It is 'parasitic on other narrative forms',[23] as its strategy is to 'turn other plot structures inside-out, upside-down, or to deconstruct and reassemble them in unrecognisable patterns'.[24]

All the Way to the Pole

The 1982 UN Convention on the Law of the Sea (UNCLOS) introduced economic zones and explained how governments should go about establishing them. Economic zones could only extend 200 nautical miles from the shoreline. In the case of continental shelves, the rules are different. All states have a right to a continental shelf of 200 miles; the rules governing shelves and water columns follow one another. The principles underlying the determination of the boundaries are also the same: governments shall attempt to find an equitable solution. In certain circumstances, however, states can claim sovereignty over their continental shelf *beyond* the 200 nautical mile line, but only if the extended shelf is a natural prolongation of the area within the 200-mile limit – which is what a shelf *is*, i.e. the relatively shallow basin between land and the deep ocean floor, the abyssal plain. There is an opportunity under UNCLOS for states to acquire jurisdiction to explore, extract and manage the natural resources on their continental shelf within 350 nautical miles, or 100 nautical miles beyond the 2,500-metre isobath (a line connecting points of equal underwater depth). In contrast to the economic zones and the continental shelf within 200 miles, however, permission is not granted automatically. Governments must file a claim with the international Commission on the Limits of the Continental Shelf in New York, along with scientific evidence that the area beyond 200 miles is, in geological terms, a prolongation of the landmass. The members of the Continental Shelf Commission are scientists and technology experts. They assess the scientific merits of the documentation provided by governments to substantiate their claims – hence, the Commission is neither a political body or a court of law.

Russia was the first Arctic state to file a claim with the Continental Shelf Commission, as early as 2000. Considered lacking in several respects, it was quickly rejected. The Russians had included large areas of the continental shelf between the eastern and western sector lines. Part of the area went all the way to the North Pole. After their submission was rejected – which the Russians accepted without orchestrating a political protest – they intensified their exploration of the Arctic shelf. During a scientific expedition in August 2007, the research team lowered a mini-submarine to the seabed at the precise point of the North Pole, and planted a metal Russian flag into the ground. The event attracted the attention of the worldwide media and political circles – Russia, it was said, is laying claim to the North Pole. In the event, it provided the starting shot for the 'race for the Arctic'. The media tended to depict the Arctic as a no-man's land, beyond the reach of international law where governments could do as they liked while the world's reserves of oil and gas elsewhere were running dry. According to estimates drawn up by the US Geological Survey (USGS), the Arctic could hold as much as 25 per cent of the world's undiscovered oil and gas deposits. This naturally provided added sustenance to the story of the race for the Arctic. At the political level, Canada, a country with significant designs on the Arctic itself, was particularly annoyed. 'You can't go around the world these days dropping flags somewhere. This isn't the fourteenth or fifteenth century', the Canadian foreign minister, Peter MacKay, was reported as saying.[25]

However the Arctic continental shelf is divided in the end – the Continental Shelf Commission has still not had its final say – the biggest winner will be Russia. The question is how much more the Russians will get than everyone else. Russia has everything to gain from cementing the application of the Law of the Sea in the Arctic.

*

Russia adopted its first Arctic policy document in 2001, back when the Arctic was still not much of an issue in international politics. The document focused mainly on the region as a potential zone of conflict among great powers. As global interest escalated, the Arctic powers all put together their own Arctic strategies. Russia's Fundamentals of the State Policy of the Russian Federation, published in 2008, was the second to be issued by a member of the 'Arctic Five', a couple of years after Norway had unveiled its High North Strategy in 2006. Canada and the USA followed suit in 2009, and Denmark in 2011. The main objective of the

Russian strategy is to transform the Arctic into the country's most important strategic natural resource base by 2020, and to preserve Russia's role as a leading Arctic power. It calls for the development of the Russian Arctic in a number of fields, most notably resource extraction, transport (primarily the Northern Sea Route) and other forms of infrastructure, but also 'softer' policy areas such as science and environmental safety. It presupposed a new Russian continental shelf claim by 2015, and also the formation of a new Arctic military unit for use in combating terrorism, smuggling and illegal immigration. While the Russian strategy is considered somewhat 'harder' than those of the other Arctic states, with its explicit emphasis on national interests and sovereignty, it downplays the potential for international tension in the Arctic, at least compared to the Russian policy plan of 2001. The need for international collaboration to preserve the Arctic as a zone of peace is among the priorities in the strategy. A follow-up strategy appeared in 2013, covering more or less the same priorities as the 2008 strategy, but as assessed by Zysk, it appears to be somewhat more realistic and dispassionate than its predecessor.[26] Acknowledging that Russia is not capable of effectively exploring the energy resources in the Arctic by itself, the document recognizes Russia's need for domestic and foreign private sector investment and experts to develop the country's northern regions.

The political leadership in Russia have generally emphasized the need to follow the rules of international law in the Arctic, and have usually downplayed threats from other countries in the region. However, senior Russian officials have expressed fear over other states' intensions in the Arctic. FSB director Nikolai Patrushev, for example, is quoted as saying that 'the United States, Norway, Denmark, and Canada are conducting a united and coordinated policy of barring Russia from the riches of the shelf'.[27] Artur Chilingarov, famous polar explorer and the president's special envoy on Arctic affairs, stated after the episode of the Russian flag planting (he was leader of the expedition and on board the submarine when the flag was planted) 'we have exercised the maritime right of the first night'.[28] Two years later he added, 'we will not give the Arctic to anyone'.[29] Even President Medvedev, who was usually inclined to emphasize the cooperative aspect of international Arctic politics, made similar statements on occasion: 'Regrettably, we have seen attempts to limit Russia's access to the exploration and development of the Arctic mineral resources … This is absolutely inadmissible from the legal viewpoint and unfair given our nation's geographical location and history'.[30]

References to Russian history and territory were key features of many of the statements made by President Medvedev and Prime Minister Putin around this time. In 2009, Putin was appointed head of the trustees of the Russian Geographical Society and in his address to the Society's congress introduced the topic of the Arctic as follows: 'When we say great, a great country, a great state – certainly, size matters … When there is no size, there is no influence, no meaning.'[31] Medvedev, in turn, in his first address as chairman of the national Security Council in 2008, entitled 'Defending Russia's National Interests in the Arctic', made the following remark:

> I want to especially underline that this is our duty, this is simply a direct debt [we owe] to those who have gone before us. We must firmly, and for the long-term future [of our country], secure the national interests of Russia in the Arctic.[32]

'The Global Fight'

Laruelle argues that there are two different Russian strategies for the Arctic: the 'security first' and the 'cooperation first'.[33] The former – supported by the Security Council (which produced the Arctic policy document), the military complex and security services – views the Arctic as a territorial arena where Russia can revive its former status as a great power. Security comes first in this strategy, and foreign presence must be curbed. The second approach – reflecting primarily the objectives of the Ministry of Natural Resources – is motivated by economic concerns and is pragmatic in its views of how best to achieve its goals: in order to develop the northern regions, Russia must be open to foreign cooperation through investments and sharing of expertise. Private businesses, both Russian and foreign, must be given greater roles in the development of the Arctic; the Russian state cannot do this alone. In addition to the revival of Russian greatness on the international scene, the 'security-first' variant is viewed as having a more immediate domestic aim: to reassert Russian patriotism in order to secure the legitimacy of the political establishment. Since 2008–9, however, Moscow has also sought external recognition by creating an 'Arctic brand' with Russia portrayed as a responsible and highly cooperative state that takes a leading role in the development of law and policy in the Arctic. When Putin speaks of 'our common Arctic home',[34] he clearly alludes to Gorbachev's 'common European home', the incarnation of modern Russian willingness to work with the West.

The Russian media sometimes frames the Arctic in the context of foreign relations; at other times as a domestic issue. The boundary between them is not impermeable, however. A common theme in foreign-policy oriented newspaper articles is the perception that the other Arctic states are 'actively flexing their muscles',[35] and that Russia must necessarily respond. The debate mainly centres on Canada's intentions in the Arctic. Canada is largely depicted as the 'aggressor' in the region. Canadian Prime Minister Stephen Harper is said to have operated under the slogan 'Conquer [the Arctic] or you'll lose it',[36] and is reported to have said: 'The Arctic is our country, our property and our ocean. The Arctic belongs to Canada.'[37] In brief, Russia's mission is to engage in 'the global fight against Canada in the Arctic'.[38]

The alleged discrepancy between Canada's assurances of no aggressive intentions in the Arctic and the country's simultaneous aggregation of military forces in the region is another recurrent theme in the Russian press. Reporting from a meeting between the Canadian and Russian ministers of foreign affairs in September 2010, *Rossiyskaya gazeta* questions the Canadian assurance that the country only has peaceful intentions in the Arctic.[39] Canada has, according to the article, recently constructed new military bases in the Arctic; it has also launched new ice-going patrol vessels for use in the region. The Canadians also conduct annual Arctic military exercises: 'All this forces Canada's partners in the "Arctic five" to question the sincerity of the Canadian party's statements [about peaceful cooperation].' While Russia is here grouped together with the three remaining 'Arctic five', Russia's position as the only non-Western state among the five is also at issue in the article. 'One of the most burning issues for the "Arctic five"', the article states, is 'NATO's interest in the region'. The Russian prime minister gives vent to a certain irritation: 'I don't think NATO behaves in an appropriate manner when it reserves for itself the right to decide who should make decisions in the Arctic', though he does not say exactly how this inappropriate behaviour takes place. Another feature article on the same meeting asks whether Foreign Minister Cannon will succeed in melting the ice of mistrust that has developed in the country's relations with Russia due to 'the Canadians' ambitious view on the ownership of the Lomonosov Ridge'.[40] Harper had recently been speaking, 'in harsh words', about Canada's ambitious programme 'Steering North' and about preserving 'the true North' strong and free, so it's 'no wonder Ottawa [subsequently] sent the minister of foreign affairs [to Russia] to clarify'. The feature writer notes that despite the 'optimistic tone' of the lecture Cannon gave to Russian politicians, journalists and academics, not everything he said sounded particularly friendly to Russian spectators: '"The Arctic has always been a part of us, it still is and always will be", Cannon said, seemingly forgetting for a moment that no country has exclusive rights in this zone.' Cannon goes on, "again without even wavering", to state that "there are territories that belong to us, where the continental shelf must be prolonged, for instance the Lomonosov Ridge, as an extension of our territory". Thus it was that Cannon managed to "[destroy] the good atmosphere of the meeting"'. The reporter was not at all convinced of Canada's peaceful intentions in the Arctic.

The other Arctic states are not only fighting to defend their own rights in the Arctic, they are actively mobilizing to wipe Russia off the board. In an article with the rather peculiar heading, 'Without fighting penguins [*sic*!]',[41] – the idea being that the establishment of a new Russian Arctic military unit does not signify the militarization of the region – ample evidence is provided to the effect that the 'USA, Norway, Denmark and Canada are pursuing a unified and coordinated policy to prevent Russia access to the riches of the continental shelf', and that the 'USA and its partners in NATO are striving to extend their economic presence in the northern waters, and to achieve internationalisation of the Northern Sea Route and, as a result, press Russia out of the region'. As proof of this development, the journalist refers to a document obtained from the Security Council's press service showing that foreign intelligence bureaus are intensifying their activities in the border areas with Russia. Norwegian research vessels are being recruited to carry out intelligence work. International NGOs are also used, especially environmental NGOs. There are foreign scientists in the areas around Novaya Zemlya and the White Sea, where Russian submarines perform military exercises. In Norway, there is talk about changing Svalbard's demilitarized status, and about a new policy of using the national armed forces in the Arctic.[42] An article entitled 'Cold NATO' claims that NATO is 'breaking into the Arctic' and that 'the question about when the Polar bears will see American hangar ships is of more than just rhetorical character' – but Russia's response to the world will be: 'We will not give the Arctic to anyone!'[43] By declaring the Arctic as 'strategically important for the alliance', NATO is meddling in the ongoing diplomatic conversations among the 'Arctic five', adding to them an element of power and thus increasing the risk that diplomacy will give way to military demonstrations. At the same time, the USA is criticized for trying to 'internationalise most of the Arctic problems, enabling them to subsequently penetrate the region by means of international law and multilateral forces'.[44] To illustrate this ominous situation, *Rossiyskaya gazeta* states that the first Russian submission to the Commission on the Continental Shelf was rejected 'not without pressure from the US, Norwegian and Canadian side'.[45] As noted above, the UN Continental Shelf Commission is neither political body nor tribunal; it is a commission of scientists, such as geologists, hydrographers and geophysicists.

There is an abundance of resources in the Arctic, the article 'Hot Arctic' notes, and the 'USA has already counted them'.[46] It also reminds the reader of how the United States around 1990 tried to take advantage of Russia's political weakness to acquire more of the Bering Sea. There was even talk of ceding Chukotka to the Americans, the environmental project 'Bering Park' being geared to that aim. The article 'On slippery ice' similarly warns readers that the Canadians are prepared to use all underhand methods to grab what's legally not theirs in the

Arctic, including 'fine-looking environmental plans' that extend sailing routes a further 100 nautical miles from the shore.[47] And 'Ice War No. 2' takes the rise in US monitoring of cruise traffic in the 'newly ice-free areas' of the Polar Ocean as yet more proof that the West is planning to start 'a tactical ice war' with Russia.[48] The Secretary of the Security Council, Nikolai Patrushev, concludes: 'If we do not act immediately, time will be lost, and then it will simply be too late – they will have squeezed us out.'[49]

Interspersed with these accounts of Western aggression we find stories depicting Russia as a peace-loving nation, one that is 'categorically against any militarisation of [the Arctic]',[50] refuses to be pulled into 'what is referred to as a conflict about access to resources',[51] and insists that 'questions about ownership must be decided exclusively by the mechanisms [provided] under UNCLOS'.[52] Even the Commander in Chief of the Russian parachute forces assures us that while he plans to put parachute troops on the North Pole, they will be 'peaceful paratroopers'.[53]

In an article named 'A slice of a Polar bear fur', the Russian Minister of Foreign Affairs comes across as more peace-loving than his Canadian colleague:

> Most of the journalists are less inclined to abandon the idea of a new world conflict unfolding in the third millennium. They asked whether the war in the Arctic was over, and Canada's representative said it was. Lavrov quickly corrected this remark. There had never been any war in the Arctic. Fellow journalists smiled, while the slightly bemused Canadian nodded his agreement.[54]

Occasionally, the straightforward narrative of 'the world is against us, but we just want peace' is interrupted. The article 'Strike below the pole' from *Kommersant* a couple of weeks after the flag planting episode is an example. It starts in recognizable form with a description of East–West antagonism and Russian heroism, but ends up by questioning Russian greatness – I discuss this further in the concluding section of this chapter. For now, let's just hear the story in its entirety.

> The sensational achievement of the 'Arktika-2007' expedition in planting the Russian flag in the seabed at the North Pole was greeted with joy by the Russian people, while our adversaries in marine matters slunked off in a huff. A completely natural response, says Vlast commentator Shamir Idiatullin. It's just the latest expression of the celebrated Russian national idea, known to everybody.
>
> Last week, the expedition team of the difficult 'Arktika-2007' voyage returned home. The expedition was led by the famous polar explorer, member of United Russia, and member and deputy speaker of the State Duma, Artur Chilingarov. Two bathyscaphes were lowered by the team to a depth of more than 4 kilometres,

where they planted a Russian flag of titanium on the seabed, and returned with a bucket of sediment and two containers of water. Not only was this the first time anyone had descended all the way down to the seabed at the geographical Pole, the 'Arktika-2007' team explained, but they had also collected material that would help Russia prove that its continental shelf extended as far north as the Pole itself. In other words, Russia owns most of the unbelievable reserves of oil and gas concealed in the eastern parts of the Arctic Sea. The US expressed doubts as to this conclusion, Canada said the North Pole was Canadian, and the world's media blew hot and cold about Moscow's scandalous act of annexation.

In reality, Chilingarov did not remonstrate in the Amundsen Sea (because it is precisely in these waters – a good distance from the Lomonosov ridge and, in consequence, the presumed Russian shelf – through which the earth's axis passes) to support [the idea of] an extension to Russia's Arctic Siberia, but rather to promote his party political, propaganda and entertainment agenda, only lightly camouflaged as economic expediency. We must not, however, believe that the conquest of the polar deep was the brainchild of some amateur Arctic explorers.

The lowering of the bathyscaphes Mir I and Mir II was a move on the part of the Russian elite (and a relatively successful one) at the shrine of the national idea. The doctrine of sovereign democracy – you can bake it with poison – only beguiles particularly disingenuous party officials. You can't get it to a Russian ideal. On the other hand, there is an ideal that's dependable and appreciated, a large, powerful country able to accomplish anything anywhere. This country is not loved, naturally; it is feared. But, first, we're not exactly a jewel in your crown; second, fear equals respect; third, we have already lived in a country like that, when the trees were higher and the water wetter. And it's a complete waste of time to create a new one by installing a proletarian dictatorship, with industrialisation and collectivisation, root and branch purges and everything else out of which the superpower emerged. The old saying is refuted by reality: if you say the word 'halva' enough times, your mouth fills with a sweet taste, and a small country can look big by putting on the airs of the superpower.

It all began in 1999 or thereabouts, this pretence, when Primakov's plane, flying over the Atlantic, turned back and Russian paratroopers were dropped over Pristina. The logic of empire was directed outwards; the Soviet ideologues believed it was possible to find lasting happiness for the state on Freedom Island, in the black continent, Antarctica – on Mars even. The Soviet Union sat firmly on the coupons and stood ankle-deep in shit – on the other hand, the country was dispatching food aid and construction workers to Asia and Africa. Russia learned a lesson. Last year, when Yakutia was paralyzed by impassable roads, a detachment of military construction workers was sent to repair roads in Lebanon. And this year, firemen were shipped to Greece and Montenegro in response to the fires in the selfsame

> Yakutia, not to mention Sakhalin, Chita and Chukotka (sure, it wasn't free, but that's not the issue).
>
> The latest advances are blatant copies of Soviet advances – such as the Olympic Games, doomed to be a celebration of Russian sports, friendship among nations, and the eviction of local inhabitants, replaced by people from other places. The achievement of the polar explorers is even more touching, because this, my boys, this is Captain Tatarinov, the SS *Chelyuskin*'s ice floe, Schmidt's beard, Papanin's Mauser and Chkalov's non-stop flight. Mercifully, most of the cost of this propaganda exercise in promoting Russian ambitions would be footed by the Swede and Australian onboard bathyscaphe number two. You may just as well get used to the idea of foreign assistance: if Russia is incapable of developing the Shtokman field itself, you can hardly expect the country in the space of fifty years or so to recover and transport even more distant and much less accessible Arctic riches.
>
> Unless, of course, quantity morphs into quality and the revival of the Soviet exploits in the form of construction troops (mentioned by Prime Minister Fradkov recently), acceleration of the space programme and all manner of changes to GTO [Soviet sports norms/sports badges] and Osoaviakhim [a civil society organization that promotes the interests of the defence industry] do not transform the country into a great-and-powerful something or other. It's not just general aesthetic considerations one can use as a pretext for speeding up the transformation – the activities of the Arctic rivals, led by the United States, who happily subscribed to the Russian idea of the polar shelf, can as well. Anyone with an inkling of American tendencies and opportunities can assume that Washington will shortly be able to discover its own continental shelf in every ocean accessible to the country – and to scientifically justify not only that the Arctic belongs to USA's natural sphere of interest but Eurasia, Africa and Australia too. After this, the discussion about spheres of interest can return to the level that was typical of the 1950s and 1960s. To the delight of people who remember those years as a golden epoch in the homeland's history.[55]

To return to the 'security-first' and 'cooperation-first' approaches in Russian Arctic policy, both are reflected in the public debate, more or less simultaneously, supporting rather than contesting each other. The debate, if we can call it a debate at all, is more descriptive than normative. Instead of discussing how Russia should angle its Arctic policies, the newspapers tell their readers 'how the world is'. By and large, it is a world where NATO is surreptitiously preparing for the rush for the Arctic, while Russia insists on international cooperation and open dialogue. Canada is the main villain, with its harsh rhetoric and alleged unilateralism. There might be an underlying normative message here that says cooperation doesn't work when your partners are not reliable and should hence be abandoned as Russia's main strategy, but it is seldom openly expressed in the debate.

'The Arctic is our Everything'

In post-Soviet Russia, the Arctic is both a 'forgotten' (economically neglected and politically marginalized) and a 'future' (the country's most important reserve, economically and spiritually) region. It is plagued with 'everything from bad roads to the notorious Russian propensity to drink'.[56] It is home to 'mythical and half-mythical resources'[57]; to a nuclear icebreaker fleet, 'which exists only in our country'[58] and is a 'convincing testimony to man's success in the duel with the ice masses'[59]; to 'the legendary Northern Sea Route', 'the Arctic's longest road', in itself 'the most genuine of ministries',[60] but desperately in need of 'a new life' – not to earn money from international transport (as often assumed in the West, and not quite unlikely), but to 'maintain life and activity in the Russian North'.[61]

Certain exclamations recur in the debate: 'The Arctic is our everything', and 'The Arctic always has been and always will remain Russian'. They often turn up without further elaboration – as in the article 'Northern lights', where the latter formulation is immediately followed by a prosaic statement that 'Russian scientists worked on oil and gas extraction projects before the Norwegians even thought about it'.[62] And there's talk about the 'rebirth' of the Arctic[63] – and countless stories of the heroic 'snow man', Artur Chilingarov, 'Hero of the Soviet Union, Hero of the Russian Federation'.[64] Two hundred journalists and thirty TV channels were waiting at the Vnukovo-3 airport terminal when he stepped onto Russian soil after the North Pole flag planting, 'trembling with excitement', and declaring – yes, you're right: 'the Arctic always has been and always will remain Russian'. Two flags were used to mark the event: the flag of the international Polar Year and the Abkhazian flag. Since Chilingarov was 'an old friend of Abkhazia', the Georgian province became the second nation on the North Pole after Russia (a year ahead of the Georgian war), beating 'far more powerful, reputable and prosperous pretenders to the riches in the Polar continental shelf'.[65] Hence, Russian Arctic policies are linked here to territorial disputes along the country's southern borders.

The notions of 'Arctic boom' (the promising future) and 'Arctic doom' (the dreary present) are combined in an article in *Argumenty i fakty* (*AiF*), from autumn 2008, entitled 'Once again the Russian flag is waving in the Arctic'.[66] The article tells the story of the journalist's trip with the border patrol vessel *Anadyr* to the Chukchi Sea.

Why sail in the Arctic?

A correspondent from *AiF-Kamchatka* accompanied a coastguard patrol vessel in the eastern sector of the Arctic, and was informed by the commander that they hadn't patrolled the area since 1993: 'It was a successful demonstration of the Russian flag. But the main thing is we showed our flag not just for the USA, but for our citizens living in Chukotka. They were no less surprised than the Americans ...'

Has anything changed in Russian policy on the Arctic? Yes, it has. The Arctic is of enormous economic interest to Russia in the form of the richest natural resources, of which oil and gas on the continental shelf are the most important.

The Russian Arctic has been thinly populated for some time, and for this reason our neighbours have been eyeing the area; envy and lust light up in their greedy eyes. America is dreaming about turning the Chukotka Sea into an open area for economic exploitation. Canada, USA, Norway and Denmark would have liked to split the Arctic four ways and push Russia out, and keep it inside the boundaries of its continental shelf. Even China wouldn't say no to a tiny piece.

But Russia is not surrendering yet and has – thank God – started taking action. The President has given his approval to a programme to utilize and protect the Arctic, and there are many references in this document to border forces as guardians of the state's economic interests.

An astounded Chukotka

[*The correspondent describes how the vessel 'not only displayed the Russian flag', but also investigated the area to make the journey easier for the next patrol. Then follows an account of Chukotka itself: In his time as governor, Roman Abramovich organized the building of lightweight modular homes, three to seven TV channels, installation of telephones, etc. But … The problem isn't just the lack of industry; unemployment is rife, especially among the indigenous peoples. The hunting of seals and marine mammals together with reindeer husbandry employ only a few, and every time a ship comes in, people dash to the harbour in case there are tourists who want to buy hides or souvenirs of walrus teeth.*]

When they heard a Russian border guard boat had arrived, the good people of Chukotka were amazed at its might and beauty. They couldn't believe Russia had military ice-rated ships capable of navigating the Arctic.

And Chukotka made an impression on the border guards with its primeval and wild beauty. The sea here proved literally to boil with whales. Every day, pod after pod, they swam alongside the boat. When *Anadyr* moved into the ice-covered areas, walrus and seal turned up as well. And precisely on Sailors' Day, a Polar bear came swimming by, scenting the aroma of *shashlik* rising from the helipad. It was impossible not to be astonished at the swimmer's dexterity – around us the sweep of the open sea – it was 20 miles to the nearest ice.

They served with honour!

[*Short interviews with a couple of the crews are reported here. A seaman from Ussuriysk:*]

'We were fortunate on this extended trip', he said sincerely. 'Before this, we were patrolling the Sea of Okhotsk, by the Kuril and Komandor islands, but the Arctic left a special impression. And here, I've finally settled on a career – I'm staying onboard as a contracted border guard.'

[*The head of the electro-technical team Ruzvelt (Roosevelt!) Gadzhimuradov also sees the voyage as an extraordinary event*:]

Obviously, the natural surroundings made an impression, but the harsh life of the people here made an even deeper one. In my opinion, the state has to take this territory seriously, the people of Chukotka deserve better.

[*The correspondent talks about the many high points of the voyage – various exercises and target shooting practice*:]

It's been misty and cold, the sea has been calm and it has been rough. The people were tired, but invigorated by their impressions, they threw themselves into it body and soul. It was the first time any of them had been to the Arctic, and they fell in love with it.

[*On plans for the future - a new boat will soon replace the Anadyr, and the area will be patrolled on a regular basis*:]

And Cape Schmidt – it's absolutely not the last stop in the new patrol area. Go further west along the Arctic Ocean! Much further! Because today the whole of Russia is thinking about the Arctic.

This story inscribes itself firmly into the Russia-against-the-rest narrative. The other Arctic nations are ready to divide the region among themselves (even to the extent of giving China a small piece), so Russia needs to remain vigilant. Surely, 'our neighbours have been eyeing the area; envy and lust light up their greedy eyes.' But more than anything, the article is an ode to the Arctic as a Russian 'homeland', and to Russia as the Arctic's patron and guardian. *Anadyr*'s voyage to these northern waters implies a 'welcome home' both to the Chukchis – the motherland does care after all – and to the young sailors who have never set foot on this genuinely Russian soil before. The local population is struck by the 'might and beauty' of the patrol vessel, the sailors by the 'primeval and wild' beauty of Chukotka; they all fell in love with the Arctic. But not only did the natural surroundings make an impression – the harsh life of the local people made an even deeper one: 'The state has to take this territory seriously, the people of Chukotka deserve better.' The Russian North has been neglected for one and a half decades (even though Abramovich set up TV channels and modular homes there), but it is ripe with natural resources: whales and walruses, oil and gas. So now the whole of Russia is talking about the Arctic: 'Go further west along the Arctic Ocean! Much further!'

Our Ocean, Our Future, Our Foes

The Russian media debate about the Arctic progresses under headings such as 'Cold NATO', 'Hot Arctic', 'Strike below the pole', 'Ice War No. 2' – and with stories of a Canada hungry for new territories: 'A Polar Bear went out to hunt'.[67] The 'Russia vs. the West' question looms large.[68] It is not in itself a question about Westernism vs. Slavophilism (whether Russia should learn from or distance itself from the West), nor, as already mentioned, about 'security first' or 'cooperation first' (whether Russia should prepare for conflict in the Arctic or seek international cooperation). The 'debaters' might be advocates of one camp or another, but here they are mostly the journalists themselves, not the interviewees. The frame of the debate is rather based on the ontological premise that states are always at loggerheads, and on the more practical premise that Russia is vulnerable to NATO's efforts in the Arctic. Western conflict-oriented intentions are taken for granted; their ultimate aim is to get Russia out of the Arctic once and for all. The NATO countries are 'breaking into the Arctic'[69] and 'flexing their muscles', while 'envy and lust light up their greedy eyes'. And, '[f]urther into the future, it will be simply too late, they will drive us away from here'. That no one appears to be urging Russia to strengthen its military presence in the region is striking. Yes, some want to see the FSB playing a bigger role in the Arctic and the Northern Sea Route and other infrastructure in the region upgraded – and there is the underlying message that 'Russia needs to remain vigilant'. But hardly anyone is urging the authorities to increase the military defence of the Russian Arctic in order to respond to Western aggression.[70] It is Russian policy that the division of the Arctic shelf should be decided by means of negotiation in international fora and in accordance with the procedural and material rules of international law. Unlike NATO, Russia is 'categorically against any militarisation of the Arctic'.

The debate also features depictions of the Arctic as a specifically Russian 'homeland' or site of a 'national idea': the Arctic belongs to Russia, and Russia belongs in the Arctic – the North Pole flag was planted 'at the shrine of the national idea'. Laruelle claims that the major Russian narrative of the Arctic can take a geopolitical, a domestic or a mythical form – and, of course, a combination of the three.[71] The geopolitical variant – which shares an interface with the 'Russia vs. the West' narrative – is multifaceted. It speaks of the Arctic as something that, by its very nature, belongs to Russia: 'the Arctic always has been and always will remain Russian'; but also as something that needs to be conquered: 'rightful compensation for the hegemony lost with the disappearance of the Soviet Union'.[72] Note, moreover, the somewhat peculiar link to the disputed republic of Abkhazia – over which Russia a year later would find itself at war with Georgia – cited in the report about Chilingarov's happy return from the North Pole. Russia and

Abkhazia were the two first 'nations' on the Pole, creating a link between two regions that Russia, in some way or other, is claiming as its own. The domestic narrative, in turn, calls for a reverse of the 'Arctic doom' to the 'Arctic boom' idea: the Russian North has been neglected since the end of the Cold War and desperately needs a new commitment and new investment. Indeed, 'the people of Chukotka deserve better'. The mythical narrative takes 'the primeval and wild beauty' of the Arctic as its base point, while raising it to a metaphysical level when speaking of Arctic 'rebirth', the Arctic as 'a promised land of abundance and freedom',[73] 'a new political and spiritual continent', 'the Arctic's mythical and half-mythical resources', and Russia's 'cosmic destiny'.[74] Or how about this one: 'From the [Russian] North comes God himself.'[75]

These sub-narratives are often interlinked, explicitly or implicitly: the Arctic needs to remain Russian (or be conquered) because it belongs to (or should belong to) Russia in a legal or political sense (by customary law, for instance), but also because it reflects the true spirit of Russia; it is a place where salvation can be found and the Russian nation can be reborn. The Russian North must be materially restored – both decaying Soviet settlements and 'the legendary Northern Sea Route' – not just because 'the people of Chukotka deserve better', but because North is good and genuine; it is 'the last empire of paradise', 'the northern Eden',[76] the 'bell, sounded long ago'.[77] Indeed, the coherence of this narrative is striking: the way geopolitics, domestic northern policies and mythical aspects are combined into one story about Russia and the Arctic as congenital twins.

Most interesting, however, is how the story is linked to territory and time, and how these, in turn, are connected with the ideas of 'pure Russia'/'holy Russia' and the Russian 'wide soul'. 'When there is no size', Putin says, 'there is no meaning'. Russian territory is *larger* than that of other countries in the world; Russia is going *higher* in the universe and *farther* north than anyone else.[78] 'Go further west along the Arctic Ocean!' the journalist from *Argumenty i fakty* exclaims after his voyage with the *Anadyr*, 'much further!' Space itself is often used as a powerful metaphor for and expression of Russianness. The 'boundless territory', the 'land with no edge', the 'flatness that curves around the horizon' – that is what makes Russia Russia.[79] And like the open territory, Russia is itself the ultimate expression of openness: openness of mind and openness of heart. The Russian landscape is wide, and so is the Russian soul, full of passion, generosity and recklessness 'in the constant need for a break-out'.[80]

The North is 'forgotten' and 'future', as we have seen; neglected and promising at the same time. It faces an imminent 'rebirth', which speaks of past glory and hopes of a bright future. 'Time' looms large in the Russian debate about the Arctic. 'This is our duty', says Medvedev, 'this is simply a debt we owe directly to *those who have gone before us*. We must firmly, and for the *long-term future*, secure the national interests of Russia in the Arctic.'[81] The *Anadyr* welcomes Chukotka back into the Russian fold, and Russia back into the Arctic's. The quintessence of the debate is that: 'The Arctic *always has been* and *always will remain* Russian.' The Russian Arctic offers 'the ultimate test of our path towards timelessness.'[82] It is the 'land with no edge', in territory and in time.

Only rarely are these 'master narratives' challenged; the article in *Kommersant* titled 'Strike below the Pole' is one example, however. It reports the planting of the flag at the North Pole a couple of weeks after it had taken place. It starts by referring to 'the sensational achievement' of the 'Arktika-2007' expedition, 'the latest expression of the celebrated Russian national idea'. It reviews the scientific purpose of the voyage before the author remarks that Mr Chilingarov did not plant the flag to demonstrate support for Russia's claim to wider jurisdiction in the Arctic, 'but rather to promote his party political, propaganda and entertainment agenda, only lightly camouflaged as economic expediency'. It was not a one-man show, however; it was staged by the Russian elite to illustrate the idea of Russia as an immense, powerful country that can do whatever it wants, wherever it wants. It is not a country it is easy to like ('not exactly a jewel in your crown'), so it has little alternative but to stoke fear in the international community in order to gain respect. However, 'we have already lived in a country like that, when the trees were higher and the water wetter' – and there's nothing to strive or yearn for. Reality will catch up with you anyway: 'if you repeat the word "halva" enough times, your mouth fills with a sweet taste, and a small country can look big by putting on the airs of a superpower'. The Soviet Union had global ambitions, but ended up 'ankle-deep in shit'. Recent events in Putin's Russia are 'blatant copies of Soviet advances', such as the Sochi Olympics, where 'friendship among nations' led to the expulsion of local inhabitants – in the mythical land where everything is built to go wrong. Oh, and Russia's old achievements in the Arctic are so touching – the *SS Chelyuskin's* ice flow, Schmidt's beard, Papanin's Mauser and Chkalov's non-stop flight – but would they have landed on the North Pole seabed had it not been for the Swede and the Australian on board the bathyscaphes? And how likely is it that Russia will have the capacity to exploit the riches of the High Arctic when it isn't even able to develop the Shtokman field in the Barents Sea without foreign assistance? The truth is, the emperor has no clothes.

This is Russia the miserable, the country plagued by 'everything from bad roads to the notorious Russian propensity to drink'. According to the nineteenth-century writer Nikolai Gogol, Russia is beset by two misfortunes: fools and bad roads. It is Anti-Disneyland and all that, but centre stage here is the foolish boldness, the lack of a sense of reality, the insistence on persuading oneself that one is something that one is not, and the desperate need to be that other. Russia is not even capable of learning from its mistakes. It repeats the grandiose gesturing of the Soviet Union in Sochi, at the North Pole, on Mars even. This is the flipside of the happy-go-lucky, the here-today-gone-tomorrow, the unbounded urge to plunge beyond the horizon, the wild ride through territory and time.

*

The Russian debate about the Arctic is constituted by at least two major metanarratives, which in Somers' typology are the epic dramas in which we are embedded as contemporary actors in history.[83] It is 'Russia vs. the West', and 'Russia and the Arctic'. The two are not mutually exclusive; indeed, they are mutually reinforcing. Adjoined to the imagery of 'Russia and the Arctic' are the more subtle narratives (which can arguably be categorized as metanarratives, too) of what it means to be Russian across space and time. It is the sense of vastness, recklessness, timelessness – in Hellberg-Hirn's words, 'soil and soul'.[84] Then there are the far less frequent 'counter narratives', stories that question the premises of the 'master narratives'.[85] *Kommersant*'s 'Strike below the Pole' ridicules Russia's Arctic ambitions specifically, and the country's inability to accomplish anything in the world more widely. It starts out as a public narrative, an account of the storyteller's cultural or institutional surroundings – here, contemporary Russian politics – but evolves into a metanarrative of Russia's eternal fate. The author refers to Soviet grandiosity and misery, to Russian pride and unwillingness to learn from past mistakes – explanations of why Russia will always remain the land of 'fools and bad roads'.

Othering takes different but not necessarily incompatible paths in the various narratives. The most conspicuous act of othering we find is in the narrative 'Russia vs. the West'. Naturally, this goes in one direction only: the Other is the West. But there are nuances in the intensity of the othering. Journalists almost exclusively portray the West as the aggressor in the Arctic, with Russia being 'categorically against any militarisation' of the region. But the West is interchangeably talked about as 'Cold NATO' and 'our neighbours'; when these foreign powers seek to maximize their interests in the Arctic, it is referred to either as a natural thing – what any reasonable state (or alliance) would do – or as outright offensive, reflecting the impudent behaviour of foreigners in Russia's backyard, or, rather, the country's core area. The latter clearly dominates the debate. Likewise, the 'soil and soul' narrative by its very nature places the West, or in principle anything non-Russian, in the position of the Other.

Russia points the finger of righteous indignation at the Canadians in response to the latter's 'harsh words', as in 'The Arctic has always been a part of us, it still is and always will be' and 'The Arctic is our country, our property and our ocean. The Arctic belongs to Canada.' Heard that before? The established Other is ridiculed for statements that sound strangely like one's own – the subconscious othering of oneself perhaps?

In the 'Russia and the Arctic' narrative, othering westwards is only indirect, implicit. If the Arctic is '*our* all', how can it also be somebody else's all? What are *they* doing here? It is not that we suspect their intentions, they've probably just not got it right – they've gone astray, but we will help them get back home. The real othering in this narrative takes place in *time*: the past of the Russian North is proud and its future bright – so why did we end up in this miserable situation? The Other is the present time itself, the 'here and now'. It took time to get here, and it will take time to get back on track. This is the slow ride home, the boring passage through time.

The 'fools and bad roads' narrative picks up the thread: there's a reason the Arctic has been neglected, like all other assets in the country. The reason is Russia itself, its never-failing ability to ruin everything that is good. Things are not the way they are because of accidental neglect, but by destined default. The Other is the hideous monster looking back at yourself in the mirror. The Other is also the picture of yourself that you present to the outside world; the image of Russia as a large, powerful country that can do whatever it wants, wherever it wants; the mirage on the horizon, your wishful thinking.

*

The dominant plot structure in the Russian media's tales about the Arctic lies somewhere between Ringmar's 'romance' and 'tragedy'.[86] Russia is the hero determined to 'save the Arctic', although perhaps more for its own than the (global) common good. The 'romance' does not necessarily speak of an end to the story; it is the process that matters, the hero's journey spreading benevolence and good deeds. In the 'tragedy', the hero rebels against the established order but is destroyed in the process. In the Arctic, tragedy is looming, with signs of NATO arming up to take control – but Russia is intent on continuing the good fight: to avoid an arms race in the High Arctic. Russia is the romantic hero that tries to pour cold (Russian) water onto hot (Western) blood. Russia is the one that has to remind the world that not only is there no war in the Arctic, or the war has been brought to an end; *there never really was one.*

The plots of the 'Russia and the Arctic' and 'soil and soul' narratives conform to the structures of the romance. Russia has a special mission in the world as the defender of the true faith, spirituality and goodness. It believes that peace can be maintained in the Arctic, and the prosperity of the Russian North restored, if only the Russians are given free rein to put their sensitivity, morality and greatness to use for the good cause.

The 'fools and bad roads' narrative takes the form of the satire. Parasitic on the other forms of narrative, it reverses the plot structures, deconstructs and reassembles them into new structures. The 'sensational achievement' of the team that planted the North Pole flag is here turned into a reflection of Soviet megalomania, incompetence and inferiority complex. Chilingarov's heroic deed is mere propaganda and showing off. The Russian heroic deed was in reality performed by a Swede and an Australian. Past achievements might have had a veneer of success, but they actually left the Soviet Union 'ankle-deep in shit'. Holy Russia is not a country it is easy to like; it is not exactly God's gift to the world.

The ultra-simple plot of the story is: 'Hey, we're Russia. And let's face it – reality's going to catch us up anyway.'

Notes

1 Typically, recent commentators on identity tend to start with a declaration such as, 'Culture and identity are staging a dramatic comeback in social theory and practice at the end of the twentieth century' (Yosef Lapid, 'Culture's ship: Returns and departures in international relations theory', in Y. Lapid and F. Kratochwil (eds), *The Return of Culture and Identity in IR Theory* (Boulder, Lynne Rienner Publishers, 1996), pp. 3–20, p. 3); 'Identity ... has become a major watchword since the 1980s' (Anssi Paasi, 'Region and place: Regional identity in question', *Progress in Human Geography* 27 (2003), pp. 475–85, p. 475); 'Identity is back. The concept of identity has made a remarkable comeback in the social sciences and humanities' (Patricia Goff and Kevin C. Dunn, 'Introduction: In defence of identity', in P. M. Goff and K. C. Dunn (eds), *Identity and Global Politics: Empirical and Theoretical Elaborations* (New York, Palgrave Macmillan, 2004), pp. 1–8, p. 1); and 'Research on language and identity has experienced an unprecedented growth in the last ten years' (Anna De Fina, Deborah Schiffrin and Michael Bamberg, 'Introduction', in A. De Fina, D. Schiffrin and M. Bamberg (eds), *Discourse and Identity* (Cambridge, Cambridge University Press, 2006), pp. 1–23, p. 1).

2 Yosef Lapid, 'Culture's ship: Returns and departures in international relations theory'.

3 Knud Erik Jørgensen, *International Relations Theory: A New Introduction* (Basingstoke, Palgrave Macmillan, 2010), pp. 173–74.

4 Alexander Wendt, 'Anarchy is what states make of it: The social construction of power politics', *International Organization* 46 (1992), pp. 391–425.

5 This does not mean that students of identity disregard the role of power in IR. Nau, for instance, holds national power and identity as two separate and independent factors defining national interests and influencing foreign policy behaviour. See Henry R. Nau, *At Home Abroad: Identity and Power in American Foreign Policy* (Ithaca, Cornell University Press, 2002).

6 Christopher S. Browning, *Constructivism, Narrative and Foreign Policy Analysis: A Case Study of Finland* (Bern, Peter Lang, 2008).

7 Ibid., p. 46.

8 Ibid., p. 275.

9 Erik Ringmar, *Identity, Interest and Action: A Cultural Explanation of Sweden's Intervention in the Thirty Years War* (Cambridge, Cambridge University Press, 1996).

10 Ibid., p. 66.

11 Ibid., p. 83.
12 Ibid., p. 85.
13 Ibid.
14 Erik Rigmar, 'The recognition game: Soviet Russia against the west', *Cooperation and Conflict* 37 (2002), pp. 115–36; The Russian word for 'house' and 'home' is the same: *dom*.
15 Ibid., p. 131.
16 Will K. Delehanty and Brent J. Steele, 'Engaging the narrative in ontological (in) security theory: Insights from feminist IR', *Cambridge Review of International Affairs* 22 (2009), pp. 523–40.
17 Ole Wæver, 'Insecurity, security and asecurity in the West European non-war community', in E. Adleer and M. Barnett (eds), *Security Communities* (Cambridge, Cambridge University Press, 1998), pp. 69–118; Felix Berenskoetter, 'Friends, there are no friends? An intimate reframing of the international', *Millennium – Journal of International Studies* 35 (2007), pp. 647–76.
18 Kuniyuki Nishimura, 'Worlds of our remembering: The agent–structure problem as the search for identity', *Cooperation and Conflict* 46 (2011), pp. 96–112, p. 105.
19 Erik Ringmar, 'Inter-textual relations: The quarrel over the Iraq War as conflict between narrative types', *Cooperation and Conflict* 41 (2006), pp. 403–21.
20 Ibid., p. 405.
21 Ibid.
22 Ibid., p. 406.
23 Ibid.
24 Ibid.
25 See, for example, *The Guardian*, 2 August 2007.
26 Katarzyna Zysk, 'Russia turns north, again: Interests, policies and the search for coherence', in L. C. Jensen and G. Hønneland (eds), *Handbook on the Politics of the Arctic* (Cheltenham, Edward Elgar, 2015), pp. 437–61.
27 'Arkticheskie territorii imeyut strategicheskoe znachenie dlya Rossii', *Rossiyskaya gazeta*, 30 March 2009. Cited from Marlene Laruelle, *Russia's Arctic Strategies and the Future of the Far North* (Armonk, M.E. Sharpe, 2014), p. 10.
28 *Rossiyskaya gazeta*, 'Shelf vzyat! V Moskvu: Uchastniki rossiyskoy arkticheskoy ekspeditsii vernulis s pobedoy', 8 August 2007.
29 *Rossiyskaya gazeta*, 'Arkticheskie territorii imeyut strategicheskoe znachenie dlya Rossii', 30 March 2009. Cited from Laruelle, *Russia's Arctic Strategies and the Future of the Far North*, p. 10.
30 Ibid., p. 11.
31 Cited from Stephen J. Blank, (ed.), 'Russia in the Arctic', *Strategic Studies Institute Monographs* (Carlisle, Strategic Studies Institute, 2011), p. 16.
32 Cited from Steven J. Main, 'If spring comes tomorrow… Russia and the Arctic', *Russian Series* (Swindon, Defence Academy of the United Kingdom, 2011), p. 10.
33 Laruelle, *Russia's Arctic Strategies and the Future of the Far North*, p. 7.
34 Ibid., p. 12.
35 *Kommersant*, 'Vozrodit rossiyski sever: Atomny ledokolny flot est tolko u nashey strany', 11 February 2011.
36 *Rossiyskaya gazeta*, '"Bely medved" vyshel na okhotu: Kanada nachala voennye uchenia v Arktike', 18 August 2009.

37 *Vzglyad*, 'Neft na dvoikh', 4 February 2010.
38 *Vzglyad*, 'Rossiya i Norvegiya podpishut soglashenie o razdele arkticheskogo dna', 15 September 2010.
39 *Rossiyskaya gazeta*, 'Na shirotnuyu nogu: Glava MID Rossii uznal plany Kanady i Ukrainy', 17 September 2010.
40 *Rossiyskaya gazeta*, 'Udar po khrebru Lomonosova: Glava MID Kanady vyskazal v Moskve svoi *Vzglyady* na Arktiku', 16 September 2010.
41 *Rossiyskaya gazeta*, 'Bez boevykh pingvinov: Rossiya sozdaet arkticheskuyu gruppu voysk bez militarizatsii regiona', 30 September 2009.
42 For the record, there has been no discussion of 'changing Svalbard's demilitarised status' in Norway; to do so would infringe international law as the 1920 Svalbard Treaty, which gives Norway sovereignty over Svalbard, stipulates that no military bases can be installed on the archipelago and that it may not be used for military purposes. Nor is there in Norway 'a new policy' of using the national armed forces in the Arctic. Debate has centred on the need not to reduce, and possibly increase, the Coast Guard's presence in the Barents Sea. The Coast Guard is a branch of the Norwegian Navy, though its tasks are mainly civilian. Its instructions come from the Ministry of Justice and the Ministry of Industry and Fisheries. And its presence in the Barents Sea (which isn't actually in the High Arctic either) is not 'new'.
43 *Rossiyskaya gazeta*, 'Kholodnoe NATO: Alyans prinyal reshenie o "vtorzhenii" v Arktiku', 16 January 2009.
44 *Rossiyskaya gazeta*, 'Novoe osvoenie Arktiki', 12 February 2009.
45 *Rossiyskaya gazeta*, 'Razdel shkury belogo medveda: Strany Arkticheskogo basseyna sobirayutsya "zabyvat kolyshki" na rossiyskikh mestorozhdeniyakh', 7 August 2007.
46 *Rossiyskaya gazeta*, 'Goryachaya Arktika: Za chetvert mirovykh zapasov nefti i gaza Rossii predstoit srazitsya s SShA, Daniey i Kanadoy', 10 October 2008.
47 *Rossiyskaya gazeta*, 'Po skolskomu ldu: Kanada rasshiraet predely sovey yurisdiktsii v Arktike', 29 September 2008.
48 *Rossiyskaya gazeta*, 'Ledovy boy nomer dva: Arktika stanovitsya arenoy takticheskikh srazheniy Rossii i Kanady', 20 May 2008.
49 *Kommersant*, 'Artur Chilingarov razrabotal proekt o Severnom Morskom Puti', 12 February 2009.
50 *Kommersant*, 'Rossiyu zatknuli za polyus', 8 August 2009.
51 *Kommesant*, 'Severny Polyus prevrashaetsya v goryachuyu tochku', 27 March 2009.
52 *Rossiyskaya gazeta*, 'Bezkhrebetnye: Kanada i SShA vystupili s rezkimi zayavleniyami po povodu rossiyskikh pretensii na Arktiku', 4 August 2007.
53 *Kommersant*, 'Rossiyu zatknuli za polyus', 8 August 2009.
54 *Rossiyskaya gazeta*, [untitled], 29 May 2009.
55 *Kommersant*, 'Udar nizhe polyusa', 13 August 2007.
56 *Rossiyskaya gazeta*, 'Arkticheski peredel: Napoleon nazyval Rossiyu "imperiey Severa"', 26 September 2005.
57 *Kommersant/Ogonyok*, 'Severnoe siyanie', 27 September 2010.
58 *Argumenty i fakty*, 'Vozrodit rossiyski sever: Atomny ledokolny flot est tolko u nashey strany', 11 February 2011.
59 *Kommersant/Ogonyok*, 'Severnoe siyanie', 27 September 2010.

60 Reference is probably made here to the elaborate system of transportation of supplies to the Russian North through the Northern Sea Route in Soviet times, the *severny zavoz*, organized by the State Committee for the North (Goskomsever).
61 *Kommersant/Ogonyok*, 'Sevmorput – eto samoe nastoyashchee ministerstvo', 27 September 2010.
62 *Kommersant/Ogonyok*, 'Severnoe siyanie', 27 September 2010.
63 *Argumenty i fakty*, 'Vozrodit rossiyski sever: Atomny ledokolny flot est tolko u nashey strany', 11 February 2011.
64 *Rossiyskaya gazeta*, 'Snezhny chelovek: Artur Chilingarov – o vkuse studnya iz stoyarnogo kleya, pro smertelnye riski vo Idakh i glubinkakh, a takzhe o tom, zachem geroyam inogda vydayut pistolety', 17 September 2010.
65 *Rossiyskaya gazeta*, 'Shelf vzyat! V Moskvu: Uchastniki rossiyskoy arkticheskoy ekspeditsii vernulis s pobedoy', 8 August 2007.
66 *Argumenty i fakty*, 'Rossiyski flag snova v Arktike', 8 October 2008.
67 *Rossiyskaya gazeta*, '"Bely medved" vyshel na okhotu: Kanada nachala voennye uchenia v Arktike', 18 August 2009.
68 Summing up the narratives in this section, I present them in truncated form, defined mostly by just a couple of words. I understand a narrative as a stretch of talk about specific events, so when I refer to the major narrative of this chapter as 'Russia vs. the West', it therefore includes the stories laid out in the preceding sections, for instance about how the other Arctic states are behaving and that behaviour is perceived in Russia.
69 For the rest of this section, I do not repeat the reference for newspaper articles that have already been cited above, only citations by other authors.
70 Admittedly, there are general calls for 'action' ('before it's too late'), but most often not specified as military action. See, e.g., *Kommersant*, 'Artur Chilingarov razrabotal proekt o Severnom Morskom Puti', 12 February 2009.
71 Laruelle, *Russia's Arctic Strategies and the Future of the Far North*, p. 39.
72 Ibid., p. 40.
73 Elena Hellberg-Hirn, 'Ambivalent space: Expressions of Russian identity', in J. Smith (ed.), *Beyond the Limits: The Concept of Space in Russian History and Culture* (Helsinki, Finnish Historical Society, 1999), pp. 49–69, p. 54.
74 Laruelle, *Russia's Arctic Strategies and the Future of the Far North*, p. 40.
75 Otto Boele, *The North in Russian Romantic Literature* (Amsterdam, Rodopi, 1996), p. 252, referring to the eighteenth/nineteenth century writer Maksim Nevzorov.
76 Ibid.
77 Franklyn Griffiths, *Arctic and North in the Russian Identity* (Toronto, Centre for Russian and East European Studies, University of Toronto, 1990), p. 53, referring to the 'countryside writer' Valentin Rasputin.
78 Laruelle, *Russia's Arctic Strategies and the Future of the Far North*, p. 39. See also presentation of Russia's 'geographical meta-narratives' above.
79 Emma Widdis, 'Russia as space' in S. Franklin and E. Widdis (eds), *National Identity in Russian Culture: An Introduction* (Cambridge, Cambridge University Press, 2004), pp. 30–49, p. 33, p. 39 (paraphrased).
80 Hellberg-Hirn, 'Ambivalent space: Expressions of Russian identity', p. 56.
81 Main (paraphrased), 'If spring comes tomorrow… Russia and the Arctic', p. 10. (All italics in this paragraph are mine.)

82 Yuri Slezkine, 'Introduction: Siberia as history', in G. Diment and Y. Slezkine (eds), *Between Heaven and Hell: The Myth of Siberia in Russian Culture* (New York, St. Martin's Press, 1993), pp. 1–6, p. 5 (edited for UK spelling).

83 Margaret R. Somers, 'The narrative constitution of identity: A relational and network approach', *Theory and Society* 23 (1994), pp. 605–49.

84 Hellberg-Hirn, 'Ambivalent space: Expressions of Russian identity', pp. 49–69.

85 I use the term 'master narrative' to indicate a narrative that dominates the debate. This is not to be confused with 'meta-narratives' (Somers, 'The narrative constitution of identity: A relational and network approach'), a category that reflects the *contents* of the narrative ('epic dramas'), not the frequency of its occurrence.

86 Ringmar, 'Inter-textual relations: The quarrel over the Iraq War as conflict between narrative types', pp. 403–21.

CHAPTER 6

SPACE AND TIMING: WHY WAS THE BARENTS SEA DELIMITATION DISPUTE RESOLVED IN 2010?

Arild Moe, Daniel Buikema Fjærtoft and Indra Øverland

Introduction

At a joint press conference on 27 April 2010, Russian President Dmitri Medvedev and Norwegian Prime Minister Jens Stoltenberg announced that a settlement had been reached on the disputed area between the two countries. This announcement signalled the end of a maritime delimitation dispute that had existed between Norway and Russia for over forty years and that involved an area in the Barents Sea and the Arctic Ocean of around 175,000 square kilometres – more than the landmass of Ireland and Portugal combined. The disputed area is not only large, but also both economically valuable and strategically important[1]: it is the gateway to Russia's only all-year ice-free port in Murmansk, the entrance to the Northern Sea Route,[2] the shipping route for oil and liquefied natural gas from the East Barents and Kara Seas[3] and is located at the centre of the most valuable fishery in Northern Europe.[4]

The settlement of the dispute came as a surprise to the public and experts alike in both Norway and Russia, as there had been no leaks in advance. Within the Norwegian Ministry of Foreign Affairs, only a handful of high-level staff directly involved in the negotiations knew that an agreement was at hand. The Russian side had been equally discreet.

This chapter is based on Arild Moe, Daniel Buikema Fjærtoft and Indra Øverland, 'Space and timing: Why was the Barents Sea delimitation dispute resolved in 2010?', *Polar Geography* 34/3 (2011), pp. 145–62.

The resulting treaty was signed in Murmansk on 15 September 2010, and the ratification documents were exchanged in Oslo on 7 June 2011. The treaty divides the disputed area, formally referred to as the 'area of overlapping claims', into two nearly equal parts. Besides specifying the maritime boundary, the treaty sets out procedures for the development of any oil or gas fields straddling the new boundary (referred to as 'unitization') and stipulates the continuation of the well-established joint management of fisheries. It also calls more generally for cooperation between the two countries in the Arctic.[5]

This chapter first lays out the possible reasons regarding why the disputed area was divided in the way it was, and then turns to the main question: *Why did the agreement come at this specific point in time?* Our concern is thus not so much the legal details of the agreement as the perceptions of national interest and the strategic, political, economic and security considerations that may have served as drivers for finalizing an agreement in 2010, rather than earlier or later.

In terms of theory and methodology, this chapter draws on Graham Allison's analysis of governmental decision making.[6] In his multi-model approach, foreign policy decisions must be explained through a comparative examination of different possible explanations involving multiple actors, levels and interests. This approach has the advantage of avoiding predetermined and rigidly generalized models of how states behave in international relations as in stereotypical versions of neo-realism, liberalism or constructivism.

In preparing the chapter we scoured all publicly available written sources from around the time of the boundary agreement, in particular all statements by Russian government officials. In addition, we carried out a review of all border treaties signed by Russia between 1990 and 2010 and examined the boundary agreement ceremony, in particular the choice of location and official representatives, as well as the public relations strategy of the Russian government. The chapter is thus based on public Russian and Norwegian sources and also draws heavily on our previous work, experience and data, including decades of interaction with both Russian and Norwegian government and petroleum actors. To supplement the written sources and to try out some of our conclusions, informal unstructured interviews were carried out with officials and commentators in Moscow in September 2010. The interviewees included officials of the Ministry of Natural Resources and the Ministry of Energy, staff of two separate divisions of Gazprom, a foreign oil company, a specialist in offshore rigs, researchers at two institutes involved in energy and foreign affairs, one researcher involved in geological studies in the Arctic and a group of researchers from a think tank close to the presidential administration.

The Dispute

Norway requested negotiations over this area in 1967. In 1970, Norwegian and Soviet representatives discussed the issue for the first time in informal meetings, and formal negotiations started in 1974. In the dispute, Norway based its claim on the 'median line' principle, according to which a boundary is drawn that is equidistant from the nearest points of the coastlines of two countries. The 1958 Convention on the Continental Shelf established the median line as a key principle when drawing continental shelf boundaries. This principle has been applied in many parts of the world, including the delimitation of the boundaries between Norway and other countries in the North Sea. The median line proposed by Norway is the eastern perimeter of the disputed area in Figure 6.1.

On the Russian side, Shtokman, Ludlovskoe and Ledovoe are all giant gas fields in terms of resources. The actual commercial potential in the latter two remains uncertain, however, due to limited exploration. Other discovered gas fields, i.e.

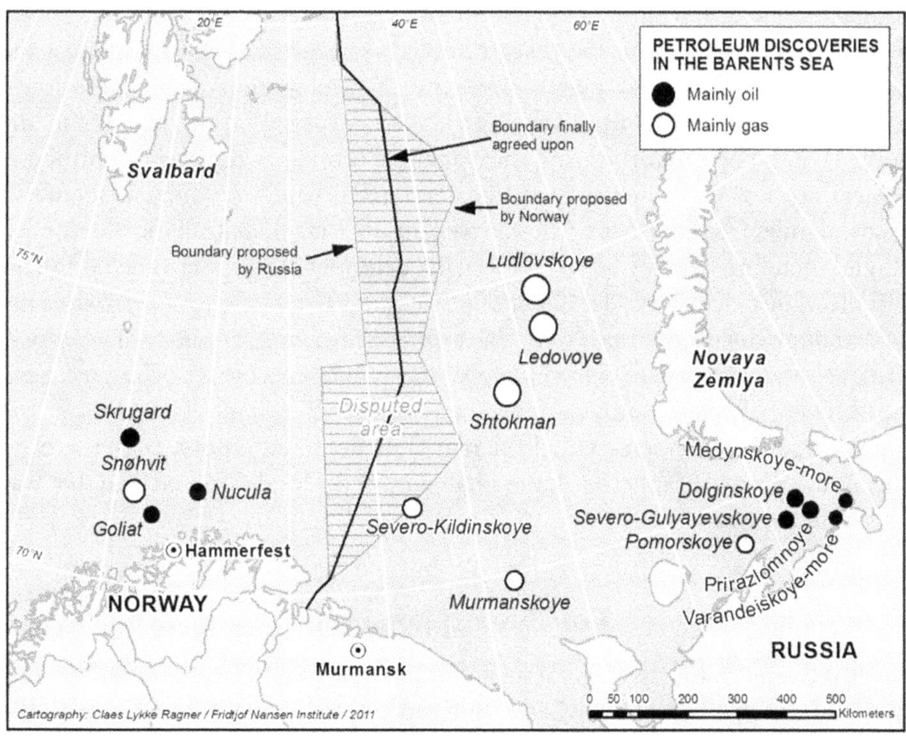

Figure 6.1 Map of the previously disputed area and petroleum discoveries in the Barents Sea.

Severo-Kildinskoye and Murmanskoye are small and complicated and have so far been considered uneconomical to develop. One relatively small oil field in the Pechora Sea, Prirazlomnoye, was expected to start producing in 2012 and other fields in that area may be connected to its infrastructure later. On the Norwegian side the gas field Snøhvit has been producing since 2007 and the development of the oil field Goliat is underway. Nucula and Skrugard are the other promising oil discoveries.

The Soviet Union also referred to the Convention on the Continental Shelf, but emphasized the 'special circumstances' that the Convention allows as reasons for deviating from the median line. The special circumstances invoked by the Soviet Union and later Russia included demographic and military considerations. The Soviet Union also pointed to a 1926 decree declaring sovereignty over islands within an Arctic 'sector', and argued that the delimitation should therefore follow a meridian that stretches from Russia's mainland border at the Varanger Fjord outlet to the North Pole. (The border proposed first by the Soviet Union and Russia corresponds to the western perimeter of the disputed area in Figure 6.1. It is not entirely straight, since it takes account of Norway's sovereignty over the Svalbard archipelago.)

It is worth noting that the disagreement concerned the delimitation of the exclusive economic zones (mainly governing the exploitation of living resources) and continental shelves (determining rights to exploration of minerals in the seabed) of the two countries, and that exclusive economic zones and continental shelves are not the same as sovereign territories, which are limited to twelve nautical miles from the shore. The Norwegian–Russian dispute in the Barents Sea should therefore be referred to as a 'marine delimitation dispute' or a 'boundary dispute' rather than a 'border dispute'.

Although the negotiations were characterized by lengthy periods of deadlock, progress was also made intermittently, most notably with the Varangerfjord Agreement of 2007, only three years before the final agreement.[7] The Varangerfjord Agreement settled the maritime delimitation of a coastal area at the mouth of the Varangerfjord, the small part of the total disputed area that was closest to the coast.

Possible Explanations

In 2010, after four decades of negotiations, Russia came to terms with a compromise that had already been contemplated by the Norwegian side in the 1970s, but never formally presented to their counterparts in the negotiations.[8] The Soviet and later Russian side had long avoided the idea of a boundary compromise altogether, instead launching various proposals for a cooperation zone without a firm boundary. All such proposals were rejected by Norway. Only in 1988 did the Soviets signal that they might be willing to negotiate a firm boundary, but there was still little scope for compromise on its location.[9] During the post-Soviet period, the Russian negotiators gradually became more forthcoming – but still, it is clear that the 2010 agreement represented a significant change in the Russian position. Explanations for the timing of the deal must therefore be sought primarily on the Russian and not the Norwegian side.

There are several possible explanations as to why the Russian authorities decided to end the dispute in the Barents Sea in 2010, and not earlier or later: (1) the gradual evolution of international law changed the premises for negotiations; (2) improvements in Norwegian–Russian bilateral relations made a solution possible; (3) the desire to start extracting the oil and gas in the disputed area was a major driver; (4) the cost of being involved in manifold unresolved territorial disputes was rising for Russia, and the agreement with Norway represents part of a general effort to finalize as many territorial negotiations as possible; (5) Russia had entered a phase where it wanted to be seen as a constructive international actor; (6) Russia wanted to bolster the UN Convention on the Law of the Sea (UNCLOS) as the framework for Arctic governance, in order to avert the involvement of non-littoral states in the region. The strength of each of these six hypotheses is examined in the following sub-sections.

Evolution of international law

Norwegian government officials emphasize that the agreement is the culmination of a long and gradual process, and that the line now drawn is based on international law. As stated by Norway's Foreign Minister Jonas Gahr Støre: 'The line has been computed in relation to the relevant coasts on either side, on the basis of modern principles of international law.'[10] Taken at face value, that statement might seem to indicate that new developments in international law made it possible to reach an agreement after forty years of negotiations.

The original Russian position focused on the 1926 Decree of the Presidium of the USSR Central Executive Committee, 'On the Proclamation of Lands and Islands Situated in the Arctic Ocean as Territory of the USSR', and what is referred to more generally in Russia as 'sector theory'.[11] This position was initially presented as non-negotiable, but implicitly became more negotiable with Russia's accession to UNCLOS in 1997.[12] According to Article 83 of UNCLOS, delimitation of neighbouring continental shelves and exclusive economic zones 'shall be effected by agreement on the basis of international law'. In practice this is a reference to the International Court of Justice, which in a series of decisions had crystallized what constitutes relevant circumstances, and had narrowed the application of that article to include permanent, natural characteristics of neighbouring territories, the length of the respective coastlines in particular. None of these decisions are based on a 'sector principle'. The court's ruling on maritime delimitation between Romania and Ukraine, which applied the median line principle, set a particularly salient precedent.[13] This ruling was made on 3 February 2009, only a year before the final agreement between Norway and Russia.

Following this legal perspective, it can be argued that legal developments had substantially narrowed the 'special circumstances', thus making the proposed compromise more acceptable from a Russian perspective. That may in turn have prompted the Russian negotiators to agree to the finalization of the deal. However, we believe this interpretation lends too much weight to the legal aspect of the negotiations. The delimitation of neighbouring continental shelves is, according to UNCLOS, an exclusively bilateral affair where the parties themselves can decide how a line should be drawn. Even if help can be found in past decisions of the International Court, the parties do not have to adhere to such precedents if they do not find them politically acceptable. Moreover, court decisions do not provide exact definitions of how lines should be drawn in other cases; they merely indicate which factors *can* be given weight. It is also striking how the delimitation resulted in a near perfect 50/50 division of the originally disputed area. This seems to underscore that willingness to find a *political* compromise lay behind the resolution. Taking into account these considerations, we conclude that although developments in international law help explain how the parties arrived at the finishing line, a legal perspective alone cannot explain why the deal was reached in 2010.

Favourable bilateral relations

Russia and Norway's bilateral relations have improved steadily over the past two decades, notwithstanding certain tensions, particularly in the fisheries sector. The autumn of 2005 was an especially low point, with the de facto kidnapping of two Norwegian coastguard officers who had boarded the Russian trawler *Elektron* in October, and a Russian ban on salmon imports from Norway in November. The feud between the Norwegian and Russian companies Telenor and Alfa Group over the Russian telecom company Vimpelcom, worth billions of US dollars, raged on and off during the second half of the 2000s and was another important thorn in the relationship.

None of these events, however, led to serious bilateral political conflict. Long-term bilateral relations developed on the back of constructive cooperation – especially in the management of Barents Sea fish stocks and the selection of the Norwegian state-controlled oil company Statoil to participate in the Shtokman Gas Field development with the Russian state-controlled gas company Gazprom.[14] Such positive overtones can help us understand why it had become politically *feasible* to reach a compromise. However, although the good bilateral relationship can be seen as a precondition for the delimitation agreement, it was a necessary but not a sufficient condition on its own for this outcome. The direction of any causal relationship between this factor and the timing of the agreement is also not self-evident: it is possible that the relatively good atmosphere between the two countries was the result of a deliberate effort by the authorities on both sides to clear the way for an agreement, rather than vice versa. The deal cannot be understood solely in terms of Norwegian–Russian bilateral relations. Also, broader developments and policy goals need to be considered, including national interests in the petroleum resources of the Barents Sea, which is the next hypothesis we examine here.

The attractiveness of the disputed area's assumed petroleum resources

The previously disputed area is believed to hold large oil and gas resources, and this may have made it particularly difficult to reach an agreement. On the other hand, considerable uncertainty is attached to this resource potential. Both Norway and the USSR/Russia have carried out some seismic surveying, Russia more so than Norway. Norway discontinued seismic surveys in 1976, whereas the USSR continued well into the 1980s. Thereafter a moratorium on all forms of exploration in the disputed area was respected by both sides.

They also agreed informally to refrain from publishing estimates of the resources in the area. The Norwegian Petroleum Directorate adhered to this practice, but on various occasions the Russian Ministry of Natural Resources and its subsidiary structures have published estimates of resources in the disputed area. According to the All-Russian Petroleum Exploration Research Institute,[15] the disputed area is expected to be gas-prone (see Table 6.1) – with 5.8 trillion m^3 in recoverable gas reserves, as well as an additional 2.7 billion barrels of recoverable oil. Similar figures were suggested in 2005 by the head of Russia's Subsoil Resource Management Agency, Rosnedra, as well. His estimates for recoverable oil were higher, at 3.9 billion barrels.[16] It is not known whether these estimates are based on seismic exploration activity or satellite data. In any case, there is a significant methodological gap between how petroleum resources are considered 'extractable'

Table 6.1 Russian resource estimates for the disputed area.[17]

	Initial total resources MMt o.e.	Oil MMt	Ass. gas BCM	Free gas BCM	Condensate MMt
In place	7,481	1,200	170		248
Recoverable	6,446	360	51	5,863	172

in the Russian system and in the approach of the international (Western) petroleum industry, so these estimates should be used with caution.

After the delimitation deal was signed, Natural Resources Minister Trutnev stressed the uncertainty of the estimates, but also announced that there were up to ten structures that *might* hold resources in the category 'very large' (more than 1 trillion cubic metres of natural gas or 1 billion tons of oil) or 'unique' (more than 5 trillion m^3 natural gas or 5 billion tons of oil).[18]

So what role can interest in these energy resources have played in the resolution of the dispute? Certainly energy was mentioned in Medvedev's official comments – both in Oslo in April 2010, when the agreement was announced,[19] and in Murmansk on 15 September 2010, when it was signed.[20] These statements, and also the official comments from the Russian Ministry of Foreign Affairs, were of a fairly general nature, acknowledging that the area might contain significant resources and expressing the wish to cooperate. Certainly, resolution of the dispute would be a prerequisite for exploiting the resources. As the comments by Medvedev and Trutnev indicate, the area's petroleum potential is a central point of interest in connection with the delimitation. However, the Russian comments did not indicate any concrete Russian programme for exploration and development of the area. This raises some initial doubts as to whether energy resources were in fact a significant driver for reaching a solution in 2010.

In our view, lobbying from energy companies to open and develop the area was not an important factor. There is no heavy Russian industrial actor with a strong interest in venturing into the previously disputed area. The Barents Sea has been reserved for development under the auspices of state-controlled Gazprom and Rosneft, but these companies were already stretched by existing commitments. Gazprom is heavily committed to the Yamal and Sakhalin projects. Considering the company's meagre results with the Prirazlomnoye Field (see Figure 6.1), it can hardly be expected to have spare capacity or appetite for another Barents Sea project beyond Shtokman. Since an appraisal of the Dolginskoye Field in 2009, Gazprom has not drilled offshore in the western part of the Russian Arctic.

Rosneft has had its hands full with onshore projects such as Vankor and can be expected to maintain its focus on Siberian projects to fill the ESPO pipeline to China. Offshore, the company's main activities are related to Black Sea licenses;

although it does carry out some exploration, this is limited to seismic surveying rather than test drilling for the time being. It is not clear what the aborted agreement between BP and Rosneft to explore three licence blocks in the Kara Sea between Yamal and Novaya Zemlya would result in if revived, with BP or another international partner, and in any case it puts these projects in the queue ahead of any future projects in the formerly disputed area.

As noted, there was an effective lid on negotiations on the Norwegian–Russian maritime boundary, with no leaks to the public. This made it possible to carry on the negotiations without nationalist, populist, oppositional or other distractions. This effectively blocked input from outside a small circle within the Russian Foreign Ministry and the Presidential Administration. Admittedly, there are strong links between key Russian political actors and the country's petroleum companies. For example, Dmitry Medvedev was Chairman of the Board of Gazprom before he became President of Russia; and Deputy Prime Minister Igor Sechin was at the time of the boundary agreement Chairman of the Board of Rosneft. However, these government-controlled companies have not expressed any interest in the disputed area, and in fact they have been criticized by the authorities for their passive stance on offshore petroleum activity. Other government agencies do not seem to have been involved in the final settlement, but for example the Ministry of Natural Resources provided data along the way and was also part of the negotiation team dealing with the technicalities of the delimitation. But that is different from taking the decision to sign a treaty – at a specific point in time.

Furthermore, after the preliminary agreement on a resolution of the delimitation dispute was announced and much of the secrecy lifted, there were no signs of expansive Russian plans for the area. Neither has there been any indication that Rosneft or Gazprom were somehow well-prepared for the agreement. Therefore, we believe there have been no secret plans for rapid development of the area. That does not mean that an assessment of the area's hydrocarbon potential did not play any role in the decision to accept a compromise, as is therefore touched upon in the official comments. These comments, however, treat energy development more as an opportunity that would arise sometime after a resolution had been found. In sum, there are few signs that specific energy-industrial considerations in Russia were a *driver* for the deal.

Increasing cost of manifold unresolved territorial disputes

The Norwegian–Russian agreement on delimitation in the Barents Sea is fully in line with the goals stated in Russia's 2008 Arctic Strategy:

> to realise active cooperation between the Russian Federation and the Arctic states with the goal of delimiting ocean areas on the basis of norms of international

> law, reciprocal agreements taking into account national interests of the Russian Federation, and also for the resolution of questions related to the international legal substantiation of the outer boundary of Arctic Zone of the Russian Federation.[21]

Such declarations need not carry much weight if they are isolated statements – but, in this case, the goal of clarifying borders and solving territorial disputes has also been followed up in practice, and not only in the Arctic. Russia has actively and systematically gone about solving the various disputes along its borders (see Table 6.2). Even if border issues have been settled earlier as well, it is remarkable how many border treaties have been concluded over the last decade. The Barents Sea deal therefore reflects a clear trend in Russian foreign policy to negotiate an end to the various disputes along the country's long borders.

Table 6.2 Border treaties negotiated by Russia, 1990–2010.[22]

3 Sept.	1990	Protocol between **North Korea** and the USSR on delimitation of the border between the two countries
16 May	1991	Border agreement between **China** and the USSR
27 Jan.	1994	Treaty on intersection of borders of **China, Mongolia** and Russia
3 Sept.	1994	Border agreement between **China** and Russia (western part of the border)
Sept.	1997	Treaty between Lithuania and Russia on the border between **Lithuania** and Kaliningrad
3 Nov.	1998	Border treaty between **China, North Korea** and Russia on the intersection of their borders at the Tumen River
5 May	1999	Agreement between **China, Kazakhstan** and Russia on the intersection of the borders between the three countries
28 Jan.	2003	Border treaty between Russia and **Ukraine**
9 Feb.	2004	Protocol between North Korea and Russia amending 1985 protocol between **North Korea** and the USSR
14 Oct.	2004	Additional agreement between China and Russia on the western part of the border, finalizing the entire border between the two countries
18 Jan.	2005	Border treaty between **Kazakhstan** and Russia
18 May	2005	Border treaty between **Estonia** and Russia (later frozen by Russia in connection with spat between the two countries)
20 June	2006	Treaty on the intersection of the borders between **Lithuania, Poland** and Russia

27 March	2007	Border treaty between **Latvia** and Russia
17 May	2010	Treaty on procedure for demarcation of borders between Russia and **Ukraine**
15 Sept.	2010	Treaty on maritime boundary delimitation between Russia and **Norway**

So why is it so important for Russia to tidy its borders? At least two explanations are plausible. Earlier it was commonly assumed, especially in small neighbouring countries such as Azerbaijan, Estonia or Norway, that unresolved disputes bear small costs for a large power like Russia, and that it could even be seen as advantageous for Russia to keep disputes open in order to use them as leverage in bilateral relationships.

While this might have been true for the Soviet Union, Russia's situation is different, and the cost of unresolved borders may have come to outweigh any benefits. Russia is more dependent on other countries now than during the Soviet period. Unresolved border conflicts put bi- and multilateral relations under strain, as well as tying up valuable political and high-level administrative capacity. Both factors may become particularly acute when the conflicts are numerous.

There is therefore a growing realization that Russia must concentrate its expertise and resources on more important issues. Furthermore, insofar as Russia seeks to be perceived as a predictable rule-based player, the potential value of an unresolved dispute as leverage in other issue areas decreases, even if Russia may still resort to such tactics occasionally. We expand on this point in the next section.

Russia as a constructive international actor

The Norwegian–Russian agreement may also be seen as reflecting a broader cooperative trend in Russian foreign policy under President Medvedev that goes beyond border management. Part of this trend is to support global governance through international law and the UN, and to take a constructive stance on many issues in international affairs. The re-set of relations with the United States (March 2009), the renewed START Treaty (April 2010) and cooperation on Iran sanctions (June 2010) are further indications of such a trend. Medvedev's proposal for a new Euro-Atlantic security architecture stretching from Vancouver to Vladivostok was first launched in June 2008, and concretized and reiterated on several occasions in 2008 and 2009.

According to the official Russian Foreign Policy Concept adopted in 2008, the main foreign policy effort should focus on achieving the following objectives:

> to influence global processes in order to ensure a just and democratic world order, based on a collective approach to finding solutions to international problems and on the supremacy of international law, in particular provisions of the UN Charter, as well as relations of equal partnership among states with a central and coordinating role in the UN, the key organisation governing international relations and possessing a unique legitimacy.[23]

In 2010, the multilateralist emphasis became even stronger in the always politically correct words of President Medvedev:

> The time when our country's foreign policy interests were implemented primarily through a network of bilateral ties is in the past. Today we need to learn how to use the resources of multilateral organisations and to operate such resources with skill, precision and assertiveness.[24]

Words are of course cheap, but such statements fit well with a sober assessment of Russia's diverse interests, limited capabilities and lack of unwavering bilateral allies. The overt support for the UN also contrasts conveniently for the Russians with the often negative stance of the United States towards that organization, allowing them to have a more progressive image in this area.

On the other hand, incidents such as the 2008 military campaign in South Ossetia, the subsequent recognition of Abkhaz and South Ossetian independence and the 2009 gas conflict with Ukraine might be seen as contradicting these positive signals in Russian foreign policy.

There are at least four possible explanations for this seeming incoherence. The first is that, in the view of the Russian foreign policy establishment (as well as some Western observers), in both conflicts Russia was the victim (its UN-mandated peacekeepers were attacked by Georgia; its gas was siphoned off by Ukraine). Thus, its actions in those conflicts were meant to be defensive rather than aggressive and did not contradict the cooperative foreign policy line.

The second is that conflicts with Georgia and Ukraine were perceived as unique bilateral issues, and the negative implications for Russia's reputation were not fully appreciated by Russian policymakers, at least not at first.

The third is that today's multilateral rhetoric and image-building got its impetus shortly after the war in South Ossetia. Although it is now difficult for the Russians to backtrack out of the cul-de-sac of Abkhaz and South Ossetian sovereignty, lessons may have been quietly learned, and there may be a desire to move on and away from that confrontation.

The fourth possible explanation emphasizes the disunity of Russian foreign policy actors: hardliners may have succeeded in getting recognition of Abkhaz and South Ossetian sovereignty, but, since then, more pragmatic and Western-oriented actors have got the upper hand. Or, they may have the upper hand in different areas. This explanation would fit with Dmitry Medvedev's slow, but gradual consolidation of his foreign policy power as president.

It is striking how the emphasis on legality in connection with the Barents Sea deal fits not only with Medvedev's broader political discourse, but also with his background in jurisprudence and with his entourage of young progressive lawyers. An emphasis on rule-bound, cooperative international behaviour is compatible with another policy orientation of this part of the Russian elite, namely a desire to reinvigorate Russia's soft power.[25] Thus a cooperative Russian foreign policy, with the Barents Sea deal as one of its expressions, is highly compatible with the worldview of Medvedev and the so-called young lawyers.

It is not easy to rank these four possible explanations in relation to each other. However, we believe that the four explanations combined are sufficiently strong to make our interpretation plausible. The delimitation treaty with Norway may thus indicate that Russia is on a cooperative and multilateralist path despite various confrontational incidents over the past few years. Even if this interpretation is correct, there is no guarantee that Russia will be on this path forever. Instead, it could be argued that if the conflicts with Georgia and Ukraine are important drivers of a current charm offensive, the charm may not last longer than the memory of those conflicts. The interpretation that Russia is on a cooperative path may, however, still be important for understanding current developments such as the resolution of the Barents Sea delimitation dispute with Norway. This line of thinking would also be in keeping with previous interpretations of Russian multilateralism as central to Russian foreign policy, but 'more about co-ordinated action than fostering and adhering to common norms'.[26] Finally, the Arctic has political characteristics that make a cooperative, multilateral approach especially valuable to Russia there, as we discuss in the next section.

Bolstering UNCLOS

Russia has explicitly linked the delimitation agreement to what is clearly the most important issue in Russian Arctic policy – its claim to an extended continental shelf in the Arctic Ocean. In fact, this was a major justification for the agreement cited by the Russian Ministry of Foreign Affairs after the deal was first announced, and also in unofficial remarks by the staff of the presidential administration.[27] According to the Foreign Ministry's spokesperson, 'The delimitation is essential also from the point of view of progress for our claim in the Commission on the Limits of the Continental Shelf.'[28] He was referring to the recommendation that the commission had given to Russia in 2002 on the need to arrive at an agreement with Norway before establishing the outer limits of the Russian continental shelf.[29] However, Norway received its final recommendations on its continental shelf in 2009, so the pending boundary delimitation did not block Norway's submission from being dealt with. Therefore, it may be questioned as to what impact an unresolved boundary could have had on the Russian claim. Nonetheless, if the Russian side made this connection, it could be because its continental shelf application is substantially larger and more complex than that of Norway, and even the slightest risk of disturbing the process in the commission could be an argument for reaching an agreement in the Barents Sea (a revised Russian continental shelf submission was received by the Commission on the Limits of the Continental Shelf in 2015).

The Norwegian–Russian deal can also be seen as supporting UNCLOS in the Arctic on a more general level. It is UNCLOS that provides the coastal states with exclusive resource rights. Russia, like Norway, would have much to lose if the authority of UNCLOS should become weakened. With the rapidly changing Arctic ice situation as well as the reordering of international politics – including the rise of new powers like China and increasing interest in the Arctic on the part of the EU and the USA – cementing UNCLOS in the Arctic has become more urgent for Russia.[30]

In the years immediately prior to 2010 there was international discussion about the need for a new governance framework for the Arctic, possibly in the form of a new international Arctic Treaty.[31] In response, Russia in close cooperation with the other Arctic littoral states (Norway, Canada, Denmark and the United States), made an effort to push this issue back off the agenda and to promote UNCLOS as the main legal framework for the Arctic. A high point came with the 27–28 May 2008 Arctic Sea Conference in Ilulissat, Greenland, which was attended by various ministers of the Arctic Sea littoral states. The littoral states did *not* invite the non-littoral Arctic states (Finland, Iceland and Sweden) or the EU to the event, and produced a declaration on UNCLOS and Arctic governance that included the following formulation:

> We remain committed to this legal framework and to the orderly settlement of any possible overlapping claims. This framework provides a solid foundation for responsible management by the five coastal States and other users of this Ocean through national implementation and application of relevant provisions. We therefore see no need to develop a new comprehensive international legal regime to govern the Arctic Ocean … The five coastal states currently cooperate closely in the Arctic Ocean with each other and with other interested parties … We will work to strengthen this cooperation, which is based on mutual trust and transparency.[32]

Many of the UNCLOS principles have yet to be applied and tried in practice in the Arctic. Hence, it is in the interest of the Arctic littoral states to avoid any statements or actions that could weaken or overshadow UNCLOS in this part of the world. Resolving the delimitation issue in ostentatious compliance with international law could be a strategic move from this perspective, both for Russia and Norway. We therefore believe that the desire to bolster UNCLOS was an important factor in explaining Russia's will to compromise in the Barents Sea in 2010. However, whereas the Russian legal experts may have been acutely aware of the importance of UNCLOS, in the broader foreign policy elite and the rest of the population such awareness may have needed more time to ripen. It may therefore have been easier for the Russian officials involved in the deal to link the delimitation agreement directly to the claim to an extended continental shelf rather than the complex legal aspects of UNCLOS in some of their statements.

Is the Deal a Firm One?

Given the centralization of power in Russia and the largely subservient parliament, the deal stood firm, and support for ratification by the State Duma was relatively unproblematic. This contrasts with the 1990s when President Yeltsin could have expected serious problems with ratification, had he signed an agreement. In light of this, the carefully steered information process surrounding the finalization of the negotiations, as well as the signing ceremony, seems striking. Both the preliminary announcement and the signing ceremony were subject to a virtual media blackout in Russia. There was no prior announcement in the Russian press on the upcoming ceremony (even though it had been widely mentioned with an accurate date in the Norwegian press eight days in advance).[33] Seemingly the Russian authorities did not want to take any risks in presenting a still unfinished process, something that could have unleashed critical voices. Information was disseminated actively to the public only after the deal was a fait accompli, signalling that any objections would be too late anyway and that Duma ratification was merely a matter of procedure.

It may be that the Russian decision to move the ceremony from Moscow to Murmansk should be seen in this light as well. That way, the agreement got less media attention, especially television coverage, than it would have in Moscow. Furthermore, the ceremony took place in a small conference room with a minimal audience – at the very same time as a meeting of the 'Maritime Collegium' with high-profile government and public figures was underway in the same city. Under normal circumstances, one might have expected the two events to be integrated, but they were kept entirely separate. Whereas Norway sent a whopping five ministers to the signing ceremony, Russia's Minister of Natural Resources Yuri Trutnev, who was in town attending the Maritime Collegium, did not attend.

The decision to downplay the agreement in the Russian public sphere contrasts with the strong official support for the deal, as reflected in President Medvedev's presence at the ceremony and his remarks afterwards. In fact, the treaty was signed by the foreign ministers of the two countries, so Medvedev could have chosen not to attend. His presence achieved two things simultaneously. Firstly, it signalled to the government apparatus and the pro-government bloc in the Duma that this was a done deal, fully backed by the president, and that objections were not welcome. Secondly, by limiting the publicity, the risk of nationalistic actors latching on to the issue and using it against the government was minimized. This interpretation is supported by the sensitivity that the Russian authorities have shown to even relatively small public manifestations of opposition beyond the print media and the internet.[34]

Nevertheless, the agreement did meet some resistance from representatives of the fisheries sector in Murmansk. They sent letters to Moscow demanding meetings with State Duma deputies and calling for the treaty to be rejected until it was amended or improved in a way that would better protect their interests. Foreign Minister Lavrov responded by publicly defending the agreement on this point.[35] Clearly the dissatisfaction in Murmansk was seen as an unwanted disturbance in the run-up to ratification.[36]

Speculation that Prime Minister Putin might distance himself from the deal in the assumed rivalry with Medvedev make little sense, especially after his public endorsement of the agreement:

> I have no doubt at all that the existing issues in the Arctic, including those related to the continental shelf, can be resolved in a spirit of partnership through negotiations and on the basis of existing international law. As an example I want to mention the recently signed Russian–Norwegian treaty on the delimitation of maritime area and cooperation in the Barents Sea and the Arctic Ocean. The negotiations were exhausting. They went on for decades and sometimes reached deadlocks. However, we finally found a way out, the treaty was concluded; I believe that it is a good example of the possibility of finding a compromise acceptable for all parties. In the given case both parties really wanted to produce a result and were taking steps to meet each other halfway.[37]

This is also, and we believe not incidentally, the very same kind of language used by the five Arctic coastal states in the Ilulissat Declaration quoted above.[38]

Conclusion

We began this chapter by arguing that Norway had long been ready for a compromise on the Barents Sea boundary dispute with Russia, and that an explanation of the resolution of the dispute in 2010 must therefore primarily be sought on the Russian side. We then asked which factors could explain the timing of the agreement and examined six hypotheses. The potential for large-scale petroleum development underlined the stakes and the importance of the outcome, but cannot explain why an agreement was reached at this specific juncture. Likewise, a positive trend in Norwegian–Russian relations and new precedents in international law may be part of the picture, but have limited explanatory power in this context. Instead, we believe that maturing negotiations, Russia's general effort to tidy up its spatial fringes by finalizing borders and boundaries and Russia's desire to be seen as a constructive and rule-abiding international actor all to some degree help to explain why an agreement was reached precisely in 2010.

Since no factor alone can explain the timing of the deal, these points must be seen in combination. There are, however, several indications that a desire to reaffirm UNCLOS as the pre-eminent framework for Arctic governance may have been a particularly important motivation for the Russian government. In light of the 2008 Ilulissat Declaration, this motivation should not be seen as unique to the Russian Federation, but to some extent part of a concerted effort of the Arctic littoral states to dispel the myth of a 'geopolitical scramble' for the Arctic.

Notes

1 Lassi Heininen, 'Impacts of globalization and the circumpolar North in world politics', *Polar Geography* 29/2 (2005), pp. 91–102, p. 92.

2 R. Douglas Brubaker and Claes Lykke Ragner, 'A review of the International Northern Sea Route Programme (INSROP) – 10 years on', *Polar Geography* 33/1–2 (2010), pp. 15–38, p. 15.

3 Maria Ivanova and Are Kristoffer Sydnes, 'Interorganizational coordination in oil spill emergency response: A case study of the Murmansk region of Northwest Russia', *Polar Geography* 33/3–4 (2010), pp. 139–64, p. 139.

4 Sveinung Eikeland, Larissa Ryabova and Lyudmila Ivanova, 'Northwest Russian fisheries after the disintegration of the USSR: Market structure and spatial impacts', *Polar Geography* 29/3 (2005), pp. 324–36, p. 325; Geir Hønneland, Lyudmila Ivanova and Frode Nilssen, 'Russia's Northern Fisheries Basin: Trends in regulation, fleet and industry', *Polar Geography* 27/3 (2003), pp. 225–39, p. 225.

5 For a map, see Figure 6.1; for an English version of the treaty with appendices, see Kingdom of Norwayand Russian Federation, 'Treaty between the Kingdom of Norway and the Russian Federation concerning Maritime Delimitation and Cooperation

in the Barents Sea and the Arctic Ocean' (2010). Available at www.regjeringen.no/upload/UD/Vedlegg/Folkerett/avtale_engelsk.pdf (accessed 19 November 2010); for a discussion of the treaty text and its provisions, see Øystein Jensen, 'Treaty between Norway and the Russian Federation concerning maritime delimitation and cooperation in the Barents Sea and the Arctic Ocean', *International Journal of Marine and Coastal Law* 26/1 (2011), pp. 151–68.

6 Graham Allison, 'Conceptual models and the Cuban Missile Crisis', *American Political Science Review* 63/3 (1969), pp. 689–718.

7 Russian Federation and Kingdom of Norway, 'Agreement between the Russian Federation and the Kingdom of Norway on the maritime delimitation in the Varangerfjord area' (11 July 2007). Available at http://www.un.org/Depts/los/doalos_publications/LOSBulletins/bulletinpdf/bulletin67e.pdf (accessed 25 January 2011).

8 Rolf Tamnes, *Oljealder 1965–1995 – Norsk utenrikspolitisk historie, bind 6* (Oslo, Universitetsforlaget, 1997), pp. 294–5.

9 Ibid., pp. 301–3.

10 Jonas Gahr Støre, '"Most is north": The High North and the way ahead – international perspective'. Lecture at the University of Tromsø, 29 April 2010. Available at https://www.regjeringen.no/en/aktuelt/Most-is-north/id602113/ (accessed 19 December 2010).

11 I. Bunik, 'Alternative approaches to delimitation of the Arctic continental shelf', *International Energy Law Review* 4 (2008), pp. 114–25, p. 118.

12 Ibid., pp. 120–1.

13 International Court of Justice, *Maritime Delimitation on the Black Sea (Romania v. Ukraine), Judgement* (International Court of Justice, 2009). Available at http://www.icj-cij.org/files/case-related/132/132-20090203-JUD-01-00-EN.pdf (accessed 21 February 2018).

14 For a long-term perspective on the Norwegian–Russian fisheries management regime, see Hønneland, Ivanova and Nilssen, 'Russia's northern fisheries basin: Trends in regulation, fleet and industry', p. 227. On Norwegian and Russian petroleum activities in the Barents Sea, see Arild Moe, 'Russian and Norwegian petroleum strategies in the Barents Sea', *Arctic Review on Law and Politics* 1/2 (2010), pp. 225–48.

15 All-Russian Petroleum Exploration Research Institute, *Osnovnye printsipy kompleksnogo osvoenia resursov uglevodorodnogo syria severo-zapadnogo regiona Rossii* (St. Petersburg, VNIGRI, 2005).

16 M.V. Ledovskikh, 'Geopoliticheskie aspekty razvitiya neftegazovogo kompleksa severo-zapadnogo regiona Rossii', *Mineral'nye resursy Rossii – Ekonomika i upravlenie* 4 (2005), pp. 2–13.

17 Data from All-Russian Petroleum Exploration Research Institute, *Osnovnye printsipy kompleksnogo osvoenia resursov uglevodorodnogo syria severo-zapadnogo regiona Rossii*.

18 RIA Novosti, 'Osvoenie arkticheskogo shelfa mozhet nachatsya lish cherez 12–15 let' (2010). Available at http://www.rosgranitsa.ru/about/international/countries/delimitation (accessed 3 January 2011).

19 Dmitry Medvedev and Jens Stoltenberg, 'Sovmestnaya press-konferentsiya possiysko-norvezhskikh peregovorov' (2010). Available at www.kremlin.ru/transcripts/8924 (accessed 7 December 2010).

20 Presidential Press Service, 'Vystuplenie na soveshchanii s rossiyskimi poslami i postoyannimi predstavitelyami v mezhdunarodnykh organizatsiyakh' (2010). Available at www.kremlin.ru/transcripts/8325 (accessed 18 December 2010).

21 Security Council of Russia, 'Osnovy gosudarstvennoy politiki Rossiyskoy Federatsii v Arktike na period do 2020 gode i dal'neyshuyu perspektivu', signed by President Dmitry Medvedev on 18 September 2008. Available at http://www.scrf.gov.ru/documents/15/98.html (accessed 19 December 2010) (our translation).

22 Data from Rosgranitsa, *Informatsiya o delimitatsii i demarkatsii gosudarstvennoy granitsy Rossiyskoy Federatsii* (Rosgranitsa, 2011). Available at http://www.rosgranitsa.ru/about/international/countries/delimitation (accessed 3 January 2011); Mikhail A. Alexeev and V. Vagin, 'Russian regions in expanding Europe: The Pskov connection', *Europe-Asia Studies* 51/1 (1999), pp. 43–64; Pavel K. Baev, 'Bear hug for the Baltic', *The World Today* 54/3 (1998), pp. 78–9; Francine Hirsch, 'Toward an empire of nations: Border-making and the formation of Soviet national identities', *Russian Review* 59/2 (2000), pp. 201–26; Bobo Lo, 'Putin's oriental puzzle', *The World Today* 61/12 (2005), pp. 15–16; Andrey Makarychev, 'Pskov at the crossroads of Russia's trans-border relations with Estonia and Latvia: Between provinciality and marginality', *Europe-Asia Studies* 57/3 (2005), pp. 481–500; Rajan Menon, 'In the shadow of the bear: Security in post-Soviet Central Asia', *International Security* 20/1 (1995), pp. 149–81; Yutaka Okuyama, 'The dispute over the Kurile Islands between Russia and Japan in the 1990s', *Pacific Affairs* 76/1 (2003), pp. 37–53; Andreas Selliaas, *Russland, Litauen og Kaliningrad – tre enheter, to land, en utfordring?*, FFI report (2002). Available at http://rapporter.ffi.no/rapporter/2002/02023.pdf (accessed 3 January 2011); Joni Virkkunen, 'Post-socialist borderland: Promoting or challenging the enlarged European Union', *Geographical Annals* 83/3 (2001), pp. 141–51; Henn-Juri Uibopuu, 'The Caspian Sea: A tangle of legal problems', *The World Today* 51/6 (1995), pp. 119–23; Bogdan Szajkowski, 'Will Russia disintegrate into Bantustans?', *The World Today* 49/8–9 (1993), pp. 172–6; Alexander Lukin, 'The image of China in Russian border regions', *Asian Survey* 38/9 (1998), pp. 821–35; Hiroshi Kimura, 'Russia and the CIS in 2004: Putin's offensive and defensive actions', *Asian Survey* 45/1 (2005), pp. 59–66; Posol'stvo Rossii v Kitae, 'Sovmestnaya Deklaratsiya Rossiyskoy Federatsii i Kitayskoy Narodnoy Respubliki 2004 godu' (2010). Available at http://www.russia.org.cn/rus/2839/31292776.html (accessed 3 January 2011); E. R. Muradyan, 'Problemy obespecheniya bezopasnosti rossiyskovo gosudarstva', *Vestnik Chelyabinskovo gosudarstvennovo universiteta* 8 (2008), pp. 12–7; M. V. Lapenko, *Rossiya i Kazakhstan na puti sozdaniya voenno-strategicheskovo prostranstva* (Saratov, Voenno-istoricheskie issledovaniya v Povolzhe, 2008), pp. 120–1; V. Mikheev, 'Potentsial vrazhdy versus sotrudnichestva', *Pro et Contra* 3/2 (1998), pp. 53–67; Presidential Press Service, 'Nachalo vstrechi s premer-ministrom Latvii Aygarsom Kalvitiso' (Presidency of the Russian Federation, 2007). Available at http://archive.kremlin.ru/text/appears/2007/03/121013.shtml (accessed 3 January 2011); A. S. Sabyrov, *Obzor pravovoy basy: Natsionalnoe zakonodatelstvo respubliki Kazakhstan* (OSCE Academy, n.d.), pp. 11–12. Available at http://www.osce-academy.org/uploads/files/Republic_of_Kazakhstan.pdf (accessed 3 January 2011).

23 Dmitry Medvedev, *The foreign policy concept of the Russian Federation* (2010). Available at http://www.mid.ru/ns-sndoc.nsf/0e9272befa34209743256c630042d1aa/

cef95560654d4ca5c32574960036cddb (accessed 15 December 2010) (official translation).

24 Dmitry Medvedev, 'Vystuplenie na soveshchanii s rossiyskimi poslami i postoyannimi predstavitelyami v mezhdunarodnykh organizatsiyakh' (2010). Available at www.kremlin.ru/transcripts/8325 (accessed 18 December 2010) (our translation).

25 Robert W. Orttung, 'Russia's use of PR as a foreign policy tool', *Russian Analytical Digest* 81 (2010), pp. 7–10, p. 7; Andrew Wilson and Nicu Popescu, 'Russian and European neighbourhood policies compared', *Southeast European and Black Sea Studies* 9/3 (2009), pp. 317–31, p. 319; Andreo P. Tsygankov, 'Russia in the post-western world: The end of the normalization paradigm?', *Post-Soviet Affairs* 25/4 (2009), pp. 347–69, p. 355; Fiona Hill, 'Moscow discovers soft power', *Current History* 105/693 (2006), pp. 341–7, p. 341.

26 Elana Wilson Rowe and Stina Torjesen, 'Key features of Russian multilateralism', in E. W. Rowe and S. Torjesen (eds), *The Multilateral Dimension in Russian Foreign Policy* (London, Routledge, 2009), pp. 1–20, p. 3.

27 See Andrei Nesterenko, Russian MFA Spokesman Andrei Nesterenko response to media question regarding Russian–Norwegian Agreement on Maritime Delimitation in the Barents Sea and the Arctic Ocean (2010). Available at http://www.mid.ru/Brp_4.nsf/arh/28A6508288DACE24C32577140029DBDC?OpenDocument (accessed 2 March 2011); MID, 'Kommentariy Departamenta informatsii i pechaty MID Rossii v svyazi s podpisaniem rossiysko-norvezhskogo Dogovora o razgranicheniem morskikh prostranstv' (2010). Available at http://www.mid.ru/brp_4.nsf/0/9350CB29FC106130C32577A00027B318 (accessed 2 March 2011); Presidential Administration, 'Dogovor o granitse v Barentsevom More ukrepit pravaoy rezhim v Arktike' (2010). Available at http://www.rian.ru/arctic_news/20100915/275973370.html (accessed 2 March 2011).

28 *Newsru*, 'Rossiya i Norvegiya razgranichili arkticheskie morskie territorii' (Russia and Norway delimited Arctic maritime territories) (2010). Available at http://www.newsru.com/russia/15sep2010/nrwrf.html#1 (accessed 26 February 2011).

29 'In the case of the Barents and Bering seas, the commission recommended to the Russian Federation, upon entry into force of the maritime boundary delimitation agreements with Norway in the Barents Sea, and with the United States of America in the Bering Sea, to transmit to the commission the charts and coordinates of the delimitation lines as they would represent the outer limits of the continental shelf of the Russian Federation extending beyond 200 nautical miles in the Barents Sea and the Bering Sea respectively': UN General Assembly, *Fifty-seventh Session, Agenda item 25 (a) Oceans and the law of the sea – Report of the Secretary-General*. Addendum A/57/57/Add.1 8 October 2002. Available at http://www.un.org/Depts/los/general_assembly/general_assembly_reports.htm (accessed 27 December 2010).

30 Claire L. Parkinson, 'Recent trend reversals in Arctic Sea ice extents: Possible connections to the North Atlantic Oscillation', *Polar Geography* 31/1–2 (2008), pp. 3–14, p. 3, 11.

31 See e.g. Olav S. Stokke, 'A legal regime for the Arctic? Interplay with the Law of the Sea Convention', *Marine Policy* 31/4 (2007), pp. 402–8.

32 Arctic Ocean Confernece, 'The Ilulissat Declaration' (2008). Available at http://www.oceanlaw.org/downloads/arctic/Ilulissat_Declaration.pdf (accessed 4 January 2011).

33 See NTB, 'Delelinjeavtalen underskrives 15. september', *Aftenposten*, 7 September 2010, p.7; NTB, 'Detaljene på plass for delelinjeavtalen', *Faedrelandsvennen*, 7 September 2010, p. 10.

34 For more on this, see for example Indra Øverland and Hilde Kutschera, 'Pricing pain: Social discontent versus political willpower in Russia's gas sector', *Europe-Asia Studies* 63/2 (2011), pp. 311–29, p. 319.

35 S. V. Lavrov, press conference, Russian Ministry of Foreign Affairs, 13 January 2011. Available at http://www.mid.ru (accessed 21 January 2011).

36 While there was little doubt about the final result, only the representatives from United Russia supported the Treaty in the Duma. Other parties listened to the vocal opposition of fisheries organizations in Murmansk, who claimed that the treaty would jeopardize their interests, also after the government had rejected these arguments.

37 Vladimir Putin, *Prime Minister Vladimir Putin addresses the international forum 'The Arctic: Territory of Dialogue'* (2010). Available at http://premier.gov.ru/eng/events/news/12304/(accessed 18 December 2010) (official translation).

38 Arctic Ocean Conference, 'The Ilulissat Declaration'.

CHAPTER 7

THE RUSSIAN ARCTIC DEBATE: THE DELIMITATION LINE IN THE BARENTS SEA

Geir Hønneland

Introduction

'What can Putin do to get the Barents Sea back?' ran the headline of an article printed in several Russian newspapers in late winter 2013.[1] The author wanted the border between Norway and Russia in the Barents Sea, established by treaty in 2010, revoked forthwith. What's more, it's time the international community stood up to Norway and its management of the waters around Svalbard. The article attracted a lot of attention in the Norwegian media, too, as winter progressed into spring. It just goes to show, some said, we still have a Russian bear as a neighbour – it's best to be on our guard and expect the worst. The viewpoints expressed in the article were pretty eccentric, commentators suggested, just an anomaly, even a misunderstanding. What more could you say about such obvious absurdities? Let's be clear, the Norwegian–Russian maritime delimitation treaty is a binding agreement between two sovereign states. It was entered into in accordance with the principles of the Law of the Sea – it's not something you withdraw from at the drop of a hat. So the issue is not so much *what* Putin should do to recover the Barents Sea, but *why* the critics of the delimitation line want him to.

Endless Negotiations, Big Compromise

When Norway and the Soviet Union established their respective 200-mile zones in the winter and spring of 1976–77, the parties were already known to differ on

---

This chapter is an extended version of Geir Hønneland, 'Delimitation of the Barents Sea', in *Russia and the Arctic: Environment, Identity and Foreign Policy* (London, I.B. Tauris, 2016), pp. 71–102.

how the boundary between their respective zones should be determined. Several years previously they had been talking about ways of dividing the continental shelf in the Barents Sea-that is the seabed and whatever lay below it. They agreed to base initial discussions on the 1958 Continental Shelf Convention. The Convention provided a three-stage list of rules regulating how governments should go about determining the border between their respective parts of a continental shelf. First, states can freely determine the boundary *by agreement*. This may sound patently obvious, but the point was to highlight the contractual freedom that applied in this area too, which is that parties can adopt whatever arrangement suits them best without worrying about external parties claiming the agreement is invalid, or indeed, unfair or biased. Second, if the parties cannot agree on a dividing line the *median line principle* will apply, which is a method whereby the dividing line offshore is determined by the direction of the boundary on land. More technically, a median line is a series of points at sea whose distance from land on both sides of the border is the same. Third, if *special circumstances* were to apply, the Shelf Convention allows states to depart from the median line.

Norway pushed the median line principle in talks with Soviet representatives; the Soviets argued against it, referring to special circumstances. The special circumstances were the area's strategic importance to the Soviet Union – its largest naval fleet, the Northern Fleet, was stationed there with access to the Barents Sea. And there was a significant disparity in population numbers on either side of the border. By then, the Kola Peninsula had over a million inhabitants, more than ten times the number in Finnmark county on the Norwegian side. Moreover, the Soviets had claimed all the islands (and later waters) between the sector lines in the east and west of the Arctic Ocean as early as 1926. A sector line is a line of longitude that starts from the terminus of the land boundary and intersects the North Pole. This, then, was the Soviet Union's official stance vis-à-vis Norway. Put simply, Norway held to the median line principle, the Soviet Union to the sector line principle. Not surprisingly, the principle Norway preferred would give Norway a larger wedge than the Soviet Union, and vice versa.

Recognizing that an immediate solution was not likely, Norway and the Soviet Union agreed to an interim arrangement in parts of the disputed area – quickly baptized in Norway as the Grey Zone (in Russian colloquially referred to as the Joint Area). Within the Grey Zone, Norway could inspect Norwegian boats and third-country vessels with a Norwegian fishing license; the Soviets could control their own vessels and again third-country vessels to which they had given permission to fish. The Grey Zone is often confused with the disputed area, but it was simply a way of organizing the supervision of the two countries' fishing activities; it had nothing to do with oil and gas. Furthermore, the Grey Zone and the disputed area were not coextensive geographically (Figure 7.1). Admittedly,

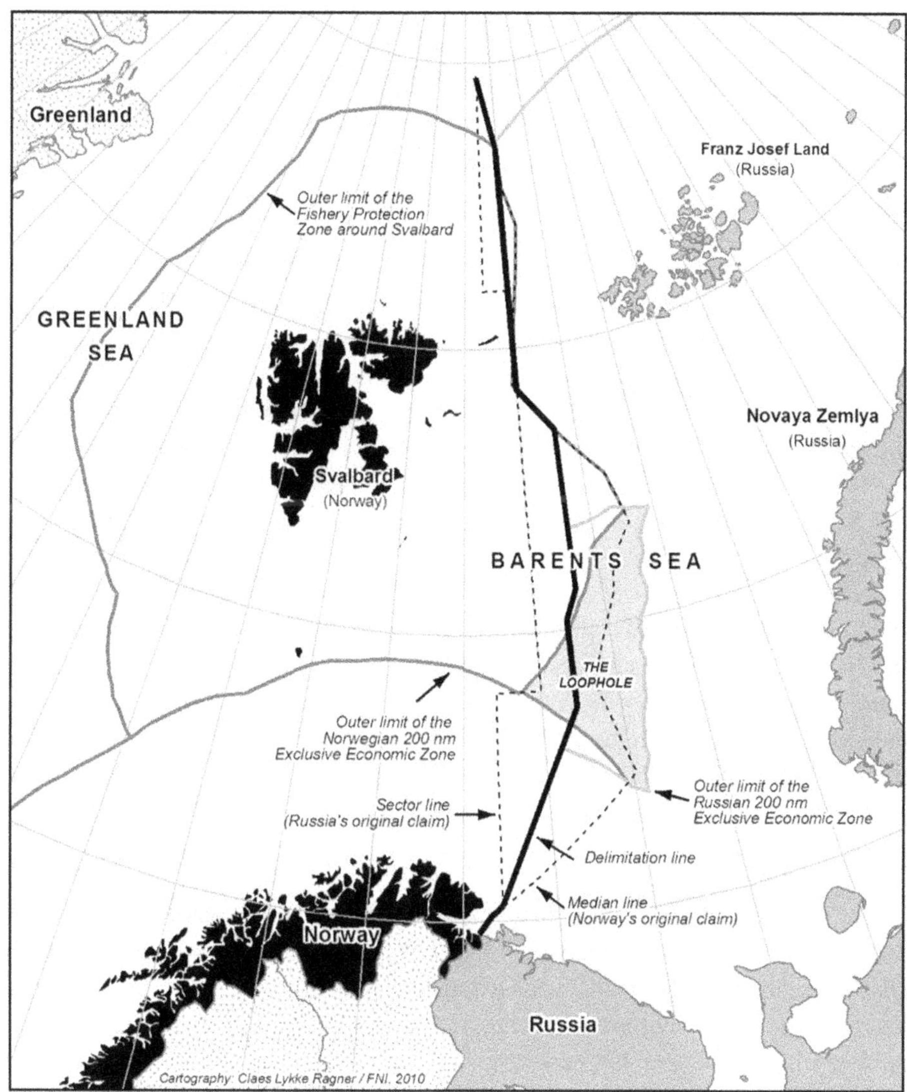

Figure 7.1 Zone configuration in the Barents Sea.[2]

the Grey Zone did overlap most of the southern parts of the disputed area, but a small wedge extended into undisputed Norwegian waters to the west (i.e., west of the sector line) and a smaller part into the undisputed Soviet waters to the east (east of the median line). This was primarily because Norway and the Soviet Union wanted the Grey Zone to cover the natural fishing grounds-that is, whole fishing banks without splitting them up.

Following the establishment of the economic zones, the maritime boundary became an item in the negotiations on the division of the shelf in the Barents Sea.[3] For years, Norway and the Soviet Union held talks on the Barents Sea border in deepest secrecy; there was no publicity nor leaks of importance to the media (at least right up until the home straight). All the same, it was widely known that the talks had been moving forward in the final years of the Soviet era, but had stalled again when the Soviet Union fell apart. In an extremely rare public statement from any political source, President Mikhail Gorbachev mentioned the delimitation negotiations when he visited Oslo in June 1991 to receive the Nobel Prize awarded to him the year before. A Norwegian journalist asked him at a press conference how the maritime delimitation talks were going. The parties, he said, had agreed on 80–85 per cent of the delimitation line; only the southernmost part of the line, down to the coast, remained in contention. In other words, the parties had drawn a boundary somewhere between the median line and sector line – a sort of compromise, which is what negotiating is all about. Progress was slow over the next ten to fifteen years, until a new coalition government took over in Norway in autumn 2005. The Labour Party's rising star, Jonas Gahr Støre, was appointed foreign minister and immediately declared the High North to be his highest priority. December 2005 saw the start of a new round of boundary talks in Moscow; and this time it was announced in the media. There was no attempt to conceal *that* talks had recommenced. While the publicity could be construed as tempting fate, it also indicated that an agreement was a distinct possibility.

*

At around midday on 27 April 2010, prime ministers Dmitri Medvedev and Jens Stoltenberg, catching most people off guard, announced during an Oslo press conference that Norway and Russia had reached agreement on the maritime delimitation of the Barents Sea and the Arctic Ocean: 'We have agreed now on every aspect of this 40-year-old issue: the maritime delimitation line',[4] said Stoltenberg. 'The agreement will be based on international law and the Law of the Sea. It is evenly balanced, and will serve both countries.' 'The essence of our policy', Stoltenberg continued, 'is not speed racing, but cooperation and mutual achievement, and today our two nations have reached an understanding in this regard'. Medvedev added: 'This has been a difficult issue and made cooperation between our countries difficult. Today we have reached agreement. We need to live with our neighbours in friendship and cooperation. Unresolved issues are always a source of tension.' How had they managed to keep news of the delimitation treaty secret, Medvedev was asked. 'In Russia, as you know, the conspiracy traditions are deep-rooted [laughter] and well-practised.'

On 15 September 2010, the Treaty on the Maritime Delimitation and Cooperation in the Barents Sea and Arctic Ocean was duly signed in Murmansk by foreign ministers Sergei Lavrov and Jonas Gahr Støre in the presence of Medvedev and Stoltenberg.[5] It was a compromise and divided the disputed area into two equal parts while also establishing a single common boundary to the continental shelf and economic zones. Entering into force on 7 July 2011 it consists of three parts: the border agreement and two annexes on fisheries and 'transboundary hydrocarbon deposits', both of which are integral parts of the treaty. The fisheries appendix broadly commits the parties to the continuance of the Joint Norwegian–Russian Fisheries Commission. On a more specific note, the 1975 agreement between Norway and the Soviet Union on cooperation in the fishing industry, and the 1976 agreement concerning mutual relations in the field of fisheries, were to remain in force for fifteen years after the entry into force of the delimitation treaty. At the end of that period, both agreements would remain in force for successive six-year terms, unless one of the parties notifies the other at least six months before the expiry of the six-year term of its intention to terminate one or both of them. In the previously disputed area within 200 nautical miles of the Norwegian or Russian mainland, the technical regulations concerning, in particular, mesh and minimum catch size, set by each of the parties for their fishing vessels, would continue to apply for a transitional period of two years from the treaty's entry into force. The appendix concerning transboundary hydrocarbon deposits provides instructions for so-called unitization in the exploitation of transboundary hydrocarbon deposits whereby such deposits would be exploited as a unit in a way that both parties had agreed on.

'They'll Squeeze us Out'

'In their talks with Norway, the Russian delegation failed to invoke Russia's preferential right to a coastline under the 1920 Svalbard Treaty, or to mention the historic borders of Russia's Arctic areas determined in 1926', writes Vyacheslav Zilanov, the author of 'What can Putin do to get the Barents Sea back?' (he is former Soviet deputy fisheries minister and now a prominent political commentator in Northwest Russia). The agreement, in other words, is seen as the result of negotiations between more or less equal parties – and the Russian side was under no compulsion when it signed over waters rightfully belonging to Russia. The effect of this 'outrageous' treaty could easily be to close off the entire western part of the Barents Sea where the biggest fish stocks were previously available to the Russian fishing industry, leaving it to fish in the much poorer waters further east. It would also allow Norway to tighten the thumbscrews on Russian fishing vessels within the fisheries protection zone around Svalbard, a zone Norway unilaterally put in place in 1977 and Moscow has never officially recognized.

Not only will the delimitation agreement in the Barents Sea treaty cost the Russians a great deal of money, according to Zilanov, the agreement is patently *unfair*. He wants a 'roadmap for the president', with instructions on how to 'repossess the Barents Sea'. It should include the appointment of a commission of Russian and foreign experts to assess whether the treaty can be said to be *reasonable* in the sense of Law of the Sea requirements. When the commission presents its conclusions, the president may then consider whether to have the treaty modified or amended, or even annulled. There should be a new 'Spitsbergen Conference' of the original signatories to the Svalbard Treaty with a view to assessing the validity of Norway's fisheries protection zone around Svalbard. Both ideas are controversial from the Norwegian point of view, to put it mildly. The delimitation treaty is, as mentioned, a binding agreement based on the principles of international law on the delimitation of areas of sea between states. Of course, national parliaments do not always ratify treaties, but to go so far as to annul one is virtually unheard of. Nor are commissions usually appointed to consider an agreement's soundness in light of international law. States can agree to whatever boundaries they like, but once the agreement is in force they have to respect it. If being bound by the treaty becomes a cause of concern to one of the signatories, it can withdraw from the agreement if the procedures for doing so are in place. The usual option, however, is simply not to ratify the treaty rather than taking the trouble to annul it. In the event of interpretative disputes, the parties can bring the case before an international court, assuming both agree – either for this particular dispute or by prior agreement – to let a court, such as the International Court of Justice in The Hague, decide the issue. It is the courts that decide whether an agreement complies with the guidelines in international law, not an international commission of experts of the sort Zilanov proposes. And to call for a new 'Spitsbergen Conference' is also a radical ploy politically speaking, even though opinion is divided on whether the treaty applies to the *waters* around Svalbard.

Former president and current Prime Minister Dmitri Medvedev is the implied villain of the piece. The article starts by noting that the agreement 'which was signed during the presidency of Dm. Medvedev in 2010', meant that Russia lost 'huge fishing grounds to Norway'. 'The document', the article continues, 'which was approved by Dm. Medvedev, fails to satisfy the basic principles [under the Law of the Sea] of *justice and fairness*' (emphasis in original). Vladimir Putin, Russia's strong man over the past fifteen or so years, was clearly needed: 'Putin, clear up the mess Medvedev left behind!', the article suggests. To an untrained eye, what the article says about Putin and Medvedev is a mixture of fact and ordinary political opinion. Medvedev happened to be president when Russia and Norway signed the agreement. Putin is in charge now. It was a bad deal for Russia – end of story. But to an eye trained in the observation of Russian affairs, there's more to it. The article's author need not have mentioned the presidents by name, or at least to repeat their roles as if to emphasize a point. Medvedev was not personally involved in the negotiations, apart possibly from the run-up to the signing in Oslo in April 2010. The author could have asked the Russian government to look at the agreement again without calling on Putin himself. Medvedev and friendly relations with the West (represented here by Norway) are linked together in the article; reading between the lines, Medvedev comes across as at best naive, at worst a traitor – weaknesses to which Putin, apparently, does not succumb. True, many Russians, it is alleged, prefer having a 'strong man' at the helm – macho Putin against brainy, flabby Medvedev – but there is more to it than that. Putin is a 'real Russian' – indeed, many would call him an 'ideal Russian', echoing the sentiments of a song performed by a female singer during Putin's first term as president. Russian men are hopeless, she sings, 'What I want is a man like Putin, a man like Putin, full of strength, a man like Putin, who keeps off the bottle.'[6] Now, Medvedev is not known to be a drunkard either, but many Russians do feel there is something indefinably alien about him. Like the last Soviet leader, Mikhail Gorbachev, he is a man the West could 'do business with'. Can the Russians trust someone who gets on so easily with foreigners? Is he really one of them?

*

'So what d'you think? Is he having us on – or is he serious?' a colleague of mine had noted on a printout of a piece in a Russian newspaper that he had put in my pigeonhole a month after the signing of the agreement. 'They'll elbow us out eventually', predicted the article's headline in the business paper *Vzglyad*.[7] My colleague knew that Vyacheslav Zilanov, the primary source of the story of Norwegian plans to despatch the Russians from the Barents Sea, was an acquaintance of mine and was wondering if I could explain what it all meant. A prank, perhaps? Or a massive misunderstanding?

'We've lost 90,000 km^2 and the opportunity to fish in the western parts of the Barents Sea', said Zilanov, now deputy head of the Federal Russian Fisheries Agency's public chamber (a public committee all Russian federal authorities are obliged to have), and vice president of the All Russian Association of Fishing Enterprises and Fish Exporters (VARPE). Zilanov was exasperated by Russia's surrender of half of the previously disputed area with Norway and concerned about the huge losses to the Russian fishing industry as a result. While 210,000–215,000 tonnes are fished annually on average in the area east of the dividing line, 300,000–315,000 tonnes are taken in the area to the west. What's more, Zilanov protests, the waters around

Svalbard – under the terms of the delimitation agreement – will all fall under Norwegian jurisdiction. 'We have lost territory, 60,000–90,000 km². We have lost the chance of fishing in the whole of the western Barents Sea – if not today, then tomorrow. They're going to force us out. It will be the end.'

> Interviewer: Did I understand you properly [when you said] the Svalbard Treaty is still in force, but only Norway can specify the fishery rules? That's to say, the Norwegians can easily 'throttle' our fisheries by, for example, banning 'outdated' fishing methods used by our Russian fishermen?
>
> Zilanov: We don't use 'outdated' methods. We use different methods to catch ground fish and pelagic fish in the Barents Sea: bottom and pelagic trawls, long lines and nets. The fisheries of Russia and Norway are asymmetric. What does that mean? Russia catches 95 per cent of its fish with bottom trawls and 5 per cent by line. The Norwegians use lines to catch 70 per cent; trawling only accounts for 30 per cent. So of course the Norwegians can introduce new rules on trawlers and say 'this isn't discriminatory because they apply to Norwegian fishermen as well'. But our fishing fleet will bear the brunt. That was the first example. Example number two: Norway could ban bottom trawls in its waters. That would be the end of the Russian fisheries.
>
> ...
>
> Interviewer: The agreement is hailed in Norway as a huge victory over Russia. Do you have any comments?
>
> Zilanov: I wouldn't put it like that, that Norway has triumphed over Russia. We're not an easily vanquished country. Let me put it like this. What Norway has done in the negotiations with the Russian Foreign Ministry is a glittering diplomatic, political and economic achievement. ... No one with any practical experience was included in the Russian delegation, only officials who don't know the difference between Novaya Zemlya and Bear Island. ... And there's another thing. This important intergovernmental document contains palpable grammatical and substantive errors. It feels like somebody was a bit unlucky with the translation – I don't know from what language – or the more likely explanation, it was all done by unprofessional people who had no conception of what they were signing.

Zilanov, in a later interview, expanded on his criticism of the treaty's language.[8] When the agreement speaks of mesh size: 'mesh size of what exactly', Zilanov wonders, 'trawls or nets?' And when it refers to 'the minimum [size of catches]',[9] he parries, 'minimum of what exactly – whales, fish, shellfish, crabs?' He also asks why the agreement fails to specify the coordinates of the disputed area. 'Are we supposed to get together with fishermen to solve the puzzle? "Oh no," the

Norwegians are going to say, "you've got it all wrong; you're getting it completely back to front, this is the mesh size for drift nets, not for trawls." I've discovered multiple examples of this kind of mumbo jumbo.' The points Zilanov is making here exemplify a long-standing difference between Norwegian and Russian legal prose. The Russians have a predilection for minutiae, the Norwegians prefer brevity – and as simply phrased as possible with a view to helping ordinary people understand legal complexities. In any case, why would one want to include the coordinates of a once disputed area in the treaty now that a new border was in place?

*

In the first few days following the signing of the agreement, the Russian media carried reports of the Oslo press conference with Medvedev and Stoltenberg and analyzed the background to the settlement. The gist of the analysis was: Norway was desperate to acquire new oil fields, and Russia wanted to get Norwegian support in its fight for the Arctic shelf, primarily against Canada (see Chapter 5 in this book) – hence the settlement. Some of the first comments on the delimitation treaty in the Russian newspapers refer to discord between Norway and Russia on fishery-related matters. *Kommersant*, for instance, writes: 'Completely unexpectedly, the leaders of Russia and Norway announced on 27 April that they had resolved an old dispute that has cost Russian fishermen quantities of blood [*sic*!], not to mention frayed nerves.'[10] Having explained that the dispute over the boundary had caused no significant problems historically, the quarrel, alleges the paper, 'did eventually lead to the wilful arrest of Russian fishing vessels in the disputed area', often for 'trivial offences' as a result of 'the obstinacy of the Norwegian border protection service'. (For the record, Norwegian authorities have never arrested Russian vessels in the disputed area, so the author must be mixing the situation in the disputed area with the Svalbard zone.)

Norwegian and Russian fishery regulations are beset by 'numerous inconsistencies', writes *Rossiyskaya gazeta* in its 28 April edition (an unfounded allegation as it happens; most monitoring and control procedures were harmonized in the 1990s). These contradictions include the 135 mm mesh size required by Norway against Russia's 125 mm. (Russia and Norway split the difference in 2009; 130 mm is the size required by both countries.) Norway even arrests Russian vessels for using nets with a width of 125 mm (also not correct).[11] But the article is not entirely negative. It mentions some of the more positive things Russian fishermen can expect from the boundary agreement. For example, by adopting 'a uniform set of regulations for the fisheries [which had in fact nothing to do with the boundary agreement; a common set of regulations evolved over many years] the Norwegian Coast Guard will no longer be able to fine Russian fishermen significantly more than Norwegian fishermen for the same offence, a system which has been benefiting the Norwegian fishing industry no end.'

The tone sharpened around the time of the signing of the treaty. 'Today', declared the title of an article from the news agency Regnum on 15 September, the day the agreement was signed, 'Russia is giving Norway a chunk of the Barents Sea'.[12] In its 22 September edition *Argumenty i fakty* fired off the following salvo: 'Right up to the last minute, Norway did not believe the agreement would be signed, but Russia took this step which today is being described as a gigantic capitulation, even indeed an act of treachery.'[13] Vyacheslav Zilanov tells the newspaper, '70 per cent of the Russian fishing fleet's annual catch is taken in waters where Norway from now on will have jurisdiction. Our fishing fleet will be consigned to an ice-filled backwater in the most eastern part of the Barents Sea.'

Like so many others, Vasili Nikitin, Director General of the Fishing Industry Union of the North, draws attention to the Soviet sector declaration from 1926 to explain the actual meaning of jurisdiction in the Barents Sea. The old declaration has still 'not been formally revoked', but with the treaty in hand, the Norwegians have all the 'leverage' they want to run Russian fishermen off the most abundant fishing grounds in the Barents Sea. Referring to the idea that the Russian fleet will never be able to meet the stringent Norwegian requirements, he concludes in some style, 'They will say to us: "We're not throwing you out, you've just got to be tall, well-built and fair-haired!"'[14] In other words, only Nordics may apply.

*

In an extensive piece in the 29 September 2010 edition of *NordNews*, Zilanov offers a more detailed account of his take on the delimitation line and management of the Barents Sea fisheries.[15] The article's title is 'Lavrov and Støre's great breakthrough in the Barents Sea: A carbon copy of the Baker–Shevardnadze breakthrough in the Bering Sea'. He is referring to the 1990 Soviet–US Maritime Boundary Agreement establishing the boundary in the Bering Sea between the United States and the Soviet Union. In Russia, most view it as an act of betrayal by Soviet foreign minister (and native of Georgia) Eduard Shevardnadze in agreeing to waive the sector line principle. There was no time to ratify the treaty before the Soviet Union collapsed, and it has not been ratified since by the Russian authorities.

Zilanov attacks the boundary agreement first under the paragraph heading 'The devil's in the details'. But what are these details, he asks:

> Why don't the boundary agreement and appendices say anything about the fate of the fishing grounds that fall within the scope of 1920 Spitsbergen Treaty? Why

> is there not a single word about the fate of the borders of Russia's Arctic Ocean dependencies from 1926, which no one has annulled and which are on every map, not only Russian but foreign as well?

'I myself', Zilanov goes on, 'have defended my homeland's fishery interests as a member of more than 35 years' standing of the Russian delegation to the delimitation talks'. However, 'the precipitate events of the past five years have occurred without the participation of fishermen, experts or practitioners in Russia's northern fishery basin'. From his time as a negotiator he remembers Norway presenting from the start an 'extraordinarily covetous median line proposal' even though they 'were well aware of the borders of our Arctic Ocean dependencies of 1926', and knew the Soviets 'would insist on the principle of fairness'. In the following years Norwegians let it be known 'in the corridors' that they would be going for a 50–50 division of the disputed area, which the Soviet leadership and the Russian Federation's first two presidents – Boris Yeltsin and Vladimir Putin – had the nerve to reject.

> [By the early 1970s] it was obvious to me that the Norwegian team had a well-defined, long-term national goal, namely to win acceptance for the median line principle as the basis for how the division of the continental shelf and the exclusive economic zones (which we then called fishery zones) should proceed. Their goal was to get the median line principle adopted in some document or another, if only informally and temporarily. And it can't be denied, they succeeded beyond belief [with the Grey Zone Agreement of 1978]. They are harvesting the fruits of this approach with their policy statement on the delimitation line: 50–50 split. So the question is, 'What area exactly is to be divided?' As it turns out, it is the area [measured] from the median line.

There is something suspicious about the Russian leadership, Zilanov seems to be hinting, for even accepting the Norwegian demand to base negotiations on the median line principle. (His annoyance would have been more understandable if the Russians had accepted the median line as the *outcome* of the negotiations.) The Norwegians are acting increasingly unilaterally in the Joint Fisheries Commission, Zilanov adds. The creation of a fisheries protection zone around Svalbard is a special case (an area to which he consistently refers as that 'covered by the Spitsbergen Treaty of 1920'). Acting on its own again, Norway increased the minimum size of mesh and fish in 1990; until then the parties had been content to have a uniform regulatory approach in the Barents Sea. After the collapse of the Soviet Union, Norwegian policy has increasingly aimed at 'impeding the work of the Russian fleet in the western Barents Sea and around Svalbard'. Under the headline 'Iraq syndrome in Russian overfishing' he takes issue with Norwegian allegations of Russian overfishing in the years 2002–8. Just as the Iraq War was in vain because the Americans found neither nuclear nor bacteriological weapons in Iraq, Norwegian allegations of Russian overfishing proved unfounded.[16] Russian fishermen were 'whipped monstrously' during these years, and inquiries were made at the highest level in Russia: 'Get those criminal fishermen out!' During the space of seven years Russian fishermen were supposed to have overfished their quotas by as much as 760,000 tonnes; in money terms between one and one and a half billion dollars. So why hadn't the market reacted? If the allegations of massive overfishing had been correct, prices would have fallen immediately. But they didn't. And apart from that, how would the fish stocks have survived this level of overfishing? The scientists say the cod population has grown consistently throughout the period during which this overfishing apparently took place. The seminal question is why the Norwegians wanted to start the debacle in the first place. It was obviously to 'compromise the Russian fishing industry in the eyes of the European market, making it difficult for our fishermen to sell their products. This is what's known as getting rid of a rival by means of "squeaky clean" methods'.

*

Criticism of the treaty was not a flash in the pan; it rumbled on and effectively delayed Russian ratification. The arguments noted above were rehearsed in open letters to Foreign Minister Lavrov, on 17 May, and to President Medvedev, on 8 September. 'The coastal population in Russia's regions', warned the writers of the letter to Medvedev, 'will suffer harshly, socially and economically', if something isn't done to renegotiate the deal so that the interests of Russian fishermen are better protected. 'Revered Dmitri Anatolevich, do not forget the astute saying "measure seven times, cut once", nor the first commandment of our fishing fleet captains: "danger is never far away"'.[17]

In October 2010, the Committee on Natural Resources Use and Agricultural Sector of the Murmansk Regional Duma discussed the delimitation treaty. The event was reported by *NordNews* on 18 October.[18] Several specialists from the regional fisheries were in attendance and repeated their arguments against ratification. In support of the alleged Norwegian plot to eject Russian fishermen from the western part of the Barents Sea, the lessons of the Bering Sea were mentioned. Although Russia has not ratified the Baker–Shevardnadze Agreement, Washington has used it to justify a number of unilateral measures, the effect of which has been to consign Russian fishermen to the worst fishing grounds, leaving them with only 'memories of fishing'. The same thing happened when Canada established its economic zone in 1976. They didn't actually throw the Soviet fishermen out, but the new regulatory regime was so rigorous, it just didn't pay to fish in Canadian waters. They are apprehensive the same thing could happen in the Barents Sea – indeed, there are tendencies in that direction already. Norway is pulling its own fishermen out of the Russian zone of the Barents, says Vasili Nikitin, Director General of the Fishing Industry Union of the North; it's only a matter of time before they tell the Russians to leave the Norwegian zone. Within two to three years, the Joint Norwegian–Russian Fisheries Commission will have lost its raison d'être. To back his argument, Nikitin points to the success of the 'greens' campaign in Norway to get the government to consider outlawing bottom trawling.

Igor Saburov, member of the Murmansk Regional Duma, remains uncommitted and asks the experts to say whether the Russian vessels can start using the long line method instead. In response, Andrei Ivanov, chair of the Committee on Natural Resources Use and Agricultural Sector, says converting the ships to line catching would cost half a billion dollars. Moreover, long line fishing has problems of its own, says Yuri Lepesevich, research director at the Knipovich Polar Research Institute of Marine Fisheries and Oceanography (PINRO). More small fish are caught and it has an adverse effect on seabirds and marine mammals. Nikitin is anxious: Norway could decide to relocate an established control point on the Norwegian–Russian border (where foreign fishermen have to report before fishing in the respective economic zones) closer to Tromsø, the city where 'Russian fishermen are taken by the Norwegian Coast Guard to face legal proceedings'. As they see it, Norway wants to 'streamline' the prosecution of Russian fishermen. It does not augur well, according to board chairman Vitali Kasatkin of the Fishing Industry Union of the North, referring to 'these expressions of elation on the part of the Norwegians after the signing of the boundary agreement … as could be seen at the session of the Joint Norwegian–Russian Fisheries Commission'. The Duma committee then adopted a resolution urging the State Duma and Federation Council (the two chambers of the Federal Assembly, Russia's parliament) not to ratify the delimitation treaty. In the Regional Duma itself, the proposal also won a majority – but not unanimity.

Our Common Kitchen Garden

On the same day that the delimitation agreement was announced, former governor of Murmansk Oblast, Yuri Yevdokimov, draws a generally sympathetic picture of Norwegian–Russian relations in an article titled 'This is Russia and Norway's promising kitchen garden': 'Now that Russia and Norway are doing such a lot of things together, like extracting deposits in the Shtokman field [which was still at a preparatory stage, and eventually did not materialize] and the global nuclear safety measures, God himself has commanded us to get rid of the inconsistencies in the Grey Zone.'[19] ('Grey Zone' is used incorrectly here for the disputed area; as we have seen, the two are not wholly coextensive.) Yevdokimov admits he is not conversant with the details of the agreement and its likely impact, but he is confident the Russian negotiators have done what they can to defend Russian interests in the best possible way. Asked by a journalist whether Russia might not have got a better deal if they had played on the fact that Norway has practically run out of oil, Yevdokimov says,

> No, that's not how I see it. The Norwegians are our neighbours – indeed, our very good neighbours – even if they do belong to a different defence alliance. They have extensive experience of working on the shelf. They have the gear and the technology. We don't. The sooner we can benefit from their lead, the better it will be for both countries. Apart from that, it was important for Russia and Norway to reach an agreement at this point in time. Many countries are looking at the disputed areas of the shelf, even countries with no connections to the sea. Everyone has something they would like to do there. In reality, the Barents Sea is our kitchen garden, useful today and promising for the future, because we are the only ones who border these immensely prolific waters. Now we have agreed that we alone can operate like rulers here, and we alone can set the rules of the game.

One month after the Murmansk Regional Duma had adopted a declaration that urged the Russian federal parliament not to ratify the delimitation agreement with Norway, the declaration was quietly withdrawn 'without explanation', according to *NordNews*.[20] When a reporter asked what the reason was, Zilanov said, 'I can only tell you what I think. The federal government, Moscow, may have leaned [on the Regional Duma]. Besides, the voting in our State Duma makes it clear where the pressure came from.' He is probably referring to the decision of the presidential party United Russia, which had a majority in the Duma and voted for a retreat. In a long interview with *Murmanski Vestnik* on 18 November 2010, Evgeni Nikora, then Speaker of the Murmansk Regional Duma, his deputy and United Russia faction leader, Igor Saburov, and Andrei Ivanov, chair of the Committee on Natural Resources Use and Agricultural Sector, are lavish in their praise of the boundary agreement.[21] Two months have passed, the article begins, since the agreement was signed. 'Passions have died down, and we can reflect more deeply about what the deal, after all, can give us.' 'The agreement', says the Speaker, 'is historic in character'; a 'serious step in a positive direction [and] a new platform for cooperation', his deputy adds. 'While Russians need to keep a close eye on how the Norwegians behave', says Igor Saburov, they 'should not anticipate anything untoward'. Last month's resolution by the Regional Duma was premature. Further delays in ratification would only give the Norwegians 'unhealthy food' to bring up in the talks ahead. 'Let's see how the agreement works in practice before we do anything', is the advice. The chair of the Committee on Natural Resources Use and Agricultural Sector explains why he changed his mind:

> Having had several important meetings in Moscow, I came to the conclusion that fishing is not the most important thing in this respect, not by a long way. The big issue is the division of the Arctic shelf; the 'race for the Arctic' has a lot of competitors already. We also need to remember the implications on the strategic national interests of the whole country, and our children and grandchildren will hopefully be grateful for the decisions we make today. The agreement will, of course, be ratified, but the work of correcting it is already in progress. We and Norway 'breathe in sync' in many areas. We understand each other, just as the residents of the [Soviet] communal apartments [*kommunalki*; council tenements where several families shared the same kitchen and bathroom] would argue and then make up again. If a broken gas valve needed replacing, they pulled together – because if the flap fell out, none of them would be safe. I don't think we should worry too much whether the Norwegians are going to institute particularly draconian measures. They are a reasonable people and would never do anything like that.

*

The State Duma ratified the delimitation treaty on 25 March 2011. Three hundred and nine Duma members (all of whom were members of United Russia) voted in favour of ratification, while the 141 representatives from other parties abstained.

The Principle of Fairness, the Ultimate Betrayal

Two very different perceptions of what constitutes Russia's relations with its northwestern neighbour are reflected above; let me use Vyacheslav Zilanov and Yuri Yevdokimov, both long-time observers of joint Norwegian–Russian ventures in the North, as representatives of the respective approaches. Zilanov has been involved in the joint Russian–Norwegian fisheries management system since it began in the mid-1970s. He led the Soviet delegation to the Joint Commission for several years in the 1980s and has since been a fisheries adviser to the Federation Council and the Governor of Murmansk. He has retained close ties with the Norwegian fisheries community, and visits Norway regularly. Yevdokimov, for his part, was the first elected Governor of Murmansk Oblast. That was in 1996, but he was re-elected three times before President Medvedev fired him in 2009. Various reasons were given by the president's administration and party, United Russia, but he was mainly accused of being too chummy by half with the

Scandinavian countries. Medvedev had allegedly given him 'one last warning' and told him to concentrate on domestic problems instead of 'fooling around abroad'.[22] Yevdokimov had indeed spent time and effort promoting cooperation with the Nordic countries in the Barents region, and was even awarded the honour of Commander of the Royal Norwegian Order of Merit by Norwegian King Harald in 2007.

According to Zilanov, the delimitation agreement was bad for Russia. First, because the Russian leaders had given ocean territory to Norway that rightly belonged to Russia. Second, the treaty would effectively banish the Russian fishing fleet from the richest fishing grounds in the Barents Sea, leaving them with the 'ice-filled backwaters' in the eastern part of the sea. The first allegation is demonstrably incorrect; the second disputable at best. The part of the Barents Sea Norway got as a result of the delimitation treaty did not belong to Russia; it was internationally recognized as *disputed* territory, and both countries accepted that the disagreement could only be solved by negotiation. Zilanov disregards this fact, preferring instead to cite a declaration from 1926 delineating Soviet Arctic possessions to prove that the waters east of the sector line were Russian. Disregarding subsequent dramatic developments in the Law of the Sea, he refers to the sector principle as *the principle of fairness* (for reasons unknown). The claim that Russia will lose fishing grounds as a result of the agreement is unfounded. Norway has the legal right to bar foreign fishing boats from the Norwegian economic zone, but it has no *interest* in doing so. The mature cod are found in the western parts of the Barents Sea and it is clearly in Norway's interest that as much as possible is fished here rather than in the ice-filled eastern waters, where the fish are much smaller. In addition, it is better for Norway if the Russians fish in the Norwegian zone because Norway can keep an eye on what they are doing. In the Russian economic zone, policing and enforcement of the regulations are believed to be less stringent.[23] Be that as it may, the point is that the delimitation agreement has not changed any of this; it merely adds a small slice of water to the Norwegian economic zone (as indeed it does to the Russian zone, too). Norway could have expelled the Russians from the Norwegian zone at any time in the past, but never did. Russian fishermen have depended on Norwegian 'good will' for nearly forty years to operate in the best fishing areas of the Barents Sea, areas which are much larger and richer than the part of the disputed area which is now Norwegian.[24] Finally, Zilanov seems to be implying that Norway's 'victory over Russia' in the delimitation question has given Norway the confidence to act in the disputed protection zone around Svalbard as it sees fit. As one of the participants in the debate put it, Norway doesn't have to close off the Svalbard zone to foreign fishing vessels, it can simply require fishermen to be 'tall, well-built and fair-haired' – a metaphor for what Russians see as an overly precautious regulatory environment. As long as the talks went on, Russia had a card up its sleeve: 'If you tighten the screw in the protection zone, we'll pay you back in the delimitation negotiations.' In this sense, the dividing line could actually be seen as making a difference. But even that idea depends on Norway *wanting* to act unilaterally and without consideration.

Zilanov inscribes himself into a narrative in which Russia is always pitted against shrewd, calculating Westerners. The plot of the story is that incompetent Russian negotiators fell prey to the clever Norwegians, and the Russians will therefore be wiped off the strategically and economically important part of the Barents Sea map. It is a 'tragedy' in Ringmar's sense, where the narrator assumes the role of the hero who – proudly and passionately – rebels against the established order (the current political leadership in Russia; Russia's pragmatic approach to the West) and relentlessly fights for their country's interests, only to become marginalized in the political play.[25] Even his like-minded comrades in the Regional Duma saw their views on the delimitation agreement turned upside down after a quick trip to Moscow; he and his allies are forcefully driven back. The West is established as the significant Other, but the external othering westwards is not of a particularly malign character. Norway is presented as a foreign country that simply pursues its own economic interests; what they did in the delimitation talks with Russia was 'a glittering diplomatic, political and economic achievement'. It is what any country would strive for, rather than a palpable act of evil.

There are other forms of othering here too: internal othering and othering in time. Zilanov repeatedly draws a line between the new delimitation agreement and the old Soviet declaration of its Arctic possessions. Implicitly, he 'others' the entire time span between these two events, a period during which the Law of the Sea changed considerably, especially from the late 1950s and, in particular, the mid-1970s – developments he himself has witnessed, and participated in. He forgets to mention Russia's global commitments under the 1958 Continental Shelf Convention and the 1982 Law of the Sea Convention; instead, he refers to the unilateral Soviet declaration of 1926, which established what he calls the *principle of fairness*. Since subsequent events are by implication *unfair*, Zilanov has tasked himself with the restoration of the old order. It is a quest for a certain form of Russian identity, a national self-image of Russia as independent, prepared and proud, as opposed to weak, unpatriotic and subservient to or envious of the West. It might not be a conscious, calculated strategy – or even a genuine fear that Norway will go mad in its desire to dominate the Barents Sea – but in its reference to past pride and future doom, the story about the big compromise between Russia and the West is given a recognizable and meaningful coherence, assembled with the various pieces available in this narrative toolbox, for this specific place, at this specific time.

Furthermore, Zilanov's argumentation includes a strong internal othering, implicating other Russian interest groups and other Russian individuals. Former president Medvedev is the big villain of the story and Putin is the hero, the saviour. Medvedev gave territory away; Putin will hopefully get it back. Medvedev's name is irrevocably linked to the cession of land, the ultimate betrayal. Behind Medvedev stands a line of incompetent Russian negotiators – notably from the Ministry of Foreign Affairs – who 'don't know the difference between [Russian] Novaya Zemlya and [Norwegian] Bear Island', are capable of 'palpable grammatical and substantive errors', mutter all kinds of 'mumbo jumbo', and had 'no conception of what they were signing'. In Russian politics, the Ministry of Foreign Affairs is considered, not unsurprisingly, to be one of the most outward- (and westward-) looking political institutions in the country, as opposed to, for example, the power structures, where the Eurasian outlook dominates.[26] The Russian fisheries establishment is also believed to be rather 'inward-looking', concerned, among other things, with reducing the export of Russian fish and increasing supplies to the home market.[27] The internal othering in this specific case is more malign than the external othering. While Norway's behaviour is fully understandable, the Russian negotiators either would not or could not defend Russian interests (the former, of course, being the far more suspicious of the two) and instead orchestrated 'a gigantic capitulation'. Beware of foreigners, beware of the new times; this narrator speaks Russia 'inwards, backwards'.

*

Former Governor Yevdokimov calls the Barents Sea 'Russia and Norway's common kitchen garden', where 'God himself commanded us to get rid of inconsistencies'. The Norwegians are 'our good neighbours – indeed, our very good neighbours'. Upon their return from Moscow where they were whipped into line, members of the Murmansk Regional Duma praise the delimitation treaty. It is 'a serious step in a positive direction', they say, and 'a new platform for cooperation'. There is no reason to 'anticipate anything untoward' from the Norwegians; they are not going to 'institute particularly draconian measures'; they are 'a reasonable people'. In fact, Russians and Norwegians 'breathe in sync', and understand each other like the residents of the Soviet *kommunalka*, where people fight but make up, where they are acutely aware of how much they depend on each other, and offer help when necessary. The plot of the story is that 'we thought our negotiators had betrayed us and we initiated this incredible hullabaloo in the Regional Duma, but we were fooled by our emotions and luckily our leaders in Moscow cleared up the misunderstanding – our grandchildren will be grateful to us for that'. The plot structure is that of the *comedy*, where oppositions and misunderstandings are resolved in the course of the narrative thanks to some fortuitous intervention, where the different twists and turns eventually lead up to a happy ending; the common good prevailing, the catastrophe averted. In hindsight, back from Moscow, cool-headed and relaxed – 'we count ourselves lucky and can laugh about what happened'. The specific kind of Russianness reflected in this narrative is the image of Russians as playful, unpredictable, emotional and game for a laugh, as opposed to the boring rationality of the West.

The 'kitchen garden narrative' is rather weak in its othering. It goes with the genre; comedy ridicules, but more subtly. This specific comedy is light-hearted; there are the mellow Moscow heroes, who gently intervene when misunderstandings reach a level of absurdity, but there are no real villains. Yet the Norwegians are not unconditional 'friends' either. Yes, they are good neighbours – very good neighbours even – but they 'do belong to a different defence alliance'. And while nothing untoward should be expected, 'Russians need to keep a close eye on how the Norwegians behave'. The West is not an enemy here and now, but they cannot be fully trusted.

But is it really a comedy, this story about the naughty Duma members from Murmansk who were summoned to Moscow to be reprimanded by the headmaster? Isn't the unexpected praise for the treaty a bit 'over the top'? The agreement isn't just 'ok after all', according to the reborn Duma members; it is suddenly 'historical in character'. Might the unexpected level of praise for the delimitation treaty, and the story about how the Duma members changed their opinion overnight, actually be a *satire*, a genre that assumes an ironic distance from the world, turns plot structures inside out and upside down? One possible interpretation is that the Regional Duma members dared challenge the political establishment in Moscow, but quickly realized they had nothing to show against Putin and his men, and returned home with their proverbial tails between their legs. Instead of expressing their (assumed) frustration or (any amount of) remaining doubt upon returning home, they engage in a convulsive tribute to Muscovite wisdom. Well aware that regional authorities enjoy practically no authority in Putin's Russia, and that their own Duma seats in reality depend on federal goodwill, there is no other narrative option than hallelujah and applause, the implicit satire. Continued protest isn't just against the interests of individual Duma members; it is something there is (practically) no word for. This is also a story of Russian absurdity, just like the comedy, but of a more malign sort. It is the story of Russian lawlessness, lack of democratic values and respect for the individual's (including the politician's) autonomy. It is the story of a Russia where criticism isn't tolerated, at least if you have even the modest level of political ambition; where lying in public isn't condemned (either by the narrator or the audience), but expected. It is the story of the country where everything that can go wrong, will go wrong. The satire, in turn, isn't necessarily (and in our case probably isn't) an open and conscious ridicule. As I imagine it, the regional politicians seem neither explicitly or implicitly disillusioned when they inform the local press about the happy news from Moscow; that would be a breach with narrative convention.

*

There is no material reason why Russian fishers would oppose the delimitation agreement with Norway; it doesn't change the *quota ratios* or any other important aspect of the bilateral fisheries management regime. It only gives Norway the opportunity to *inspect* Russian fishing vessels in a *marginally larger area* of the Barents Sea than before – and Russia to inspect Norwegian vessels in an equally larger area. By repeating the story of the dismantling of old Soviet practices, how the Cold War never really came to an end, 'Soviet' identity is recreated and maintained in the form of a tragedy. The post-Soviet period has been a 'formative moment' in Russian history when new metaphors have been launched, when new stories have been told about Russia's place in the world, when what passes as meaningful is 'up for grabs' – and, some would say, Russia has lost face geopolitically. Zilanov and his companions perform a forceful defence of traditional Russian (at least Soviet) identity, in the face of radical change: something's wrong – we don't know exactly what, but it's something about the new times, things going too fast. To come to grips with this fluidity, the opponents of the delimitation agreement – consciously or subconsciously knowing how a story is expected to be composed – read into the plot a structure that it, strictly speaking, does not have, crafting a story that hangs together, makes sense and gives your actions credibility; narrating a sense of meaningfulness here and now, between past and future.

The comedy-slash-satire is less prevalent in the public debate about the delimitation treaty; it is also 'lighter' and less tangible than the forceful tragedy. The story of the Duma members who happily return from Moscow with new insight about a bright future is more difficult to grasp. The explicit shorthand plot of this story is the same whether we understand it as a comedy or a satire: 'misunderstandings cleared up, everything fine now'. The *implicit* plot of the satire variant is, 'Hey, this is Russia, you know how it is.' Inherent here are different expressions of Russian absurdity, either good or bad.[28] It is the Russia where people are able to, and sometimes forced to, change position at the drop of a hat; where black and white predominate the narrative platter; where narrative convention fosters categorical expression rather than doubt and nuance – though the inherent plot of the story is that in Russia reality is never what meets the eye. It is a Russia where everything is seen through a veil, where the colours are unclear, where black is white and right is wrong, where stories circulate at ever-greater speed, and where you can't do anything but freeze the frame, live in the present, raise the glass.

Societal fluidity is tackled at a distance, as it were, but in recognizable patterns. The narrated sense of meaningfulness is, in fact, a Russia of meaninglessness.

*

As we saw in Chapter 5, most international relations (IR) studies of identity presuppose some form of othering, either external (of other states), internal (within the state) or historical (in relation to previous and future selves). In our case, external othering comes through loud and clear. In the debate about general Arctic politics, 'a Polar bear went out to hunt' – and it was not Russia. Canada is Russia's quintessential Other in the Arctic, with the other NATO countries lined up behind. In the debate about the delimitation line and resource management in the Barents Sea, Norway is the obvious Other, again with NATO indiscreetly lurking in the background. But the West is not a uniform and static Other – I will have more to say on that presently. Internal othering is limited here, although there is an explicit othering of Moscow in regional criticism of the delimitation line. More pronounced is the othering in time: we are not what we used to be, and we will strive to become someone else than who we are now (in practice, return to our former self). And, most conspicuously, we find an 'inverted' othering: the Other is actually ourselves.

I have repeatedly referred to Ringmar's literary categories of romance, tragedy, comedy and satire.[29] Only in one instance did I find the plot structure of the romance, but that was in the most fundamental story about Russia and the Arctic. Russia is the hero who is determined to 'save the Arctic'; Russia believes peace can be maintained in the region if only Russians are given free rein to use their sensitivity, morality and greatness for the greater good. The most forceful narrative, however, takes the form of the tragedy. It is less prevalent in the general story about Russia and the Arctic, where Russia is still proactive, but all the more powerful in the stories about Russia and Norway in the Barents Sea region, where Russia has been given a more defensive role. This is somewhat ironic since Norway is at the same time spoken of as the good neighbour, the most trustworthy of the 'Arctic five', all of whom (except Russia, of course) are members of NATO. The comedy is not very prevalent in my narratives, but there are subtle reflections of this genre in the stories of Russian absurdities, the blurred line between good and bad, the unexpected twists and turns. Satire does not occur frequently either, but it is blatant and noisy when it does: 'Hey, who do we think we are really: God's gift to the world, or what?'

In brief, tragedy and satire dominate – that sums up the story about Russia.

Defending the Other Self

The discussion in this chapter and Chapter 5 says something about the narrative environment in which Russian Arctic politics is formulated, but it provides only bits and pieces of the analytical framework needed to explain Russian foreign policy. The theory on narrative and IR is actually quite simple – it claims that the available narratives form state identities, which in turn determine state interest, which then determines action. Alternatively, 'interest' is left out of the equation: in some situations, states simply act in defence of their identity, without explicitly considering whether it is in their 'interest' to do so. Typically, such actions take place at the expense of apparent political and economic gain. It could happen, for example, if Russia decided to flout the recommendations of the Continental Shelf Commission and unilaterally establish the limits of Russia's Arctic shelf. It would certainly lead to economic sanctions (in some form or other) and raise tensions between East and West. (Needless to say, we're already there since Russia's annexation of Crimea and involvement in the conflict in Ukraine from 2014 onwards, but unilateral action in the Arctic would not improve the situation.) An 'annexation' of the Arctic would clearly not be in Russia's political or economic interest – yes, it would secure Russian jurisdiction over potential reserves of oil and gas in the High Arctic shelf, but these resources are practically inaccessible and at least not economically viable to extract at the moment. (Most of the Arctic's hydrocarbon resources are on land and on the shelf within 200 nautical miles from the baselines, and therefore much easier to extract.) Furthermore, the foreign experts Russia needs in order to develop even the most accessible resources beneath the shallow waters close to land would leave the country (which they have already done in response to the Ukrainian crisis, but it would also reduce the chances of Western companies resuming their work on the Russian shelf).

Such an action would have nothing to do with political or economic interests – it would be an action, perhaps more spontaneous than considered, performed in defence of the self: what would Russia be without (dominance in) the Arctic? Russia would not be Russia. We must act to ensure the survival of who we are, whatever the cost. The stories people tell about Russian heroism in the Arctic (ranging from the great eighteenth-century Arctic expeditions to the Soviet conquest of the North) must be kept alive. Only action can do this (and that is even more important since one of the other constitutive stories, that of Russia the great power, evaporated with the dissolution of the Soviet Union). By acting, one makes 'the constant attempt to surmount time in exactly the way the story-teller does … to dominate the flow of events by gathering them together in the forward-backward grasp of the narrative act'.[30] We change the events, by acting, to accommodate the story.

As we saw in Chapter 5, Ringmar emphasizes the importance of *recognition* for state identity.[31] Identity is a precondition of interest, and in certain situations identity-driven explanations of foreign policy can substitute for interest-driven explanations altogether. This can happen, for instance, when a state has experienced loss of recognition under humiliating circumstances ('lost face'), or at 'formative moments' when new metaphors are launched and individuals tell new stories about themselves, and new sets of rules emerge through which identities are classified – in short, 'when the very definition of the meaningful is up for grabs'.[32] At these moments, there is an urgent need to have one's own constitutive stories recognized. Needless to say, Russia lost face when the Soviet Union (or the old Russian Empire) fell apart. It lost face, domestically and abroad, when it lost its capacity to take care of its Arctic possessions: infrastructure disintegrated and the population fled. New stories about the self were in the air – about a 'new Russia' totally different from the old – but things didn't work out, and the old stories provide a safe haven, away from contemporary chaos.

So far, however, Russia has opted for the opposite strategy in the Arctic: openness to the outside world, strict adherence to the rules of international law and other norms of good political behaviour. As we have seen, this is not in opposition to the narrative where the West is out to get Russia in the Arctic. Incorporated in this narrative is the idea of Russia as the guarantor of law and order in the region. One might speculate as to whether the political elite actually wanted to add a new layer to the old narratives in order to ensure popular support for the chosen policy: to act responsibly in the Arctic despite overt Western aggression. The scales could easily have tipped, with the other variant of this overarching narrative determining the actions of the president: the West is out to get us, they cannot be trusted, so we should shun them. The Ministry of Foreign Affairs is generally outward-looking while the power structures in Russia tend to be more inward-looking. In Arctic affairs, the hardliners have been rewarded with increased security investments in the region. But the views of the Ministry of Foreign Affairs have determined action: strict compliance with the country's international obligations (which was Putin's more general foreign-policy outlook up to the Ukrainian crisis). The power structures are not necessarily against this, but they would probably be less concerned were Russia to pull out of the international club.

The same goes for the Barents Sea delimitation agreement. In the opinion of almost all the public commentators, it was a bad deal for Russia, and it was largely seen through the lens of East–West conflict. Furthermore, this is not just a debate that emerged with the conclusion of the delimitation line agreement – stories about Norwegian aggression in the Barents Sea have flourished for years. But action went against the (implicit) recommendations of these stories: Norway was to be trusted, according to the country's leadership, and a compromise was warranted. The accepted explanation in the Western foreign-policy literature is that Russia agreed to the delimitation line in order to further strengthen the status of the Law of the Sea in the Arctic.[33] By acting according to the principles of the Law of the Sea in establishing a delimitation line with a neighbouring state (following the guidelines of the Law of the Sea Convention to find *equitable* solutions, in practice a compromise), it would be harder for other states to challenge these principles in the establishment of the shelf's outer limits (i.e., the political costs would be higher the stronger the international norm). Interestingly, this explanation was not mentioned in my media material; slightly reminiscent, though, is the claim that the agreement was necessary in order to ensure Norwegian support for the future primacy of the existing Law of the Sea in the Arctic.

Similarly, the dominant narrative has not determined Russian action in the Barents Sea fisheries management. While the anti-Western narrative is clearly dominant in the public debate, Russian behaviour has been markedly accommodating. Russia is a constructive participant on the International Council for the Exploration of the Sea, the Northeast Atlantic Fisheries Commission and, not least, the Joint Norwegian–Russian Fisheries Commission. Even in the contested Svalbard zone, Russian authorities let the Norwegian Coast Guard inspect their vessels. They have also stopped protesting against Norwegian arrests of Russian vessels in the area.

Where does all this land us, in theoretical terms? Is my study a refutation of the claim that narrative equals identity equals (interest and) action? Of course not; reality is never that simple, nor is the theory. Narrative doesn't operate alone – a full explanation of a state's foreign policy requires a variety of theoretical tools, including, not least, a study of internal power struggles at the domestic level. Moreover, narrative theory's fundamental claim that narratives define (or at least contribute to defining) identities and that understanding who we are influences our understanding of what we want, can hardly be refuted. This is not only for epistemological reasons (How can it be falsified?), but also ontologically most IR theorists would arguably agree that identities (possibly determined narratively) can influence interest and action (even hardcore realists would agree; they just have their analytical focus elsewhere). The question is what explanatory *force* it has. And even constructivists, among whom narrative theorists are normally grouped, would stop short of claiming that foreign policy can be explained by discourse, identity or narrative alone. Realists are normally content to explain a few important things in international politics (often state security and international economy), and leave the rest of the (IR) field to others. Constructivists, on the other hand, have no intention of taking over the whole field, but of enriching it, filling in the nooks and crannies overlooked by the 'grand theories' and, perhaps, of modifying their conclusions.

The lack of apparent congruence between the dominant narratives and actual politics makes for two further comments. First, there is the temporal aspect: a narrative that maintains its force over time will not necessarily display a high 'impact' on action (here, foreign policy) incessantly – it will fluctuate. And the impact of an emergent narrative can be either immediate or gradual, if it has any effect at all. Second, and this is one of my main points: *acting (consciously or subconsciously) in opposition to a particular (e.g. dominant) constitutive story of oneself may imply acting consciously in defence of another (e.g. challenging or declining) constitutive story.* Not playing by the rules of anti-Western rhetoric in the Arctic, Putin has acted in defence of another story about Russia: we're not the backyard of Europe; we're a normal country.

In any event, actors in international politics are not, as Ringmar reminds us, faceless. That Russia is exactly Russia makes all the difference in the world.[34]

Between Past and Future

I have identified four metanarratives in the Russian public debate about the Arctic (see Chapter 5): 'Russia vs. the West', 'Russia and the Arctic', 'soil and soul' and 'fools and bad roads'. Most conspicuous is the story of NATO chasing Russia in the Arctic – fiercely, persistently and often surreptitiously. Othering westwards is omnipresent, but it grows in strength as the topics under discussion become more specialized and less highly profiled. In the general debate about the Arctic, with the imminent division of the Arctic continental shelf as the main issue, the Western states – especially Canada – are accused of acting improperly. The Russian response, however, is more righteous indignation than outright anger. When the Canadian Minister of Foreign Affairs said at a press conference that the Arctic war was now over, his Russian colleague corrected him. There had never been any war in the Arctic. 'Fellow journalists smiled, while the slightly bemused Canadian nodded his agreement.'[35] Othering of the West is more distinct, and possibly harsher, in the public debate about the Barents Sea delimitation agreement, but it is still milder than the internal othering of those in Moscow responsible for the agreement (primarily the Ministry of Foreign Affairs). Norway does what it can to take advantage of Russian incompetence – that is natural; it's Russia's President Medvedev who has committed the ultimate act of treachery. In the debate about the management of marine resources in the Barents Sea, the tone is even sharper. Norway conducts raids on behalf of NATO with the purpose of breaking Russia's neck. All forms of subterfuge are allowed; the rules are those of the intelligence world, not petty international law.

The anti-Western position reflected in the 'Russia vs. the West' narrative is taken for granted as a point of departure for further discussion, but it can be reproduced, nuanced or challenged. The point is, it is here that the story starts, whether the conclusion is in line with this narrative or in opposition to it. You can praise the Barents Sea delimitation agreement or Norwegian diligence in managing the marine resources for the good of future generations, but you first have to refer to the prevailing truth about NATO-Norway and its determination to get you, *and actively distance yourself from it*. The West is the axis around which Russian identity production revolves, just as it has been for centuries. But it is not a fixed entity. Everyday Russian chitchat about Scandinavian neighbours is a cheerful genre, a blissful mix of comedy's 'Aha!' moments and satire's playfulness. It is a place where you can throw out exaggerations, absurdities, whatever comes to mind in the situation, twist and turn established truths, laugh and provoke. It is a joyful commonplace for the cultivation of Russianness.

The Other is the West, loud and clear. But it is not a fixed entity; it changes with circumstance, evades definition. It's not actually so important who the Other is, it just has to be someone. And the West is always there to play with.

*

'Russia and the Arctic' represents a temporary low, between a glorious past and a promising future – 'fools and bad roads' are Russia's eternal fate. 'Russia and the Arctic' is the story of the Arctic as the shrine of Russia's national idea, where 'Arktika-2007' planted the titanium flag. It is a new political and spiritual continent, a promised land, Russia's cosmic destiny. Russia is the land with no limits, territorially or temporally. It stretches infinitely, it lasts eternally. The Russian landscape is wide, and so is the Russian soul – full of passion, generosity and recklessness. Russia is the ultimate expression of openness: openness of space and openness of heart – 'soil and soul'. The Arctic is all that; the Arctic is more Russian than Russia itself. The Arctic is the picture you present of yourself to the outside world, your wishful thinking: Russia as a great power that can do whatever it wants, wherever it wants. But the Arctic is also the monster returning your gaze in the mirror: rubbish, decay – hubris and escapism.

This is the 'fairy-tale life', the noisy existence of extremes incessantly flying through the air: brutally categorical, with nothing in-between. This is Russia the Janus-faced, the obscure, where reality is never what meets the eye, but the choices are few and deceitful. So you move along the plain, exhilarated and numb at the same time, always part of the intense Russian drama.

Notes

1 See for example 'Kak Putinu vernut Barentsevo more?', *Tikhookeanski Vestnik*, 13 February 2013.

2 Map created by Claes Lykke Ragner, Fridtjof Nansen Institute.

3 The Grey Zone agreement was in force one year at a time and renewed annually until the delimitation treaty came into effect in 2011, making the Grey Zone agreement redundant. Contrary to popular belief, the Grey Zone agreement worked perfectly from start to finish.

4 www.nrk.no, 27 April 2010.

5 For a detailed examination, see Øystein Jensen, 'The Barents Sea: Treaty between Norway and the Russian Federation concerning maritime delimitation and cooperation in the Barents Sea and the Arctic Ocean', *International Journal of Marine and Coastal Law* 26 (2011), pp. 151–68.

6 *Takogo kak Putin*, Poyushchie vmeste (pop group), 2002.

7 *Vzglyad*, 'Postepenno nas vydavyat ottuda', 27 October 2010.

8 *NordNews*, 'Vyacheslav Zilanov: – Rossiya budet vynuzhdena vesti rybolovstvo, kak eto delalos v 50–60-gody proshlogo veka', 23 November 2010.

9 The adjective *promyslovy* occurs quite frequently in Russian fisheries terminology. Strictly speaking it means 'catch' whereas in English we would say 'fishery'.

10 *Kommersant*, 'Rossiya i Norvegiya dogovorilis o razgranichenii morskikh prostranstv', 27 April 2010.

11 *Rossiyskaya gazeta*, 'More po-polam: Rossiya i Norvegiya dogovorilis o demarkatsii granits', 28 April 2010.

12 *Regnum*, 'Segodnya Norvegiya poluchit ot Rossii chast Barentseva morya', 15 September 2010.

13 *Argumenty i fakty*, 'Murmanski proryv: Glavy Norvegii i Rossii reshili problemu, desyatiletiya oslozhnyavshuyu otnosheniya', 22 September 2010.

14 *Regnum*, 'Dogovor o delimitatsii v Barentsevom more pozvolit Norvegii nas vyzhit: rossiyskie rybaki', 28 October 2010. *Vysoki stroyny blondin* is translated rather broadly as 'tall, strapping blonds' by Århus (2012). *Blondin* is the masculine form of the noun derived from the adjective 'blond' (the feminine form is *blondinka*). While his variant is flamboyant – I considered using it myself – I ended up with a more literal translation.

15 *NordNews*, 'Barentsevomorski proryv Lavrova-Stere – klon beringomorskogo proryva Beykera-Shevardnadze', 29 September 2010.

16 Around the turn of the millennium, Russian fishing vessels resumed the old Soviet practice of delivering their catches to transport ships at sea. Instead of going to Murmansk with the fish, however, these transport vessels now headed for other European countries: Denmark, the UK, the Netherlands, Spain and Portugal. Norway took the initiative to assess the possibility of overfishing, but the Russians were unwilling. Thereupon, Norway took unilateral measures to calculate overfishing in the Barents Sea, and presented figures that indicated Russian overfishing from 2002, rising to nearly 75 per cent of the total Russian quota in 2005, gradually declining to zero in 2009. The Russian side never accepted these figures, claiming they were deficient at best, and an expression of anti-Russian sentiments at worst. The International Council for the Exploration of the Sea (ICES), however, used them in their estimates of total catches in the Barents Sea during the 2000s, thereby providing these figures with some level of approval. For details see Geir Hønneland, *Making Fishery Agreements Work: Post-Agreement Bargaining in the Barents Sea* (Cheltenham, Edward Elgar, 2012), pp. 73–6.

17 *NordNews*, 'Podpisanie Dogovora o razgranichenii morskikh prostranstv vBarentsevom more i Severnom Ledovitom okeane prezhdevremennoe i pospeshnoe', 10 September 2010.
18 *NordNews*, 'Pritormozit ratifikatsiyu dogovora po razgranicheniyu morskikh prostranstv', 18 October 2010.
19 *Vzgljad*, 'Eto nash s Norvegiey perspektivny ogorod', 27 April 2010.
20 *NordNews*, 'Vyacheslav Zilanov: – Rossiya budet vynuzhdena vesti rybolovstvo, kak eto delalos v 50–60-gody proshlogo veka', 23 November 2010.
21 *Murmanski Vestnik*, 'Sosedski mir luchshe konfrontatsiy: V Moskve ponimayut trevogi rybakov i gotovy pomogat', 18 November 2010.
22 *Barents Observer*, 5 March 2009. Other reasons suggested for Yevdokimov's removal were economic circumstances and the fact that he had supported a mayoral candidate in Murmansk city who did not belong to the presidential party United Russia. Of course, different factors could have played together here.
23 See Hønneland, *Making Fishery Agreements Work: Post-Agreement Bargaining in the Barents Sea.*
24 When Zilanov talks about how much fish the Russians are 'losing', he is talking about everything caught on the western side of the new delimitation line – including in the Norwegian economic zone and the Svalbard zone – not just the part of the old, disputed area which became Norwegian with the signing of the treaty.
25 Erik Ringmar, 'Inter-textual relations: The quarrel over the Iraq War as conflict between narrative types', *Cooperation and Conflict* 41 (2006), pp. 403–21.
26 Jeffrey Mankoff, *Russian Foreign Policy: The Return of Great Power Politics* (Lanham, Rowman & Littlefield, 2012).
27 Geir Hønneland, *Russian Fisheries Management: The Precautionary Approach in Theory and Practice* (Leiden, Martinus Nijhoff, 2004); Anne-Kristin Jørgensen, 'Recent developments in the Russian fisheries sector', in E. W. Rowe (ed.), *Russia and the North* (Ottawa, University of Ottawa Press, 2009), pp. 87–106.
28 Cf. also President Medvedev's cheerful remark that in Russia conspiracy traditions are deep-rooted and well-practised.
29 Ringmar, 'Inter-textual relations: The quarrel over the Iraq War as conflict between narrative types'.
30 David Carr, *Time, Narrative, and History* (Bloomington, Indiana University Press, 1986), pp. 61–2.
31 Erik Ringmar, *Identity, Interest and Action: A Cultural Explanation of Sweden's Intervention in the Thirty Years War* (Cambridge, Cambridge University Press, 1996).
32 Ibid., p. 85.
33 See, for instance, Arild Moe, Daniel Buikema Fjærtoft and Indra Øverland, 'Space and timing: Why was the Barents Sea delimitation dispute resolved in 2010?', *Polar Geography* 34 (2011), pp. 145–62.
34 Erik Ringmar, 'The recognition game: Soviet Russia against the west', *Cooperation and Conflict* 37 (2002), pp. 115–36.
35 *Rossiyskaya gazeta*, [untitled], 29 May 2009.

CHAPTER 8

RUSSIA'S REVISED ARCTIC SEABED SUBMISSION

Øystein Jensen

Introduction

On 3 August 2015, the Russian Federation submitted to the Commission on the Limits of the Continental Shelf (the Commission), in accordance with Article 76, paragraph 8, of the UN Convention on the Law of the Sea (the LOS Convention),[1] information on the limits of the continental shelf beyond 200 nautical miles from the baselines from which the breadth of its territorial sea is measured in respect of the Arctic Ocean.[2] In accordance with Article 8 of Annex II to the LOS Convention, Russia's submission is a partially revised one. The area was included in the Russian continental shelf submission of 10 December 2001,[3] for which the Commission on 27 June 2002 adopted Recommendations.[4] Consideration of Russia's new and partly revised submission will be included on the provisional agenda of the Commission, and upon completion of its consideration the Commission will issue recommendations. Pursuant to the Rules of Procedure,[5] the Commission has published an Executive Summary of the 2015 submission, including all charts and coordinates. The Executive Summary provides a good basis for examining the main features of Russia's claim to an extended continental shelf in the Arctic Ocean, and prompts discussion of a number of substantive and procedural legal issues.

This chapter begins by examining the key aspects of Russia's revised Arctic seabed submission and by presenting the international legal framework, Article

---

This chapter is based on Øystein Jensen, 'Russia's revised Arctic seabed submission', *Ocean Development & International Law* 47/1 (2016), pp. 72–88.

76 of the LOS Convention, that applies to Russia with respect to establishing the outer limits of its continental shelf. The major legal issues related to the implementation of Article 76 in the Arctic Ocean are addressed. The chapter subsequently turns to Russia's revised submission and gives a description of the provisionally delineated outer limits. Procedural and substantive legal issues with respect to the submission are addressed, including how seafloor highs have been classified, and Russia's application of apparent sector lines in determining its outer limits. Next, some remarks on future maritime delimitation issues and the key role of the Commission in implementing Article 76 in the Arctic Ocean are offered. The chapter concludes with a summation of the key points and views on a number of issues.

Applicable Law

The truth about the 'race' to the North Pole and regarding the Arctic Ocean seafloor begins and ends with Article 76 of the LOS Convention. Basically, the issue is about one thing only: which part of the seabed, in legal terms, constitutes a state's continental shelf, and which does not? The question may sound easy, but Article 76 is a complex provision. It consists of ten paragraphs, most of which (paragraphs 2 to 8) relate exclusively to the outer limits of the continental shelf extending beyond 200 nautical miles from the baselines from which the breadth of the territorial sea is measured.

Under Article 76 of the LOS Convention, the basis for a coastal state to determine the outer limits of its continental shelf is either the natural prolongation of the land mass to the end of the continental margin or a distance of 200 nautical miles from the baselines from which the breadth of the territorial sea is measured.

When a state seeks to delineate the outer limits of its shelf beyond 200 nautical miles the detailed provisions of Article 76 come into play. The provision is designed to ensure that a coastal state is entitled to its continental shelf floor extending 'beyond its territorial sea throughout the natural prolongation of its land territory to the outer edge of the continental margin'.[6] Thus, the continental shelf can include all or part of the ocean floor considered by scientists to comprise the continental shelf, the continental slope, and the continental rise.

Beyond the complexities of the language of Article 76, which are described in detail in the following, the LOS Convention has introduced a specific process to be followed by coastal states respecting the outer limits of shelf areas beyond 200 nautical miles. The most distinctive element of this process concerns the specialized treaty body: the Commission.

The Commission was established by Annex II of the LOS Convention. To support its proposed outer limit of a shelf area beyond 200 nautical miles a coastal state has to present a submission to the Commission.[7] The Commission has twenty-one members, all of whom are scientists elected by the states that are parties to the convention.[8] According to Article 3 of Annex II to the LOS Convention, the Commission has two functions: first, to consider the data and other material submitted by coastal states concerning the outer limits of the continental shelf in areas where those limits extend beyond 200 nautical miles and make recommendations in accordance with Article 76; and second, to provide scientific and technical advice, if requested by the coastal state concerned, during the preparation of such data.

The process for establishing the outer limits beyond 200 nautical miles under the LOS Convention can be summarized as follows. After a coastal state has provisionally delineated the outer limits on the basis of the provisions of the LOS Convention, it is to submit information on these limits to the Commission. The Commission, following the procedure set out in Annex II to the LOS Convention, prepares recommendations for the coastal state on the establishment of the outer limits and submits these recommendations to the coastal state. The coastal state is to establish the outer limits in domestic law. If a coastal state disagrees with the recommendations of the Commission, it can, within a reasonable time, lodge a revised or new submission with the Commission.[9]

Specific Legal Issues Related to the Continental Margin Beyond 200 Nautical Miles in the Arctic Ocean

In implementing Article 76 in the Arctic Ocean, at least two substantive issues stand out. First is the criterion of natural prolongation. Second is the application of constraint lines for determining the maximum seaward extent of the continental shelf.

Natural prolongation

For any coastal state, the process of establishing the outer limits of its continental shelf under the LOS Convention begins by determining whether it is legally entitled to delineate the outer limits throughout the natural prolongation of its land territory to either the outer edge of the continental margin, or only to a distance of 200 nautical miles from the baselines. This process is described by the Commission in its Scientific and Technical Guidelines as the 'test of appurtenance'.[10]

The test of appurtenance may create some challenges for Russia in delineating the outer limits of its continental shelf in the Arctic Ocean. Notably, the criterion of natural prolongation is challenging from the perspective of treaty interpretation.

In Article 76, as reflected in the practice of both coastal states and the Commission, determining whether the legal continental shelf extends beyond 200 nautical miles is both a geological and geomorphological exercise. Geological measurements, such as sampling crust types and so on, can indicate whether the more seaward part of the seafloor is, or used to be, naturally linked to the seafloor near the coast. There is also the issue of geomorphology, that is, the form and structure of the seafloor. For instance, does the Lomonosov Ridge have features that indicate a present or former relationship with the Barents–Kara shelf? Possible discontinuities in the continental margin may arise as an acute problem in relation to the seafloor highs that extend across the Arctic Ocean. A cursory glance at charts and maps of the Arctic Ocean seafloor seems to reveal contours of ruptures separating the Lomonosov Ridge and the Alpha-Mendeleev from the Russian continent.

Maximum constraint lines and classification of seafloor highs

In delineating the outer limits of the continental shelf beyond 200 nautical miles in the Arctic, an issue that is problematic in the interpretation and application of Article 76 concerns whether the seafloor highs that stretch across the Arctic Ocean are submerged prolongations of the surrounding coastal state's land territory such that they can be considered as submarine ridges or submarine elevations.

This is a critical distinction, as the category of submarine elevation confers a more favourable maximum limitation on the extent of the continental shelf under the LOS Convention. According to Article 76, paragraphs 5 and 6, the continental shelf can extend to 350 nautical miles from the baselines on submarine ridges, but to either 350 nautical miles or 100 nautical miles beyond the 2,500-metre isobath on submarine elevations. If the seafloor highs in the Arctic are legally classified as elevations, there may not be any areas of the seafloor in the Central Arctic Ocean beyond the Gakkel Ridge (see later discussion) that are not under coastal state jurisdiction.[11]

The distinction between ridges and elevations is not clear in Article 76. Nor is it clear in the Scientific and Technical Guidelines of the Commission.[12] However, the term 'submarine elevations' in Article 76(6) is followed by the qualification 'that they 'are natural components of the continental margin, such as its plateaux, rises, caps, banks and spurs'. Thus, a basis for the distinction may lie in the fact that submarine elevations can be distinguished as separate features that are a more integral part of the prolongation of the land mass than ridges.[13] It is also argued that a basis for the distinction between ridges and elevations could lie in the geomorphological, geological, and tectonic relationship of the seafloor high to the land mass.[14]

The 2001 Russian Submission portrayed its continental shelf as extending all the way to the North Pole. The North Pole is, however, located beyond 350 nautical miles from the baselines of Russia, and hence, at a more seaward position than a continental shelf may extend on submarine ridges under the LOS Convention. Thus, the ridges must have been classified by Russia as submarine elevations. The same position is taken in Denmark's 2014 Submission.[15] Canada will also have to take a position on the issue of the classification of the seafloor highs in the central Arctic Ocean. For the United States, a non-party to the LOS Convention, the question is also relevant in relation to the Chukchi Plateau off the north coast of Alaska.[16] During the Third United Nations Conference on the Law of the Sea (UNCLOS III), the United States argued that seafloor highs such as the Chukchi Plateau were covered by the term 'submarine elevations', and thus not subject to the 350-nautical-mile limitation provided for under Article 76, paragraph 6, of the LOS Convention.[17]

General Description of the Russian Outer Limit

In the 2015 Partial Revised Russian Submission, the area of continental shelf beyond 200 nautical miles in the Arctic Ocean covers 1,191,347 square kilometres, that is, approximately 100,000 square kilometres more than in Russia's 2001 Submission.[18] Segments of the outer limits and the sea floor areas bounded by these limits – as shown in Figure 8.1 – are divided into six main areas.

In addition, one section of the Submission is devoted to describing the intersection of the last segment of the western outer limit and the delimitation line between Norway and Russia in the Barents Sea and the Arctic Ocean.[20] For the purpose of describing the outer limit in this chapter, however, it is appropriate to examine the outer limit in terms of three main areas.

Western outer limit

The western segment of the outer limit (Figure 8.2) bounds the area of the Southern Gakkel Ridge and the adjacent ocean area of the Nansen Basin. The Russian proposed outer limit of its shelf begins here from the agreed Norwegian–Russian endpoint of the bilateral maritime boundary between Norway and Russia in the Barents Sea and the Arctic Ocean. Article 2 of the 2010 Agreement describes how the endpoint of the delimitation line is to be established:

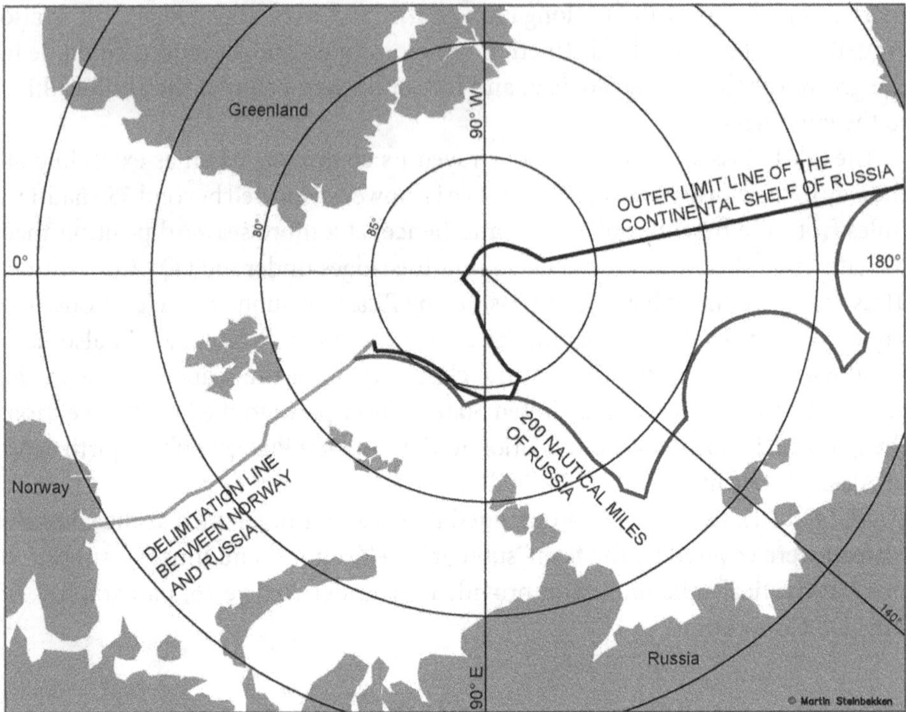

Figure 8.1 Outer limit line of Russia in the Arctic Ocean.[19]

> The terminal point of the delimitation line is defined as the point of intersection of a geodetic line drawn through the points 7 and 8 and the geodetic line connecting the easternmost point of the outer limit of the continental shelf of Norway and the westernmost point of the outer limit of the continental shelf of the Russian Federation, as established in accordance with Article 76 and Annex II of the Convention. (Translated from Norwegian.)

In its Submission, Russia draws a geodetic line from its westernmost outer limit fixed point to the geodetic line through coordinates 7 and 8 of the delimitation agreement. It is the point at which this geodetic line intersects the delimitation line that denotes the initial westernmost point of the outer limit of Russia's continental shelf in the Arctic Ocean. Thus, the outer limit of the Russian continental shelf begins in the west slightly to the south of the coordinates of point 8 set by the 2010 delimitation treaty between Norway and Russia.

The outer limit then runs eastward in the western Nansen Basin through seven fixed points constructed on the basis of both Article 76(4)(b) – sixty nautical

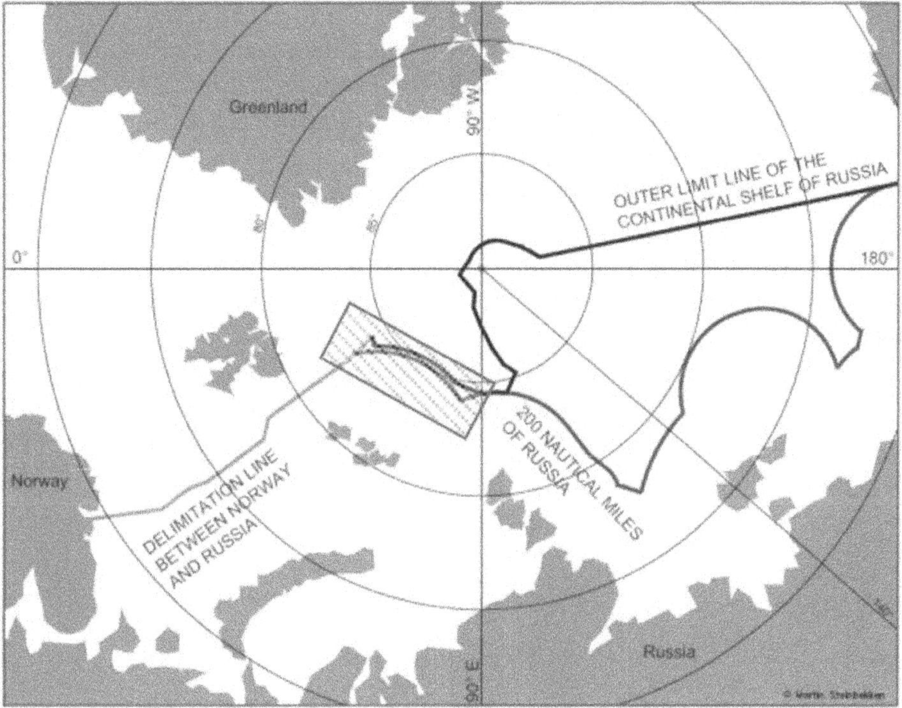

Figure 8.2 Western segment of the outer limit line.[21]

miles from the foot of the continental slope (the Hedberg formula) for one fixed point and Article 76(4)(a) – where the thickness of sedimentary rocks is at least 1 per cent of the shortest distance to the foot of the slope (the Gardiner formula) for the remaining six fixed points.

In this area, none of the fixed points comprising the line of the outer limit of the continental shelf goes beyond 350 nautical miles from the territorial sea baselines of Russia.

The outer limit ends in the eastern Nansen Basin on a line drawn along twenty-four fixed points coinciding with the outer limit of Russia's exclusive economic zone (EEZ). Therefore, in this section there is no area of continental shelf that extends beyond 200 nautical miles. A part of the seabed in this area within Russia's EEZ is undoubtedly deep ocean floor in terms of the LOS Convention.

Northern outer limit

The northern segment of the outer limit in the Revised Russian Submission is centred on the Lomonosov Ridge and bounds Russia's northernmost continental shelf areas, including the North Pole, and shelf areas to the North American side of the North Pole (Figure 8.3). The outer limit begins from a point on Russia's 200 nautical mile zone in the eastern Amundsen Basin and stretches northward through three fixed points constructed on the basis of the Gardiner formula (sediment thickness) and one fixed point calculated on the basis of the Hedberg formula (foot-of-the-slope plus 60), with the result of incorporating a portion of continental shelf area beyond 200 nautical miles not included in Russia's 2001 Submission. In accordance with paragraph 7 of Article 76, the fixed points are connected by straight lines not exceeding sixty nautical miles.

The outer limit continues through the central Amundsen Basin, where twenty fixed points are constructed on the basis of the Hedberg formula (foot-of-the-slope plus 60), while one fixed point is constructed on the basis of the Gardiner formula (sediment thickness). Noticeably, the outer limit in this

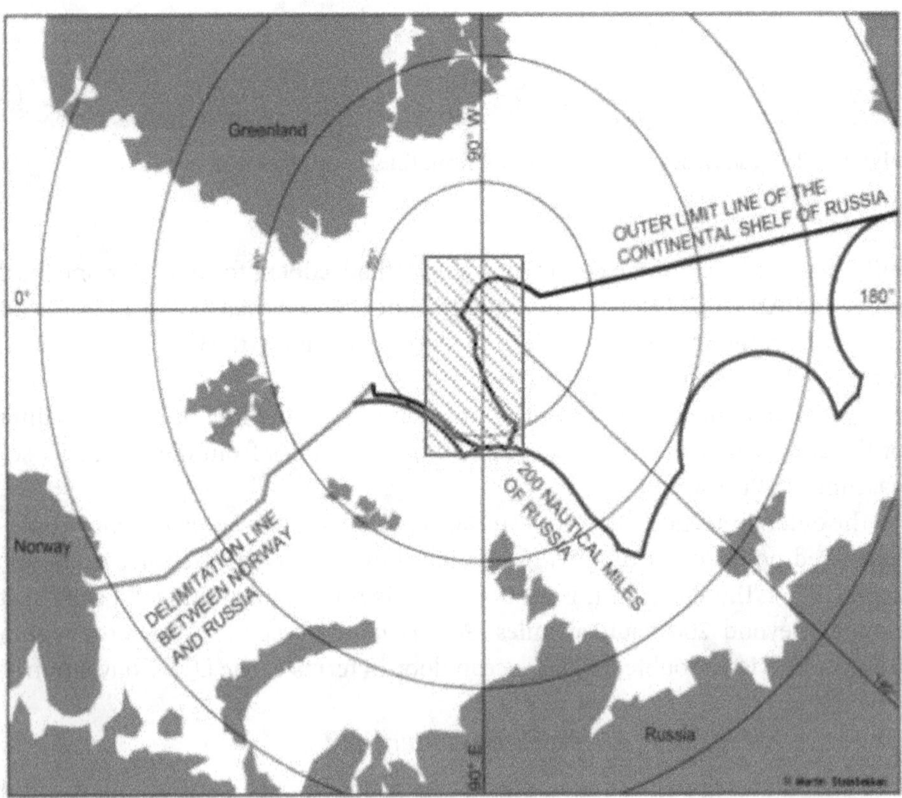

Figure 8.3 Northern segment of the outer limit line.[22]

seabed area is delineated at a slightly more landward position than was the case in Russia's 2001 Submission.

Then the final segment of the northern outer limit continues through fifty-two fixed points in the Amundsen Basin and the Makarov Basin, constructed on the basis of both the Gardiner and Hedberg formulas. This last segment of the outer limit connects to the northbound straight line described in the following and covers seabed areas not included in Russia's 2001 Submission. The continental shelf area enclosed by the Russian outer limits in the North Pole region can expect to be part of future maritime boundary negotiations involving Russia, Canada, and Denmark (Greenland).

In this region, parts of the Russian outer limits lie beyond 350 nautical miles from its territorial sea baselines. Russia is clearly of the view that the Lomonosov Ridge is a submarine elevation, naturally affiliated with the continental margin of Eurasia, which permits the use of the LOS Convention's most favourable constraint rule with respect to outer shelf limits (100 nautical miles from the 2,500-metre isobaths).

Eastern outer limit

The eastern outer limit of Russia's Submission bounds shelf areas within the Makarov Basin and the Mendeleev Rise (Figure 8.4). The proposed outer limit here runs along the line coinciding with the eastern so-called sector line of Russia in the Arctic Ocean.[23] Thus, the intermediate point of the outer limit of the shelf is the point where the straight line intersects the outer limit of Russia's EEZ in the Chukchi Sea. The outer limit (sector line) is an extension of the conditional delimitation line of the maritime spaces between Russia and the United States set out in the 1990 Agreement between the USA and the Soviet Union on the Maritime Boundary.[24] The northernmost part of this straight line outer limit in the eastern segment will potentially be the subject of delimitation negotiations between Russia, Canada and Denmark (Greenland).

Sections of the submitted outer limit lie beyond 350 nautical miles from Russia's territorial sea baselines. The delineation seems to be based on an affiliation of the Mendeleev Rise with the natural components of the Russian continental margin, with the elevation wording again being invoked.

Legal Assessment

Russia's Revised 2015 continental shelf Submission prompts a discussion of a number of legal questions.

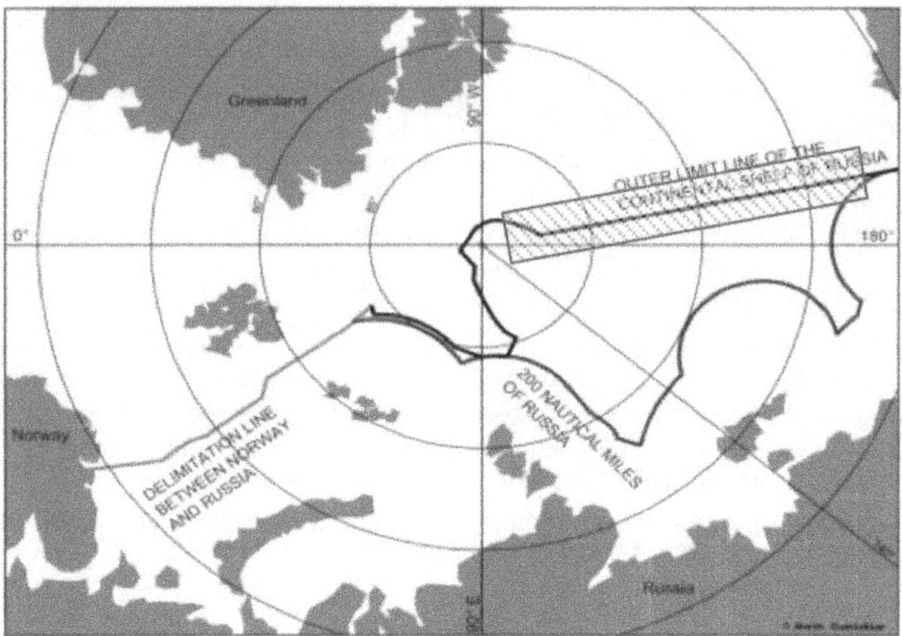

Figure 8.4 Eastern segment of the outer limit line.[25]

Procedural issues

Time and a revised submission

According to Article 8 of Annex II to the LOS Convention, following a difference of view between the Commission and a submitting state, the coastal state is to make a new or revised submission to the Commission 'within [a] reasonable time'. Russia received its Recommendations in 2002. The Partial Revised Submission was thus lodged thirteen years later. Does this constitute a reasonable time?

The wording of Article 8 of Annex II indicates that the coastal state should be granted a great deal of flexibility. While the preparatory work provides little help and state practice is sparse, as only four revised submissions have been submitted,[26] the relevant context is important. Article 4 of Annex II, which determines that the original submission is to be lodged no later than ten years after ratification, suggests that thirteen years to prepare and lodge a revised submission is too long to fall within the reasonable time limit.

However, in order to respond to the Commission's recommendations a coastal state may have to undertake new surveys of the seafloor. A revision may easily take at least as long as the preparation of the original submission. Russia's Revised Submission seems to be an example of this. In 2002, the Commission not only advised Russia that based on the submitted information, the Lomonosov Ridge and the Alpha-Mendeleev Ridge Complex could not be considered submarine elevations under the LOS Convention,[27] but more generally advised that Russia, in making revisions to its proposed outer limit, should be more scrupulous in following the Commission's Scientific and Technical Guidelines.[28] The Commission basically urged Russia to go back to the drawing board. With regard to the Arctic Ocean, the additional constraints are caused by natural conditions, with the presence of ice being but one complicating factor.

Purposive considerations also suggest that coastal states should have great flexibility with regard to the time limit. The purpose of the Convention's continental shelf regime is to attain a correct interpretation and application of Article 76. It serves neither a coastal state nor other states if the former must run against the clock to meet a deadline to delineate its outer limits. The argument is especially pertinent with respect to the Arctic Ocean, where any commercial exploitation of the continental shelf's resources lies far off into the future. Both Russia and other states are better served by Russia taking enough time to fully prepare its submission. This must be reflected in the legal interpretation of what a reasonable time means in the context of Annex II.

When will the partial revised submission be processed by the Commission?

Rule 51, paragraph 4 ter, of the Rules of Procedure of the Commission reads: 'The submissions shall be queued in the order they are received.'[29] Since the Russian Submission is a revised one, at issue is whether it will move to the front of the queue of the submissions lodged. Neither the LOS Convention nor the Commission's Rules of Procedure address this issue specifically. At its twenty-sixth session in 2010, however, the Commission discussed the order in which revised submissions would be considered were the need to arise.[30] They decided that any revised submission in the future would be considered as a priority notwithstanding the queue. This decision was followed respecting the revised submission made by Barbados in 2011[31] and Russia's resubmission for the Sea of Okhotsk in 2013.[32] At the time of writing no information is available concerning the processing of the two other resubmissions to the Commission – that of Brazil, made on 15 April 2015, and of Russia with respect to the Arctic. There seems to be no reason, however, why the Commission should deviate from its 2010 decision. Russia's resubmission will thus probably be considered before Denmark's 2014 Arctic Submission. This is something Russia expects.[33]

Changes in the membership of the Commission

Having received Russia's Submission in 2001, the Commission established a subcommission as per Article 5 of Annex II to the LOS Convention and Section

X of the (current) Rules of Procedure.[34] Seven members of the Commission were nominated to serve on the subcommission and, in order to ensure the highest possible integrity of the proceedings, the members of the Commission who were nationals of a state with opposite or adjacent coasts, or of a state that might have a dispute with Russia regarding the submission, were not selected as members of the subcommission.[35] The following commissioners were on the subcommission: Alexandre Tagore Medeiros de Albuquerque, Lawrence Folajimi Awosika, Galo Carrera Hurtado, Peter F. Croker, Karl H. F. Hinz, Iain C. Lamont and Yong Ahn Park. The subcommission elected Hurtado as its chairperson, Hinz as its vice-chairperson, and Croker as the rapporteur.

The Commission's practice is not to dissolve a subcommission once established. It continues to exist, if only on paper. As of 2015, however, only Awosika and Park are currently members of the Commission; therefore, even though the subcommission of 2001 has been in operation for thirteen years, many vacancies have to be filled and its composition will be very different from the original. This is the inevitable result of the LOS Convention's system of five-year terms for commissioners and that they are not necessarily re-elected. The subcommission tasked with examining Russia's Partial Revised Submission for the Sea of Okhotsk[36] also had vacancies to fill.[37]

Substantive Issues

The Lomonosov Ridge and the Alpha-Mendeleev Rise

In its 2001 Submission, Russia clearly took the view that the Lomonosov Ridge and the Alpha-Mendeleev Rise were submarine elevations under paragraph 6 of Article 76 and, accordingly, that these seafloor highs fit the wording 'natural components of the continental margin, such as its plateaux, rises, caps, banks and spurs'.

In its Recommendations, the Commission expressed the view that based on the evidence, neither the Lomonosov Ridge nor the Alpha-Mendeleev Rise could be considered a submarine elevation under the Convention.[38] In the Executive Summary of its Revised Submission, Russia describes the main conclusion drawn by the Commission in 2002 as indeed indicative of the 'state of scientific knowledge' at the time.[39] Russia noted that the original submission was based on seismic surveys carried out before 1990 from drifting ice stations, and that modern technology and extensive activity support the Russian Revised Submission. One figure in the Executive Summary shows clearly the vast differences of seismic reflections received on multichannel surveys before 2002 – which served as the basis for the 2001 submission – and those received between 2012 and 2015 – serving as the basis of the resubmission.[40]

The notable finding of Russia's recent surveys of the Arctic Ocean seabed is that the bathymetric and seismic surveys demonstrate 'a natural morphological prolongation without traces of any interruption' of the shallow shelves of the East Siberian and Chukchi Seas to the Lomonosov Ridge and the Mendeleev Rise.[41] Thus, Russia asserts that it is now 'clearly' demonstrated that the Lomonosov Ridge, the Mendeleev Rise, the Chukchi Rise, and separating them, the Podvodnikov Basin and the Chukchi Basin form a single consolidated block of continental crust, which is elevated to 1.5 kilometres above the level of the deep seabed of the Canada and Amundsen Basins.[42] From Russia's perspective, the seafloor highs, including the Lomonosov Ridge and the Mendeleev-Alpha Rise, are components of the continental margin of the Arctic Ocean and constitute a natural prolongation of the continental margin of Eurasia. Noticeably, a new term has been introduced in the Russian Revised Submission to describe how these seabed areas are both natural prolongations and submarine elevations according to Article 76, paragraph 6, of the LOS Convention: 'Complex of the Central Arctic Submarine Elevations'.[43] What is considered deep seabed, however, is the Gakkel Ridge, the geomorphology of which seems to be completely different (Figure 8.5).

In terms of origin and tectonic evolution, Russia claims that the entire area of the Complex of the Central Arctic Submarine Elevations comprises structures of rifting extension and expansion of the earth's crust, with an approximate north–south orientation, that is, similar to the directions mapped on the shallow shelves adjacent to the Russian Arctic territories. Notably, Russia begins from the premise in the Commission's Scientific and Technical Guidelines, under which both the geological crust type (paragraph 7.2.9) and the formation processes of continental margins and growth of continents (paragraph 7.3.1) are relevant qualifiers in the classification of ridges and elevations in paragraph 6 of Article 76.

Regarding crust types, it appears that the seismic sounding lines run by Russia on the Arctic seabed have not allowed for any reliable determination of the crust types.[44] With respect to formation processes of continental margins and growth of continents, however, Russia asserts that it has developed a reliable geological model of the evolution of the Arctic Basin.[45]

The 2015 Revised Submission emphasizes that the mapping of the seafloor since 2002 does not confirm the viewpoint of the Commission's recommendations that the Mendeleev-Alpha Rise was formed by volcanic activity creating an oceanic plateau built on the oceanic crust of the Canada Basin. Rather, a three-stage model is described for the formation of the Arctic Basin, which demonstrates submarine elevations and not ridges. First, after the opening of the Canada Basin during the Late Jurassic–Early Cretaceous, the Complex of the Central Arctic Submarine Elevations became part of the Siberian shelf, and thus a natural component of

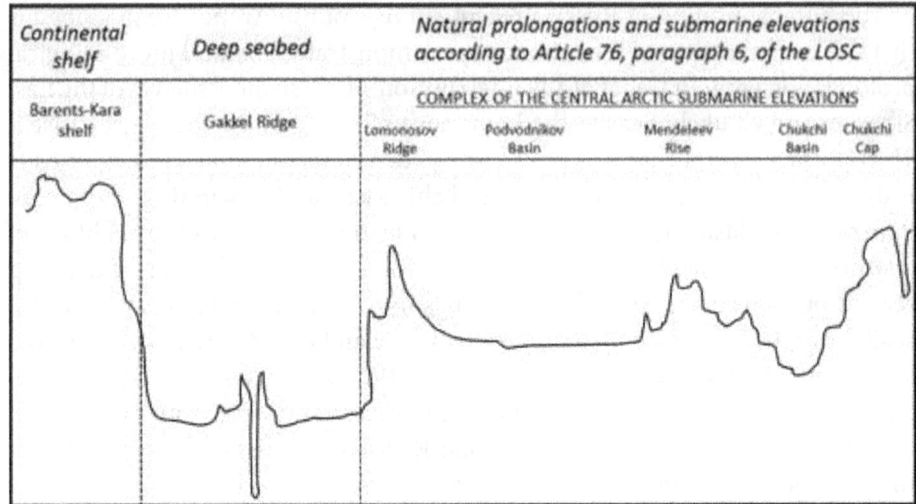

Figure 8.5 Scheme of elements in the seabed areas in the Russian submission.[46]

the Chukchi–Siberian continental margin.[47] Second, submarine elevations were created following rift stretching, which occurred from the continental crust from the Lomonosov Ridge and eastwards. This rifting and stretching led to the subsiding of the Podvodnikov Basin and the Chukchi Basin. Third, the opening of the Eurasian Basin as a result of spreading along the Gakkel Ridge led to the Lomonosov Ridge splitting off and moving away from the Barents–Kara shelf. The rifting then continued in the Amerasian Basin, within the Chukchi Borderland and the Mendeleev-Alpha Rise, and in the Chukchi and Podvodnikov Basins. Whether the Commission is convinced by this explanation remains to be seen.

Northbound extension of the shelf

With regard to the seaward extension of the outer limit line proposed by Russia, there are two aspects to be noted. First, as compared to Russia's 2001 Submission, the outer limit extends past the North Pole and south in the direction of the Greenlandic and North American continents. In the 2001 Submission, the North Pole was the northern geographical maximum of Russia's outer limit.

It is difficult to understand why Russia has defined a larger shelf area towards the North American continent. The question is whether the Lomonosov Ridge would allow the outer limit to be extended even farther in the direction of the Greenlandic and Canadian continents, or, phrased differently, why is the outer limit established only marginally beyond the North Pole? Here, it is helpful to make reference to Denmark's 2014 continental shelf Submission, in which it was proposed that the shelf related to the Greenlandic continent extended across the Arctic basin, stopping only at the outer limit of Russia's EEZ.[48] According to Denmark, there are areas seaward of Russia's proposed outer limit that are continental shelf under the LOS Convention. Judging from Denmark's Submission, it appears that Russia could have extended its outer limit as far as Greenland's and Canada's respective 200-nautical-mile limits.

There are several possible explanations for the discrepancy in Russia's and Denmark's Submissions with respect to the geographical extension of the continental shelf. First, it may be that Russia did not collect scientific evidence to underpin an extension of the shelf in this area. Second, Russia may simply have found it opportune not to delineate the outer limit at a more seaward position. A coastal state has no obligation to maximize its shelf area. The rationale behind the decision may thus be the result of political considerations. It is worth noting that the shelf area beyond the proposed Russian outer limit most likely would end up on the Danish/Canadian side of any future delimitated boundaries based on equidistance,[49] so surveying this part of the seafloor might have been seen as of little value. A third explanation may be that Russia believes that the continental shelf does not extend beyond its proposed outer limit.

The 'sector' line

The proposed outer limit in the easternmost segment of Russia's extended continental shelf merits special attention. In this area – 'Area VII' in the Russian Submission – the outer limit is a straight line coinciding with the so-called sector line of Russia in the Arctic Ocean.[50] As already noted, the segment is drawn along the conditional delimitation line between Russia and the United States. As noted in Article 2 of the 1990 Agreement, the maritime boundary extends north along the 168°58′37″ W across the Bering Strait and Chukchi Sea into the Arctic Ocean as far as permitted under international law.[51]

Based on the Executive Summary, Russia has not used Article 76 to delineate the outer limit of its shelf in this area. One question that arises is whether the sector line or the 1990 delimitation is a basis for delineating the outer limit of the continental shelf beyond 200 nautical miles in accordance with Article 76 of the LOS Convention.

The answer is no. Having ratified the LOS Convention, Russia has removed any legal support that might have existed for a pie-shaped section of the Arctic Ocean extending from its eastern and western borders to the North Pole based on a sector principle argument. It is, therefore, surprising to see Russia now refer to the sector approach in the 2015 Submission, and even more so considering that sector lines were not used for the other segments of the outer limit or in the maritime delimitation with Norway.[52]

Regarding the Delimitation Agreement between Russia and the United States, states can and do delimit shelf areas beyond 200 nautical miles prior to implementing Article 76.[53] States are free to use sectors for such delimitation. But a delimitation agreement in itself does not indicate whether or not a legal continental shelf exists. Separate rules of the LOS Convention determine what in legal terms a continental shelf is (Article 76) and how a state's shelf is to be delimited if it overlaps with that of another state (Article 83). Thus, notwithstanding a preceding delimitation agreement, the seafloor area beyond 200 nautical miles to which an agreement applies must be surveyed to affirm the existence of a legal continental shelf. This appears to have been understood in the 1990 US–Soviet Union Agreement, where it states in Article 2, 'into the Arctic Ocean as far as permitted under international law'.[54]

'International law' in Article 2 refers to the definition of continental shelf in Article 76 and corresponding rules of customary international law.[55] Based on the 2015 Executive Summary, Russia has done nothing to clarify how 'far' the delimitation line between the two states extends into the Arctic Ocean. The eastern segment of the Russian outer limit is nothing more than a provisional delimitation line, with no scientific evidence to indicate whether a continental shelf exists in this area or not. It will not be possible for the Commission to evaluate and make recommendations on an outer limit in this area.

Future Maritime Delimitations

If the Commission finds that a continental shelf exists along the seafloor highs and emerges at the opposite side of the Arctic Basin and in the direction of the land masses of North America and Greenland, this will still be only half the story. As noted, Denmark has made a Submission in which the continental shelf areas portrayed overlap with those in Russia's Submission.[56] Canada will undoubtedly follow suit, though details of Canada's submission have not yet been made public. In time, the United States will also finalize the establishment of the outer limits of its continental shelf in the Arctic. Three of the coastal states may have a continental shelf that extends throughout the Arctic basin, overlapping with that of Russia. And continental shelf areas – if they are demonstrated to exist and overlap – may need to be delimited.

Russia may have to negotiate boundary agreements with two of its Arctic neighbours. This eventuality is clearly anticipated in the 2015 Revised Submission. Mention is made of delimitation disputes that have been resolved, including the 2010 Norwegian–Russian Delimitation Agreement[57] and the 1990 Agreement with the United States.[58]

Russia, in accordance with paragraph 2 of Annex 1 of the Rules of Procedure of the Commission,[59] has informed the Commission of the presence of two unresolved maritime areas in the Arctic Ocean. One area is in the Amundsen Basin, on the Lomonosov Ridge and in the Makarov and Podvodnikov Basins with Denmark (Greenland).[60] The continental shelf areas in Denmark's 2014 Submission north of Greenland overlap with shelf areas included in Russia's Revised Submission. However, Russia and Denmark have held talks on the issue and have agreed on procedures for moving forward.[61] A similar understanding has been reached by Russia and Canada regarding areas in the Arctic Ocean included in Russia's revised submission, that is, the Makarov Basin and on the Mendeleev Rise,[62] which may also be covered in the Canadian submission. The Commission has been requested to consider the Russian submission without prejudice towards unresolved delimitation disputes concerning the continental shelf.

The Fundamental Role of the Commission: Some Procedural Challenges

Under the LOS Convention, the Commission's role is crucial to the process of a coastal state delineating the outer limits of its continental shelf beyond 200 nautical miles. The Commission is not an adversarial institution. Judging from its composition, it is to be a scientific body, but such nomenclature does not indicate a true picture. The Commission must interpret and apply Article 76 respecting each submission. It frequently relies on its Scientific and Technical Guidelines, which are clearly interpretations of the LOS Convention. Even though establishing which part of the seafloor is part of a state's legal continental shelf (and which is not) is ultimately determined by coastal states and not based on the views of the Commission; nevertheless, the recommendations have important legal effects, notably as interpretations of Article 76 as understood under the rules on treaty interpretation in international law.[63]

The role of the Commission is further reinforced by the interests of other states in the Arctic region. Legally, while the discussion is about unilateral limits, the continental shelf in the Arctic is subject to wider interests, driven by the likelihood of petroleum deposits. Canada and Denmark (Greenland) will be keeping a watchful eye on the handling by the Commission of Russia's Submission and the Commission's recommendations. The Commission will likely also attract broader public interest, as indeed have all Arctic matters in recent years.

A process issue of importance raised by the Russian Arctic Submission concerns the assessment by the Commission of the evidence. It is up to the coastal state to demonstrate, through its submission, the existence of a continental shelf beyond 200 nautical miles. Under the LOS Convention, only the coastal state may provide the Commission with scientific data and information on the limits of its continental shelf.[64]

The Commission is to assess the evidence in the coastal state's submission, including hypotheses on the geological evolution of different parts of the seafloor. What standard of proof is to apply to statements and hypotheses in a state's submission? For instance, has the Lomonosov Ridge split off and moved away from the Barents–Kara shelf? In law, this is a point of fact: that is, a question to be answered by reference to facts and evidence and inferences arising from those facts. Such questions of fact are amenable to proof or disproof by reference to a certain standard of proof. The LOS Convention and the Rules of Procedure of the Commission are, however, silent on the sufficiency of the evidence a coastal state must present. Put a different way, is what is necessary a preponderance of the evidence, meaning that the coastal state has to demonstrate that its contentions are more likely to be true than false? Is a higher standard of proof required? Is evidence beyond a reasonable doubt required, meaning that the commissioners in making up their minds should have no reasonable doubts over whether what the coastal state asserts is correct? The complexity of the Arctic Ocean seafloor brings such issues to the fore.

Conclusion

Russia's much-discussed foray into the Arctic Ocean has nothing to do with occupying or annexing new territory. Neither is it the expression of a fading superpower's expansionist foreign policy. In seeking to show that the seafloor in the Arctic Ocean is the natural prolongation of its land mass – its continental shelf in the sense of the LOS Convention – Russia has observed and applied the relevant international law.

Certain substantive matters are, nevertheless, put to the test, including the concept of natural prolongation and the classification of seafloor highs into the categories of Article 76, paragraph 6, of the LOS Convention. Also with respect to the easternmost seabed area (Chukchi Sea), where it seems as if Article 76 has not been applied by Russia, questions may arise. Based on the Executive Summary, the Revised Submission appears to be founded on more extensive scientific documentation than the 2001 Submission.

The new Submission will, in line with Commission practice, be put at the front of a long and growing queue of first-time submissions. The Commission's recommendations may be forthcoming in not too many years, and before the Commission issues recommendations respecting Denmark's 2014 Submission.

The scientific complexity of Russia's 2015 continental shelf Submission may be the biggest challenge for the Commission. Russia's Revised Submission goes back millions of years and explores the theories of the geological origins of the different parts of the Arctic seafloor. The uncertainty regarding the proof/evidence of facts to be utilized by the Commission is one of the challenges raised by the 2015 Russian Revised Submission.

Notes

1 United Nations Convention on the Law of the Sea, 10 December 1982, 1833 UNTS (hereinafter LOS Convention).

2 Russian Federation, 'Partial Revised Submission of the Russian Federation to the Commission on the Limits of the Continental Shelf in Respect of the Continental Shelf in the Arctic Ocean', Executive Summary (2015). Available at http://www.un.org/depts/los/clcs_new/clcs_home.htm (accessed 24 April 2018).

3 Russian Federation, 'Russian Federation Submission to the Commission on the Limits of the Continental Shelf', Executive Summary (2001). Available at http://www.un.org/depts/los/clcs_new/clcs_home.htm (accessed 24 April 2018).

4 See: Commission on the Limits of the Continental Shelf (CLCS), 'Statement by the Chair on the Progress of Work', Doc. CLCS/34, 1 July 2002, paragraph 33. Available at http://www.un.org/depts/los/clcs_new/clcs_home.htm (accessed 24 April 2018). For an overview of the 2001 Russian Submission, see David Colson, 'The delimitation of the outer continental shelf between neighbouring states', *American Journal of International Law* 97 (2003), pp. 91–107, pp. 97–9.

5 Commission on the Limits of the Continental Shelf (CLCS), 'Rules of Procedure of the Commission on the Limits of the Continental Shelf', Doc. CLCS/40/Rev.1, 17 April 2008. Available at http://www.un.org/depts/los/clcs_new/clcs_home.htm (accessed 24 April 2018).

6 LOS Convention, Article 76, paragraph 1.

7 Ibid., Article 76(8).

8 Ibid., Article 2 of Annex II.

9 Ibid., Article 8 of Annex II.

10 Commission on the Limits of the Continental Shelf (CLCS), 'Scientific and Technical Guidelines', Doc. CLCS/11, 13 May 1999, paragraph 2.2. Available at http://www.un.org/depts/los/clcs_new/clcs_home.htm (accessed 24 April 2018).

11 See Ron Macnab, 'The outer limits of the continental shelf in the Arctic Ocean', in M. Nordquist, J. N. Moore and Tomas Heidar (eds), *Legal and Scientific Aspects of Continental Shelf Limits* (Hague, Martinus Nijhoff, 2004), pp. 301–11, p. 302.

12 CLCS, 'Scientific and Technical Guidelines', paragraphs 7.2. and 7.3.

13 See International Law Association, *Legal Issues of the Outer Continental Shelf*, Second Report (2006), Toronto Conference, pp. 4–7. Available at http://www.ila-hq.org/ (accessed 24 April 2018).

14 Harald Brekke and Philip Symonds, 'The ridge provisions of article 76 of the UN Convention on the Law of the Sea', in Nordquist, Moore and Heidar (eds), *Legal and Scientific Aspects of Continental Shelf Limits*, pp. 169–200, p. 187.

15 Denmark, 'Partial Submission to the Commission on the Limits of the Continental Shelf – The Northern Continental Shelf of Greenland', Executive Summary (2014). Available at http://www.un.org/depts/los/clcs_new/clcs_home.htm (accessed 24 April 2018).

16 On the relationship between the substantive definition of the continental shelf in Article 76 of the LOS Convention and US policy with respect to delineation of the continental shelf beyond 200 nautical miles, see generally J. Ashley Roach and Robert W. Smith, 'Policy governing the continental shelf of the United States of America', in J. A. Roach and R. W. Smith (eds), *Excessive Maritime Claims* (Hague, Martinus Nijhoff, 2012), p. 188.

17 Third United Nations Conference on the Law of the Sea, Official Records, Vol. VIII, United Nations (1977), p. 36: The United States understands that features such as the Chukchi plateau and its component elevations, situated to the north of Alaska, are covered by this exemption, and thus not subject to the 350 mile limitation set forth in paragraph 6. Because of the potential for significant oil and gas reserves in the Chukchi plateau, it is important to recall the US statement made to this effect on April 3, 1980 during a Plenary session of the Third United Nations Conference on the Law of the Sea, which has never given rise to any contrary interpretation. In the statement, the United States representative expressed support for the provision now set forth in Article 76(6) on the understanding that it is recognized that features such as the Chukchi plateau situated to the north of Alaska and its component elevations cannot be considered a ridge and are covered by the last sentence of paragraph 6.

18 Russian Federation, 'Partial Revised Submission of the Russian Federation to the Commission on the Limits of the Continental Shelf in Respect of the Continental Shelf in the Arctic Ocean', p. 20.

19 Map created by Martin Steinbekken.

20 Norwegian Ministry of Foreign Affairs, 'Treaty between Norway and the Russian Federation Concerning Maritime Delimitation and Cooperation in the Barents Sea and the Arctic Ocean' (Oslo, Norwegian Ministry of Foreign Affairs, 2010), reprinted in *Overenskomster med fremmede stater*, 2011, p. 575 and *Law of the Sea Bulletin*, vol. 77 (2012), p. 24. See Geir Ulfstein and Tore Henriksen, 'Maritime delimitation in the Arctic: The Barents Sea Treaty', *Ocean Development & International Law* 42 (2011), pp. 1–21, and; Øystein Jensen, 'The Barents Sea: Treaty between Norway and the Russian Federation concerning maritime delimitation and cooperation in the Barents Sea and the Arctic Ocean', *International Journal of Marine and Coastal Law* 26 (2011), pp. 151–68.

21 Map created by Martin Steinbekken.

22 Map created by Martin Steinbekken.

23 The sector line was approved by Decree of the Presidium of the Supreme Council of the USSR No. 8908, dated 21 February 1979, and provided for 'making clarification to presentation in the Soviet maps of the eastern boundary of polar domains of the USSR in the Arctic Ocean'. See Russian Federation, 'Partial Revised Submission of the Russian Federation to the Commission on the Limits of the Continental Shelf in Respect of the Continental Shelf in the Arctic Ocean', p. 29.

24 United States of America and Russian Federation, 'Agreement between the United States and the Soviet Union on the Maritime Boundary', 1 June 1990, in *International*

Legal Materials, 29 (1990), p. 941. See generally: Robert W. Smith, 'United States–Russia maritime boundary', in G. H. Blake (ed.), *Maritime Boundaries* (New York, Routledge, 1994), p. 91.

25 Map created by Martin Steinbekken.

26 It took Russia eleven years to make a Revised Submission with respect to the Sea of Okhotsk after having received the Commission's recommendations in 2002 (Recommendations were adopted on 27 June 2002, and the Resubmission was lodged on 28 February 2013). Russian Federation, 'Revision of the Partial Submission to Commission on the Limits of the Continental Shelf Related to the Sea of Okhotsk', Executive Summary (2013). It took Brazil eight years to lodge a Partial Revised Submission in respect of the Brazilian Southern Region (Recommendations were adopted on 4 April 2007, and the Resubmission was lodged on 10 April 2015). It took Barbados only one year to make a Revised Submission with respect of its seabed areas beyond 200 nautical miles (Recommendations were adopted on 15 April 2010, and the Resubmission was lodged on 25 July 2011).
Respecting the submissions and recommendations, see http://www.un.org/depts/los/clcs_new/clcs_home.htm (accessed 24 April 2018).

27 Russian Federation, 'Partial Revised Submission of the Russian Federation to the Commission on the Limits of the Continental Shelf in Respect of the Continental Shelf in the Arctic Ocean', p. 5.

28 A short summary of the 2002 Recommendations as it relates to the Arctic Ocean is contained in the 'Report of the UN Secretary-General to the Fifty-Seventh Session of the UN General Assembly under the agenda item "Oceans and the Law of the Sea"', Doc. A/57/57/Add.1, 8 October 2002, paragraph 41.

29 CLCS, 'Rules of Procedure of the Commission on the Limits of the Continental Shelf'.

30 Commission on the Limits of the Continental Shelf (CLCS), 'Statement by the Chairperson of the Commission on the Limits of the Continental Shelf on the Progress of Work in the Commission', Doc. CLCS/68, 17 September 2010, paragraph 57. Available at http://www.un.org/depts/los/clcs_new/clcs_home.htm (accessed 24 April 2018).

31 Commission on the Limits of the Continental Shelf (CLCS), 'Progress of Work of the Commission on the Limits of the Continental Shelf – Statement by the Chairperson', Doc. CLCS/72, 16 September 2011, paragraph 49. Available at http://www.un.org/depts/los/clcs_new/clcs_home.htm (accessed 24 April 2018).

32 Commission on the Limits of the Continental Shelf (CLCS), 'Progress of Work of the Commission on the Limits of the Continental Shelf – Statement by the Chairperson', Doc. CLCS/80, 24 September 2013, paragraph 38. Available at http://www.un.org/depts/los/clcs_new/clcs_home.htm (accessed 24 April 2018).

33 Russian Ministry of Foreign Affairs, 'Comment by the Information and Press Department on Russia's application for Arctic shelf expansion', 4 August 2015. Available at http://en.mid.ru/en/%20web/guest/foreign_policy/news/-/asset_publisher/cKNonkJE02Bw/content/id/1633205 (accessed 24 April 2018).

34 The Rules of Procedure of the Commission applicable at the time of Russia's Submission were contained in 'Internal procedure of the subcommission of the Commission on the Limits on the Continental Shelf', Doc. CLCS/L.12, issued 25 May 2001. Available at http://www.un.org/depts/los/clcs_new/clcs_home.htm (accessed 24 April 2018).

35 See generally: Commission on the Continental Shelf (CLCS), 'Statement by the Chairperson of the Commission on the Limits of the Continental Shelf on the Progress of Work in the Commission', Doc. CLCS/32, 12 April 2002. Available at http://www.un.org/depts/los/clcs_new/clcs_home.htm (accessed 24 April 2018).
36 Russian Federation, 'Revision of the Partial Submission to Commission on the Limits of the Continental Shelf Related to the Sea of Okhotsk'.
37 CLCS, 'Progress of Work of the Commission on the Limits of the Continental Shelf – Statement by the Chairperson', paragraphs 33–34.
38 Russian Federation, 'Partial Revised Submission of the Russian Federation to the Commission on the Limits of the Continental Shelf in Respect of the Continental Shelf in the Arctic Ocean', p. 5.
39 Ibid., p. 12.
40 Ibid., p. 15.
41 Ibid., p. 13.
42 Ibid.
43 Ibid., p. 13.
44 Ibid., p. 17.
45 Ibid.
46 Created by Øystein Jensen, FNI.
47 Russian Federation, 'Partial Revised Submission of the Russian Federation to the Commission on the Limits of the Continental Shelf in Respect of the Continental Shelf in the Arctic Ocean', p. 18.
48 Denmark, 'Partial Submission to the Commission on the Limits of the Continental Shelf – The Northern Continental Shelf of Greenland'.
49 On maritime claims and boundaries in the Arctic region, see generally Ted L. McDorman and Clive Schofield, 'Maritime limits and boundaries in the Arctic Ocean: Agreements and disputes', in L. C. Jensen and G. Hønneland (eds.), *Handbook of the Politics of the Arctic* (Cheltenham, Edward Elgar Publishing, 2015), pp. 207–26.
50 On doctrinal views and State practice of the Soviet Union and Russia relating to the sector principle, see generally Leonid Timtchenko, 'The Russian Arctic sectoral concept: Past and present', *Arctic* 50 (1997), pp. 29–35.
51 United States of America and Russian Federation, 'Agreement between the United States and the Soviet Union on the Maritime Boundary'.
52 'Treaty between Norway and the Russian Federation Concerning Maritime Delimitation and Cooperation in the Barents Sea and the Arctic Ocean'.
53 States are not obliged to enter into a delimitation agreement within a specific time frame and there is practice that states delimit shelf areas beyond 200 nautical miles before proceeding to delineate the outer limits. See Øystein Jensen, 'Maritime boundary delimitation beyond 200 nautical miles: The international judiciary and the Commission on the Limits of the Continental Shelf', *Nordic Journal of International Law* 84 (2015), pp. 580–604, pp. 583–4. A useful compilation of State practices regarding delimitation of the continental shelf beyond 200 nautical miles is provided in B. M. Magnusson, 'Outer continental shelf boundary agreements', *International and Comparative Law Quarterly* 62 (2013), pp. 345–72.
54 United States of America and Russian Federation, 'Agreement between the United States and the Soviet Union on the Maritime Boundary'.

55 On the assertion that the substantive rights of Article 76 are part of customary international law, see Ted L. McDorman, 'The outer continental shelf in the Arctic Ocean: Legal framework and recent developments', in D. Vidas (ed.), *Law, Technology and Science for Oceans in Globalisation – IUU Fishing, Oil Pollution, Bioprospecting, Outer Continental Shelf* (Hague, Martinus Nijhoff Publishers, 2010), p. 505.

56 Denmark, 'Partial Submission to the Commission on the Limits of the Continental Shelf – The Northern Continental Shelf of Greenland'.

57 'Treaty between Norway and the Russian Federation Concerning Maritime Delimitation and Cooperation in the Barents Sea and the Arctic Ocean'.

58 United States of America and Russian Federation, 'Agreement between the United States and the Soviet Union on the Maritime Boundary'.

59 'Treaty between Norway and the Russian Federation Concerning Maritime Delimitation and Cooperation in the Barents Sea and the Arctic Ocean'.

60 CLCS, Rules of Procedure of the Commission on the Limits of the Continental Shelf'.

61 Ibid., p. 11.

62 Ibid.

63 On legal effects of the Commission's recommendations, see Øystein Jensen, *The Commission on the Limits of the Continental Shelf: Law and Legitimacy* (Leiden, Brill/Nijhoff, 2014), pp. 92–152.

64 LOS Convention, Article 76, paragrah 8, indicates that information on the limits of the continental shelf beyond 200 nautical miles is to be submitted by 'the coastal State' to the Commission. In Article 4 of Annex II, this is restated: 'Where a coastal intends to establish the outer limits of its continental shelf, the coastal State shall submit particulars of such limits to the Commission along with supporting scientific and technical data.'

PART III

ASIA

CHAPTER 9

ASIA IN THE ARCTIC: POLICIES, STAKES AND INVOLVEMENT

Olav Schram Stokke

Introduction

During the past decade, China, India, Japan and the Republic of Korea have considerably increased the attention they pay to Arctic developments and governance, evident also in the observer status they now enjoy in the Arctic Council – a high-level intergovernmental forum on Arctic affairs. In January 2018, China published its long-awaited Arctic policy, joining Japan and South Korea, which several years earlier had provided formal statements of the goals and priorities they pursue in the Arctic region. This chapter shows how these policies reflect considerable sensitivity towards the worries expressed by some regional actors over the effects that broader great-power involvement might have on the privileged position of Arctic coastal states in the governance of economic activities, on the visibility of indigenous concerns and on the protection of the Arctic environment.

I begin by linking the Asian-state policy documents on the Arctic to the notion of stakeholder salience, which refers to the attention and priority that a stakeholder may expect to receive in the governance of an activity or a region. The subsequent empirical review of Arctic economic activities and environmental

Parts of this chapter builds on material previously published in Olav S. Stokke, 'The promise of involvement: Asia in the Arctic', *Strategic Analysis* 37/4 (2013), pp. 474–9, and 'Asian stakes and Arctic governance', *Strategic Analysis* 38/6 (2014), pp. 770–83. The work has received funding from the Research Council of Norway, most recently under the POLARPROG, project no. 257614, and appears here with kind permission from Taylor & Francis Group.

protection reveals that Asian states obtain high scores on stakeholder salience, especially in the many issue areas where Asian players have formal roles to play in regulatory decision making or possess resources relevant to problem solving. Although governments are the foremost actors in Arctic governance, non-state actors such as scientific advisory bodies, transnational corporations, environmental groups and indigenous peoples' organizations also participate in the creation and operation of relevant institutions.[1] The final substantive section relates these patterns of stakeholder salience to the distinctive roles of the Arctic Council in key areas of Arctic governance and derives some policy implications regarding the depth of Asian-state involvement in that institution.

Arctic Policies and Stakeholder Salience

Stakeholder salience has emerged on the Arctic policy agenda because a wide range of actors who previously paid scant attention to this region are now jockeying for positions to influence political decisions or to acquire a share in regional industrial activities. The flow of governmental policy documents on the Arctic began shortly after the planting of a Russian flag on the North Pole seafloor by an expedition led by the Russian scientist, explorer and politician Artur Chilingarov in 2007.[2] Prior to that event, only Norway had published a High North Strategy, defining this region as its 'most important strategic priority area in the years ahead'.[3] Only a few years later, all eight member states of the Arctic Council as well as one Permanent Participant had specified their Arctic priorities and objectives, and by 2018 the same was true for six European and Asian observer states.[4] Common to all of these strategy documents, including those by Asian states, is an emphasis on scientific research, economic opportunities, environmental protection, and the human dimension-typically highlighting the traditions and living conditions of indigenous peoples.

Geopolitical setting

The growing interest among non-Arctic states in regional affairs evolved against the backdrop of broader geopolitical and geo-economic shifts, reinforced by the recent debate on the adequacy of the legal framework for Arctic governance. The USA is still well ahead of any Asian or other competitor in its capacity for military power projection and remains the world's strongest economy by far, not least in terms of technology and innovation.[5] Yet, many years of growth rates considerably lower than those achieved by several large 'emerging economies', like China and India, have made clear that this ranking is not written in stone. Although another Arctic state, Russia, remains the world's number two military power, China is rapidly narrowing the gap, especially as regards conventional capability.[6] Moreover, Russia's economic structure is in general less diversified and more dependent on resource extraction than are those of the leading Asian states. And Moscow has somewhat mixed feelings about the surge in Chinese investments in, and immigration to, the Russian Far East.[7] This larger geopolitical backdrop influences how Arctic states view the stakeholder claims of non-regional players.

Arctic-state wariness of outside interest has also been fuelled by Arctic policy documents issued by the European Union, especially the European Parliament's controversial call in 2008 for a comprehensive international environmental treaty applicable to the Arctic Ocean.[8] That resolution coincided with similar suggestions by some environmental NGOs and scholars that a firmer legal framework might be needed for adequate Arctic governance.[9] Such suggestions and especially the EU resolution were very negatively received by the five coastal states with maritime zones adjacent to the Arctic Ocean, often referred to as the 'Arctic Five': Canada, Denmark/Greenland, Norway, Russia and the USA. The Arctic Five responded by issuing the 2008 Ilulissat Declaration, highlighting the UN Law of the Sea Convention (UNCLOS) and pointing to their 'sovereignty, sovereign rights and jurisdiction in large areas of the Arctic Ocean [which imply] … a stewardship role in protecting' Arctic ecosystems.[10] This declaration was intended and perceived as a reminder that the geopolitical struggle over regulatory competence in the Arctic had in fact been settled in 1982 with the UNCLOS, which is no less applicable in the Arctic than elsewhere.[11] That Convention differentiates the competence to regulate ocean use by activity and distance from the coast, placing the coastal states at the helm regarding the exploitation of hydrocarbon and mineral resources on generously defined continental shelves and regarding the exploitation of living resources in these states' exclusive economic zones (EEZs). Unlike all other major states, the USA has not yet ratified the Convention but core UNCLOS provisions like the allocation of regulatory competence simply codify international customary law and are, therefore, legally binding on non-parties as well.

The Ilulissat Declaration and the diplomatic activity that surrounded it served to infuse greater caution in subsequent policy statements by the EU as well as other non-Arctic players, including the Asian states in focus here.[12] In Japan's policy document, for instance, at the first mention of the word 'resources' a footnote has been added pointing out that not only the land areas but also a 'large part of the Arctic Ocean consists of the territorial waters of the coastal states, and these have sovereignty or sovereign rights to EEZs and continental shelves'.[13] In a similar vein, the Korean policy document blends attention to Arctic maritime business opportunities' sea routes with sensitivity to the interests of the Arctic Five, aiming 'to contribute to [the] sustainable future of the Arctic by enhancing cooperation with the Arctic coastal states and relevant international organisations'.[14] Only slightly more assertive, China highlights the vast territorial and maritime areas subject to coastal-state jurisdiction in the Arctic, noting that 'all activities to explore and utilise the Arctic should … respect the laws of the coastal states', adding, however, that other states too 'share maritime rights and interests in accordance with international law … [and that c]ertain areas of the Arctic Ocean form part of the high seas and the Area'.[15]

This sober language contrasts with earlier statements by some Asian observers or practitioners who tended to frame their stakeholder claims in Arctic affairs by concepts and arguments that imply shared ownership, notably 'the common heritage of mankind'. This term has enjoyed some currency in debates over Antarctica, where various national claims to sovereignty are unrecognized beyond the group of claimants,[16] but it lacks relevance in the economically attractive parts of the Arctic where coastal-state sovereignty is not at issue. A much-cited example of the common-heritage argument is the remark in 2010 by Chinese Retired Rear Admiral Yin Zhuo that 'the North Pole and the sea area around the North Pole belong to all the people in the world' and that 'China must play an indispensable role in Arctic exploration as we have one-fifth of the world's population'.[17] Those sceptical of non-Arctic state involvement (or with budgetary interest in such scepticism) quickly blew the sovereignty whistle: for instance, Russian Navy Commander-in-Chief Vladimir Vysotsky warned about 'the penetration of a host of states which … are advancing their interests very intensively, in every possible way, in particular China', adding that Russia will 'not give up a single inch' of Arctic ground.[18] Russia and Canada generally place sovereignty issues higher up on their list of Arctic priorities than do other regional states – partly because theirs are by far the longest Arctic coastlines, and partly because some of their unilateral and stricter-than-global Arctic shipping regulations have been challenged on legal grounds by other states.[19]

Keeping in mind this wider geopolitical setting is helpful when examining the steadily more numerous claims by non-regional states, including Asian ones, for stakeholder status in Arctic affairs.

The salience of stakeholder claims

The broad concept of stakeholders applies here (actors who are either significantly affected by an institution or capable of affecting it) and derives from strategic management analysis, which holds that stakeholder status extends beyond those with the legal competence or recognized right to participate in institutional decision making.[20] Contributors to stakeholder theory have focused on private corporations, but the basic problem they address is equally relevant for international governance[21]: what factors should those operating institutions take into consideration in managing stakeholder relations – that is, when setting priorities among the stakes that different actors claim to have in its decisions?

Those who advocate a restrictive approach to stakeholder management typically emphasize the first part of the stakeholder definition – the ability to affect – arguing that priority should be given to those stakeholders who are crucial to institutional performance and survival. A more inclusive approach is often taken by those who place equal emphasis on the second part – affectedness – advocating attention to a range of stakeholders and seeking ways to reconcile possible conflicting demands. My approach to this question is instrumental, with the focus on how exclusiveness or inclusiveness is likely to affect institutional performance.[22] Thus, differences among stakeholders as to their ability to provide resources for – or to impede – the realization of institutional objectives loom large in this chapter.

Mitchell and colleagues usefully differentiate an organization's stakeholders by reference to three attributes: power, legitimacy and urgency.[23] *Power* refers to the ability to impose one's will in a relationship, including by controlling outcomes of interest to the institution. *Legitimacy* concerns the perceived or assumed appropriateness of the claim an actor makes for institutional attention, whereas *urgency* is about the insistence on such attention. These authors hold that the actual attention and priority accorded to such claims – stakeholder salience – can be derived from the accumulation of those three attributes. Thus, actors who combine power, legitimacy and urgency are 'definite' stakeholders, and can be expected to receive substantially more attention from those operating an institution than will stakeholders possessing only one or two of those attributes – 'latent' and 'expectant' stakeholders, respectively.[24]

In these terms, the Arctic Five coastal states are clearly definite stakeholders in any area of Arctic governance, and whatever international institution is in focus. As will be elaborated presently, coastal-state power and legitimacy in any governance process pertaining to the Arctic derives from the state's recognized sovereignty over land, internal waters and the territorial sea, and from its sovereign rights to natural resources in its EEZ and continental shelves. Urgency is also high, as emphasized by the Ilulissat Declaration. This combination of power, legitimacy and urgency would lead Mitchell and colleagues to predict that any international institution aspiring to influence the management of Arctic fish resources, for instance, or to strengthen environmental standards for Arctic petroleum activities, will pay very close attention to coastal-state concerns, in its procedures for decision making as well as in the content of its standards.

Other stakeholders too are salient in Arctic affairs to varying extents. The three Arctic Council members not littoral to the Arctic Ocean as such – Finland, Iceland and Sweden – are clearly definite stakeholders in issues decided upon in the Council, although we note shortly that this set of issues is rather narrow. In key Arctic issue areas like natural resource management, shipping or protection of the marine environment, neither the power nor the legitimacy of the three non-coastal state members of the Council significantly exceeds that of other actors interested in Arctic affairs, such as the European Union or the Asian states in focus here. As will be shown in the following, the salience of stakeholders other than the five coastal states in Arctic international governance institutions tends to be either 'latent' or 'expectant', depending on the urgency of their claims and the issue-specific power and legitimacy they hold in other institutions in the Arctic governance complex.

Economic Opportunities

The Arctic region is rich in natural resources such as petroleum, strategic minerals and fish; and the steep growth of Asian economies like China and India during the past decade has raised commodity prices to levels that make recovery of more of those resources economically feasible. Like other stakeholders lacking coastal-state rights in the region, Asian states cannot legitimately demand a role in the exploitation of Arctic natural resources – but their financial and technological muscle has already made Asian firms attractive partners.

Economically recoverable resources in the Arctic are overwhelmingly found either on land or in marine areas that lie undisputedly under coastal-state jurisdiction. This allocation of regulatory competence, codified in UNCLOS, reflects a political balance struck in the mid-1970s between coastal-state demands for natural-resource control and maritime-state requests for unrestricted navigation.[25] Coastal states are endowed with sovereign rights to regulate and exploit natural resources in the water masses, the seabed and the subsoil of their EEZs, which may extend 200 nautical miles from the baselines. For seabed and subsoil resources – which include oil, gas and mineral nodules – those rights extend even further, throughout the natural prolongation of the coastal state's land territory (the continental shelf), within certain overall limits. Although the exact outer limits of most Arctic continental shelves are yet to be determined, it is already clear that practically all recoverable oil and gas resources will be located inside national jurisdiction, and the situation is similar for marine living resources.

Placing the coastal states at the helm as regards regulation as well as use of Arctic natural resources, the UNCLOS framework derives its legitimacy from global acceptance and its political stability from good alignment between such legitimacy and the global distribution of power. The balance struck between coastal-state and navigational concerns was favoured by the two superpowers at the time: the USA and the Soviet Union. Those two as well as the other Arctic states were among the greatest winners in terms of spatially extended jurisdiction; the same holds true for China and India. The basic deal underlying the legal order for Arctic resource management is likely to remain stable, due to universal acceptance and the long-standing support of not only all Arctic states but the geo-economically rising Asian states as well. This section examines more closely the salience of Asian economic stakes in the Arctic.

Energy and minerals

While management authority over practically all economically recoverable resources in the Arctic rests with the coastal states, industries from non-regional states can derive benefits from the business opportunities those resources provide. That is why large companies operating worldwide now include the Arctic in their assessments of future resource bases. Greater attention to the potential profits from Arctic resources is spurring technological advances in areas that can facilitate operations in cold-water and harsh environments. Asian-state policy documents emphasize that their industries tend to be well placed to participate in the realization of Arctic commercial opportunities – but alongside such self-confidence we find considerable soberness with respect to the economic potentials. Closest to the upbeat end of the continuum, the Chinese policy 'encourages its enterprises to engage in international cooperation on the exploration for and utilisation of Arctic resources by making the best use of their advantages in capital, technology and [the] domestic market'.[26] Somewhat more cautiously, Korea plans to contribute to joint research, geological survey and other explorative activities, whereas Japan points to the difficult operational circumstances posed by 'extreme cold with sea ice ... [implying that] resource development should be addressed steadily over the mid and long term'.[27]

The biggest Arctic deal involving Asian companies to date is the twenty-five-year oil-for-cash agreement between Russia's largest oil company, Rosneft, and the state-owned China National Petroleum Corporation. That agreement will more than double the level of oil trade between the two countries and might generate Chinese involvement in the exploration of three Arctic offshore fields.[28] Indian companies have reportedly engaged in commercial negotiations with license holders in Yamal-Nenets in western Siberia, the core area for Russian petroleum activity, and in Sakhalin.[29] Companies from China, Japan and Korea are already at work on the Norwegian continental shelf.[30] The China Investment Corporation is among the biggest owners of GDF Suez, a multilateral petroleum company with a share in Snøhvit, Norway's first Arctic gas field to reach the production stage, as well as holding operator responsibility further south. Another Chinese company has recently acquired a share in a licence to explore a field in Icelandic waters, and Chinese mining firms are considering involvement in the development of Greenlandic onshore rare-earth mineral resources.[31]

The urgency inherent in this demonstration of serious interest in joining Arctic mining and petroleum activities, backed up by governmental support and the power that stems from commercial competitiveness, renders Asian companies as expectant stakeholders in Arctic mineral resources. They may have roles to play in the exploitation of such resources but only if the Asian players are perceived as attractive partners by regional actors, since mineral resources are found overwhelmingly within coastal-state jurisdiction. In the petroleum sector in particular, Asian firms have emerged as expectant stakeholders due to the urgency inherent in their preparedness to invest in Arctic resource development and the power inherent in their ability to offer globally competitive technological solutions, equipment, or venture capital.

Marine living resources

In the case of Arctic fishery resources, any involvement of Asian players must also occur largely by invitation, but the likelihood of such involvement seems much slimmer than for mineral resources. That is because the harvesting capacity of the Arctic coastal states, and of neighbouring states with reciprocal access agreements with them, far exceeds the available resources in the region.[32] Some Arctic stocks have historically been subject to large-scale fisheries by distant-water fishing fleets, also from Asia, most prominently Alaska pollock, a semi-pelagic species taken in the Central Bering Sea. Throughout much of the 1980s, this stock fed one of the world's largest fisheries, involving vessels from China, Japan, Korea and Taiwan.[33] From around 1990, however, Alaska pollock has not been available in recoverable quantities outside the EEZs of Russia and the USA, and the same is true today for most other Arctic fish stocks. Northeast Arctic cod, currently the world's largest cod stock, is shared between Norway and Russia, with limited fishing rights being granted to certain other states under reciprocal access agreements.[34] Even though higher temperatures might affect the migratory patterns of commercially important fish stocks in the Arctic, only a few pelagic stocks, such as redfish and capelin, are likely to be available in the high seas outside the 200-mile zones of coastal states. The process of negotiating a regional high-seas fisheries management organization for the Arctic Ocean, initiated by the United States and confined during the early stages to the Arctic Five, was therefore precautionary in the sense that no one expects any commercial opportunities of significance in the foreseeable future. That initiative met with some success with the 2014 agreement among the Arctic coastal states on 'the need for interim precautionary measures to prevent any future commercial fisheries without the prior establishment of appropriate regulatory mechanisms'.[35]

Asian stakes in future high-seas fisheries in the Arctic derives from the limits that international law imposes on coastal-state fisheries jurisdiction. Conservation and use of fisheries resources that cross national boundaries are among the issues where the UNCLOS encourages regional management regimes (Articles 63–64 and 116–119); for stocks straddling the high seas and coastal-state zones, parties to the 1995 UN Fish Stocks Agreement are obliged to create or join a regional fisheries regime. Unlike in the EEZ, however, that obligation does not come with the right to exclude non-regional states that might claim a 'real interest' in the stock based on one or more of a long list of criteria (Article 8), with zonal attachment and historical catches as the most weighty.[36] Given the vast expanses of the Arctic Ocean, a fish stock that adapts to rising temperatures by moving northward is unlikely to have been exploited by all the Arctic states and also unlikely to have avoided exploitation by states outside the region. Thus, several non-Arctic states that are now members of the European Union were among the founders of the North–East Atlantic Fisheries Commission (NEAFC), which has regulatory competence with respect to high-seas areas in the European segment of the Arctic Ocean. Under such circumstances, a regime with a membership confined to Arctic coastal states would run counter to the spirit as well as the letter of international fisheries law.[37]

Among the Asian policy documents on the Arctic, that of China is clearly the most assertive and elaborate with respect to fisheries interests but Japan and Korea also signal clear interest in participating 'in discussions with coastal states and other states toward the formulation of rules for preservation and management of fishery resources in the high seas of the Arctic Ocean'.[38] Thus, China 'supports efforts to formulate a legally binding international agreement on the management of fisheries in the high seas portion of the Arctic Ocean' but also remind readers of its 'lawful right to conduct fisheries research and development' in those waters and rubs in its view that 'all States should fulfil their obligations to conserve the fishery resources and the ecosystem in the region'.[39] Responding to the salience of other stakeholders, the Arctic Five decided to broaden the negotiations to also include China, Japan and Korea, along with Iceland and the European Union. In December 2017, these so-called 'Five plus Five' negotiations produced an agreement that commits parties to prohibit their nationals from engaging in high-seas fisheries in the Central Arctic Ocean for at least sixteen years and to contribute to scientific investigations on Arctic stocks and their associated ecosystems.[40]

Since the overwhelming part of Arctic marine living resources are found inside the EEZs of coastal states, however, the Asian states are in practice no more than expectant stakeholders in the fisheries sector – and their roles here are likely to remain more modest than for energy resources because the Arctic coastal states are more than capable of taking the total allowable catches of the most lucrative species themselves.

Maritime transport

Arctic sea routes have been eyed with expectation by many generations of shippers due to the relatively short sailing distances these routes offer between important ports in Asia and in Europe or the eastern coast of the USA. Like for fisheries, China makes the boldest claims among the Asian states as to the roles they envisage for themselves: 'The utilization of sea routes and exploration and development of the resources in the Arctic may have a huge impact on the energy strategy and economic development of China … [and] China's capital, technology, market, knowledge and experience is expected to play a major role in expanding the network of shipping routes in the Arctic and facilitating the economic and social progress of the coastal States along the routes.'[41] More modestly, Japan pledges to '[i]dentify the natural, technical, systemic, and economic challenges of the Arctic Sea Route, and preparation of an environment for its utilization by Japanese shipping companies and others.'[42] Finally, Korea's document pays considerable attention to shipping opportunities but is even more specific and elaborate on the business options associated with shipbuilding for polar conditions.[43]

Unlike the case of Arctic natural resources, Asian stakeholders are well placed to influence decisions concerning Arctic sea lanes, because international law severely limits the measures that coastal states may legitimately impose on foreign vessels outside their internal waters. That is why the negotiations for a legally binding Polar Code were conducted within the framework of the International Maritime Organization (IMO), which also involves Asian states and industries, and not in a more select group of Arctic coastal states. Yet, as this section shows, the level of activity by Asian states in these global negotiations was modest indeed.

Marine transport is a global industry, and leading actors have been eager to avoid spatially-fragmented regulation – especially for aspects that are costly or difficult to modify, like vessel design, construction, manning or equipment. That is why the UNCLOS sets *maximum* standards for what states may demand of a vessel flagged by another state – and those regulatory ceilings become lower the further away from the coastline a vessel operates. In ports and internal waters, coastal states have the same monopoly on regulation and rule enforcement as on land. In the territorial sea, they may 'adopt laws and regulations for the prevention, reduction and control of marine pollution from foreign vessels' as long as these laws and regulations do not impede 'innocent passage' or go beyond generally accepted international rules and standards as regards 'the design, construction, manning or equipment of foreign ships'.[44] In their EEZs, however, coastal states may not normally set any rules beyond those 'conforming to and giving effect to generally accepted international rules and standards established through' the IMO. Since treaty-making in this organization in practice proceeds by consensus, these provisions confer legitimacy as well as power on any IMO member interested in maritime transport in the Arctic.

The extent of such non-coastal power over regulatory decisions on Arctic shipping is tempered by the provisions of UNCLOS Article 234, which for 'ice-covered areas' within EEZs grants coastal states 'the right to adopt and enforce non-discriminatory laws and regulations for the prevention, reduction and control of marine pollution from vessels', on condition that those rules 'have due regard to navigation'. However, ambiguity as to the precise meaning of 'due regard' and whether these rights also apply in the territorial sea (and, therefore, might restrict the right to unimpeded transit passage that foreign vessels have in straits used for international navigation) renders Article 234 contestable as a basis for ambitious coastal-state regulation of Arctic shipping.[45] Both Canada and Russia have adopted standards on the design, construction, equipment and manning of vessels operating in Arctic waters adjacent to their coasts that are stricter than those agreed in IMO instruments.[46] However, neither state relies primarily on Article 234 for these standards: both claim that parts of the shipping lanes in question are internal waters – claims that are explicitly contested by the USA, and in the case of Canada also by the EU.[47] In sum, international law provides some basis for unilateral coastal-state regulation in ice-covered waters – but the substantive extent of that basis is ambiguous, contestable, and set to diminish spatially with the retreat of the Arctic sea ice.

These ambiguities and contestations were important drivers of the 2009 decision by the IMO Council to negotiate a legally binding Polar Code, adopted in 2015 and setting forth mandatory regulations and standards for ships operating in ice-covered waters with respect to vessel design, construction, equipment, manning and training.[48] With the exception of India, all the Asian observer states to the Arctic Council were members of the IMO Correspondence Group tasked with developing an agreed text of the Polar Code. Although such participation indicates a certain level of urgency on the part of Asian stakeholders, the intensity of their actual involvement was modest indeed. An overwhelming proportion of documents for these meetings was submitted by Arctic states or by European states with observer status in the Arctic Council, such as Germany and France.

Among the 141 documents on the matter submitted to this subcommittee before the adoption of the Polar Code, none originated from an Asian state.[49] This changed somewhat towards the end of the process, when the draft text had reached the committee level. China and Korea co-sponsored two papers prior to the final adoption by the Council, including a successful proposal for more stringent language concerning the scope of the Code's double hull and double bottom requirement for new vessels.[50] In contrast, Japan's single submission to the same committee took the shipper's rather than the shipbuilder's or environmental perspective, joining a successful industry-backed proposal to widen an exemption for small tankers from the same requirement.[51] Environmental groups such as the World Wide Fund for Nature (WWF), industrial organizations like the Cruise Lines International Association, and even the South Pacific micro-state Vanuatu were all considerably more active in submitting papers to the Polar Code negotiations than were any of the Asian shipping giants examined here.

Also indicating low urgency with respect to Arctic shipping governance is the fact that, unlike the USA and the EU, none of the Asian states in focus here has objected to the unilateral environmental measures taken by Russia or Canada in Arctic waters. When China's governmental research vessel *Xue Long* (snow dragon) made its transit through the Northern Sea Route in 2012, it duly complied with Russian passage procedures; the same holds true for the commercial transits that Asian-flagged and other vessels have conducted with rising frequency in recent years.

In summary, the salience of Asian stakeholders in Arctic shipping governance is high on the legitimacy dimension, and substantial as to power – but low with respect to the third property, urgency. Legitimacy is high because international law recognizes their right to participate prominently in global regulatory processes on Arctic shipping, as illustrated by the process that created a legally binding Polar Code. The power held by Asian states in such negotiations is substantial because the IMO in practice proceeds by consensus, although the veto implied by that practice is limited by political pressure as well as the special rights that coastal states have to establish especially stringent regulation in ice-covered parts of their 200-mile zones. As yet, however, there have been few indications that the Asian states in focus here seriously tried to influence the substantive direction of the Polar Code negotiations. This low urgency implies salience in the shipping sector somewhere between that of a latent and an expectant stakeholder.

Environmental Protection

Asian stakeholders are major contributors to several of the most severe environmental challenges faced in the Arctic, thereby holding power over the performance of any institution aspiring to protect the regional environment. The most important of those institutions are global in scope. As in the case of shipping, the Asian states under study are highly legitimate participants in the UN-based regimes that address discharges of greenhouse gases (GHGs), persistent organic pollutants (POPs) or heavy metals. In contrast to the shipping case, those states also score high on the urgency dimension of stakeholder salience – but, except for Japan, they have typically supported the laggard side in negotiations with high Arctic relevance.

Most of the changes currently underway in the Arctic are associated with a rise in mean temperatures roughly twice the global average, driven mainly by GHG emissions in industrial and urban centres further south. For a quarter of a century, international regulation of such emissions has been centred on the UN Framework Convention on Climate Change. The universal membership of that regime makes it better placed for regulatory action than narrower institutions, because in order to be effective, mitigation of GHG emissions must involve major contributors throughout the world. The deadlocked and generally weak regulatory performance that marked the post-Kyoto climate regime up until the 2015 Paris Agreement reflected an inability to find a burden-sharing formula that can induce those contributors to assume legally binding mitigation commitments.[52] Among those who most stubbornly resisted specific emissions reductions commitments were two Arctic states (the USA and Canada), as well as Asian and Latin American states with rapidly growing economies such as China, India and Brazil. In the climate change area, therefore, the Arctic-interested Asian states are legitimate as well as powerful players in the main international institution; but among them, only Japan had translated its urgency into regulatory leadership before the adoption of the Paris Agreement with its near-universal and legally binding national pledges.[53]

Significant dependency on action taken outside the region also marks another severe environmental threat: the hazardous substances that bio-accumulate in Arctic food chains and threaten regional ecosystems. The Pole-bound atmospheric and oceanic circulation systems, as well as rivers draining into the Arctic seas, transport a range of toxic substances that originate or volatilize further south, including a string of POPs and heavy metals such as mercury.[54] That is why several UN-based regulatory processes have been central in the negotiation of binding rules restricting the use, production and trading of hazardous substances that end up in the Arctic. Of particular interest here are the 2001 Stockholm Convention on POPs and the 2013 Minamata Convention on Mercury.

Arctic states, especially Canada, were among the early pushers for stronger international regulations on POPs. The fact that long-range transported organic and non-organic toxic substances appear in very high concentrations in the fat of

Arctic animals, and in the breast milk of some Inuit women, had been discovered prior to the establishment of Arctic cooperative institutions in the early 1990s.[55] It was also known that this might impair immune systems and reproduction, and cause neuro-behavioural disorders. As part of the Arctic Environmental Protection Strategy, a precursor to the Arctic Council, delegates from the eight Arctic states expressed their concern about the Arctic health effects of POPs before the executive body of a regional treaty, the Convention on Long-Range Transboundary Air Pollution. Given the political weight of this group of states, this is likely to have contributed to a subsequent strengthening of the mandate given to the task force examining the basis for a separate POPs protocol, one that would provide a model for the subsequent global Stockholm Convention.[56] According to the chair of the Stockholm Conference, other Arctic stakeholders – notably indigenous and environmental organizations – also influenced the multilateral negotiations in a productive way, not least by ensuring continued publicity for the process.[57]

Compared to these various Arctic stakeholders, the Asian states under study played much more marginal roles in the process that generated the Stockholm POPs Convention. China, India and Korea coordinated their positions within the 'Group of 77 and China', focusing mainly on financial mechanisms for developing countries, whereas Japan was lukewarm towards the idea of restricting trade in toxic substances or banning trade with non-parties and was strongly opposed to any reference to the precautionary approach.[58]

A similar contrast between environmental leadership provided by Arctic stakeholders and recalcitrance on the part of Asian states has marked the international combat of mercury release, which for nearly a decade has been high on the list of priorities expressed in the biennial Ministerial Declarations by the Arctic Council.[59] China is by far the world's biggest emitter of this heavy metal, with India as a strong number three. Unlike Japan, those two states worked actively to prevent the process from generating a legally binding instrument, and, when that failed, they sought to water down the commitments that were finally adopted.[60] Although India and Korea are both prominent members of the United Nations Environment Programme (UNEP), neither of them has ratified the Mercury Convention.[61]

In sum, major drivers of Arctic environmental problems originate outside the region, which means that the most important Arctic environmental institutions are not regional but global ones. Leading Asian states are among the definite stakeholders to these institutions, combining high scores on power, legitimacy and urgency. With the exception of Japan in the climate area, these states refrained from translating such salience into regulatory leadership roles in the global processes for mitigating discharges of GHGs, POPs and heavy metals.

Asian States and the Arctic Council

It is clear from the previous discussion that the Arctic Council is only one of many international bodies in the larger institutional complex for governing the Arctic. In most of the issue areas likely to see increasing activity in this region, other institutions are more important.[62] Narrower institutions, either coastal states or international bodies involving subsets of them, will manage the rise of regional offshore petroleum activities or any increases in commercial fisheries. Broader institutions will continue to predominate in the governance of international shipping or of the wide range of activities that generate GHGs or hazardous compounds affecting Arctic ecosystems. However, the Arctic Council provides some valuable support for those other institutions, a provision that is likely to benefit from deeper involvement of Asian stakeholders in Council activities: building knowledge, catalysing regulatory advances and raising capacity to implement international commitments.

Knowledge building was the early specialization of the Arctic Council, evident in a series of collaborative assessments of the state of the Arctic environment and of the risks and opportunities associated with climate change, regional oil and gas development and Arctic shipping. It still is: the project 'Adaptation Actions for a Changing Arctic' under the Arctic Monitoring and Assessment Programme (AMAP) was aimed at analysing the combination of these various dynamics.[63] Involving a broader set of states in the often-demanding Arctic monitoring and research activities would be advantageous not only for reasons of cost-efficiency; it would also imply access to relevant expertise and activities found as well as financed beyond this region. More than sixty states participated in the research coordinated under the International Polar Year 2007–8, including the leading Asian states that have now obtained permanent observer status on the Arctic Council. Among them, Japan has the longest Arctic-research record, with an Arctic-research station already established in the early 1990s and heavy involvement in an early comprehensive multinational research project on the physical, economic and political conditions for broader use of the Northern Sea Route.[64] China is catching up rapidly: its ice-capable research vessel, the *Xue Long*, was acquired two decades ago, and the government agency responsible for polar activities added 'Arctic' to its name in 1996. All the largest Asian states now have research stations in Norway's Arctic archipelago, Svalbard, and a recent study has shown that they are now significant contributors to Arctic research.[65] The Arctic Council clearly stands to gain from the greater involvement of Asian states in the research and assessment work conducted in connection with its knowledge-building role.

Capacity enhancement is a second governance task assumed by the Arctic Council in areas such as environmental protection and safety at sea. A range of projects under the Council's Arctic Contaminants Action Plan have mapped stockpiles of various categories of toxic substances, including obsolete or prohibited pesticides, mercury, dioxins, and brominated flame retardants, and have helped to improve the storage or destruction of such toxic compounds. These projects could also generate business opportunities for Asian chemicals technology firms, but only Western companies have been involved as yet. Other instances of Arctic Council contributions to capacity building are the recent agreements on search and rescue, and oil-spills preparedness and response, negotiated under the Council but adopted specifically by the member states since the Council lacks binding powers.[66] While cooperation among the coastal states can be vital in maritime search and rescue, the Arctic Marine Shipping Assessment points out that in practice such operations often involve nearby commercial vessels.[67] Systems of communication and coordination among vessel-based tourism companies operating in the most popular destinations, including Svalbard and the eastern coast of Greenland, can therefore complement coastal-state capacities – and major Asian vessel operators are now considering a move into Arctic tourism. Among the messages of the Arctic Marine Shipping Assessment is that the maritime infrastructure is generally inadequate throughout most of the circumpolar area – also with respect to technologies for dealing with emergency situations and oil spills. Involving Asian maritime clusters in Arctic capacity-enhancement efforts can therefore prove highly beneficial for stakeholders not only in Asia but in the Arctic as well.

Similar comments are in order regarding a third way in which Arctic Council activities may influence the overall governance of this region: by serving as a catalyst for stronger regulatory provisions in broader institutions. Such catalytic aspirations are evident in the recommendation in the Arctic Marine Shipping Assessment to upgrade the voluntary Polar Guidelines to a legally binding Polar Code under the IMO. An even clearer example is the role of Arctic Council activities in the strengthening of international rules on hazardous compounds, as outlined earlier. A major finding from the environmental assessment reports produced during the early years of the Council was that the effects of POPs and heavy metals on humans were more dramatic in the Arctic than those documented at lower latitudes.[68] The focus of these assessments on transport pathways and health impacts fit the four criteria developed under the broader institution to identify chemical substances in particular need of regulation: transport range, persistency, toxicity and bioaccumulation.[69] The substances that were selected from an initial list of more than a hundred included those of greatest relevance to Arctic ecosystems.

Furthermore, the ambitious 2005 Arctic Climate Impact Assessment (ACIA) aimed to contribute to regulatory progress under broader regimes, by factoring into the broader assessment work under the Intergovernmental Panel on Climate Change.[70] Indeed, the ACIA reports and a Policy Document containing some of the clearest statements subscribed to by the George W. Bush administration on the need for action on global warming were widely disseminated in the USA, where policymakers and the general public have traditionally viewed 'climate science' with considerable scepticism.[71] Thus we see that, whether the subject matter is shipping, toxic substances or climate change, knowledge-building efforts under the Arctic Council have highlighted the Arctic dimension of broader problems and also helped to mobilize political energy among non-regional states. The wider involvement of Asian states in such activities can only enhance the ability to catalyze regulatory advances in broader institutions with relevant competence, by expanding the set of states and actors with ownership in Arctic Council assessments and recommendations.

To summarize, the limited but valuable contributions of the Arctic Council to better governance of the activities affecting the Arctic will be further enhanced if the Council can manage to involve Asian stakeholders in ways that raise their participation and ownership in knowledge-building and recommendation work. Such involvement in knowledge building might promote the regulatory dynamics within broader international institutions crucial to Arctic governance, as well as encouraging collaboration in mutually beneficial capacity enhancement.

Conclusion

The Asian states that have observer status in the Arctic Council are all influenced by Arctic developments and they are capable of influencing those developments. Their stakeholder salience is particularly high in issue areas governed largely by global regimes – as with shipping, climate change and environmental toxicity. In those areas, Asian states combine power, legitimacy and in most cases also urgency. Especially as regards environmental issues, Asian states are definite stakeholders, highly capable of influencing the performance of relevant international regimes. These are areas where the Arctic Council plays supportive, subordinate roles, building knowledge that could enhance regulatory progress in broader institutions or helping to put such regulations into practice by bolstering administrative and industrial capacities in parts of the Arctic. Deeper involvement of the Asian observer states in such activities holds the promise of mobilizing additional resources for Arctic problem solving, improving awareness of Arctic concerns among actors who are central to global regulation, and facilitating the identification of political or industrial synergies among Asian and Arctic players.

In other issue areas, like petroleum, minerals and fisheries, the salience of Asian stakeholders will depend on their ability to compete commercially for lucrative roles in the production and distribution chains – and that ability is clearly on the rise.

Stakeholder theory has structured the argument in this chapter. The findings reported here shed light on the substantive scope of this theory, which is rooted in corporate management analysis: when applied to international governance, stakeholder salience analysis should include the broader complex of institutions that are relevant to a policy domain. Such a macro-approach is necessary because evaluation of stakeholder power in one institution must also take into consideration the stakeholder's power, legitimacy and urgency in other institutions that are crucial to problem solving. An institutionally narrow stakeholder salience evaluation, limited to the Arctic Council itself, would misrepresent the real stakeholder salience that Asian states have, because it would fail to take into account their legitimacy, power and urgency in broader institutions. The more comprehensive approach advocated here is especially relevant when the stakeholders in question have assumed a laggard or a leader role in such broader institutions. Among the reasons why those operating the Arctic Council should pay greater attention to Asian stakeholders is that greater involvement in the Council's assessment and guidance activities might influence the policy positions these stakeholders take in a whole range of global institutions crucial to governance of the Arctic.

Notes

1 On this definition of governance, see Oran R. Young, *International Governance: Protecting the Environment in a Stateless Society* (Ithaca, Cornell University Press, 1994), p. 15.

2 For example Klaus Dodds, 'Flag planting and finger pointing: The Law of the Sea, the Arctic and the political geographies of the outer continental shelf', *Political Geography* 29/2 (2010), pp. 63–73.

3 Norwegian Ministry of Foreign Affairs, *Norwegian Government's High North Strategy* (Oslo, Norwegian Ministry of Foreign Affairs, 2006).

4 These Arctic policy documents, except China's, are available at https://arcticportal.org/arctic-governance/arctic-policies-database (accessed 5 June 2018), whereas China's policy is available at http://english.gov.cn/archive/white_paper/2018/01/26/content_281476026660336.htm (accessed 5 June 2018). The Permanent Participant in question is the Inuit Circumpolar Congress, one of six transnational indigenous-peoples organizations that enjoy a prominent position in the Arctic Council, higher than that of observer states.

5 For an instructive analysis, see Michael Beckley, 'China's Century? Why America's Edge Will Endure', *International Security* 36 (2011/12), pp. 41–78.

6 According to the SIPRI Military Expenditure Database, China's military spending (in constant US dollars) rose by 75 per cent from 2009–17, to a level that was roughly four times that of Russia but less than half of US military spending: see https://sipri.org (accessed 30 May 2018).

7 Mikhail A. Alexseev and C. Richard Hofstetter, 'Russia, China, and the Immigration Security Dilemma', *Political Science Quarterly* 121 (2006), pp. 1–32.

8 European Parliament, 'Resolution of 9 October 2008 on Arctic Governance', Doc. P6_TA(2008)0474 (2008). Available at http://www.europarl.europa.eu/sides/getDoc.do?type=TA&reference=P6-TA-2008-0474&language=EN (accessed 30 May 2018).

9 See, respectively, Linda Nowlan, 'Arctic legal regime for environmental protection', in *IUCN Environmental Policy and Law Paper* (Cambridge, IUCN, 2001) and Timo Koivurova, 'Alternatives for an Arctic Treaty – evaluation and a new proposal', *Review of European, Comparative & International Environmental Law* 17/1 (2008), pp.14–26.

10 Arctic Ocean Conference, 'The Ilulissat Declaration' (2008). Available at http://www.oceanlaw.org/downloads/arctic/Ilulissat_Declaration.pdf (accessed 30 May 2018).

11 Olav S. Stokke, 'A legal regime for the Arctic? Interplay with the Law of the Sea Convention', *Marine Policy* 31/4 (2007), pp. 402–8.

12 On the greater caution on this matter displayed by EU bodies with greater authority on foreign affairs than the European Parliament has, see Kristine Offerdal, 'The EU in the Arctic: In pursuit of legitimacy and influence', *International Journal* 66/44 (2011), pp. 861–77. The most recent instance of such caution is the report by the High Representative of the Union for Foreign Affairs and Security Policy, *An integrated European Union policy for the Arctic*, JOIN (2016) 21 final (2016). Available at https://eeas.europa.eu/arctic_region/docs/160427_joint-communication-an-integrated-european-union-policy-for-the-arctic_en.pdf (accessed 30 May 2018).

13 Japan, 'Japan's Arctic Policy' (Tokyo, Headquarters for Ocean Policy, 2015), paragraph 1.

14 Korea, 'Arctic Policy of the Republic of Korea' (Seoul, Korea Maritime Institute, 2013), p. 4.

15 State Council, 'China's Arctic Policy' (The State Council Information Office of the People's Republic of China, 26 January 2018), paragraphs IV.3 and I; 'the Area' is an UNCLOS term that refers to 'the seabed and ocean floor and subsoil thereof, beyond the limits of national jurisdiction': see United Nations Convention on the Law of the Sea (UNCLOS), 10 December 1982, 1833 UNTS, Article 1 and Part XI.

16 For an in-depth discussion of Antarctic governance, including relationships between external (UN) interests and regional measures concerning science, resource management, tourism and environmental protection, see Olav S. Stokke and Davor Vidas (eds), *Governing the Antarctic: The Effectiveness and Legitimacy of the Antarctic Treaty System* (Cambridge, Cambridge University Press, 1996).

17 J. Juo, China News Service, 5 March 2010, translated and cited by Linda Jakobson and Jingchao Peng, *China's Arctic aspirations*, SIPRI policy paper 34 (Stockholm, Stockholm International Peace Research Institute, 2012), p. 15.

18 Guy Faulconbride, 'Russian Navy Boss Warns of China's Race for Arctic', *Reuters*, 4 October 2010. Available at https://www.reuters.com/article/russia-arctic-idAFLDE6931GL20101004 (accessed 30 May 2018).

19 See the following discussion; and Olav S. Stokke, 'Regime interplay in Arctic shipping governance: Explaining regional niche selection', *International Environmental Agreements: Politics, Law and Economics* 13 (2013), pp. 65–85.
20 R. Edward Freeman, *Strategic Management: A Stakeholder Approach* (Boston, Pitman, 1984).
21 For overviews of stakeholder theory, see e.g. Thomas Donaldson and Lee E. Preston, 'The stakeholder theory of the corporation: Concepts, evidence and implications', *Academy of Management Review* 20 (1995), pp. 65–91; Ronald K. Mitchell, Bradley R. Agle and Donna J. Wood, 'Toward a theory of stakeholder identification and salience: Defining the principle of who and what really counts', *Academy of Management Review* 22/4 (1997), pp. 865–9; Jeff Frooman, 'Stakeholder influence strategies', *Academy of Management Review*, 24 (1999), pp. 191–205; and the debate in Bradley R. Agle, Thomas Donaldson, R. Edward Freeman, Michael C. Jensen, Ronald K. Mitchell and Donna J. Wood, 'Dialogue: Toward superior stakeholder theory', *Business Ethics Quarterly* 18 (2008), pp. 153–90.
22 On the distinctions between descriptive, instrumental and normative stakeholder theories, see Donaldson and Preston, 'The stakeholder theory of the corporation: Concepts, evidence, and implications'.
23 See Mitchell et al., 'Toward a theory of stakeholder identification and salience: Defining the principle of who and what really counts'.
24 Ibid., p. 869.
25 Olav S. Stokke, 'The Law of the Sea', in G. Ritzer (ed.), *Wiley–Blackwell Encyclopedia of Globalization*, vol. 3 (New York, Wiley-Blackwell, 2012), pp. 1280–2.
26 State Council, 'China's Arctic Policy', paragraph VI.3.
27 Respectively, Korea, 'Arctic Policy of the Republic of Korea', pp. 12–13, and Japan, 'Japan's Arctic Policy', paragraph 3.
28 Tom Røseth, 'Russia's China policy in the Arctic', *Strategic Analysis* 38/6 (2014), pp. 841–59.
29 Rakesh Sharma, 'ONGC in Talks with Rosneft, Novatek for Russia Energy Assets', *Wall Street Journal*, 14 December 2011; see also Neil Gadihoke, 'Arctic melt: The outlook for India', *Maritime Affairs: Journal of the National Maritime Foundation of India* 8 (2012), pp. 1–12.
30 Norwegian Ministry of Foreign Affairs, *Nordområdene: Visjon og virkemidler*, Meld. st.7 (2011–12) (Oslo, Norwegian Ministry of Foreign Affairs, 2011), p. 49.
31 Miguel Martin, 'China in Greenland: Mines, Science, and Nods to Independence', *China Brief* 18/4 (Jamestown Foundation, 2018). Available at https://jamestown.org/program/china-greenland-mines-science-nods-independence/ (accessed 15 May 2018).
32 On overcapacity in the world's fisheries, including in the North Pacific and the North Atlantic, see FAO, *The State of World Fisheries and Aquaculture 2013* (Rome, FAO, 2013).
33 David A. Balton, 'The Bering Sea Doughnut Hole Convention: Regional solution, global implications', in O. S. Stokke (ed.), *Governing High Seas Fisheries: The Interplay of Global and Regional Regimes* (Oxford, Oxford University Press, 2001), pp. 143–78.
34 Olav S. Stokke, *Disaggregating International Regimes: A New Approach to Evaluation and Comparison* (Cambridge, MIT Press, 2012).

35 Government of Greenland, 'Consensus to protect the central Arctic Ocean from unregulated fisheries', Press Release, 25 February 2014. Available at http://www.pewtrusts.org/~/media/legacy/oceans_north_legacy/attachments/greenlandpress-release-english.pdf (accessed 5 June 2018).
36 Olav S. Stokke, 'Managing straddling stocks: The interplay of global and regional regimes', *Ocean & Coastal Management* 43/2–3 (2000), pp. 205–34.
37 Olav S. Stokke, 'Geopolitics, governance, and Arctic fisheries politics', in E. Conde and S. S. Iglesias (eds), *Global Challenges in the Arctic Region: Sovereignty, the Environment and Geopolitical Balance* (London, Routledge, 2017), pp. 170–96.
38 Japan, 'Japan's Arctic Policy', paragraph 4 (2).
39 State Council, 'China's Arctic Policy', paragraph IV.3(3).
40 Hanna Hoag, 'Nations agree to ban fishing in Arctic Ocean for at least 16 years', *Science*, 1 December 2017. Available at http://www.sciencemag.org/news/2017/12/nations-agree-ban-fishing-arctic-ocean-least-16-years (accessed 30 May 2018).
41 State Council, 'China's Arctic Policy', paragraph IV.3(1).
42 Japan, 'Japan's Arctic Policy', paragraph 4 (3).
43 Korea, 'Arctic Policy of the Republic of Korea', especially paragraphs on Strengthening International Cooperation and Pursuing Sustainable Arctic Businesses.
44 UNCLOS, Article 211, paragraph 4 (providing for innocent passage) and Article 21, paragraph 2 (restricting rules on design, construction, manning and equipment). Passage is 'innocent so long as it is not prejudicial to the peace, good order or security of the coastal State'; among the acts considered as prejudicial in those respects are 'wilful and serious pollution contrary to this Convention' (Article 19, paragraphs 1 and 2(h)). Available at http://www.un.org/depts/los/convention_agreements/texts/unclos/closindx.htm (accessed 30 May 2018).
45 Kristin Bartenstein, 'The "Arctic exception" in the Law of the Sea Convention: A contribution to safer navigation in the Northwest Passage?', *Ocean Development and International Law*, 42 (2011), pp. 22–52, p. 45.
46 Donat Pharand, 'The Arctic Waters and the Northwest Passage: A final revisit', *Ocean Development and International Law* 38 (2007), pp. 3–69; David VanderZwaag, Aldo Chircop, Erik Franckx, Hugh Kindred, Kenneth MacInnis, *Governance of Arctic Marine Shipping* (Halifax, Dalhousie University, 2008). Available at http://arcticportal.org/uploads/bC/JU/bCJUaKAo52XTtHDZ359QNA/5.novAMSA-Governance-of-Arctic-Marine-Shipping-Final-Report-1-Aug.pdf (accessed 20 May 2014).
47 On Russia, see R. Douglas Brubaker, 'Straits in the Russian Arctic', *Ocean Development and International Law* 32 (2001), pp. 263–87; on Canada, see Bartenstein, 'The "Arctic exception" in the Law of the Sea Convention: A contribution to safer navigation in the Northwest Passage?', p. 35.
48 The Polar Code is available at http://www.imo.org/en/MediaCentre/HotTopics/polar/Documents/POLAR%20CODE%20TEXT%20AS%20ADOPTED.pdf (accessed 8 May 2018).
49 Two Chinese documents relevant to the Polar Code were submitted to another subcommittee, that on Human Element, Training and Watchkeeping, concerning certification and training requirements; see IMO Docs. HTW 1/11/2 and HTW 2/9/1.
50 See IMO Docs. MEPC 68/6/4. The second co-sponsored failed to convince the Marine Safety Committee to introduce simplified certification procedures for single voyages; see MSC 94/3/15.

51 See IMO Doc. MEPC 67/9/8, co-submitted with Iceland, the Marshall Islands, Panama and the Cruise Lines International Association.

52 See e.g. David G. Victor, *Global Warming Gridlock: Creating More Effective Strategies for Protecting the Planet* (Cambridge, Cambridge University Press, 2011).

53 For example Robert O. Keohane and David G. Victor, 'Cooperation and discord in global climate policy', *Nature and Climate Change* 6/6 (2016), pp. 570–5.

54 Olav S. Stokke, Geir Hønneland and Peter Johan Schei, 'Pollution and Conservation', in O. S. Stokke and G. Hønneland (eds), *International Cooperation and Arctic Governance: Regime Effectiveness and Northern Region Building* (London, Routledge, 2007), pp. 78–111.

55 Eric Dewailly and Chris Furgal, 'POPs, the environment, and public health', in D. L. Downie and T. Fenge (eds), *Northern Lights Against POPs: Combatting Toxic Threats in the Arctic* (Montreal, McGill-Queen's University Press, 2003), pp. 3–21.

56 On Arctic-state influence on the mandate of the toxics task force, see Lars-Otto Reiersen, Simon J. Wilson and V. Kimstach, 'Circumpolar perspectives on persistent organic pollutants: the Arctic Monitoring and Assessment Programme', in Downie and Fenge (eds), *Northern Lights Against POPs: Combatting Toxic Threats in the Arctic*, pp. 60–86, at p. 61.

57 John Anthony Buccini, 'The long and winding road to Stockholm: The view from the chair', Downie and Fenge (eds), *Northern Lights Against POPs: Combatting Toxic Threats in the Arctic*, pp. 224–56, p. 250.

58 Georg Karlaganis, Renato Marioni, Ivo Sieber and Andreas Weber, 'The elaboration of the Stockholm Convention on Persistent Organic Pollutants (POPs): A negotiation process fraught with obstacles and opportunities', *Environmental Science and Pollution Research* 8 (2001), pp. 216–21.

59 See the Arctic Council Ministerial Declarations from 2006 to 2013, available at http://www.arctic-council.org (accessed 30 May 2018).

60 Steinar Andresen, G. Kristin Rosendal and Jon Birger Skjærseth, 'Why negotiate a legally binding mercury treaty', *International Environmental Agreements: Politics, Law and Economics* 13 (2013), pp. 425–40.

61 See http://www.mercuryconvention.org/Countries/Parties/tabid/3428/language/en-US/Default.aspx (accessed 30 May 2018).

62 Olav S. Stokke, 'Interplay management, niche selection, and Arctic environmental governance', in S. Oberthür and O. S. Stokke (eds), *Managing Institutional Complexity: Regime Interplay and Global Environmental Change* (Cambridge, MIT Press, 2011), pp. 143–70.

63 See https://www.amap.no/adaptation-actions-for-a-changing-arctic-part-c (accessed 30 May 2018).

64 On the International Northern Sea Route Programme, see Willy Østreng (ed.), *The Natural and Societal Challenges of the Northern Sea Route: A Reference Work* (Dordrecht, Kluwer Academic, 1999).

65 Iselin Stensdal, 'Coming of age? Asian Arctic research, 2004–2013', *Polar Record* 52/2 (2016), pp. 134–43.

66 Svein Vigeland Rottem, 'A note on the Arctic Council agreements', *Ocean Development & International Law* 46/1 (2015), pp. 50–9.

67 On the Arctic Marine Shipping Assessment, see Stokke, 'Regime interplay in Arctic shipping governance: Explaining regional niche selection'.
68 AMAP (Arctic Monitoring and Assessment Programme), *Arctic Pollution Issues* (Oslo, AMAP, 1997).
69 Henrik Selin, *Towards International Chemical Safety: Taking Action on Persistent Organic Pollutants (POPs)* (Linköping, Department of Water and Environmental Studies, Linköping University, 2007).
70 AMAP (Arctic Monitoring and Assessment Programme), CAFF (Conservation of Arctic Flora and Fauna) and IASC (International Arctic Science Committee), *Arctic Climate Impact Assessment* (Cambridge, Cambridge University Press, 2005).
71 Alf Håkon Hoel, 'Climate change', in Stokke and Hønneland (eds), *International Cooperation and Arctic Governance: Regime Effectiveness and Northern Region Building*, pp. 112–37.

CHAPTER 10

COMING OF AGE? ASIAN ARCTIC RESEARCH, 2004–13

Iselin Stensdal

Introduction

The Arctic is changing, not only as regards climatic fluctuation, but also in socio-economic and political terms.[1] At its Kiruna meeting in May 2013, the Arctic Council (AC) granted permanent observer status to China, India, Italy, Japan, Singapore and South Korea. In the years prior to this, the Asian candidates had convinced the Nordic countries, and eventually the Unites States that they should be granted such status. During the Kiruna negotiations, Canada and Russia, which had previously been opposed also gave in.[2]

The years leading up to the Kiruna meeting were marked by increased international attention towards the Arctic. One milestone in this 'Arctic-hype' period was the assertive planting of the Russian flag on the Arctic seabed in August 2007. This action did not go unnoticed internationally, but the Russian government was at the time sending mixed messages to the international community, signalling both provocation and wishes for peace and stability in the region.[3] Another important indication of international attention to the Arctic came when the US Geological Survey (USGS) published its Circum-Arctic Resource Appraisal in 2008. Although the report duly emphasized the data challenges and

This chapter builds on parts of Iselin Stensdal, *Asian Arctic Research 2005–2012: Harder, Better, Faster, Stronger*, FNI Report 3/2013 (Lysaker, Fridtjof Nansen Institute, 2013); and 'Coming of age? Asian Arctic research, 2004–2013', *Polar Record* 52/2 (2016), pp. 134–43. Special thanks to Elisabeth Råstad and Sebastien Barrault at Kings Bay A/S and Kirsten Haraldsen, University of Oslo, for assistance in obtaining data.

uncertainties, its conclusions – that up to 30 per cent of the world's undiscovered natural gas resources, and up to 13 per cent of the world's undiscovered oil resources may be located in the Arctic – were received with enthusiasm and global interest.[4] The potential geopolitical consequences became a topic of scholarly focus as well.[5] When it became evident that the Arctic was particularly vulnerable to climate change, the world was alarmed on ecological grounds – but many also saw new opportunities emerging through easier utilization of Arctic sea routes and sub-soil resources becoming more accessible. International attention came from many countries, but the media were particularly attentive to the interest shown by Chinese actors.[6]

In a worldview of grand politics, any actions of a country or its representatives may be interpreted as part of a power play. Governments frequently use soft power – the ability to influence others so as to obtain the desired outcomes through attraction rather than coercion or payment[7] – and public diplomacy to win credibility among the public, the media, businesses and intergovernmental organizations.[8] In several cases, science has been employed as part of a two-track diplomacy.[9] The Arctic-research efforts of Asian countries preceded their applications for AC observer status, but have been little examined. Occasionally, their research activity in the region has been interpreted as an expression of wider interests concerning the Arctic. One example is the Indian news outlet Zee News's coverage of Indian President Pranab Mukherjee's visit to Norway and Finland in 2014: the research efforts he mentioned were understood as an Indian endeavour to establish a presence in the Arctic.[10] Often the focus is on China, as with *The Economist's* linking of China's sixth Arctic scientific sea expedition to interests in commercial shipping along the Northern Sea Route.[11] The Arctic scientific activities of Asian countries – of China in particular – are sometimes seen as part of a deliberate diplomatic strategy, also in academic writing.[12]

However, these assessments lack a factual foundation. Jakobson and Peng note research institutions as Chinese Arctic actors, and assert that their job is to provide recommendations to policymakers[13]; and Chen interprets China's increasing allocation of resources to Arctic science and the ordering of a second icebreaker as part of a wider Arctic diplomatic strategy.[14] Such studies take research as an agent, a site and object in the political landscape – without going more deeply into what the research actually entails in terms of disciplinary areas, research locations, funding models, places of publication, and whether international cooperation was involved. Too often, the assumption is made that there is a clear connection between the Arctic research conducted by researchers from Asian countries and the grander Arctic strategies of these countries.

While not studying these possible connections in detail, this chapter aims to take a first step in bringing to the table hard facts about Asian Arctic research.

How is Arctic research organized by governments in Asian countries? How has Asian Arctic research changed over the last decade? What aspects of the Arctic have Asian researchers studied, and where? How do China, India, Japan and South Korea compare? Surely, opinion is best formed on the basis of facts; likewise, the best conditions and starting point for any debate, scholarly or public, is that participants are informed by facts and reality. In this chapter I focus on the period 2004–13, to shed light on the development of Asian research on the Arctic as regards Asia's four largest economies: China, India, Japan and South Korea. The Russian Federation has territory in Asia, but it is also an Arctic country. This survey concerns only non-Arctic countries.

After explaining my choices in mapping Asian Arctic research, I examine how the governments have institutionalized Arctic research, and then investigate the parameters of science: research activities in the Arctic, government spending on Arctic research and infrastructure, journal publications, and international memberships and cooperation. The ten-year period shows a marked increase in research infrastructure, and in publication volume as well as new Asian initiatives involving networks for researchers residing in Arctic and in Asian countries.

Method, Data and Definitions

'Arctic research' is understood as referring to 'research on the basis of material from the Arctic region, around Arctic-based phenomena or which is directly aimed at usage in the Arctic region'.[15] This definition does not necessarily require the scientist(s) to have been physically present in the Arctic area.

I have concentrated on parameters that were obtainable and comparable. Funding for research usually gives a good indication of how serious a government is in pursuing a given topic, but comparable data for the four Asian countries proved difficult to obtain. I consulted a range of sources: statistics, databases, relevant publications and information from these countries' own polar institutes: the Polar Research Institute of China, India's National Centre for Antarctic and Ocean Research, Japan's National Institute of Polar Research and the Korea Polar Research Institute. The following indicators were chosen: the role of the national polar institutes, investments in infrastructure and scientific funding, research activities such as scientific cruises, and publication output. Scientific publishing is important in science, both for the standing of the institutions involved, and for the scientific debate. I used the worldwide databases Web of Science and Scopus to collect Asian Arctic-research articles. However, while these are excellent for locating work published in Europe or North America, they are not comprehensive regarding publications in Asia, although journals in Asian languages are covered by the databases. Therefore, I checked several Asian national science websites:

China Knowledge Resource Integrated Database, India's National Institute of Science Communication and Information Resources Online Periodicals Repository, Japan's ScienceLinks and KoreaScience.

My findings are not exhaustive, and there may well exist Arctic research that I have not located, perhaps published in Asian languages. However, the findings give an indication of publication trends. Further, only scientific articles have been included, not monographs or edited volumes. The articles were whole-counted: for each article with at least one, say, Indian (co-) author, that article counted as one.[16] When counting articles in this manner, one cannot simply add co-authorships: a figure of, say, 25 per cent Chinese co-authors and 25 per cent Korean co-authors does not necessarily mean that there were Chinese and Korean co-authors for exactly half of the articles. Most probably, some articles had both Chinese and Korean co-authors, and these were counted twice. Further, as not every article with 'Arctic' in its abstract, keywords or title that came up in searches actually concerned the Arctic, I checked every article to ensure only those that did involve the Arctic were included in the count. Articles are arranged by country on the basis of the author's institutional affiliation. Quite a few researchers work abroad, which meant they were coded with another country than their native one. On the macro-level, however, my figures should give a fair indication of publication trends. I found most of the articles in Scopus and Web of Science. While journals indexed in those two databases are peer-reviewed, that might not be the case for all the Asian journals found on the Asian science websites. However, assuming that the articles found on the science websites were selected on the basis of their scientific qualities, I have not distinguished further between refereed and non-refereed journals, unless explicitly stated.

National Polar Institutes: Governmental Links and Research Hubs

Much of the Arctic research conducted in Asian countries is undertaken by scientists working at universities, research institutes and research centres. However, the various national polar research institutes are central to the coordination of polar and Arctic research; they also act as links between the government and the research communities.

China has two national polar organizations: the Chinese Arctic and Antarctic Administration (CAA) in Beijing, and the Polar Research Institute of China (PRIC) in Shanghai. Both report to the State Oceanic Administration (SOA), which in turn reports to the Ministry of Land and Resources. The CAA, with a staff of around forty, holds a more administrative function, organizing and drafting national polar research strategies and plans. PRIC has a more hands-on role, supervising and managing polar research expeditions, research stations, the research vessel and icebreaker *Xue Long*, and acting as a domestic hub. In 2006 PRIC had a staff of 124, rising to around 220 by 2013. The institute also conducts polar research.[17]

India's National Centre for Antarctic and Ocean Research (NCAOR) in Goa has overall responsibility for implementation of India's polar research programmes, which includes undertaking research. The centre is autonomous but is part of the Ministry of Earth Sciences, which also incorporated the India Meteorological Department in 2006. NCAOR has a core staff of about fifty; with affiliated researchers and project members, the total is approximately 110. In connection with the International Polar Year 2007/8, the government decided to extend India's polar research to include the Arctic and to open a research station in Norway's Arctic Svalbard archipelago. Station management was delegated to NCAOR.[18]

Japan's National Institute of Polar Research (NIPR) was established in 1973 under the Ministry of Education, Culture, Sports, Science and Technology (MEXT). It is Japan's key institution for polar science, with management responsibility for the country's polar stations. It has some 250 employees, with a further 300 affiliated scientists. Within NIPR, the Arctic Environment Research Centre (AERC) manages the Ny-Ålesund research station on Svalbard, facilitates research activities for Japan's research organs in the Arctic region and collects Arctic data.[19] NIPR also serves as secretariat to the network Japan Consortium for Arctic Environmental Research (JCAR), with some 300 members. In addition to supporting its members' research, JCAR organizes research plans and infrastructure, makes recommendations to MEXT and disseminates research outcomes to the public.[20] Polar research is an integral part of Japan's overall science structure. In 2004, the Research Organization of Information and Systems (ROIS) became the parent organization to NIPR and other Japanese national institutes of informatics, mathematics and genetics. The aim is to facilitate holistic and interdisciplinary research on issues vital to humanity in the twenty-first century. In turn, ROIS is one of Japan's four inter-university research institute corporations. Under ROIS, NIPR is part of the Transdisciplinary Research Integration Centre, which works to create new paradigms in the fields of earth environment, life sciences and human and social systems. Here NIPR contributes in the fields of life and earth sciences.[21] Unlike the other national polar institutes, NIPR does not manage Japan's research vessels and other sea-vessel research equipment: that is the job of the Japan Agency for Marine-Earth Science and Technology (JAMSTEC).

The Korea Polar Research Institute (KOPRI) conducts scientific research and long-term observations on issues that require data from the polar regions, and coordinates domestic research projects and international cooperation. It also contributes to Korean policy and public services by delivering information to the government and other stakeholders.[22] KOPRI has an annual budget of around US$ 50 million and close to 300 employees in total, some 220 of whom are scientists.[23] Korea's 2011 Marine Technology Road Map prescribed strengthening national competitiveness in the marine and polar fields. Following this, the Ministry of Land, Transport, and Maritime Affairs (MLTM) established the Korea Institute of Ocean Science and Technology (KIOST) in July 2012, as a modern replacement of the Korea Ocean Research and Development Institute (KORDI), which opened in 1973. KOPRI is hierarchically under KIOST, but operates independently. There are plans to increase KIOST personnel to more than 1,700 towards 2020, with promises of accompanying governmental budgeted funds.[24]

Asian Polar Research Historically and Geographically: Antarctica First

In all these countries, research on Antarctica preceded Arctic research, and the four Asian countries studied here are all signatories to the 1959 Antarctic Treaty. Japan was among the original signatories – in fact, its first polar expedition had reached Antarctica in January 1912. Some forty-five years later, the Japanese established their Syowa Station in Antarctica. China, India and South Korea all commenced Antarctic-research expeditions and established research stations in Antarctica in the 1980s. At present, the four countries have more research stations and personnel located in Antarctica than in the Arctic: China has three camps and one station, India has three stations, Japan has one camp and four stations, and South Korea has two stations in the Antarctic.[25] Despite an increase in Arctic-research efforts between 2004 and 2013, more resources, time and personnel are still devoted to research in Antarctica.[26]

Concerning the Arctic, Japan's NIPR was again the first of the four to set up a research station there, in Ny-Ålesund on Svalbard in 1991. Chinese researchers joined in the Arctic expeditions of other countries in the 1990s, and in 1999 China launched its first national Arctic expedition. In 2002, eleven years after the Japanese station was inaugurated, the Korean research station Dasan was opened in Ny-Ålesund. China's CAA followed suit in 2004, with its Yellow River station, and India's NCAOR opened its Himadri Ny-Ålesund station in 2008. Much of the explanation for this recent expansion of Asian polar research from Antarctica to the Arctic lies in the growing acknowledgement that climatic changes in the Arctic affect the Asian countries as well. For example, studies have indicated connections between developments in the Arctic region and changes in Indian monsoon intensity.[27] Researchers from elsewhere in Asia are also conducting polar research. For example, researchers at Taiwan's National University and National Ocean University publish frequently on polar research, and in 2009 scientists from Taiwan were scheduled to participate in China's Antarctic expedition, marking the first cross-straits polar research cooperation.[28] In 2004 the Asian Forum for Polar Sciences (AFoPS) was established by the national polar research institutes of China, India, Japan, Malaysia and South Korea, to facilitate research cooperation on polar science. Indonesian, Philippine, Vietnamese and Thai research institutions are observers to the AFoPS.[29]

Svalbard: The Increasing Asian Presence in Ny-Ålesund

Norway's Svalbard archipelago is the world's most northerly location equipped with modern infrastructure and research facilities, and is ideal for tracking satellites with polar orbits. This is where the four Asian national polar institutes have set up permanent research stations. The 1920 Spitsbergen Treaty gives Norway full sovereignty over the archipelago and Norwegian law applies. However, the treaty grants certain rights to the subjects of other signatories, including free access to the islands and equal rights to pursue certain economic activities, notably mining, fishing, hunting and trade. Scientific research is not listed among these activities, but Norway has practised a liberal policy here. In recent years, the Norwegian government has actively encouraged the establishment of research stations in Ny-Ålesund, a former mining settlement now designated as the international base for natural sciences. Here the national polar institute of Norway as well as Dutch, French, German, Italian and British research institutions have research stations, in addition to the four Asian stations. The Russian research base on Svalbard is located in the mining settlement of Barentsburg; and Poland's Academy of Sciences' Institute of Geophysics has a Svalbard research station at Hornsund near the southern tip of the main island.[30]

In Ny-Ålesund, all overnight stays are registered according to the scientists' institutional affiliation. The Asian share is shown in Figure 10.1. Between 2004 and 2007, Asia sent only Chinese, Japanese and Korean researchers: that might explain the 3 per cent increase from 2007 to 2008, when the Indian station opened. Especially notable is the change from 2010 to 2011, with the Asian share jumping from 15 per cent to 21 per cent.

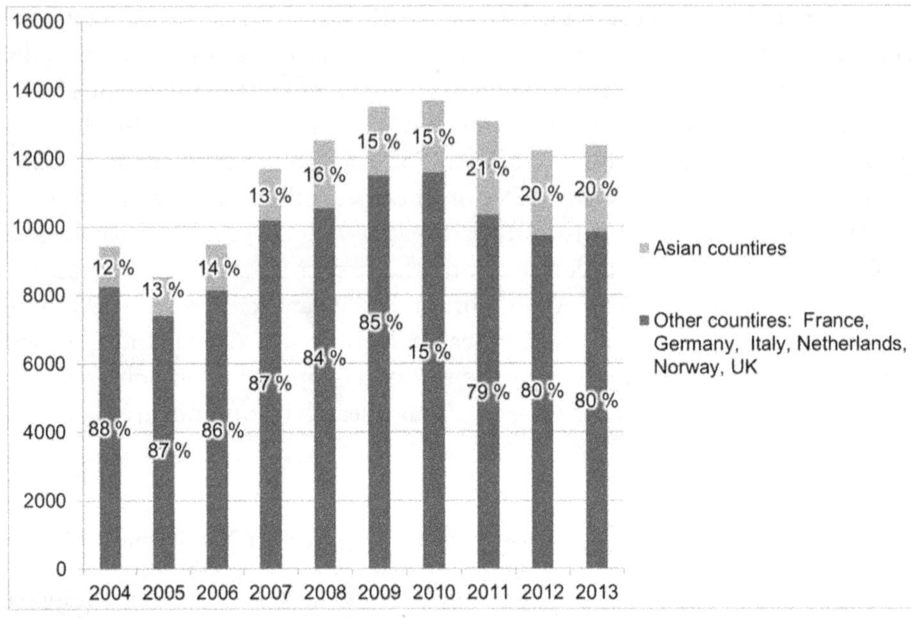

Figure 10.1 Asian share of researcher overnight stays in Ny-Ålesund, 2004–13.

That increase was driven largely by heightened activity on the part of Chinese as well as Indian researchers. Since 2011, the Asian share of overnight stays has remained stable at around 20 per cent. The overall peak year in Ny-Ålesund was 2010: total stays have declined somewhat since then, but the general trend for the whole period 2004–13 was an increase in overnight stays, combined with a greater Asian share of those stays. The Chinese constituted the third largest group of Ny-Ålesund overnight stays in 2010–13, after Norwegian and French/German operations. Between 2004 and 2013 there was almost a doubling in Chinese and in Indian overnight stays. The trend was less clear for the Japanese and Korean stations, with annual overnight stays in the period covered here fluctuating between 90 and 417 at the Japanese and between 204 and 541 at the Korean stations. That Japanese researchers had comparatively the lowest presence in Ny-Ålesund can probably be explained by the presence of Japanese scientists elsewhere in the Arctic. NIPR also has an office at the University Centre in Longyearbyen, the largest settlement on Svalbard.[31] All in all, the Asian presence in Ny-Ålesund has increased significantly, in total numbers and in percentage terms, but is still much less than that of Norwegian or French/German activities.

Scientific Cruises

Scientific cruises organized by Asian polar institutes increased in volume in the period 2004–13, with most Asian-managed sea expeditions being conducted after 2007. The Chinese *Xue Long* set out on its third, fourth and fifth Arctic Ocean expeditions in 2008, 2010 and 2012. The Japanese research vessel *Mirai* undertook six scientific cruises between 2004 and 2013; between 2008 and 2013, it was only in 2011 that the *Mirai* did not visit the Arctic. KOPRI has sent its research vessel *Araon* on scientific cruises annually since the vessel was completed in 2009. Scientific cruises are international in nature, normally involving researchers from outside the host country as well. For example, scientists from institutions in ten countries were involved in the *Araon*'s 2012 Arctic cruise, Chinese and Japanese included.[32] On launching the Indian Arctic Programme in 2007, India's NCAOR sent its first team of scientists to Svalbard; it has since sent researchers to the Ny-Ålesund station several times a year. Indian scientific cruises are conducted mainly in the Southern Ocean, with no Arctic cruises between 2004 and 2013.[33] Of the above-mentioned scientific cruises, one is noteworthy for conducting more than scientific data collection: the fifth Chinese Arctic expedition in August 2012 made a five-day stop at Iceland, at the invitation of the Icelandic President Olafur Ragnar Grimsson. This was four months after Chinese Premier Wen Jiabao's official visit to Iceland, where China's SOA and Iceland's Ministry of Foreign Affairs signed a bilateral framework agreement on Arctic cooperation and a memorandum of understanding (MoU) on cooperation on marine and polar science and technology. In August the cruise members were invited to the presidential residence, and PRIC and the Icelandic Centre for Research signed research cooperation MoUs on Arctic issues such as climate change and sustainable development, Asian and Nordic economic cooperation, and Arctic strategies, policies and legislation. President Grimsson referred to the cruise delegation's visit as a new pillar of bilateral cooperation between China and Iceland.[34] On its return, *Xue Long* sailed not along the Northern Sea Route and through Russian waters, as it had on its outward journey, but took the transpolar route crossing the Arctic Ocean, to investigate future shipping possibilities in the Arctic connecting East Asia and Europe.[35]

Increased Investments in Infrastructure and Research Funding

The polar institutes and governments of the four countries in focus made substantial investments in infrastructure and research programmes in the period under study. By early 2004, Chinese, Japanese and Korean polar research institutions had established research stations in Ny-Ålesund, and India made a considerable investment when it established a research station in the Arctic in 2008. Moreover, in line with the 2012 framework MoU on cooperation on marine polar science and technology, in 2013 the Chinese PRIC and the Icelandic Centre for Research (RANNIS) signed an agreement on constructing a joint Aurora Observatory in northern Iceland, at Karholl near Akureyri. Several Chinese and Icelandic research institutions are affiliated with the observatory, which will focus on aurora, space and physics studies. The observatory was set up in 2013 as a non-profit foundation, with the Chinese side putting forward ISK 300 million (US$ 2.4 million). A cornerstone-laying ceremony was held in October 2016, and the observatory's management committee had its first meeting in October 2013.[36]

Research institutions may seek funding from many sources, and thereby pursue research topics on their own. Major boosts in scientific fields usually require specific government allocations in funding. Moreover, some infrastructure – icebreakers, for example – is so costly that only governments can pay. Between 2004 and 2013, both China's PRIC and Korea's KOPRI ordered new research vessels with icebreaker capabilities. Construction of the Korean *Araon* was started in 2007; since completion in 2009, it has visited the Arctic and the Antarctic annually. China's CAA and PRIC signed a contract in 2012 with the Finnish company Aker Arctic for a new research vessel. In 2013, work started on building this vessel, estimated to cost RMB 1.25 billion (US$ 198 million). With their considerable activity in Antarctica, the Chinese have not been able to conduct scientific cruises in the Arctic annually, and the new ship is expected to help meet this logistical challenge.[37]

Most of the four governments have earmarked funding to Arctic research, often in combination or as part of larger national strategies for the future. In 2006 China's SOA established the research fund for the Chinese polar science strategy, which in the course of three years awarded a total of RMB 5,600,000 (US$ 900,000) in funding to more than seventy research applications. Furthermore, in 2012 SOA announced a new five-year polar research project on environmental issues and climate change, involving three Arctic missions and five Antarctic expeditions.[38] In 2006 the Chinese government decided to boost the country's research and development efforts, aiming to devote 2.5 per cent of GDP to research and development by 2020. As of 2012 China had achieved 2.0 per cent of GDP, up from 1.4 per cent in 2006.[39] This increase in Arctic research should be viewed in light of China's overall emphasis on science.

Following recommendations in a report by Japan's working group on Arctic research examination, in 2011 MEXT instigated a five-year programme, the Arctic Climate Change Project, under the Green Network of Excellence (GRENE). GRENE was established in the same year in a strategic effort aimed at national growth, where 'green' innovation was singled out as important to Japan's future.

The Arctic Climate Change Project ran from 2011 to 2016, involving altogether thirty-five institutions and more than 300 scientists. The project had four main goals: to understand the mechanisms of increased warming in the Arctic; to understand the Arctic system's impact on global climate and future change; to evaluate impacts of Arctic change on weather and climate in Japan, marine ecosystems and fisheries; and to prepare projections of sea-ice distribution and Arctic sea routes.[40]

In addition, the South Korean government has placed Arctic research within a broader strategic context. After the Marine Technology Road Map (adopted in 2011), the MLTM allocated some KRW 3.6 trillion (US$ 3.3 billion) up to 2020 for marine and polar technology development. As well as research funding, support goes to KIOST, Korea's only government-run ocean science research institute, and towards the goal of making the coastal cities of Busan and Incheon hubs of the ocean and polar research and industry.[41]

Journal Publications

Publishing research findings is a major goal: for contributing new insights and information and building one's career. Asian annual publication output of articles concerning the Arctic has more than doubled over the ten years studied here, although Japan's output remained fairly stable. In 2004 Japan published more Arctic articles than the other three countries combined. China surpassed Japan in terms of article output in 2009. Especially notable are China's two jumps in output volume, in 2008–9 and 2011–12. The fairly low total volume of articles from India reflects the fact that the Arctic is a new research area for the country's research institutions (Figure 10.2).

In line with the international orientation of the polar science community, co-authorship with scientists from other countries is common, as shown in Table 10.1. India stands out because its articles are mostly written by Indian authors, but the total number of articles is modest. Japan is the most outward-focused, with 77 per cent of its articles co-written with authors from other countries. As a group, scientists from the eight AC member states, writing together with Japanese and Korean scientists, are co-authors of more than half of the articles. The USA is the most frequent collaboration country for all four Asian countries, followed by the UK, with 10 per cent for China, then Germany at 8 per cent for India, and Canada at 15 per cent for Japan. China is Korea's second-largest collaboration partner, with co-authoring of 11 per cent of the articles. Collaboration among the four Asian countries is not as prevalent as with the AC countries, but Korea stands out, with co-authors from the other Asian countries in 18 per cent of the articles. Publication outlets provide further confirmation of the international orientation

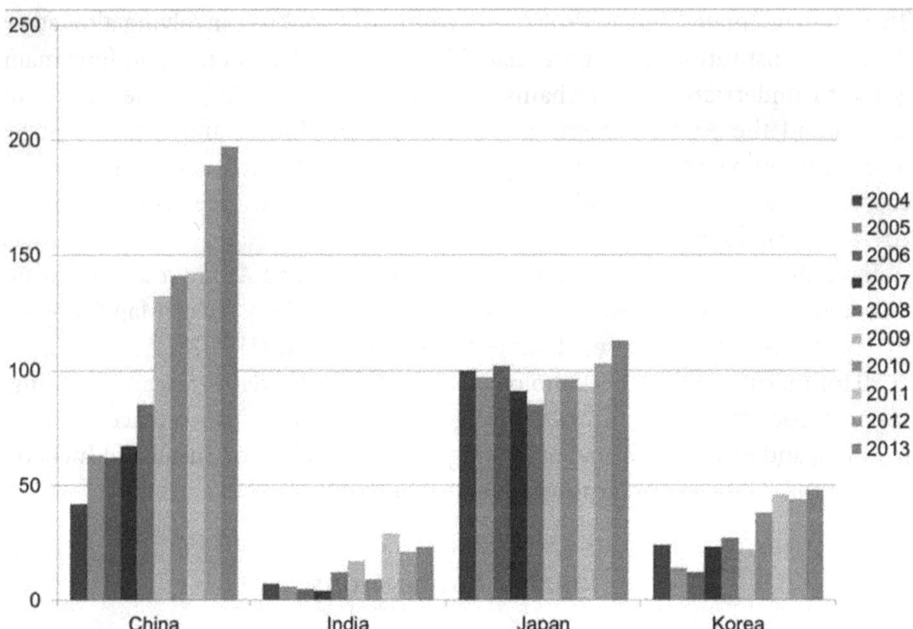

Figure 10.2 Arctic article output by country, 2004–13.

of Asian researchers: between 71 per cent and 83 per cent of the articles analyzed here were published in journals not originating nationally. During the ten-year period, Asian researchers published frequently in such acclaimed international journals as *The Journal of Geophysical Research: Atmospheres*, *Geophysical Research Letters*, *The Journal of Climate* and *Polar Biology*. There are also many articles published in thematic national peer-reviewed journals, such as China's *Advances in Atmospheric Sciences*, India's *Mausam*, the *Journal of the Meteorological Society of Japan* and South Korea's *Ocean and Polar Research*. The remaining articles are published in a wide range of international and national journals, many with only one article, and equally many with two to five articles. Not all of these national journals are necessarily peer-reviewed.

Topically, the natural sciences dominate. Climate change and climate-related issues were featured in most Asian Arctic publications, with proportions varying from country to country (see Table 10.1). The number of citations is an indication of the influence of a given article on the scientific dialogue. One of the most-cited articles with Chinese authors is that by Liu and colleagues,[42] on the impact of declining Arctic sea ice on winters in Europe and parts of the USA, resulting in cold and snowy winters in recent years. Among the most cited articles involving Indian authors is Srinivas and colleagues, on bacterial diversity in Kongsfjorden

Table 10.1 Academic articles on Arctic issues by Asian authors, 2004–13.

	China	**India**	**Japan**	**S. Korea**
Co-author(s) nationality, in per cent				
Only nationals	45	65	33	40
AC member-states	41	26	52	51
USA	39	18	35	41
Other Asian countries*	9	10	10	18
Topic: Climate change, per cent	65	46	59	50
Published: in national periodicals, per cent	29	23	17	23
Number of articles published	1120	133	976	298

* ***At least one author from one of the other three Asian countries in the study.***

and Ny-Ålesund on Svalbard, mapping the bacteria's fatty acid profiles.[43] One of the most cited articles with Japanese authors is Shimada and colleagues, also on the ice cover of the Arctic Ocean: their 2006 article links receding ice cover in the Bering Sea to inflow of warm summer water from the Pacific.[44] Concerning South Korean authors, among the most cited articles is that by Jhun and Lee, which finds a close relation between the East Asian winter monsoon intensity and Arctic Oscillation.[45]

There is some variation regarding themes. Some 5 per cent of the Chinese articles focused on governance aspects of the Arctic, from a social science or legal angle; 21 per cent of India's articles pertained to bacterial studies, 22 per cent of the Japanese articles dealt with various aspects of oceanography, and 12 per cent of the Korean articles concern shipping and navigation. This focus on shipping is in line with Korea's economic profile, where shipbuilding is a cornerstone industry. Interestingly, between 2004 and 2013 only Chinese researchers published a significant amount of social science articles. These articles were all published after 2008, which coincides with and reflects the rise in global attention on Arctic natural resources that started around 2008/9, when the US Geological Service published estimates on the undiscovered oil and gas potential in the Arctic. The Chinese articles present studies of the Arctic countries' own Arctic policies, of Arctic governance structures and mechanisms such as the AC and UNCLOS, of sea route administration and resources like oil and gas; some also discuss the implications for China. Most of these articles were published in national journals in Chinese, some of these probably non-peer-reviewed, and targeted at a Chinese readership.

That there were very few policy-related articles with Indian, Japanese and South Korean authors but considerably more articles with Chinese authors may be due to various reasons. Firstly, Chinese authors became interested in governance and politics related to the Arctic earlier than their counterparts in neighbouring countries. Secondly, authors from other Asian countries have also written on Arctic governance and policy implications, but have published elsewhere and not in scholarly journals – for example, the *Indian Society for the Study of Peace and Conflict* and the *Indian Council of World Affairs* have published issue briefs and policy notes on Arctic issues. This difference probably also reflects researchers' perceptions of which issues are worth studying in the context of their own countries. For instance, a Japanese business approaching investment in the Arctic would probably not create more attention beyond the standard business-buzz surrounding any new venture. In 2011, a group of Japanese companies, with the Japan Oil, Gas and Metals National Corporation (JOGMEC), Japan's stockpiling agency, as the major shareholder, formed the Greenland Petroleum Exploitation Co. Ltd. (GreenPeX). In 2013 GreenPeX was granted two petroleum exploration licenses by the Greenlandic authorities.[46] By contrast, a similar case involving Chinese companies would probably receive much more attention.

Altogether, Asian output more than doubled over the ten years studied here, due mainly to the Chinese increase. Responsiveness towards the international science community is evident in co-authorships and publication outlets. Articles are generally based in natural science disciplines, with climate change as a major focus.

International Memberships and Cooperation

While some of the government funding for Arctic research can be linked to national strategy rationales, researchers and scientific organizations are outwardly focused on the international scientific community. This is shown by the co-authorships noted here, and is also reflected in the affiliations with Arctic science committees, such as the International Arctic Science Committee (IASC) and the Ny-Ålesund Science Managers Committee (NySmac), and international research networks like the international cooperation network on ocean-ridge crest research (Interridge) and the polar earth-observation network, Polenet. Of the four countries studied here, Japan has the largest number of affiliations to international scientific bodies, and India the fewest. This is probably explained by how long each country has focused on the Arctic: Japan has a longer history of Arctic research than the other three.

Asian institutions are not only involved in existing mechanisms for scientific cooperation, they are also creating their own. In 2004, AFoPS was established as a forum aimed at strengthening cooperation among Asian scientists on polar research. It was first an initiative with Chinese, Japanese and Korean members, but India and Malaysia also joined in 2007.[47] Most Arctic research is within the natural sciences, but Asian initiatives for social science cooperation have also emerged recently. In 2011 the Korea Maritime Institute, the Korea Transport Institute of the Republic of Korea, and the US East–West Centre together established the North Pacific Arctic Conference (NPAC), which has since become an annual event. These conferences bring together participants from the Arctic and non-Arctic countries, to share ideas and thoughts on challenges in the Arctic. From the Asian countries, researchers have come from China, Japan and Korea. Climate change, Arctic sea routes, safety and security in Arctic shipping, natural resources and governance are among the issues discussed at the NPACs.[48]

In June 2013, China's PRIC held a China–Nordic Arctic Cooperation Symposium in China, with Chinese and Nordic researchers participating. At the symposium, PRIC proposed establishing a China–Nordic Arctic Research Center. In December the same year the China–Nordic Arctic Research Center (CNARC) was officially launched in Shanghai, with ten member institutions–Chinese and Nordic. Serving as a platform for academic Arctic-research cooperation, CNARC aims to increase awareness of the Arctic globally, to support sustainable development in the Nordic Arctic and the coherent development of China globally. In addition to an annual conference, CNARC was established with the intention of facilitating Chinese–Nordic joint research projects and supporting researchers for visiting scholar exchanges. The PRIC Director serves as CNARC Director, and PRIC also serves as the secretariat for CNARC.[49] Both NPAC and CNARC have been positively received by researchers from the Arctic countries.

Research and Politics

Since 2004, there has been an increase in government funding allocations to Arctic research and scientific infrastructure in China, India, Japan and South Korea. Asian scientists spent more time in the Arctic in 2012 and 2013 at the Svalbard research stations and on scientific cruises than in 2004 and 2005. We have also noted the marked increase in article output, dominated by the natural sciences and climate-change research, but with an emerging body of literature within the social sciences from 2008. That Asian scientists study climate change should come as no surprise. In 2004, Asian Arctic research was just emerging: by 2013 it had become consolidated, mature and intensified, national variations notwithstanding.

Asian Arctic research picked up from 2008, reflecting surging global interest in the Arctic. However, the context of Asian Arctic research should not be forgotten. In 2013, Asian Arctic research was still the 'little brother' of Asian Antarctic research, with more resources and personnel devoted to expeditions and science in the Antarctic. Nor are Asian countries the only non-Arctic countries to increase their research focus on the Arctic. France, Germany, Italy, the Netherlands and the UK are not Arctic states, but they all have research stations in Ny-Ålesund, where they, together with Norway, account for around 80 per cent of overnight stays. Despite its recent growth, Asian Arctic research has remained less comprehensive than the Arctic-research activities and output of other countries.

Earlier accounts have emphasized Asian Arctic research as politically motivated, but without prior examination to back up the claims. What does the study presented here indicate about the relationship between science and researchers on the one side, and policies and government officials on the other?

There exist several connecting areas between Arctic science and politics, domestically and internationally. As is common practice worldwide, Asian scientists offer advice to their home governments. China incorporated the concept of a 'scientific outlook on development' into its constitution in 2008, emphasizing the importance of scientific advice in the future growth of the country.[50] As research and development are national priorities in China, the increase in Arctic research should be understood in this context. India's NCAOR did the work of mapping the country's seabed in support of India's UNCLOS submission for delimitation of the country's continental shelf beyond 200 nautical miles.[51] Korea's KOPRI has provided input to the Ministry of Education, Science and Technology, the MLTM, the Ministry of the Environment and the Ministry of Foreign Affairs and Trade. KOPRI also assisted the government in South Korea's application for permanent observer status on the AC.[52] Furthermore, the Asian polar institutes execute their governments' research agendas and manage the national science infrastructure.

Internationally, the Arctic Council is a prime example of a setting in which the scientific community supplies advice to decision makers. Its working groups, task forces and expert groups provide important input to this political-level forum. The AC observer manual for subsidiary bodies prescribes the working groups as the primary body where observers may contribute. Topics dealt with in the working groups are often technical and scientific in nature, and the meetings provide a venue for experts and bureaucratic representatives to discuss the issues at hand. These working groups are thus important arenas for the Asian states in their new status as permanent observers. Engaging in the activities of the working groups can provide information and contacts, but it is also there that they have opportunities to contribute relevant insights and information. It is too early to come to conclusions concerning the Asian effort here, as the time frame studied goes only to 2013, the year when permanent observer status was granted. The recent CNARC and NPAC initiatives of China's PRIC and South Korea's Korea Maritime Institute and Korea Transport Institute are creating arenas for bringing

Arctic and non-Arctic researchers together on Arctic legal and social science issues. These collaborative ventures can provide governments with input from the meetings and findings.

Of the parameters investigated here, the strongest candidate for an instance where scientific activities also served political goals was the Icelandic invitation to the Chinese scientific cruise expedition in 2012, where President Grimsson explicitly identified the visit as a pillar in bilateral relations between the two countries. The Chinese side seemed happy to engage, but it should be noted that the initiative was not Asian, but Arctic, coming from Iceland. In examining Asian interest in the Arctic, we should bear in mind the relative importance of the region. While the Arctic might be of high importance to the foreign policies of smaller Nordic countries, it ranks further down the foreign-policy agendas of other Arctic countries like the USA; and for Asian countries, there are other areas closer to home that are more important. The heightened political and scientific focus on Arctic resources since 2008 is not exclusively Asian, but is more a global phenomenon. Conclusively proving aspirations of achieving political impact by the use of research is difficult, unless they are made explicit – as in the case of the Icelandic president.

Postscript: After 2013

Once China, India, Japan, Korea and Singapore had been granted permanent observer status on the Arctic Council in 2013, the 'Arctic-hype' as such began to wind down. However, research activities have continued with the same vigour as in previous years.

After 2013, the Asian polar institutes' Antarctic-research facilities continue to outnumber their Arctic ones. Both Chinese PRIC and Korean KOPRI opened Antarctic facilities in 2014 – a seasonal camp, Taishan, and a year-round camp, Jang Bogo, respectively.

The national polar institutes have maintained their pace and size, or increased somewhat. India's NCAOR has expanded all its operations, including opening a glaciological research station, Himansh, in the High Himalayas in October 2016. Staff numbers have increased from around 110 to 142 as of 2017.[53] China's PRIC is planning to move to a larger national polar-research base campus, but no date has yet been confirmed.[54]

As for research publications, a rough search indicates that researchers in all four countries have continued to increase their Arctic-research publishing. Asian research on the Antarctic still outnumbers the Arctic publications, but the difference is less for 2014–18 (January) than for 2009–13. The natural sciences continue to dominate over the social sciences.

It is worth noting that few of the investments decided on in the 2004–13 period had been completed by the time of writing (early 2018). As for the Chinese–Icelandic aurora observatory, originally expected to be completed in 2016, some research activities began in October 2017, but the observatory's webpage indicates an estimated full opening in autumn 2018.[55] The commissioned Chinese research vessel, *Xue Long 2*, is now expected to be completed in 2019.[56]

Politically, official government strategies for the Arctic have been released. South Korea launched its Master Plan in December 2013, followed by Japan's Arctic Policy in October 2015, and finally China's Arctic Policy in January 2018. No similar document has been issued by the Indian government. All three strategies mention research and scientific activities as national goals, which indicates that Arctic research is something Asian governments value and support. Research that can contribute to international knowledge building should be welcomed, regardless of the institution or the author's postal address. Observers and scholars bent on interpreting Asian governments' support for science as a sign of greater political power plays will still need to bring hard evidence to prove the causal connection.

Notes

1 Oran R. Young, 'If an Arctic treaty is not the solution, what is the alternative?', *Polar Record* 47/4 (2011), pp. 327–34, p. 327.

2 Leiv Lunde, 'Introduction', in I. Stensdal, L. Lunde and Y. Jian (eds), *Asian Countries and the Arctic Future* (Singapore, World Scientific Publishing, 2016), pp. 7–11, at pp. 8–10.

3 Marlene Laruelle, *Russia's Arctic Strategies and the Future of the Far North* (New York, Routledge, 2015), p. 12.

4 Katarzyna Zysk, 'The evolving Arctic security environment: An assessment', in S. Blank (ed.), *Russia in the Arctic* (Carlisle, Strategic Studies Institute of the US Army War College, 2011), pp. 91–138, at p. 96.

5 As in Scott G. Borgerson, 'Arctic meltdown: The economic and security implications of global warming', *Foreign Affairs* 87/2 (2008), pp. 63–77.

6 Such as Clifford Coonan, 'The east looks north as China moves in on Iceland', *The Independent*, 30 August 2011. Available at http://www.independent.co.uk/news/business/news/the-east-looks-north-as-china-moves-in-on-iceland-2346482.html (accessed 1 March 2018); Øyvind Paasche, 'The race for Arctic energy resources', *oilprice.com*, 11 April 2011. Available at https://oilprice.com/Geopolitics/International/The-Race-For-Arctic-Energy-Resources.html (accessed 7 March 2018).

7 Joseph S. Nye, 'Public diplomacy and soft power', *Annals of the American Academy of Political and Social Science* 616/1 (2008), pp. 94–109, p. 94.

8 Ibid., p. 95, p. 100.

9 National Research Council, *Scientists, Engineers, and Track-Two Diplomacy: A Half-Century of US–Russian Interacademy Cooperation* (Washington, DC, National Academies Press, 2004).

10 *Zee News*, 'Presidential visit helps India establish presence in key Arctic region', 20 October 2014. Available at http://zeenews.india.com/news/india/presidential-visit-helps-india-establish-presence-in-key-arctic-region_1487403.html (accessed 5 April 2018).

11 *The Economist*, 'China and the Arctic: Polar bearings', 15 July 2014, p. 47.

12 Such as S. Blank, 'China's Arctic strategy', *The Diplomat*, 20 June 2013. Available at https://thediplomat.com/2013/06/chinas-arctic-strategy/?allpages=yes (accessed 5 April 2018); Rasmus G. Berthelsen, Li Xing and Mette Højris Gregersen, 'Chinese Arctic science diplomacy: An instrument for achieving the Chinese dream?', in E. Conde and S. I. Sánchez (eds), *Global Challenges in the Arctic Region: Sovereignty, Environment and Geopolitical Balance* (New York, Routledge, 2016), pp. 442–60; Jingchao Peng and Njord Wegge, 'China's bilateral diplomacy in the Arctic', *Polar Geography* 38/3 (2015), pp. 233–49, at p. 237.

13 Linda Jacobson and Jingchao Peng, *China's Arctic aspirations*, SIPRI policy paper 34 (Stockholm, Stockholm International Peace Research Institute, 2012), pp. 4–6.

14 Gang Chen, 'China's emerging Arctic strategy', *The Polar Journal* 2/2 (2012), pp. 358–71.

15 Dag W. Aksnes, Kristoffer Rørstad and Trude Røsdal, *Norsk polarforskning – forskning på Svalbard. Ressursinnsats og vitenskapelig publisering – indikatorer 2010* (Norwegian Polar Research – research at Svalbard. Resource input and scientific publishing – Indicators 2010), report 3/2012 (Oslo, Nordic Institute for Studies in Innovation, Research and Education, 2012), pp. 12–13.

16 Another option would have been fractional counting: taking one article and dividing it by the number of authors; see David A. Pendlebury, *White paper: Using bibliometrics in evaluating research* (Sydney, Thomson Reuters, 2008), p. 4.

17 Anne-Marie Brady, 'China's rise in Antarctica?', *Asian Survey* 50/4 (2010), pp. 759–85, p. 764; CAA (Chinese Arctic and Antarctic Administration), 'CAA's main responsibilities' (in Chinese) (2011). Available at http://www.chinare.cn/caa/gb_article.php/%7b?\\\\\\\%7dmodid=02001 (accessed 2 October 2014).

18 Neloy Khare, 'Indian scientific endeavors in Ny-Alesund, Arctic', *Antarctic Record* 53/1 (2009), pp. 110–13, pp. 110–11; NCAOR (National Centre for Antarctic and Ocean Research), 'NCAOR' (Goa, NCAOR, 2012). Available at http://www.ncaor.gov.in/annualreports (accessed 5 April 2018); SaGAA (National Conference on Science and Geopolitics of Arctic and Antarctic), *Brochure* (New Delhi, SaGAA, 2011), on file with author.

19 NIPR (National Institute of Polar Research), 'Arctic environment research center' (Tokyo, NIPR, Division for Polar Research, Arctic Environment Research Center, 2012). Available at http://www.nipr.ac.jp/english/polar-research02.html (accessed 1 November 2014); NIPR (National Institute of Polar Research), 'National Institute of Polar Research Japan 2012–2013' (Tokyo, NIPR, 2012).

20 JCAR (Japan Consortium for Arctic Environmental Research), 'Japan Consortium for Arctic Environmental Research' (Tokyo, JCAR, 2012). Available at http://www.jcar.org/english/menu01/(accessed 5 April 2018).

21 NIPR, 'National Institute of Polar Research Japan 2012–2013', p. 4, p. 32; ROIS (Research Organization of Information and Systems), *Research Organization of Information and Systems 2011* (Tokyo, ROIS, 2011). Available at http://www.rois.ac.jp/pdf/youran_2011e.pdf (accessed 5 April 2018).

22 KOPRI (Korea Polar Research Institute), 'KOPRI staff' (Incheon, KOPRI, 2012). Available at http://eng.kopri.re.kr/home_e/contents/e_1600000/eng_staff/staffEng.do (accessed 1 November 2014); KOPRI, 'KOPRI vision and mission' (Incheon, KOPRI, 2012). Available at http://eng.kopri.re.kr/home_e/contents/e_1200000/view.cms (accessed 1 November 2014).

23 Jean de Pomereu, *Korea's polar ambitions* (Brussels, International Polar Foundation, 2012). Available at http://www.sciencepoles.org/interview/koreas-polar-ambitions (accessed 5 April 2018); KOPRI, 'KOPRI staff'.

24 KIOST (Korea Institute of Ocean Science and Technology), 'KIOST backs new future for marine and polar fields' (Ansan, KIOST, 2012). Available at http://eng.kiost.ac/kordi_eng/main.jsp?sub_num=336&state=view&idx=661&ord=0 (accessed 3 October 2014); KIOST, 'Organization' (Ansan, KIOST, 2014). Available at http://eng.kiost.ac/kordi_eng/?sub_num=423 (accessed 1 November 2014).

25 COMNAP (Council of Managers of National Antarctic Programs), 'Our members' (Christchurch, Council of Managers of National Antarctic Programs, 2014). Available at https://www.comnap.aq/Members/SitePages/Home.aspx (accessed 2 July 2014).

26 Jean de Pomereu, *China spreads its polar wings: investigating the infrastructure* (Brussels, International Polar Foundation, 2012). Available at http://www.sciencepoles.org/article/china-spreads-its-polar-wings-investing-in-infrastructure (accessed 5 April 2018); Pomereu, *Korea's polar ambitions*; NCAOR (National Centre for Antarctic and Ocean Research), *Annual report 2012–2013* (Goa, NCAOR, 2013); NIPR, 'National Institute of Polar Research Japan 2012–2013'.

27 CAA (Chinese Arctic and Antarctic Administration), 'Arctic research activities of the Chinese' (in Chinese) (2008). Available at http://www.chinare.cn/caa/gb_article.php?modid=04010 (accessed 3 October 2014); KOPRI (Korea Polar Research Institute), *KOPRI history* (Incheon, KOPRI, 2012). Available at http://eng.kopri.re.kr/home_e/contents/e_1300000/view.cms (accessed 1 November 2014); Shailesh Nayak, 'Polar research in India', *Indian Journal of Marine Sciences* 37/4 (2008), pp. 352–57, at p. 356; NIPR, 'National Institute of Polar Research Japan 2012–2013', p. 39.

28 *China Post*, 'Taiwan, China to conduct polar research', 29 March 2009. Available at http://www.chinapost.com.tw/china/national-news/2009/03/29/202074/Taiwan-China.htm (accessed 29 May 2015).

29 AFoPS (Asian Forum for Polar Sciences), *Who are we?* (Incheon, AfoPS, 2015). Available at http://www.afops.org/m11.php (accessed 5 April 2018).

30 Dag W. Aksnes, Kristoffer Rørstad and Trude Røsdal, *Norsk polarforskning – forskning på Svalbard. Ressursinnsats og vitenskapelig publisering – indikatorer 2010*, report 3/2012 (Oslo, Nordic Institute for Studies in Innovation, Research and Education, 2012), pp. 57–9.

31 NIPR, 'Arctic environment research center'.

32 Sung-Ho Kang, Seung Il Nam, Jung Han Yim, Kyung Ho Chung and Jong Kuk Hong, *Cruise report: RV 'Araon' ARA03B, August 1–September 10, 2012.Chukchi borderland and Mendeleyev Ridge.* (Incheon, Korea Polar Research Institute, 2012).

33 Khare, 'Indian scientific endeavors', pp. 111–12; NCAOR, *Annual report 2012–2013*, pp. 72–6.

34 Egill Thor Nielsson, 'The Arctic at a crossroads: north meets east', *Arctic Update* (2013). Available at http://www.dnv.com/industry/oil_gas/publications/updates/arctic_update/2012/01_2012/the_arctic_at_a_crossroads.asp (accessed 3 March 2015).

35 Ibid.; PRIC (Polar Research Institute of China), 'Substantial progress has been made on the China–Iceland Joint Aurora Observatory' (Shanghai, PRIC, 2013). Available at http://www.pric.gov.cn/detail/News.aspx?id=92739a68-d8d3-4f2c-87d2-637677274d14 (accessed 6 June 2014).

36 PRIC, 'Substantial progress has been made on the China–Iceland Joint Aurora Observatory'; RUV (Icelandic National Broadcasting Service) *300 milljónir í norðurljósarannsóknir* (300 millions to northern research) (Reykjavik, RUV, 2014). Available at http://www.ruv.is/frett/300-milljonir-i-nordurljosarannsoknir (accessed 5 April 2018).

37 CAST (China Association for Science and Technology), *China to boost Arctic research* (Beijing, CAST, 2012). Available at http://english.cast.org.cn/n1181872/n1182018/n1182078/13722719.html (accessed 2 October 2014); de Pomereu, *China spreads its polar wing*; KOPRI, *KOPRI history*.

38 CAST (China Association for Science and Technology), *China launches polar environmental assessments* (Beijing, CAST, 2012). Available at http://english.cast.org.cn/n1181872/n1182018/n1182078/13722705.html (accessed 2 October 2014).

39 Government of China, *China issues guidelines on scitech development program* (Beijing, Government of China, 2006). Available at http://www.gov.cn/english/2006–02/09/content_184426.htm (accessed 2 October 2014); World Bank, 'World databank' (Washington, DC, World Bank, 2014). Available at http://databank.worldbank.org/data/home.aspx (accessed 5 April 2018).

40 GRENE (Green Network of Excellence), 'Introduction of GRENE' (Tokyo, GRENE, 2011). Available at http://grene.jp/english/about/ (accessed 5 November 2014); NIPR (National Institute of Polar Research), 'Arctic climate change research project' (Tokyo, NIPR, 2014). Available at http://www.nipr.ac.jp/grene/e/index.html (accessed 5 April 2018); Fujio Ohnishi, 'Japan's Arctic policy development: From engagement to a strategy', in Lunde, Yang and Stensdal (eds), *Asian countries and the Arctic future*.

41 KIOST, 'KIOST backs new future for marine and polar fields'; KIOST (Korea Institute of Ocean Science and Technology), 'KIOST celebrates opening for Korea's marine science development' (Ansan, KIOST, 2012). Available at http://eng.kiost.ac/kordi_eng/main.jsp?sub_num=360&state=view&idx=663 (accessed 1 November 2014).

42 Jiping Liu, Judith A. Curry, Huijun Wang, Mirong Song and Radley M. Horton, 'Impact of declining Arctic sea ice on winter snowfall', *Proceedings of the National Academy of Sciences of the United States of America* 109/11 (2012), pp. 4074–9.

43 T. N. Srinivas, S. S. N. Rao, P. V. V. Reddy, M. S. Pratibha, B. Sailaja, B. Kavya, K. H. Kishore, Z. Begum, S. M. Singh and S. Shivaji, 'Bacterial diversity and bioprospecting for cold-active lipases, amylases and proteases, from culturable bacteria of Kongsfjorden and Ny-Alesund, Svalbard, Arctic', *Current Microbiology* 59/5 (2009), pp. 537–47.

44 Koji Shimada, Takashi Kamoshida, Motoyo Itoh, Shigeto Nishino, Eddy Carmack, Fiona McLaughlin, Sarah Zimmermann and Andrey Proshutinsky, 'Pacific Ocean

inflow: Influence on catastrophic reduction of sea ice cover in the Arctic Ocean', *Geophysical Research Letters* 33/8 (2006), pp. 1–4, p. 1.

45 Jong-Ghap Jhun and Eun-Jeong Lee, 'A new East Asian winter monsoon index and associated characteristics of the winter monsoon', *Journal of Climate* 17/4 (2004), pp. 711–26.

46 Ohnishi, 'Japan's Arctic policy development'.

47 NIPR (National Institute of Polar Research), *Asian forum for polar sciences (AFoPS). Report to XXXII ATCM* (Buenos Aires, Secretariat of the Antarctic Treaty, 2009). Available at www.ats.aq/documents/ATCM32/ip/Atcm32_ip089_e.doc (accessed 5 April 2018).

48 Jong-Deong Kim, 'Findings and challenges of the North Pacific Arctic Conference', in Lunde, Yang and Stensdal (eds), *Asian countries and the Arctic future*.

49 CNARC (China–Nordic Arctic Research Center), 'Background' (Shanghai, PRIC, 2018). Available at https://www.cnarc.info/organization (accessed 5 April 2018).

50 Karl Hallding, Guoyl Han and Marie Olsson, 'China's climate and energy security dilemma: Shaping a new path of economic growth', *Journal of Current Chinese Affairs* 38/3 (2009), pp. 119–34, at p. 124.

51 NCAOR (National Centre for Antarctic and Ocean Research), *Delimitation of the outer limits of the continental shelf* (Goa, NCAOR, 2014). Available at http://www.ncaor.gov.in/pages/researchview/8 (accessed 5 April 2018).

52 KOPRI (Korea Polar Research Institute) *KOPRI annual report 2008* (Incheon, KOPRI, 2009), p. 49.

53 NCAOR (National Centre for Antarctic and Ocean Research), *Annual report 2016–2017* (2017), p. 74. Available at http://www.ncaor.gov.in/annualreports (accessed 5 April 2018).

54 PRIC (Polar Research Institute of China), '中心介绍(Center introduction)' (2018). Available at http://www.pric.org.cn/detail/sub.aspx?c=29 (accessed 10 April 2018).

55 Karholl Aurora Observatory, 'Kynning' (Information) (2018). Available at https://karholl.is/is/kynning (accessed 11 January 2018).

56 *China Daily*, 'China's first home-built icebreaker named Snow Dragon 2', 27 September 2017. Available at http://www.chinadaily.com.cn/china/2017-09/27/content_32544019.htm (accessed 11 April 2018).

CHAPTER 11

MUCH ADO ABOUT SOMETHING? CHINA IN ARCTIC RESOURCE DEVELOPMENT: GREENLAND AND THE ISUA IRON-ORE PROJECT

Iselin Stensdal

Introduction

Change is underway in the Arctic region – as regards climate and the environment, as well as socio-economic circumstances. China is among the non-Arctic states that have shown interest in the Arctic. It has presented itself as a 'near-Arctic' country[1]; and, along with India, Italy, Japan, Singapore and South Korea, obtained permanent observer status on the Arctic Council in 2013. What makes China different from these countries is how Chinese actors have been received and perceived. Some observers have expressed suspicion about China's intentions in the Arctic.[2] Others, however, have been enthusiastically welcoming – like the Icelandic government under President Ólafur Ragnar Grímsson.[3]

Before China released its Arctic strategy in late January 2018,[4] many speculated about the future, analysing China's actions in the Arctic.[5] These authors seem to have viewed 'China' as one coherent unitary actor, without distinguishing between China's private and state companies, or between Chinese companies and the Chinese government. However, there are a few noteworthy exceptions: some contributions have sought to clarify misconceptions and offer detailed analyses of Chinese interests in the Arctic.[6]

Further reliable evidence and facts are needed to understand the new Arctic actors. In this chapter, I present one case that has featured both reported and rumoured Chinese involvement: the Isua iron-ore mine project on Greenland.

My aim is to describe the events as closely to what happened as possible, differentiating between alleged and actual Chinese connections.

Under the headline 'Race Is On as Ice Melt Reveals Arctic Treasures', the *New York Times* in September 2012 detailed how the Arctic, and Greenland in particular, had risen on China's foreign policy agenda.[7] A major Danish newspaper, *Berlingske Tidende*, told its readers: 'Smile, the Chinese are coming'[8] – and reported that a 'Chinese-controlled' company, London Mining, had applied to the Greenlandic government for permission to extract iron ore, and that China was willing to invest DKK 14 billion (approx. EUR 1.9 billion) in the project.[9] The news spread around the world: 3,000 Chinese workers would soon flood Greenland to work on London Mining's Isua mining project.[10] For a population of 56,000, that is more than 5 per cent of the inhabitants. The *Financial Times* called it 'the big deal' that would decide the future of Greenland.[11] As recently as 2016, an academic text reported that the Isua project 'could attract as many as 5,000 imported Chinese workers'.[12] The link to China in the Isua case has repeatedly been mentioned in the literature,[13] but there has been little research to provide a factual basis for the 'China connection'. Moreover, by April 2018, no activity had commenced on this much-hyped project.

The Isua iron-ore project went from glaring headlines to silence and no activity in just a few years. Exactly what happened? To what extent was or is there Chinese involvement in the Isua project? Was London Mining 'Chinese-controlled'? What about China–Greenland government relations and the alleged 3,000 Chinese workers? If London Mining was ready to start developing the project, why has nothing happened? In examining these questions, I seek to provide a fact-based understanding of 'China' in the Arctic.

This chapter begins by describing the licensing process, from exploration until all permits were granted and construction could commence. Next, London Mining's China connection is evaluated, followed by an examination of the claims that thousands of Chinese workers would come to Greenland because of the mining project. In the following sections, the focus shifts to Greenland: its history and political arrangements are key factors for understanding this case. For hundreds of years, natural resources have been important to Greenland's economy, and central to political developments. Around 2009, mineral resources appeared as a possible solution that could facilitate total independence from Denmark, leading the Greenlandic government to seek investments from abroad, including China. However, public opinion and expert advice have been mixed, as we shall see. Much of the explanation as to why there is no activity yet in the Isua project probably lies in economic factors. This is discussed in the final section, where I also offer some concluding observations.

This work draws on a range of materials: public government documents, hearing documentation, letters, statements, reports, London Mining's statements and annual reports, and local news coverage. I have aimed to identify the most trustworthy and original sources, and to uncover the realities that more shallow analyses may have skipped, got wrong, or merely approximated. I draw also on personal communications with mineral-resource experts in China, Greenland, and Europe, and a Greenlandic state employee, as well as participation at seminars and meetings in Denmark in 2013 and 2014 on resource development on Greenland and the Isua project.

From Exploration to Exploitation Licence to No Activity

The Isua iron-ore deposit is situated in the Isua Greenstone Belt, located at Isukasia, 150 km northeast of Nuuk, the capital of Greenland (Figure 11.1).[14] These deposits hold more than one billion tons of iron ore.[15] The Isua deposit was first explored in 1962[16]; in 1997, Rio Tinto identified the resource potential at Isua.[17] London Mining estimated that the mine would run for twenty-one years and produce ten million tons per year (Mtpa),[18] yielding a high-grade concentrate with 70.2 per cent iron content.[19]

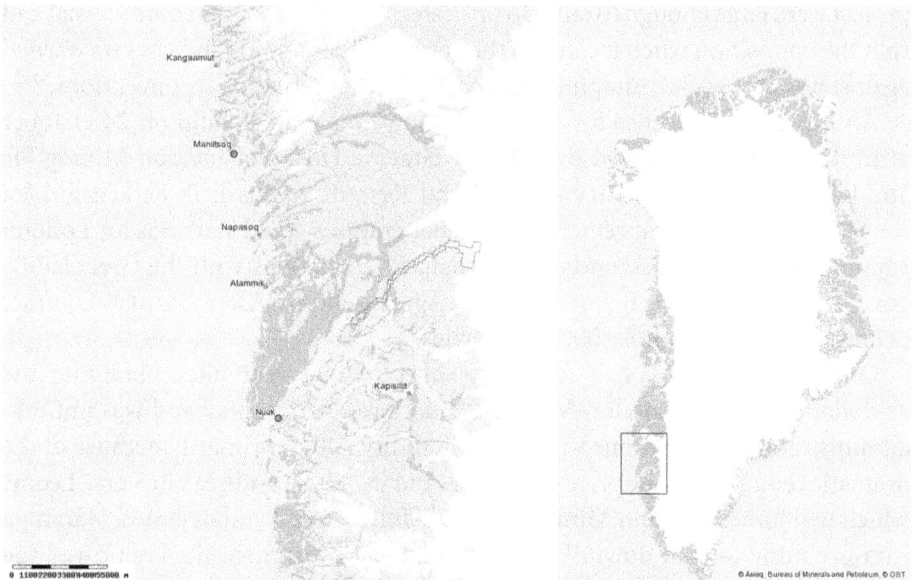

Figure 11.1 Maps of the Isua exploitation license area and Greenland.[20]

In 2006, London Mining obtained an exploration license for the Isua deposits,[21] through its subsidiary London Mining Greenland A/S, as licensee companies are required to be registered as corporations on Greenland. As is common in mining projects, lengthy preparations were needed before an exploitation permit could be granted: from 2007 to 2009 there were preparatory studies, as well as environmental and archaeological surveys. In 2008, a base camp, shared with Alcoa,[22] was set up.[23] London Mining expected Isua to deliver around five to ten million tons of iron ore per year by 2015 – roughly 25 per cent of the company's expected global production.[24] Statements from London Mining CEO Graeme Hossie on the occasion of the completed feasibility study in June 2010 were optimistic.[25] In September 2012, London Mining Greenland A/S applied for an exploitation license. The application documents explained that the construction phase would require an estimated 1,500 to 3,000 skilled and experienced workers, whereas in the operational phase the number would drop below 1,000.[26] Four rounds of public hearings were held between August and October 2012,[27] but the government was heavily criticized for not involving the public sufficiently in this process.[28]

In December 2012 the Parliament of Greenland passed a law on large-scale projects, defined as any project entailing more than DKK 5 billion in construction costs. The Act allowed foreign workers to work on large-scale constructions for less than what Greenlandic workers would be paid, albeit still within minimum wage levels.[29] At the time only the Isua project and the Alcoa aluminium smelter project were large enough to fall into this category.[30] The Act was controversial and split the opposition when it came to the vote.[31] Trades unions and lawyers warned against possible social dumping and conflict with international conventions.[32]

An exploitation license for London Mining was granted, and on 24 October 2013 the permit was signed by Director Graeme Hossie of London Mining Plc and the Minister of Industry and Mineral Resources Jens-Erik Kirkegaard (of the Siumut Party). What remained before operations could start was for London Mining to find investors, and also to finalize negotiations with the Greenlandic government over the Impact Benefit Agreement (IBA), a formal contract delineating responsibilities between parties.[33]

On 16 October 2014, a few days short of one year after obtaining the exploitation license, London Mining Plc declared bankruptcy and was put into administration. The reasons were grave liquidity issues, primarily because of the dramatic reduction in the price of iron ore, and the Ebola outbreak in Sierra Leone, which had forced London Mining Plc's only fully-owned and operated Marampa iron-ore mine to shut down.[34] The Greenlandic government then approved the sale of London Mining Greenland A/S shares to General Nice Development Limited, a subsidiary of the General Nice Group, a Hong Kong-based corporation involved in mineral resource investments and trading, as well as real-estate investment. It has more than ninety subsidiaries worldwide, as well as operating in over twenty provinces in China.[35] Calling the company 'a new strong force', the Greenlandic government stated that they were confident that General Nice would raise the financing needed for the Isua project.[36] However, as of April 2018 there was still no activity. The flagship project of Greenland's mining development has ground to a halt.

London Mining: China as Financing Source and Target Market

How 'Chinese-controlled' was London Mining? London Mining Plc was established in early 2005.[37] It was listed on Oslo Axess in October 2007 and on London AIM in November 2009.[38] In its ten years of operations it focused on producing high-quality iron ore for the global steel industry. Greenland was not the only location where London Mining had stakes, however. Its main properties were two fully owned assets – the license on Greenland, and an iron-ore mine in Sierra Leone – but the company also owned shares in iron-ore projects in Brazil, Chile, China, Mexico and Saudi Arabia, as well as shares in coal-mining projects in Colombia and South Africa.[39] Moreover, in 2010 London Mining entered into a joint venture for iron-ore production in the Atacama region of Chile, with Chinese and Chilean partners.[40]

In April 2009 London Mining also acquired 50 per cent shares in an operative iron-ore mine in China, the Xiaonanshan mine, and processing plants in Anhui and Jiangsu provinces; it also created a joint venture, China Global Mining Resources (CGMR), with Wits Basin Precious Metals.[41] That investment was seen as a regional consolidation and the doorway to future opportunities in the region.[42] However, in 2010 production at the joint venture in China was halted, and a litigation process with the original vendors began.[43] In 2011 London Mining opened a representation office in China, but lost the Xiaonanshan mine, which was written down to nil.[44]

London Mining began seeking Chinese cooperation partners for the mining project on Greenland. In June 2010, announcing the completed feasibility study, London Mining CEO Graeme Hossie stated: 'We are particularly excited about the opportunity to develop further mutually beneficial relationships with Chinese partners in order to fund and build Isua.'[45] More specifically, the scoping study that London Mining reported in February 2011 was based on estimates using two Chinese state-owned engineering and construction companies as contractors: Sinosteel and CCCC (China Communications Construction Company).[46] No contract was signed with any Chinese partner, but in August 2011 the UK-based Anglo Pacific Group Plc entered into a royalty agreement for future iron-ore production. US$ 30 million was paid to London Mining in return for 1 per cent royalties on future iron-ore sales from the Isua mine. London Mining used this funding to complete a bankable feasibility study to present to potential investors.[47] In November 2012, Sichuan Xinye Mining Investment Company confirmed that it had been in negotiations with London Mining concerning the Isua mine for more than a year,[48] but no contract was ever signed. There might have been discussions and negotiations with Chinese companies; but, as no concrete agreement had materialized, China's Foreign Ministry's spokesperson said in March 2013:

> I think that current discussions about China's investment in Greenland have gone way beyond the truth … there is no Chinese worker in Greenland … The intention of some media and people's groundless hype of 'China making a big push into Greenland' is worth pondering.[49]

On Greenland, London Mining's Project Director for Isua, Xiaogang Hu, was Chinese. He joined the company in 2009, with previous mining experience from the Canadian Arctic.[50] In April 2013 he left the company for personal reasons, but stated that in the preceding months Danish media had spread many false speculations about the project, causing problems for the project and potential investors.[51]

London Mining Plc was *not* Chinese-owned: it saw China as a potential source of financing and as a target market for its steel. True, London Mining Greenland A/S had some Chinese nationals as employees, but that can hardly be called 'Chinese-controlled'.

3,000 Chinese Workers: Making a Mountain Out of a Molehill?

Sensational news reports told the world that as many as 3,000 Chinese workers would enter Greenland to work at the Isua mine.[52] In 2015, only 975 individuals (1.7 per cent) on Greenland were foreign nationals,[53] so 3,000 would unquestionably have a major impact. What were the realities? Reading of the London Mining documentation in preparation for the exploitation license shows that the company never intended to bring 3,000 Chinese to Greenland. In the Social Impact Assessment (SIA) report accompanying the exploitation application in September 2012, it was estimated that in the construction phase between 1,000 and 3,000 skilled and experienced workers would be required. Recognizing that the population of Greenland could not supply such a demand,[54] the plan described in the report during the four-year construction phase was for the workforce to be 20 per cent Greenlandic, 35 per cent Western and 45 per cent Chinese or Asian.[55] At the lowest range of 1,000 workers, there could be at most

450 Chinese or Asians; with the highest range, the maximum number of estimated Asian workers would be 1,350. That is still a high number for Greenland, roughly 2.4 per cent of the population and more than the total number of foreigners there already – but it is less than half of 3,000. In the operational mining phase, numbers would be reduced to around 300 Chinese or Asian workers in the first year; from the fifth year, no Asian workers were expected to be needed.[56]

The figure of 3,000 stuck in people's minds, however. Even politicians who should have read the assessment reports operated with overly high figures. At the fourth public hearing, responding to the question of whether the government had taken precautions to ensure that the project would give jobs to locals and ensure revenues if Chinese workers were to come and work for low wages, Minister of Industry and Mineral Resources Ove Karl Berthelsen (of the social liberal Inuit Ataqatigiit Party) replied:

> The Chinese are coming, we hear that often, and … it looks like it's just around the corner, not least when there's talk about 2,000–3,000 Chinese who will come and work in the construction phase the next 4 to 5 years ….[57]

He went on to reassure the audience that the government was taking all necessary precautions, but failed to mention that the report had estimated a lower maximum of Chinese workers than 3,000. London Mining addressed the misconception of 3,000 in the SIA report:

> There is a perception among Greenlandic people that there will be an invasion of international workers, especially during the construction phase of the Isua project. This perception is strengthened as the issue of international workers has been raised on a number of projects e.g. for the Alcoa project where around 3,000 Chinese workers would be expected for the construction.[58]

However, this clarification was not taken up by politicians, the public or the media. The misconceptions lived on, despite the facts having been presented in written form. That politicians seemed eager to get the project up and running is connected to the special situation of the country. Greenland's history and political situation are crucial to understanding the circumstances of the Isua iron-ore project, and will be discussed in the following sections.

Greenland: Cursed or Blessed by Resources?

Mineral resources have been important throughout Greenland's recorded history. They were one reason for the Danish expeditions that started in the seventeenth century. Graphite and coal were among the first minerals to attract interest.[59] Cryolite, used for soda and enamel production, was discovered; systematic extraction began in 1854 in Ivittuut in south-western Greenland.[60] From 1973 to 1990 the Black Angel lead, zinc and silver mine in Maarmorilik, west Greenland, was in operation; there are still ore reserves in this deposit. The Ivittuut cryolite mine closed in 1987, after 130 years of activity. Both the Ivittuut and Maarmorilik mines were very profitable and of considerable socio-economic importance at the time.[61]

Politically Greenland has been under Danish influence since 1721, first through merchant and missionary activity, and since 1814 as a colony. The first debates about greater autonomy for Greenland emerged among well-educated Greenlanders in the late 1950s and early 1960s. A broader independence debate was prompted in 1973 when, despite a referendum with 70 per cent of the vote opposed to Greenland joining the EU-predecessor, the European Community (EC), Greenland was forced to join the EC with Denmark.[62] In 1979, Greenlandic Home Rule was established by law, with recognition of the special position of Greenland in the Danish realm, as a distinct nation (*et særligt folkesamfund*). Negotiations prior to the law were amicable, except for the question of soil and subsoil jurisdiction. The Greenlanders wanted such jurisdiction for themselves, but the Danes were concerned with security of oil supply, and wanted the Danish state to be retained as co-owner. The solution became equal rule, with veto power granted to both sides. From 1980 the system of a block grant from Denmark to Greenland's budget was started, replacing specified allocations.[63] In July 1998, responsibility for onshore and offshore mineral and petroleum resources, including licensing management, was transferred from the Danish Mineral Resources Administration for Greenland in Copenhagen, which was shut down, to the newly-established Bureau of Minerals and Petroleum (BMP) in Nuuk. The change did not affect the awarding of licenses, which were granted, as before, by the Danish–Greenland Joint Committee on Mineral Resources in Greenland.[64] Desiring greater influence over foreign policy concerning Greenland, the Home Rule government announced its wish to have Home Rule replaced by a Self-Rule system that would grant Greenland more power in matters of foreign policy, without exiting the Danish realm. A proposal on Self-Rule was put to a referendum in 2008, with 76 per cent of voters favouring the new system.[65]

Self-Rule and the need for economic activity

Self-Rule entered into effect on 21 June 2009, Greenland's National Day. Foreign policy, defence and security policy have remained under Danish jurisdiction. Under the Self-Rule government, the Greenlanders are recognized as a people under international law, with the right to independence if and when so desired. As part of the agreement, ownership of resources on- and sub-soil was transferred to the Self-Rule government.[66] This was followed by the preparation and publication of relevant documents. The 2004 Mineral Strategy, which had emphasized greater exploration for gold and diamonds, was updated. The 2009 Mineral Strategy put the focus on all economically viable minerals. Encouraging the mineral industry to conduct exploratory activities in Greenland was a strategic objective.[67]

As another part of the Self-Rule arrangement, the block grant is locked in value, but with correction for inflation. Furthermore, it was decided that if Greenland's income from oil or mineral production should reach DKK 75 million, the block grant would be reduced by 50 per cent of the Self-Rule government's minerals income that year.[68] Should the block grant be reduced to zero in the future, new negotiations on the economic relationship between Greenland and Denmark will commence.[69] In 2009, the grant from Denmark was close to DKK 3.5 billion, equal to 37 per cent of total public income.[70]

Increasing economic activity and government revenues was not only a question of the desire for future independence: it also concerned the need to increase economic activity, as well as government revenues, in order to sustain current levels of public services. Without any changes in economic activity, an ageing population and the prospects of increased public spending are expected to bring the budget into deficit.[71] Except for 2010 and 2011, Greenland's GDP has had negative real growth since 2009, due largely to reduced activity in the construction industry.[72] Some 39 per cent of the workforce were employed in public administration between 2008 and 2014. The second largest sector in terms of employment was fisheries and agriculture, at 14–16 per cent in the same period, followed closely by commerce at 12 per cent. The mineral and oil sector accounted for less than 1 per cent, employing between 110 and 143 people.[73] Unemployment rates had risen somewhat, from close to 8 per cent in 2010 to 10 per cent in 2014.[74]

Thus, the London Mining project came at the right time for the Self-Rule government. According to its SIA report, London Mining anticipated eventually achieving 55 per cent local employment at the mine, with accessibility to apprenticeship positions for local higher education institutions, and expected 70 per cent of business opportunities to be awarded to local companies – all this with few adverse social and health impacts being foreseen.[75] Even with two changes of Self-Rule government, all of Greenland's governments supported the London Mining project. In March 2014, at the Conference of Prospectors & Developers Association of Canada held in Toronto, the Greenlandic government awarded London Mining the prize and title of 'Prospector and Developer of the Year 2014'. As Minister of Industry and Mineral Resources Jens-Erik Kirkegaard (Siumut) commented in a press release: 'It's a pleasure to work with London Mining. They are extremely professional, and always work solution-oriented, which is positive for all parties.'[76]

Greenlandic Officials Courting the Chinese?

London Mining was not alone in looking for foreign investors. The 2009 Self-Rule agreement spurred the Greenlandic government to encourage large-scale mineral production. All prime ministers in office expressed such sentiments, including Aleqa Hammond (Inuit Ataqatigiit), who had been more reserved before becoming prime minister. From 2011, the China Mining Congress & Expo in Tianjin was added to the list of annual events visited by representatives from Greenland. In 2011 the delegation to China was headed by Minister of Industry and Mineral Resources, Ove Karl Berthelsen (Inuit Ataqatigiit), joined by Greenlandic companies. In addition to expo participation, Berthelsen met with Vice-Minister for Land and Resources Wang Min and numerous Chinese company representatives, as well as meeting Vice Premier Li Keqiang in Beijing.[77] Also, in 2012 and 2013, BMP (renamed the Mineral License and Safety Authority, MLSA, from 2013) had stands and hosted events at the expo in Tianjin.[78] They were joined by the minister of industry and mineral resources on both occasions: Ove Karl Berthelsen in 2012 and Jens-Erik Kirkegaard in 2013. In 2013, the day after London Mining's exploitation license was granted, Kirkegaard travelled to China at the invitation of the Chinese Minister of Land and Resources, Jiang Daming, for a week-long stay 'to discuss the further cooperation between the two countries in the field of mineral resources'.[79]

However, China was not Greenland's sole focus. Even before Self-Rule was introduced, the government actively solicited foreign investments and foreign actors to establish mineral resource activities on Greenland. Between 2006 and 2009, BMP representatives regularly attended trade fairs in Canada to promote and make Greenland internationally known as a place for mineral exploration.[80] After the introduction of Self-Rule, BMP representatives also attended several mining fairs in Australia each year, as well as European arrangements like the Mining Journal Conference in London.[81] Bilateral agreements were also signed: in 2012 a Memorandum of Understanding (MoU) with South Korea on mineral resources and a Letter of Intent with the EU Commissioner for Industry and Entrepreneurship regarding minerals.[82]

Mixed Feedback from Experts and the Public

Governments were not the only stakeholders in mineral resource development. Experts on the Economic Council of Greenland affirmed the need to expand economic activity; they concluded that since the main industry, fisheries, lacked potential for large-scale expansion, mineral extraction was the most realistic industry to focus on.[83] However, another expert group questioned how much large-scale mineral projects would help the Greenlandic economy. In January 2014, the Committee for Greenlandic Mineral Resources to the Benefit of Society released its report 'To the Benefit of Greenland'. The Committee's calculations showed that twenty-four large-scale mining projects would be needed to bring the block grant from Denmark down to zero – which was not only unrealistic in the foreseeable future, but would also have a massive impact on Greenlandic society.[84] The Committee concluded that large-scale mining projects alone could not bring enough revenue to Greenland, also noting that public participation earlier in the decision-making phases should be improved. Discussions on the future direction of Greenland and what kind of society the people wanted were proposed.[85]

Public acceptance – or what Koivurova and colleagues call 'social license to operate'[86] – is crucial to the success of any new mining project, in addition to government approval and licenses. Following the application for resource exploitation, public hearings were held between August and October 2012. Stakeholders were invited by the Greenlandic government to comment on the environmental impact assessment (EIA) and the SIA reports. In all, thirty-three written comments were submitted.[87] Meeting attendance figures nearly trebled: from fewer than sixty participants at the first meeting to 160 at the fourth and final one.[88] The government's lack of public involvement was criticized. Some asked whether the people would be consulted through a referendum; it was also noted that presenters used the word 'when', not 'if', in talking about the mine.[89] Regarding social issues, concern for securing revenues for Greenland through taxes and jobs for the local workforce was strong. People wanted assurance that the project would in fact bring economic benefits to Greenland. Furthermore, reports of an influx of Chinese workers were mentioned on several occasions. The public wanted confirmation that the negative impacts of the project would be minimal. However, public opinions presented at the hearings and in the written questions and statements were not in unison. Few supported the project unreservedly, but some saw it as a necessity for Greenland.

In sum, mineral resources have played an important role in Greenland's history. Future independence may also depend on resource development, although this cannot be a quick fix. The Greenlandic government worked actively to support the Isua iron-ore project and London Mining, while also seeking to attract investments not only from China, but also from other countries. The Chinese government invited Greenlandic officials to China in 2013 to discuss mineral resources, but China was not the only country to which the Greenlandic government looked to attract investments.

Price Tag

General Nice Development Limited's acquisition of the bankrupt London Mining Greenland A/S was approved by the Greenlandic government in December 2014 – but, more than three years later, the project has not yet started. Why? The main reason lies in the cost-return calculations. A new project requires considerable investment, and future profits depend on both the selling price and production costs.

As for the costs, the feasibility of a mining project hinges on the costs of production, transportation and transactions. Production costs are high in the Arctic, due to climatic conditions and poor infrastructure.[90] Greenland is the world's northernmost land area – and 81 per cent of it is covered by ice.[91] London Mining's plans included construction of the necessary infrastructure; the Isua mine would be an open pit, and ice would have to be removed to access the ore body. A primary crusher to reduce the size of the blocks and a processing plant with a power station would be constructed a few kilometres from the pit. At 105 km from the processing plant and 70 km from Nuuk, a port with the necessary facilities would be constructed.[92] In 2011 London Mining estimated that operational costs would be US$ 29 per ton, but one year later that estimate had been revised to US$ 45 per ton.[93] Transaction costs include dealing with local governments, complying with regulations and gaining public acceptance.[94] London Mining was well-received by the government, but acceptance by the general public was a more complicated matter.

Most companies with exploration licenses on Greenland are junior companies, normally dependent on external financing for each exploration project.[95] Investors are usually interested only in projects likely to bring good returns on their investment.[96] London Mining had not managed to secure the necessary funding to begin construction work before it went bankrupt in 2014. However, London Mining was not alone in this situation: Nunaminerals, the most active exploring company on Greenland, also went bankrupt a few months later, in 2015.[97] Also under General Nice Development Ltd, London Mining Greenland A/S has experienced a bumpy ride. The local paper *Sermitsiaq* reported that in the autumn of 2016 the company was forced into compulsory dissolution due to its failure to submit annual reports to the government. That was averted in December 2016: fresh capital was also injected, and the company could resume activities.[98]

The price of iron ore had remained stable and relatively low from 1980 to 2003, ranging from US$ 10 to US$ 14 per ton.[99] In 2004 it rose to US$ 16; then to US$ 28 in 2005; and by 2006, when London Mining acquired its exploration license on Greenland, it had risen to US$ 33 – doubling in the course of two

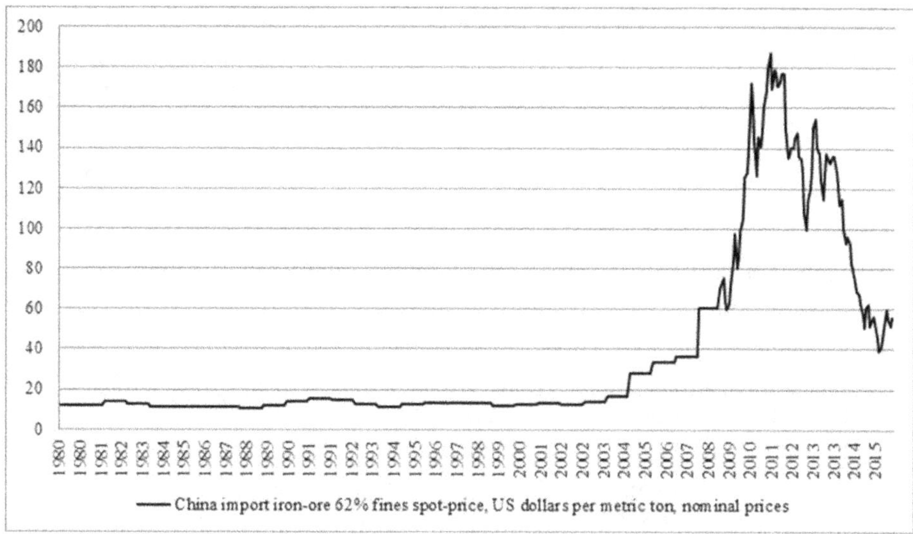

Figure 11.2 Spot prices of China's iron-ore imports, January 1980–July 2016, monthly data.[100]

years. The price continued to rise, passing US$ 100 in December 2009. London Mining's Greenland project came at a highly favourable time indeed.

As the world's largest producer of steel, China exerts great influence on the global price of iron ore.[101] Whereas its global share of iron-ore imports in 2000 had been around 10 per cent, by 2008 this had soared to almost 70 per cent.[102] Prices continued to rise (Figure 11.2), peaking in 2011 at more than US$ 180 per ton.[103] Since then, however, the combination of reduced steel production in China and oversupply in the market after production increased in the two largest iron-ore-producing countries, Australia and Brazil, led to a price collapse.[104] In a presentation in Copenhagen in October 2015, representatives from General Nice indicated that, at current market prices, around US$ 54 at the time, the Isua project had no commercial value.[105] Since then prices have fluctuated, up to US$ 89 in February 2017, but falling sharply in the following months.[106] As long as price-cost calculations fail to indicate profitable returns, construction of the mine is unlikely to commence.

Conclusion

After the wave of high expectations for greater resource extraction, and the scramble for the Arctic and its resources,[107] reality as of spring 2018 is more sombre. Fewer projects than anticipated have got underway in Greenland and elsewhere in the Arctic region. There have been both positive and negative responses to Chinese involvement in Arctic resource development and utilization. Needing investments to sustain and expand their economies, business with Chinese actors has been welcomed in the Arctic region – in Iceland, which signed a free-trade agreement with China in 2013, and in Greenland by the government, as shown in this chapter. On the negative side, there has been inherent scepticism towards Chinese companies and investments. Even in Iceland, where the government has maintained a positive attitude towards Chinese investments, plans by the Chinese real-estate developer Huang Nubo to buy 300 square kilometres of land (0.3 per cent of Iceland's territory) in order to establish a US$ 200 million tourism project with its own airport, hotel and golf course were halted at the ministerial level in 2012. Public opinion suspected ulterior political motives for the project.[108] The Isua case is an example where both types of response have been evident: the government was positive, but the public had mixed feelings.

What became of the 'Chinese' involvement in Isua? In fact, it was London Mining and the Greenlandic government that solicited Chinese partners and investors, rather than the other way around. True, there was some potential Chinese interest, as seen from London Mining's talks and negotiations with CCCC, Sinosteel, and Sichuan Xinye Mining Investment Company. However, the project did not appear sufficiently appealing for any of these companies to sign agreements. The Chinese government also invited Greenlandic officials to China for talks about resource opportunities on Greenland, and Isua may very well have been mentioned. However, it is not uncommon for the Chinese government to invite foreign governments to Beijing to discuss bilateral opportunities, including possible resource ventures. Moreover, the many headlines foretelling a Chinese 'invasion' of Greenland were well off the mark. London Mining had never indicated that 3,000 Chinese would be needed; the highest number they estimated would have been 1,350, had the project started. The magic number of 3,000 lived on, however – in the public hearings, in the minds of politicians, and in the media. Adding to the news-value was the juxtaposition of such a small population in dire need of economic growth, on the one hand, and, on the other, the world's most populous country, with decades of economic growth and a seemingly unending demand for resources.

The comment made by the Chinese Foreign Ministry in March 2013, that the Chinese presence on Greenland was over-hyped, might also point to the broader political situation at the time, with China lobbying for, and receiving, permanent observer status on the Arctic Council. Being portrayed as having already settled in on Greenland was not helpful to China. Whereas official Japanese and South Korean plans and statements have openly expressed interest in Arctic resources, the official Chinese line until the release of its Arctic strategy in late January 2018 has been more modest, emphasizing climate-change issues and research in the Arctic.[109] This tone has been kept in the 2018 strategy, which acknowledges that China is well aware of the resource potential in the Arctic, but also firmly states that Arctic resources are to be utilized in a lawful and rational manner:

> China advocates protection and rational use of the region and encourages its enterprises to engage in international cooperation on the exploration for and utilization of Arctic resources … China maintains that all activities to explore and utilize the Arctic should abide by … international law, respect the laws of the Arctic States, and proceed in a sustainable way on the condition of properly protecting the eco-environment of the Arctic and respecting the interests and concerns of the indigenous peoples in the region.[110]

This case makes clear the importance of hard facts and details. Had politicians and the media been more diligent in seeking answers, there might have been a more informed public debate in Greenland. For academics whose opinions are often treated as expert counsel by non-academics, grounding the analysis on realities and details, and taking care to explicate important distinctions, should be the norm – not the exception. The field of 'China in the Arctic' needs accurate, in-depth analyses. This chapter has aimed to contribute to that end.

Notes

1 Peng Zhang and Jian Yang, 'Changes in the Arctic and China's participation in Arctic governance', in L. Lunde, J. Yang and I. Stensdal (eds), *Asian Countries and the Arctic Future* (Singapore, World Scientific, 2015), p. 217.

2 David Curtis Wright, 'The dragon eyes the top of the world – Arctic policy debate and discussion in China', *China Maritime Study* 8/47 (2011). Available at http://www.andrewerickson.com/wp-content/uploads/2017/09/China-Maritime-Study-8_China-Arctic-Policy-Debate_Wright_201108.pdf (accessed 13 March 2018).

3 Atle Staalesen, 'Iceland invites China to Arctic shipping', *Barents Observer*, 22 September 2010. Available at http://www.andrewerickson.com/wp-content/uploads/2017/09/China-Maritime-Study-8_China-Arctic-Policy-Debate_Wright_201108.pdf (accessed 13 March 2018).

4 Xinhua, 'Full text: China's Arctic Policy', *China Daily*, 26 January 2018. Available at https://www.chinadailyasia.com/articles/188/159/234/1516941033919.html (accessed 13 March 2018).

5 Gang Chen, 'China's emerging Arctic strategy', *Polar Journal* 2/2 (2012), pp. 358–71; Nong Hong, 'Emerging interests of non-Arctic countries in the Arctic: A Chinese perspective', *Polar Journal* 4/2 (2014), pp. 271–86; Marc Lanteigne, '"Have you entered the storehouses of the snow?" China as a norm entrepreneur in the Arctic', *Polar Record* 53/2 (2017), pp. 117–30; Frédéric Lasserre, Linyan Huang and Olga V. Alexeeva, 'China's strategy in the Arctic: Threatening or opportunistic?', *Polar*

Record 53/1 (2017), pp. 31–42; Jingchao Peng and Njord Wegge, 'China's bilateral diplomacy in the Arctic', *Polar Geography* 38/3 (2015), pp. 233–49; Li Xing and Rasmus Gjedssø Bertelsen, 'The drivers of Chinese Arctic interests: Political stability and energy and transportation security', *Arctic Yearbook* (2013). Available at https://www.arcticyearbook.com/2013-articles/57-the-drivers-of-chinese-arctic-interests-political-stability-and-energy-and-transportation-security (accessed 14 March 2018).

6 Such as Aki Tonami, 'The Arctic policy of China and Japan: Multi-layered economic and strategic motivations', *Polar Journal* 4/1 (2014), pp. 105–26; and Christopher Weidacher Hsiung, 'China and Arctic energy: Drivers and limitations', *Polar Journal* 6/2 (2016), pp. 243–58.

7 Elisabeth Rosenthal, 'Race is on as ice melt reveals Arctic treasures', *New York Times*, 18 September 2012.

8 Christian Steffens Nielsen and Niels Philip Kjeldsen, 'Smil, kineserne kommer' ('Smile, the Chinese are coming'), *BT Denmark*, 14 June 2012.

9 Ibid.

10 BBC, 'Greenland awards London Mining huge iron ore project', 17 January 2018; Øyvind Rønning Nyborg, 'Flere tusen kinesere klare til å innta Grønland', *NRK*, 14 March 2013.

11 Philip Stephens, 'The grab for Greenland', *Financial Times*, 6 December 2013.

12 Adam Lajeunesse and P. Whitney Lackenbauer, 'Chinese mining interests and the Arctic', in D. A. Berry, N. Bowles and J. Halbert (eds), *Governing the North American Arctic: Sovereignty, Security, and Institutions* (New York, Palgrave Macmillan, 2016), pp. 74–102.

13 Such as Min Pan and Henry P. Huntington, 'A precautionary approach to fisheries in the Central Arctic Ocean: Policy, Science, and China', *Marine Policy* 63 (2016), pp. 153–7; and Jørgen Taagholt and Kent Brooks, 'Mineral riches: A route to Greenland's independence?', *Polar Record* 52/3 (2016), pp. 360–71.

14 Mark Nuttall, 'The Isukasia iron ore mine controversy: Extractive industries and public consultation in Greenland', *Nordia Geographical Publications* 45/5 (2012), pp. 23–34, p. 26.

15 GEUS/MIMR, *The Government of Greenland and London Mining sign mining permit* (Nuuk, Geological Survey of Denmark and Greenland Ministry of Industry and Mineral, 2014), p. 1. Available at http://www.geus.dk/minex/minex45.pdf (accessed 14 March 2018).

16 Mark Nuttal, 'Zero-tolerance, uranium and Greenland's mining future', *Polar Journal* 3/2 (2013), pp. 368–83, at p. 371.

17 London Mining, *Annual report 2011* (London, London Mining, 2012), p. 27.

18 London Mining, 'Isua, Greenland – Prefeasibility study for 10mtpa' (2010).

19 Grontmij A/S, *Social Impact Assessment for the ISUA Iron Ore Project for London Mining Greenland A/S. Final.* (2013), p. 15.

20 Maps from Asiaq, Bureau of Minerals and Petroleum; and the Danish Geodata Agency (GST).

21 Mark Nuttall, 'Subsurface politics: Greenlandic discourses on extractive industries', in L. C. Jensen and G. Hønneland (eds), *Handbook of the Politics of the Arctic* (Cheltenham, Edward Elgar, 2015), pp. 105–27, at p. 114.

22 American Alcoa's project involved an aluminium smelter near the Isua deposit. This project too has stopped; the last website update (January 2013) explained that work on environmental, health, and social impact assessments had been halted. Alcoa, 'Project updates' (2016). Available at http://www.alcoa.com/greenland/en/proposed_smelter/project_updates.asp (accessed 10 August 2016).

23 Government of Greenland, *Høring ved borgermøde vedr. London Minings ansøgning om udnyttelse af jern ved Isua – fjerde møde af 4 høringsmøder (Public hearing on London Mining's application for iron exploration at Isua – fourth meeting of four hearings)* (2012), p. 6. Available at http://naalakkersuisut.gl/~/media/Nanoq/Files/Hearings/2012/London%20Mining%20ISUA/Referat%204%20dansk.pdf (accessed 14 March 2018); London Mining, *Annual report 2008* (London, London Mining, 2009), p. 8.

24 Ibid., p. 6.

25 London Mining, 'Isua, Greenland – Prefeasibility study for 10mtpa'.

26 Grontmij A/S, *Social Impact Assessment for the ISUA Iron Ore Project for London Mining Greenland A/S*, p. ix.

27 Government of Greenland, *Høring ved borgermøde vedr. London Minings ansøgning om udnyttelse av jern ved Isua – første møe av 4 høringsmøder (Public hearing on London Mining's application for iron exploitation at Isua – first meeting of four hearings)* (2012). Available at http://naalakkersuisut.gl/~/media/Nanoq/Files/Hearings/2012/London%20Mining%20ISUA/Referat%201%20dansk.pdf (accessed 14 March 2018); Government of Greenland, *Høring ved borgermøde vedr. London Minings ansøgning om udnyttelse av jern ved Isua – tredje møde af 4 høringsmøder (Public hearing on London Mining's application for iron exploitation at Isua – third meeting of four hearings)* (2012). Available at http://naalakkersuisut.gl/~/media/Nanoq/Files/Hearings/2012/London%20Mining%20ISUA/Referat%201%20dansk.pdf (accessed 14 March 2018); Government of Greenland, *Høring ved borgermøde verd. London Minings ansøgning om udnyttelse av jern ved Isua - fjerde møde af 4 høringsmøder (Public hearing on London Mining's application for iron exploitation at Isua – fourth meeting of four hearings).*

28 Nuttall, 'Subsurface politics: Greenlandic discourse on extractive industries', pp. 118–23.

29 Kurt Kristensen, 'Så blev storskalaloven vedtaget' ('And so the large-scale act was adopted'), *Sermitsiaq*, 7 December 2012. Available at http://sermitsiaq.ag/node/142536 (accessed 20 April 2018); Parliament of Greenland, 'Inatsisartutlov nr. 25 af 18. december 2012 om bygge- og anlægsarbejder ved storskalaprojekter' ('Parliament of Greenland's Act 25 of 18 December 2012 regarding construction of large-scale projects') (2012). Available at http://lovgivning.gl/lov?rid={6D7F52B4-6893-4BDC-A943-601817D309A0 (accessed 10 August 2016).

30 Kristensen, 'Så blev storskalaloven vedtaget'.

31 Ibid.

32 Emil Rottbøll, 'Grønland omskriver storskalalov over en weekend' ('Greenland rewrites large-scale act in the course of a weekend'), *Information*, 6 March 2014. Available at https://www.information.dk/indland/2013/11/groenland-omskriver-storskalalov-weekend (accessed 19 March 2018).

33 GEUS/MIMR, *The Government of Greenland and London Mining sign mining permit*, p. 1.

34 Kathrine Kruse, 'Kinesiske minegogant ejer nu London Mining Greenland' ('Chinese mining giant now owns London Mining Greenland'), *Sermitsiaq*, 8 January 2015. Available at http://sermitsiaq.ag/kinesisk-minegigant-ejer-london-mining-greenland (accessed 19 March 2018); PwC, 'London Mining Plc – in administration ("the Company")', 2015. Available at https://www.pwc.co.uk/services/business-recovery/administrations/london-mining-plc.html (accessed 19 March 2018).
35 General Nice, 'About us', 2016. Available at http://www.generalnice.com.hk/about-us/ (accessed 10 August 2016).
36 Government of Greenland, 'New strong force behind London Mining Greenland' (2015). Available at http://naalakkersuisut.gl/en/Naalakkersuisut/News/2015/01/080115-London-Mining (accessed 27 January 2016).
37 London Mining, *Annual report 2008*, p. 16.
38 London Mining, *Annual report 2009* (London, London Mining, 2010). It de-listed from Oslo Axess in September 2011 to focus on the London Stock Exchange; London Mining, *Annual report 2011*, p. 9.
39 London Mining, *Annual report 2008*, pp. 9–13.
40 London Mining, *Annual report 2010* (London, London Mining, 2011), p. 19.
41 London Mining, *Annual report 2009*, p. 9.
42 Ibid., pp. 2–4.
43 London Mining, *Annual report 2010*, p. 19.
44 London Mining, *Annual report 2011*, p. 31.
45 London Mining, 'Isua Greenland – Prefeasibility study for 10mtpa'.
46 London Mining, *Annual report 2010*, p. 14.
47 London Mining, *Annual report 2011*, p. 28.
48 Jun Pu, 'After year of talks, Sichuan miner still no closer to Greenland deal', *Caixin*, 6 November 2012.
49 Chinese Ministry of Foreign Affairs, 'Foreign Ministry spokesperson Hua Chunying's regular press conference on March 15, 2013' (2013). Available at http://www.mfa.gov.cn/ce/ceil/eng/fyrth/t1022074.htm (accessed 10 August 2016).
50 London Mining, *Annual report 2011*, p. 51.
51 Søren Duran Duus, 'London Mining-direktør stopper' ('London Mining Director quits'), *Sermitsiaq*, 10 April 2013. Available at http://sermitsiaq.ag/node/151841 (accessed 20 April 2018).
52 Such as BBC, 'Greenland awards London Mining huge iron ore project'; Nyborg, 'Flere tusen kinesere klare til å innta Grønland'; Stephens, 'The grab of Greenland'.
53 Statistics Greenland, *Statistisk årbog 2016* ('Statistical Yearbook 2016') (2016). Available at http://www.stat.gl/sa/saD2016.pdf (accessed 10 August 2016).
54 Grontmij A/S, *Social Impact Assessment for the ISUA Iron Ore Project for London Mining Greenland A/S. Final*, p. 107.
55 Ibid., pp. 102–4.
56 Ibid., p. ix.
57 Government of Greenland, *Høring ved borgermøde vedr. London Minings ansøgning om udnyttelse af jern ved Isua –4. møde af 4 høringsmøder*, p. 7.
58 Grontmij A/S, *Social Impact Assessment for the ISUA Iron Ore Project for London Mining Greenland A/S. Final*, p. 148.
59 GOVMIN, 'Mining history' (2016). Available at https://www.govmin.gl/index.php/minerals/mining-history (accessed 15 January 2016).

60 Mark Nuttall, 'The Isukasia iron ore mine controversy: Extracting industries and public consultation in Greenland', *Nordia Geographical Publications* 45/5 (2012), pp. 23–34, p. 371.
61 GOVMIN, 'Mining history'; 'The Isukasia iron ore mine controversy: Extracting industries and public consultation in Greenland', p. 371.
62 Alex Kjær Sørensen, 'Grønnland' ('Greenland') (2015). Available at http://danmarkshistorien.dk/leksikon-og-kilder/vis/materiale/groenland/ (accessed 11 December 2015).
63 Ibid.
64 GEUS/BMP, *Minex* (No.15) (1998), p. 1. Available at http://www.geus.dk/minex/MINEX15.pdf (accessed 20 March 2018).
65 Sørensen, 'Grønnland'.
66 Ibid.
67 Government of Greenland, *Mineral Strategy 2009. Update of objectives and plans for mineral exploration activities in Greenland* (2009), pp. 9–11. Available at https://govmin.gl/images/stories/about_bmp/publications/mineral_strategy_2009.pdf (accessed 20 March 2018).
68 Statistics Greenland, *Statistisk årbog* 2016 ('Statistical yearbook 2016') (2016). Available at http://www.stat.gl/sa/saD2016.pdf (accessed 10 August 2016), p. 5.
69 Ibid., p. 1.
70 Statistics Greenland, *Statbank Greenland* (data set) (2016). Available at http://bank.stat.gl/pxweb/en/?rxid=d427561b-fde7-411d-a2c1-191223cb0f83 (accessed 10 August 2016).
71 Committee for Greenlandic Mineral Resources to the Benefit of Greenland, *To the benefit of Greenland* (Nuuk, University of Greenland and University of Copenhagen, 2014), pp. 9–10.
72 Statistics Greenland, *Statbank Greenland; Statistisk årbog*,
73 Ibid.
74 Ibid.
75 Grontmij A/S, *Social Impact Assessment for the ISUA Iron Ore Project for London Mining Greenland A/S. Final*, pp. 172–85.
76 *Sermitsiaq*, 'Kirkegaard giver London Mining årets pris' ('Kirkegaard awards London Mining this year's prize', 6 March 2014. Available at http://sermitsiaq.ag/kirkegaard-giver-london-mining-aarets-pris (accessed 20 April 2018).
77 GEUS/BMP, Minex (No.41) (2012), pp. 4–5. Available at http://www.geus.dk/minex/minex41.pdf (accessed 20 March 2018).
78 GEUS/MIMR, *The Government of Greenland and London Mining sign mining permit*, p. 1.
79 Danish Ministry of Foreign Affairs in China, 'Greenland event at embassy on 5th November' (2013).
80 Government of Greenland, *Mineral Strategy 2009. Update of objectives and plans for mineral exploration activities in Greenland*, p. 23.
81 Government of Greenland, *Greenland's oil and mineral strategy 2014–2018* (Report FM 2014/133) (2014), p. 67. Available at https://govmin.gl/images/stories/about_bmp/publications/mineral_strategy_2009.pdf (accessed 20 March 2018).

82 Government of Greenland, *Udenrigspolitisk Redegørelse 2014* (*Foreign Policy Report 2014*) (2014), p. 50. Available at https://govmin.gl/images/stories/about_bmp/publications/mineral_strategy_2009.pdf (accessed 20 March 2018).

83 Economic Council of Greenland, *Grønlands økonomi i 2013* (Greenland's economy 2013) (Nuuk, Economic Council of Greenland, 2013), p. 3.

84 Committee for Greenlandic Mineral Resources to the Benefit of Greenland, *To the benefit of Greenland*, pp. 18–19.

85 Ibid., pp. 27–33.

86 Timo Koivurova, Arild Buanes, Larissa Riabova, Vladimir Didyk, Thomas Ejdemo, Gregory Poelzer, Päivi Taavo and Pamela Lesser, '"Social license to operate": a relevant term in Northern European mining?', *Polar Geography* 38 (2015), pp. 194–227.

87 Grontmij A/S, *Social Impact Assessment for the ISUA Iron Ore Project for London Mining Greenland A/S. Final*, p. 131.

88 Government of Greenland, *Høring ved borgermøde vedr. London Minings ansøgning om udnyttelse af jern ved Isua – første møde af 14 høringsmøder*, p. 1; *Høring vedborgermøde vedr. London Minings ansøgning om udnyttelse af jern ved Isua – tredje møde af 4 høringsmøder*, p. 1.

89 Ibid., p. 3.

90 Iselin Stensdal, 'Arctic mining: Asian interests and opportunities', in Lunde, Yang and Stensdal (eds), *Asian Countries and the Arctic Future*, pp. 154–67, p. 164.

91 Statistics Greenland, *Statistisk årbog 2016*, p. 1.

92 Grontmij A/S, *Social Impact Assessment for the ISUA Iron Ore Project for London Mining Greenland A/S. Final*, pp. 15–6.

93 Gwladys Fouche, 'Chinese firm unlikely to develop $2 billion Greenland iron ore mine soon: minister', *Reuters*, 26 January 2016; London Mining Greenland, *Isua Iron Ore Project* (2011), p. 5. Available at https://www.govmin.gl/images/stories/minerals/events/suppliers_seminar_jan_2011/london_mining_eng.pdf (accessed 20 March 2018).

94 Stensdal, 'Arctic mining: Asian interests and opportunities', p. 164.

95 Government of Greenland, *Mineral Strategy 2009. Update of objectives and plans for mineral exploration activities in Greenland*, p. 5.

96 For a discussion of strategic investments that do not return the investment in the short term, see Stensdal, 'Arctic mining: Asian interests and opportunities', pp. 164–65.

97 Niels Krogh Søndergaard, 'Landets mest aktive efterforskningsselskab konkurs' ('the country's most active exploration company bankrupt'), *Sermitsiaq*, 21 April 2015. Available at http://sermitsiaq.ag/landets-mest-aktive-efterforskningsselskab-konkurs (accessed 20 April 2018).

98 Walter Turnowsky, 'Berigtigelse: London Mining Greenland genoptaget' ('Corrigendum: London Mining Greenland resumed'), *Sermitsiaq*, 3 January 2017. Available at http://sermitsiaq.ag/node/192945 (accessed 20 April 2018).

99 Prices are stated as nominal prices, i.e. the price paid at the time, not adjusted for inflation (as in the case of real price).

100 In the past few years, the standard reference price for a metric ton of iron ore has been the spot price in US$ for iron ore with 2 per cent iron content at the Tianjin

port in China. See MacroBusiness, 'A brief history of iron markets' (2013). Available at https://www.macrobusiness.com.au/2013/08/a-brief-history-of-iron-ore-markets/(accessed 20 March 2018); IMF, 'IMF primary commodity prices' (2016). Available at https://www.imf.org/external/np/res/commod/index.aspx (accessed 5 April 2018).

101 Rodney Nelson, *Iron Ore* (Quarterly Commodity Insights Bulletin March 2013) (2013), p. 1. Available at https://assets.kpmg.com/content/dam/kpmg/pdf/2015/06/iron-ore-q4-2012-march-2013.pdf (accessed 20 March 2018).

102 Shaun K. Roache, 'China's impact on world commodity markets (IMF Working Paper no. 12/115) (Washington, DC, IMF, 2012), p. 5.

103 IMF, 'IMF primary commodity prices'.

104 Pieter van Dijk, *Iron Ore (Q2, 2015-Q3, 2015)* (Quarterly Commodity Insights Bulletin December 2015) (2015), p. 2. Available at https://assets.kpmg.com/content/dam/kpmg/pdf/2015/12/iron-ore-2015-Q4.pdf (accessed 20 March 2018).

105 Jenny Yang, Yikang Liu and David Dou, 'Chinese perspectives on Greenland Isua project', Presentation at Arctic Cluster of Raw Materials meeting, 6 October 2015. Available at http://acrm.dk/wp-content/uploads/2015/09/Chinese-Perspectives-on-Greenland-and-the-Isua-Project.pdf (accessed 20 March 2018).

106 IMF, 'IMF primary commodity prices'.

107 Klaus Dodds and Mark Nuttall, *The Scramble for the Poles: The Geopolitics of the Arctic and Antarctic* (Cambridge, Polity Press, 2016).

108 Valur Ingimundarson, 'Framing the national interest: the political uses of the Arctic in Iceland's foreign and domestic policies', *Polar Journal* 5/1 (2015), pp. 82–100, p. 93.

109 Zhang and Yang, 'Changes in the Arctic and China's participation in Arctic governance', pp. 229–30.

110 Xinhua, 'Full text: China's Arctic Policy'.

CHAPTER 12

CHINA'S CLIMATE POLICY: DOES AN ARCTIC DIMENSION EXIST?

Gørild Heggelund and Han Cheng

Introduction

China's climate policy and actions are of global relevance given that it is the world's largest greenhouse gas (GHG) emitter. Furthermore, the Arctic is regarded as an important source of knowledge for future climate development. In recent years, China has shown a growing interest in the Arctic region and a number of studies and reports have discussed whether China has geopolitical intentions in the Arctic linked to global security, shipping routes and resource interests.[1] However, these studies have not looked into a possible climate policy strand in China's engagement in the Arctic. This study aims to fill this knowledge gap.

The overarching question is whether and to what extent an Arctic dimension in Chinese climate policy exists, and whether there are signs of potential linkages between China's engagement in the Arctic and its domestic climate policies. Consequently, this chapter analyzes China's climate change policy developments, and institutions involved in Arctic policymaking and research. Equally important, this chapter explores the possible implications of climatic change in the Arctic for Chinese domestic climate policy by examining the evidence of climate-related engagement in the region. Trends related to rapidly evolving policy contexts, such as progress in China's scientific research in the Arctic, are evaluated. Based on climate science and policy prospects in relation to the Arctic, the chapter

---

This chapter is a revised and updated version of Gørild Heggelund and Han Cheng, 'China's climate policy: Does an Arctic dimension exist?', *Advances in Polar Science* 27/3 (2016), pp. 139–45.

discusses the signs of possible linkages and their potential implications, as well as China's Arctic policy (white paper) that was launched in January 2018.

China has a long history of engagement in the Arctic and considers itself a near-Arctic country.[2] China's presence in the Arctic comprises the Polar Research Institute of China's research station on the Svalbard archipelago, which is under Norwegian sovereignty.[3] A milestone in China's Arctic history came in 2013 when the country obtained observer status on the Arctic Council; Japan, South Korea, India, Singapore and Italy were also granted observer status at the Ministerial meeting in Kiruna, Sweden in 2013.[4] That same year, the China–Nordic Arctic Research Center was established in Shanghai to strengthen research collaboration between China and Nordic research institutions on Arctic matters.[5] In addition to engaging with smaller Nordic states (e.g., Norway, Denmark and Iceland), China also collaborates with bigger Arctic states (USA, Russia and Canada).[6]

The chapter begins with a brief overview of China's Arctic interests. The subsequent section presents the policies and institutions that are key to the development of China's climate agenda, climate policy and governance. In the third section, China's climate research and central research institutions are introduced. The fourth section is a discussion of possible links between China's climate and the Arctic/Arctic Council. Finally, the chapter ends with a concluding section, summarizing the findings and thoughts on future trends.

Rationale for China's Engagement

China is regarded as a 'near-Arctic' country situated in the peripheral region near yet outside the Arctic region.[7] Scientific literature discusses the Arctic region as having great influence on China's climate, environment and agricultural production, as well as economic and social development. Research shows that Arctic warming is linked to extreme weather events in China,[8] as well as precipitation patterns and temperature rise.[9] For instance, the sea-ice melt in the Arctic sends cold streams towards South China and causes the summer monsoon to move north[10]; the 2016 January low sea-ice extent allowed cold air outbreaks in many regions of the world, including Asia and the Pacific.[11] Additionally, simulated ice thickness data were used to investigate the relationship between Arctic sea-ice distribution and the climate of China. The results imply that Arctic sea-ice thickness is closely related to various rainfall patterns in different areas of the country.[12] It is thus necessary for China to keep a close watch on global warming impacts in the Arctic, and incorporate this interest in the country's climate science and policy efforts.

The Arctic is very sensitive to global climate change. Natural variations in the Arctic will result in climate instability in the world, especially in the climate system of the northern hemisphere. Atmospheric changes in the Arctic therefore have a direct impact on China's weather and climate, ecological environment, and agriculture.[13] Moreover, melting in Greenland has accelerated global sea-level rise, which will severely threaten the socio-economic development of China's east coast.[14] Consequently, many aspects of Arctic climate affairs are a cause of core policy concern for China. In particular the following:

- **Climate science** Climate change in the Arctic has global implications. As part of the northern hemisphere, China is also heavily affected by shifting climate conditions in the Arctic, with concerns, including its national ecosystem, agriculture, and coastal security.[15]
- **Natural resources** The Arctic is rich in energy, mineral and fishery resources that are of economic interest to China, and climate change has generated natural conditions conducive to prospective resource exploration in the region.

Despite China's gradually slowing annual economic growth rate under the 'new normal', estimated at approximately 6.5 per cent (13th Five-Year Plan, FYP),[16] the demand for energy, resources and animal protein has encouraged investment in research, economic and political capital towards involvement in future Arctic affairs.

- **Shipping routes** The acceleration of ice melting in the Arctic has opened up new shipping routes for commercial use that could have a significant impact on China's global trade patterns. In 2017 China included the Arctic into the Belt and Road Initiative.[17] 'The Silk Road on Ice' is 'seen as the third arch of the Belt and Road Initiative'.[18] Among other potential targets and gains, developing the new shipping routes is one of China's most achievable and viable pursuits in the Arctic.

Policies and Institutions

China's climate-policy agenda and governance

Climate policy in China has evolved in recent decades from largely focusing on mitigation and energy-related issues to a growing awareness of resilience, adaptation and vulnerability to climatic change. China's mitigation challenges come as a result of heavy reliance on coal, which has led to excessive GHG emissions. In recognition of the need for mitigation efforts, climate change was introduced as a topic in the 10th FYP in 2001 (2001–5) when energy targets were introduced. In 2007, China was ranked as the world's largest overall emitter of GHG, although its per capita emissions were lower than the global average.[19] The period 2000–13 was an energy-intensive growth period when China's coal consumption nearly tripled.[20] Attempts to control emissions became a priority in the 11th and 12th FYPs. Coal constituted 66 per cent of China's overall annual energy consumption in 2015. Approximately 90 per cent of China's carbon emissions are attributed to the consumption of fossil fuels, 68 per cent of which comes from coal combustion alone.[21]

Adaptation and resilience to reduce climate risk has increased in importance in climate policy, particularly since 2007 in China's National Climate Change Programme.[22] China has experienced considerable warming with a mean temperature rise of about 1.4 degrees Celsius for the whole year between 1951 and 2009.[23] In particular, the Tibetan Plateau, part of the so-called Third Pole in the Himalayas, has seen rising temperatures.[24] The period 2005–14 was marked by extensive retreating of glaciers in the Tibetan Plateau. China launched the National Adaptation Strategy in November 2013, which demonstrates a more strategic approach to managing climate risk, and advancing the priority work areas outlined in the 2007 National Programme.[25] A follow-up to the strategy is the Action Plan for Climate Change Adaptation in Cities.[26] China's Third National Assessment Report published in 2015 illustrated the severity of the climate impact on China.[27] The report compiles the latest science and policy options from state-appointed experts[28] and highlights China's vulnerability to climate change, exemplified by rising sea levels, as well as shifting rainfall and snow patterns. Recent reports state that the biggest emitters are also among the most threatened, with China's coastal cities being among the most vulnerable in terms of socio-economic developments and assets.[29] China now views climatic change as a serious threat to the nation's socio-economic development, and has incorporated the issue into the country's development policy.[30]

On the climate governance side, the need for a deeper understanding among policymakers regarding climate change saw the establishment of China's National Coordination Committee on Climate Change in 2007 during the 11th FYP (2006–10), led by the Chinese Premier.[31] This demonstrated the importance of climate issues at the highest levels of Chinese government. Several of the stakeholders involved in Arctic climate research are members of the leading group such as the State Oceanic Administration (SOA),[32] the Chinese Academy of Sciences (CAS) and the China Meteorological Administration (CMA) (the Leading Group on Addressing Climate Change, Energy Saving and Emissions Reduction: 国家应对气候变化及节能减排工作领导小组).[33]

China's international engagement through the United Nations Framework Convention on Climate Change (UNFCCC), along with multilateral and bilateral collaboration, has been important for domestic climate policymaking.[34] Recent policy developments are found in its Intended National Determined Contribution (INDC), which was submitted to the UNFCCC in 2015 before the 2015 United Nations Climate Change Conference (COP21) in Paris.[35] Of utmost priority was China's pledge to curb its CO_2 emission growth by 2030 or earlier. The INDC goals are to lower CO_2 emissions per unit of Gross Domestic Product (GDP) by 60–65 per cent from the 2005 level; to increase share of non-fossil energy by up to 20 per cent by 2030; to increase its forest stock volume by around 4.5 billion cubic metres from the 2005 level; and to control coal consumption by setting a cap on coal use. Less attention was paid to other objectives that have direct relevance for the research question of this chapter: enhancing risk and resilience work, including strengthening assessment and risk management of climate change, and improving national monitoring, early-warning and communication systems on climate change.[36] Additionally, it is important to strengthen research on the mechanisms and assessment methodology of climate change impacts and risks. China approved the Paris Agreement, which further cements commitments to emissions reductions and resilience building.[37] The 13th FYP, approved in March 2016 at the annual session of the National People's Congress (NPC), further consolidates efforts to work on adaptation and mitigation in parallel. Following the endorsement of the final draft of the 13th FYP by the NPC, provincial, local and district governments, as well as ministries, government agencies and industry regulators are expected to draft their five-year and thematic plans, within the guiding principles detailed in the national five-year plan, and implement the plan over the subsequent years. The national–thematic sub-plans were released in the first year of the 13th FYP, and the follow-on implementation documents will be released in the coming months and year.[38]

The Arctic in national policies

China's strategic and trade interests are perceived to be the main drivers for its diplomacy in the Arctic[39]; however, China is eager to maintain a low profile in the Arctic region and around its Arctic interests.[40] China's Assistant Minister of Foreign Affairs, Hu Zhengyue, stated in 2009 that 'China does not have an Arctic strategy',[41] and no significant policies have been announced until now. China launched its long anticipated Arctic policy (white paper) in early 2018.[42] Before the white paper, China's Arctic policy was best understood as the six points raised by Vice Foreign Minister Zhang Ming in his speech in 2015.[43] In later years, the Ministry of Foreign Affairs (MoFA) and SOA officials have made statements on China's Arctic-related interests and activities, such as China's Special Representative for Climate Change Negotiations Gao Feng from MoFA.[44] Gao highlighted the need to understand natural science, the political environment and the legal environment as China lags behind other countries. Gao also emphasized the need to protect the Arctic environment and climate system that influences China's domestic climate, as well as protecting the Arctic.[45] This perspective is reflected in the white paper, where environmental protection and climate change stand out and form the backdrop to China's engagement in the Arctic.[46]

China becoming an observer nation in the Arctic Council highlights its interest in the region. Attention to the Arctic has largely been reflected in China's national plans for scientific expeditions as well as science and technology development plans, albeit only in general terms. For example, in the 12th FYP, the Arctic is mentioned mainly in two documents. First, in the National Oceanic Development section of the 12th FYP (2011–15) there is a chapter titled 'Deepening Polar Scientific Expedition', in which the Arctic is mentioned:

> Implementing comprehensive studies of the Antarctic continent and its surrounding waters, as well as the Arctic marine environment and Deepening the polar scientific investigation and research, focusing on scientific research on glaciers, oceans, atmosphere, geology and geophysics, astronomy and other basic areas.

Second, the 12th FYP on Science and Technology focuses on 'Strengthening ecological, resource and environmental scientific investigation of the three poles (Antarctica, the Arctic, the Tibetan Plateau)'.

China's involvement in the Arctic has mainly been linked to scientific research.[47] China's climate-related policies in the Arctic have been fairly consistent over the past few decades, focusing on scientific expeditions and basic scientific climate research. The government has been investing its resources mainly in understanding the biological and climatic conditions of the region, as well as building the country's scientific capacity in climate research in the region.

One recent change noted in the policy chapter in the National Oceanic Development 12th FYP, however, is the government's evident interest in Arctic shipping routes and in collaborating internationally for their potential development. This trend shows that the Chinese government has started to link its long-time climate research in the Arctic with its global policy development and international economic engagement. Climate change impacts in the Arctic are likely to draw increasing policy attention from the Chinese government.

The 13th FYP, which puts equal emphasis on the need to address adaptation and mitigation, is a general document that does not explicitly refer to the Arctic. The specific FYPs for various sectors/themes were developed and introduced in the subsequent year.[48] For instance, the Ministry of Science and Technology (MOST), Ministry of Land and Resources, and Ministry of Water Resources in 2017 jointly issued the 13th Five-Year Plan on scientific and technological innovation in the marine field.[49] One of the Seven Major Tasks is to improve China's polar scientific research ability and technical support capacity and provide technical support for the protection of China's polar rights and interests.[50] Nevertheless, China's objectives for climate-resilient, green, low-carbon development paths to tackle climate-change challenges are coherent, referring to both its domestic and international actions. These aspects are relevant for the Arctic and protection of the Arctic is one of the stated policy goals in China's Arctic policy.

China's Climate Research in the Arctic

Institutional structure and stakeholders

A number of stakeholders influence policymaking processes in China, and it is useful to understand whether they contribute to an Arctic dimension in China's climate policy. Multiple government, research and business bodies are involved in the policy development process relating to Arctic issues. The policy formation process of China's Arctic policy is largely dominated by input from experts and scholars engaged in polar science. Any analysis focusing on China's Arctic policy should start from understanding its polar research.

The main managing institution for Arctic affairs is the SOA. It proposes policies and plans, and oversees overall Arctic activities. Institutional restructuring introduced during the National People's Congress in March 2018, means that the SOA is incorporated into the Ministry of Natural Resources, and the impact of this change is not yet clear.[51] The subordinate Chinese Arctic and Antarctic Administration founded in 1981 (formerly named the Office of the National Antarctic Expedition Committee) is responsible for the implementation of planned activities, organizing expeditions, and engaging with international treaties and conventions. The official Chinese research programme of the Arctic was formally established in 1989 when the Polar Research Institute of China (PRIC) was founded as a research arm for the Chinese Arctic and Antarctic Administration (CAA).[52]

The Chinese Advisory Committee for Polar Research was set up in 1994 by the Ministry of Science and Technology and now has sixteen member institutions, including MoFA, the National Development and Reform Commission (NDRC), the Ministry of Education, the Ministry of Industry and Information Technology, the Ministry of Finance, and the Ministry of Land and Resources. The Advisory Committee is led by the SOA.[53] The Advisory Committee monitors, consults, and evaluates scientific expeditions and research. There is broad participation of institutions engaged in Arctic matters, ranging from economic development, science, climate change and meteorology to foreign policy issues. Interestingly, a number of these stakeholders are also members of China's National Coordination Committee on Climate Change.

China's primary Arctic-focused research institutions are: PRIC in Shanghai, with a staff of 142 people, which is in charge of polar expeditions on the *Xue Long* icebreaker and conducts comprehensive studies of polar regions; the China Institute for Marine Affairs, the research department of the SOA in Beijing, which mainly does research on international maritime law and China's ocean development strategy; and the Institute of Oceanology, a multidisciplinary marine-science research and development institute under the Chinese Academy of Sciences.

The SOA, the main government agency in charge of China's Arctic activities, sits on China's National Coordination Committee on Climate Change, and in this capacity takes part in China's design and implementation of climate change policies. China's National Climate Change Programme, launched in June 2007, identified marine and coastal zones as one of its four adaptation focus areas, from which the SOA was given the mandate of incorporating climate change into its oceanic planning and management.[54] The SOA immediately followed the national directive with its own work plans to address climate change issues in oceanic zones. In 2014, the Chinese government released its National Plan on Climate Change for 2014–20,[55] which specifically discussed work relating to oceanic areas. These include prevention and reduction of natural disasters, capacity building of monitoring and forecasting, and treatment and restoration of sea islands.[56] Although the Arctic is not mentioned in any of these key documents and action plans, the SOA appears to be strongly involved in climate-change policymaking and implementation. This indicates the possibility that an Arctic dimension can be included in China's national climate agenda via the SOA.

China's Arctic research and expeditions

China's Arctic-research activities largely focus on environmental issues, such as the impact of melting polar ice on China's continental and oceanic environment, and implications for the country's agricultural and economic development.[57] Specifically, China's research in the Arctic has centred on aerial physics, climate change, ecology, and marine aspects.[58] China formally joined the International Arctic Science Committee in 1996 and the Polar Research Institute of China (PRIC) established the research station Yellow River in 2004 in Svalbard.[59]

Although there is no Chinese institution devoted specifically to research on Arctic politics, there are individual researchers who have published articles and book chapters that focus on Arctic strategies and geopolitics.[60] As a major step to enhance China's understanding of the political, legal and military dimensions of the Arctic, in September 2007, the SOA launched a research project entitled 'Arctic Issues Research', which involved scholars and officials from around China and focused on ten research topics, including climate-related topics.[61]

Since its first official scientific expedition to the Arctic in 1999, China has successfully completed eight expeditions to the region for multidisciplinary research, focusing on polar environmental research, as well as systematic observation of the sea ice, ocean and atmosphere. These expeditions have contributed to exploring the relationship between the rapid changes in the Arctic oceanic environment and climate change in China, revealing the role of the Arctic in global climate and environmental systems, and improving China's understanding and capability to respond to climate change. It has been announced that such expeditions from now on will take place annually.[62] Expeditions have focused closely on the rapid changes taking place in the Arctic and their impact on China's climate.[63] The scientific findings provide basic information and support for further research on global climate change, Arctic waterways and polar ocean databases.

The Chinese government released the 12th FYP for Polar Expeditions in 2012, which also announced the State Council's special project of comprehensive investigation and evaluation of the Antarctic and Arctic environment, the largest study in China's three-decade history of polar studies.[64] The focus was environmental and climate research, including three Arctic expeditions from 2011 to 2015, and the purpose was to study major areas in the Arctic Ocean as well as the impact of climate change in the Arctic on China and the rest of the world. More importantly, this special project was expected to lead to a strategic assessment of China's national interest in polar regions.[65] The participating institutions in China's Arctic expeditions are mostly direct affiliates of the SOA and national research bodies, such as the CAS, CMA, or various ministries (of Education and Land and Resources).

China's climate research in the Arctic is transitioning from the previous stage of ad hoc observation and data collection to formalized systematic knowledge production to provide a better understanding of domestic climatic changes. It also indicates a transition in the function of China's Arctic expedition teams, from purely scientific research to a mixture of research, development and policy formation.

China's Climate Change Policy and the Arctic

Through expeditions and research, China has gradually improved its understanding of the Arctic climate through initiatives such as the State Council's special project mentioned in the previous section. Over the years, China has established a preliminary observation system of Arctic atmospheric physics, climate, ecology and ocean, supported by a growing team of experts. Reports also illustrate the numerous activities being carried out by Chinese institutions, such as the annual reports issued by the Chinese Antarctic and Arctic Administration.[66] There is a long tradition in Chinese climate policymaking of including advice from scientists and scholars, including the climate expert group.[67] As argued in earlier sections, much of China's science activities in the Arctic has comprehensively enhanced awareness, understanding and significance of the climate-change agenda. This was done through contributions to government-led research projects, policy discussions and reports, even if there is no concrete evidence showing direct input from such scientific findings from the Arctic to China's domestic climate policy. Yet, we do see a connection between climate science and climate policymaking through China's domestic institutional climate arrangement. The members of China's National Coordination Committee on Climate Change are line ministries of the State Council, coordinated by the NDRC. The formation of China's Arctic-climate science research is largely dominated by government-affiliated research bodies, experts and scholars engaged in polar science research over a number of years. Research findings and recommendations are provided to decision makers and officials through established communication channels. These are central to the formation of the climate change agenda in the Arctic and to future Arctic strategy. MoFA is responsible for coordinating the work and input for such a strategy. It is also one of the key ministries involved in climate-change negotiations. The SOA also plays a role and has incorporated climate change into its oceanic planning and management. The SOA has several institutes under its authority that are involved in polar research, and is a major contributor to the growing capacity in climate science.

Furthermore, a growing number of Chinese experts contribute to global research on climate change, for instance through the IPCC processes.[68] It is therefore very likely that Chinese experts will also be able to contribute to research through the Arctic Council's working groups: for example, the IPPC adopted the global climate model of the National Climate Center under the CMA.[69] Likewise, Chinese experts will possibly 'bring home' relevant expertise for Chinese climate efforts from working group research. Black carbon is a research topic for the Arctic Council that is also an issue in China.[70] A framework for 'Enhanced Black Carbon and Methane Emissions Reductions' was agreed upon at the Arctic

Council Ministerial in Iqaluit in April 2015, in which 'each Arctic Council Observer States were invited to join the actions described in the framework including sharing a national report'.[71] To date, only one developing country, India, has submitted a national report.[72] However, a parallel task force on short-lived climate pollutants, including black carbon, was undertaken in 2015 by the China Council for International Cooperation on Environment and Development (CCICED), a high-level policy advisory body.[73] It refers to the Arctic Council efforts and framework on this issue, as part of a broader discussion of relevant international policy actions. China's involvement in Arctic affairs thus appears to play a role in raising the profile of some domestic climate policies. An extensive assessment regarding China's role in the Arctic Council may be premature at this time. The Arctic Council is the region's key intergovernmental forum: it has an opportunity to leverage China's interest in the Arctic and to encourage China to add an Arctic pillar to its national climate-change strategies. There is a vast underexplored space for Arctic countries to explore and build a climate dialogue and partnership with China and other non-Arctic observer countries.

Conclusion

Initially, we asked whether there is an Arctic dimension in China's climate policies. This chapter has therefore explored a number of signs, based on publicly available evidence, where both the recent development and future prospects of China's Arctic-climate nexus may be put into perspective. We have found that an Arctic dimension exists in domestic climate policy, although the link is not direct. However, there are points of convergence between the Arctic climate and China's domestic climate policymaking summarized here. The Arctic policy white paper launched in January 2018, confirms this observation: environmental protection and climate change stand out and form the backdrop to China's engagement in the Arctic.

Climate change continues to climb up the political agenda in China. On a global level, China has shown growing ambition, leadership and practices in climate change through international negotiations and collaboration. China's achievement of Arctic Council observer status in 2013 is a milestone in this regard. The Council's work is closely linked with China's key domestic policies and priorities on the environment and climate change. Domestically, China has recently approved the 13th FYP that further strengthens policies to address climate change. China's vulnerability to climatic change and the subsequent social impacts and economic losses have brought to the fore the challenges of adaptation, climate risk and resilience that increasingly play a role in domestic climate policymaking as illustrated in the Third Assessment Report for China. The

13th FYP places equal emphasis on mitigation and adaptation. The need to better understand climatic impacts on China has made the Arctic an attractive area for scientific research. Moreover, the rapid climatic changes in the Arctic and their impact on China's climate are receiving mounting attention, and policymakers have become increasingly aware of the complexities and risks of climate change.

China's engagement in the Arctic thus far has been dominated by scientific climate and polar research; polar scientific research plays an important role in determining China's Arctic climate agenda. China's climate research in the Arctic is now transitioning into systematic knowledge production to provide better understanding of climatic changes at home. In addition to scientific research, we anticipate that social-science research and geopolitical research will be further strengthened. The Arctic policy white paper promotes international research collaboration on Arctic issues, for instance through the work of the China-Nordic Arctic Research Center in Shanghai.

Notes

1 Sanjay Chaturvedi, 'Arctic geopolitics then and now', in M. Nuttall and T. V. Callaghan (eds), *The Arctic: Environment, People, Policy* (Singapore, Harwood Academic Publishers, 2000), pp. 441–58; Margaret Blunden, 'Geopolitics and the Northern Sea Route', *International Affairs* 88 (2012), pp. 115–29; Leiv Lunde, 'Potential for co-operation over Arctic', *Financial Times*, 20 December 2013; Jongchao Peng and Njord Wegge, 'China's bilateral diplomacy in the Arctic', *Polar Geography* 38 (2015), pp. 233–49; Iselin Stensdal, 'Coming of age? Asian Arctic research, 2004–2013', *Polar Record* 52/2 (2016), pp. 134–43; Ping Su and Marc Lanteigne, 'China's developing Arctic policies: Myths and misconceptions', *Journal of China and International Relations* 3/1 (2015).

2 Pei Zhang and Yang Jian, 'Changes in the Arctic and China's participation in Arctic governance', in L. Lunde, J. Yang and I. Stensdal (eds), *Asian Countries and the Arctic Future* (Singapore, World Scientific Publishing, 2016), p. 292; State Council, *China's Arctic Policy* (The State Council Information Office of the People's Republic of China, 26 January 2018). Available at http://english.gov.cn/archive/white_paper/2018/01/26/content_2814 76026660336.htm (accessed 4 May 2018).

3 Stensdal, 'Coming of age? Asian Arctic research, 2004–2013'.

4 Peng and Wegge, 'China's bilateral diplomacy in the Arctic'; Richard Milne, 'China wins observer status in Arctic Council, *Financial Times*, 15 May 2013.

5 Stensdal, 'Coming of age? Asian Arctic research, 2004–2013'.

6 Peng and Wegge, 'China's bilateral diplomacy in the Arctic'.

7 Zhang and Jian, 'Changes in the Arctic and China's participation in Arctic governance'.

8 Ibid.

9 Xuezhong Wang, Sun Zhaobo and Hu Banghui, 'Relationship between Arctic sea-ice thickness distribution and climate of China', *Acta Meteor Sinica* 26/2 (2012), pp. 189–204.

10 Timo Vihma, 'Effects of Arctic sea ice decline on weather and climate: A review', *Surveys in Geophysics* 35/5 (2014).
11 Brandon Miller, 'Amid higher global temperatures, sea ice at record lows at poles', *CNN*, 20 November 2016.
12 Bingyi Wu, Renhe Zhang, Rosanne D'Arrigo and Junzhi Su, 'On the relationship between winter sea ice and summer atmospheric circulation over Eurasia', *Journal of Climate* 26 (2013), pp. 5523–36.
13 Wang, Zhaobo and Banghui, 'Relationship between Arctic sea ice thickness distribution and climate of China'; Wu, Zhang, D'Arrigo and Su, 'On the relationship between winter sea ice and summer atmospheric circulation over Eurasia'.
14 Charlotte Middlehurst, 'Chinese cities most at risk from rising sea', *China Dialogue*, 6 January 2016.
15 Vihma, 'Effects of Arctic sea ice decline on weather and climate: A review'; Wu, Zhang, D'Arrigo and Su, 'On the relationship between winter sea ice and summer atmospheric circulation over Eurasia'.
16 Mark Magnier, 'China's economic growth in 2015 is slowest in 25 years', *The Wall Street Journal*, 19 January 2016.
17 SOA (State Oceanic Administration), 国家发展改革委、国家海洋局联合发布《'一带一路'建设海上合作设想》(*National Development and Reform Commission, the State Oceanic Administration jointly published Maritime Cooperation among 'the Belt and Road'*) (20 June 2017). Available at http://www.soa.gov.cn/xw/hyyw_90/201706/t20170620_56591.html (accessed 3 November 2017).
18 *Xinhua News Agency*, 'Belt & Road Initiative reaches the Arctic', 3 November 2017.
19 Gørild Heggelund and Rebecca Nadin, 'Climate change policy and governance', in E. Sternfeld (ed.), *Routledge Handbook of Environmental Policy in China* (Abingdon, Routledge, 2017), pp. 97–112.
20 Fergus Green and Nicholas Stern, 'China's changing economy: Implications for its carbon dioxide emissions', *Climate Policy* 17/4 (2016), pp. 1–15.
21 Zhu Liu, *China's Carbon Emissions Report 2015*, Belfer Center Discussion paper #2015-02 (Cambridge, Harvard Kennedy School of Government, 2015). Available at https://www.belfercenter.org/sites/default/files/legacy/files/carbon-emissions-report-2015-final.pdf (accessed 4 May 2018).
22 NDRC (National Development and Reform Commission), *China's National Climate Change Programme* (2007).
23 Rebecca Nadin, Sarah Opitz-Stapleton and Xu Yinlong (eds), *Climate Risk and Resilience in China* (London, Routledge, 2015).
24 ICIMOD (The International Centre for Integrated Mountain Development), 'What is the Third Pole?' (no date). Available at http://www.icimod.org/?q=3487 (accessed 4 May 2018).
25 Heggelund and Nadin, 'Climate change policy and governance'.
26 NDRC (National Development and Reform Commission) and MOHURD (Ministry of Housing and Urban-Rural Development), *Action Plan for Climate Change Adaptation in Cities* (in Chinese) (2016). Available at http://bgt.ndrc.gov.cn/zcfb/201602/t20160216_774739.html (accessed 4 May 2018).
27 The Third National Assessment of Climate Change Writing Committee, *The Third National Assessment of Climate Change* (in Chinese) (2015).

28 Chris Buckley, 'Chinese Report on Climate Change Depicts Sombre Scenarios', *New York Times*, 29 November 2015; The Third National Assessment of Climate Change Writing Committee, *The Third National Assessment of Climate Change.*
29 Alison Doig and Joe Ware, 'Act nor or pay later: Protecting a billion people in climate-threatened coastal cities', *Christian Aid*, May 2016.
30 Heggelund and Nadin, 'Climate change policy and governance'.
31 Ibid.
32 The National People's Congress (NPC) 5–20 March 2018 has introduced structural changes to the ministries under the State Council, see Ministry of Ecology and Environment, 'China to establish ministry of ecological environment' (2018). Available at http://english.mep.gov.cn/News_service/media_news/201803/t20180314_432393.shtml (accessed 28 May 2018); Renminwang, 'Overview of the institutional reform plan of the State Council' (一文读懂国务院机构改革方案) (2018). Available at http://lianghui.people.com.cn/2018npc/n1/2018/0313/c417507-29865242.html (28 May 2018). Nearly all of SOA's portfolio will be incorporated into the Ministry of Natural resources (formerly Ministry of Land and Resources). Marine environmental protection has been included in the Ministry of Ecology and Environment (MEE; formerly Ministry of Environmental protection). Climate-change responsibility, including the carbon market, is to be incorporated into MEE, see Stian Reklev and Kathy Chen, 'China to merge climate change, ETS into new ministry in major government shuffle', *Carbon Pulse*, 13 March 2018. Available at https://carbon-pulse.com/48836/(accessed 28 May 2018).
33 China's National Coordination Committee on Climate Change, see http://en.ccchina.gov.cn/list.aspx?c lmId=104.
34 Simon Denyer, 'China tries to recast itself as a global leader in climate-change fight', *Washington Post*, 2 November 2015; Urmi Goswami, 'Brazil, South Africa, India and China chalk out plan for climate negotiations', *Economic Times*, 8 August 2014; Alicia Parlapiano, 'Climate Goals Pledged by China and the US', *New York Times*, 2 October 2015.
35 NDRC (National Development and Reform Commission), *China's Intended Nationally Determined Contributions Enhanced Actions on Climate Change* (2015). Available at http://www4.unfccc.int/submissions/INDC/Published%20Documents/China/1/China's%20INDC%20-%20on%2030%20June%202015.pdf (accessed 4 May 2018).
36 Ibid.
37 UNFCCC, 'Adoption of the Paris Agreement. Proposals of the President' (12 December 2015). Available at https://unfccc.int/resource/docs/2015/cop21/eng/l09r01.pdf (accessed 4 May 2018).
38 Koh Fui Pin, Rebecca Nadin and Jessie Liu, 'Want to know by who and how China's 13th Five Year Plan was drafted? Mapping the drafting process of China's 13th Five-Year Plan', 4 March 2016. Available at https://www.linkedin.com/pulse/want-know-who-how-chinas-13th-five-year-plan-drafted-rebecca-nadin (accessed 4 May 2018).
39 Peng and Wegge, 'China's bilateral diplomacy in the Arctic'; Doig and Ware, 'Act now or pay later: Protecting a billion people in climate-threatened coastal cities'.
40 Sanna Kopra, 'China's Arctic interests', in *Arctic Yearbook* (2013). Available at https://www.arcticyearbook.com/images/Articles_2013/KOPRA_AY13_FINAL.pdf (accessed 4 May 2018).

41 Yao Dongqin, 'Join the Arctic Council, China's test has only just begun – exclusive interview with Foreign Ministry Special Representative for Climate Change Negotiations Gao Feng', *China Economic Weekly*, 21 May 2013.
42 State Council, *China's Arctic Policy*.
43 Ministry of Foreign Affairs of the Republic of China, Keynote Speech by Vice Foreign Minister Zhang Ming at the China Country Session of the Third Arctic Circle Assembly in October 2015. Available at http://www.fmprc.gov.cn/mfa_eng/wjbxw/t1306858.shtml (accessed 4 May 2018).
44 Linda Jakobson, 'China prepares for an ice-free Arctic', *SIPRI Insights on Peace and Security* 2010/2 (2010), p. 9. Available at https://www.sipri.org/sites/default/files/files/insight/SIPRIInsight1002.pdf (accessed 4 May 2018).
45 Sanna Kopra, 'China's Arctic interests'; Jakobson, 'China prepares for an ice-free Arctic', p. 9; David Curtis Wright, 'The dragon eyes the top of the world' (Washington DC, US Naval War College, China Maritime Studies Institute, 2011), pp. 28–32; *Beijing Times*, 'China dismisses accusations of its activities in the Arctic', 3 February 2012.
46 State Council, *China's Arctic Policy*.
47 Peng and Wegge, 'China's bilateral diplomacy in the Arctic'; Zhang and Jian, 'Changes in the Arctic and China's participation in Arctic governance'.
48 Pin, Nadin and Liu, 'Want to know by who and how China's 13th Five Year Plan was drafted? Mapping the drafting process of China's 13th Five-Year Plan'.
49 Ministry of Science and Technology, Ministry of Land and Resources, Ministry of Water Resources of the Republic of China, *13th Five-Year Plan* ('十三五' 海洋领域科技创新专项规划) (2017). Available at http://www.most.gov.cn/kjbgz/201705/P020170523667975005919.pdf (accessed 4 May 2018).
50 Ibid.
51 Ma Tianjie and Liu Qin, 'China reshapes ministries to better protect environment', *China Dialogue*, 14 March 2018; See note 33.
52 Olga Alexeeva and Frédéric Lasserre, 'China and the Arctic', *Arctic Yearbook* (2012). Available at https://arcticyearbook.com/images/Articles_2012/Alexeeva_and_Lassere.pdf (accessed 4 May 2018).
53 Linda Jakobson and Peng Jingchao, *China's Arctic aspirations*, SIPRI Policy Paper 34 (Stockholm, Stockholm International Peace Research Institute, 2012). Available at https://www.sipri.org/sites/default/files/files/PP/SIPRIPP34.pdf (accessed 4 May 2018).
54 Xuan Yang, 'State Oceanic Administration has taken measures to strengthen the capacity to address climate change in the marine sector' (in Chinese) (2008). Available at http://www.gov.cn/gzdt/2008-04/29/content_957843.htm (accessed 4 May 2018).
55 NDRC (National Development and Reform Commission), *National plan on climate change (2014–2020)* (2014). Available at http://www.scio.gov.cn/xwfbh/xwbfbh/wqfbh/33978/35364/xgzc35370/Document/1514527/1514527.htm/ (accessed 29 November 2016).
56 SOA (State Oceanic Administration), 'SOA Office issued Division of labour regarding work for National plan on climate change (2014–20)' (in Chinese) (2015). Available at http://www.soa.gov.cn/xw/hyyw_90/201505/t20150512_37312.html (accessed 4 May 2018).

57 Dongqin, 'Join the Arctic Council, China's test has only just begun – exclusive interview with Foreign Ministry Special Representative for Climate Change Negotiations Gao Feng'.

58 Zhang and Jian, 'Changes in the Arctic and China's participation in Arctic governance'.

59 Ibid.

60 Gang Cheng, 'China's emerging Arctic strategy', *Polar Journal* 2/2 (2012), pp. 358–71; SOA (State Oceanic Administration), 'Tour to begin exploring the relationship between Arctic marine environment and climate change; Interview with China's sixth Arctic expedition team leader Qu Tanzhou' (in Chinese) (15 July 2014). Available at http://www.soa.gov.cn/xw/dfdwdt/jsdw_157/201407/t20140715_33071.html (accessed 7 May 2018).

61 Xuan Yang, 'State Oceanic Administration has taken measures to strengthen the capacity to address climate change in the marine sector'(in Chinese)(2008). Available at http://www.gov.cn/gzdt/2008-04/29/content_957843.htm (accessed 7 May 2018).

62 CAA, 'China's Arctic expeditions'; Xinhua News Agency, 国家海洋局：我国北极科考频次增至每年一次 ('State Oceanic Administration: China Arctic expedition frequency increased to once a year') (2017). Available at http://www.cma.gov.cn/2011xwzx/2011xmtjj/201710/t20171011_451274.html (accessed 3 November 2017).

63 SOA, 'Tour to begin exploring the relationship between Arctic marine environment and climate change; Interview with China's sixth Arctic expedition team leader Qu Tanzhou'.

64 *China News*, 'Polar environment comprehensive survey and special assessment have started' (in Chinese), 24 February 2012. Available at http://news.sina.com.cn/c/2012-02-24/201023989363.shtml (accessed 7 May 2018).

65 SOA (State Oceanic Administration), *The 12th five-year-development plan for China's polar expeditions* (in Chinese) (2011). Available at http://www.soa.gov.cn/zwgk/hygb/gjhyjgb/2011_2/201508/t20150827_39802.html (accessed 7 May 2018).

66 Chinese Antarctic and Arctic Administration (CAA), *2015 National Annual Report on Polar Programme* (2015). Available at http://www.chinare.gov.cn/caa/userfiles/chinare2015en.pdf (accessed 7 May 2018).

67 Jost Wübbeke, 'China's climate change expert community – principles, mechanisms and influence', *Journal of Contemporary China* 22/82 (2013), pp. 712–31.

68 IPPC, 'Working Group II, Final Draft Assessment Report V, Chapter 24' (2013). Available at http://ipcc.ch/pdf/assessment-report/ar5/wg2/drafts/fd/WGIIAR5-Chap24_FGDall.pdf (accessed 7 May 2018); Laura Poppick, 'Black carbon soot greater in China, India than thought', *Live Science*, 27 January 2014. Available at https://www.livescience.com/42872-black-carbon-exposure.html (accessed 7 May 2018).

69 Wübbeke, 'China's climate change expert community – principles, mechanisms and influence'.

70 CCICED, *A Report to the China Council for International Cooperation on Environment and Development (CCICED). Coordinated Actions for Addressing Climate Change and Air Pollution* (2015). Available at http://www.cciced.net/cciceden/POLICY/rr/prr/2015/201511/P020160810466251190363.pdf (accessed 7 May 2018); India, *National Report by India – January 2016. Enhanced Black Carbon and Methane Emissions Reduction – an Arctic Council Framework for Actions* (2016).

Available at https://oaarchive.arctic-council.org/bitstream/handle/11374/1169/EDOCS-3137-v1-India_2016_Black_Carbon_Methane_National_Report.PDF?sequence=26&isAllowed=y (accessed 7 May 2018).

71 Arctic Council, *Arctic Council Observer States 2015 National Reports on Enhanced Black Carbon and Methane Emissions Reductions* (2015). Available at https://oaarchive.arctic-council.org/handle/11374/1169 (accessed 7 May 2018).

72 Ibid.

73 India, *National Report by India – January 2016. Enhanced Black Carbon and Methane Emissions Reduction – an Arctic Council Framework for Actions.*

EPILOGUE

We started this book series with an examination, in the first volume, of key governance structures in the Arctic. The law of the sea is the prevailing legal framework and the Arctic Council is regarded as the most important forum for inter-state cooperation in the region. In the second book in the series, we identified commercial and resource-related potentials in the Arctic. In both books, states are clearly identified as the most important actors. They are the ones that legitimize which governance structures shall apply and the degree to which potential resources are to be harvested. These two introductory books segue naturally into the third and final book in the series where we examine the behaviour of certain states in the Arctic. A key insight here, despite the agreement on the basic governance and management structures in the region, is that there is no single Arctic. Opportunities and challenges identified in different parts of the region are perceived differently. The reasons are climatic, geographical, economic and cultural. Researchers at FNI have traditionally concentrated on analyzing Russia and Norway, but in recent years, Asia's engagement in the region has caught the attention of researchers at the institute. New actors with a taste for the north have globalized the region and the consequences are as yet difficult to specify.

Given this globalization of the Arctic, it is absolutely essential to avoid falling for simple, overconfident analyses of what is happening and going to happen in the region. Climate change, technological advances and increasing numbers of actors looking to the north have nevertheless changed our understanding of what the Arctic is and can be. Once one of the least explored areas in the world, it is now a region with a recurring place on the international agenda. We are seeing the emergence of a 'new' Arctic. The conflict discourse that prevailed between 2007 and 2012 spawned interest in the region, but resulted in several inaccurate analyses of opportunities for the shipping and petroleum sectors. It also resulted, however, in a number of more robust analyses probing the likelihood of conflict, resource utilization and other commercial activity. Here, researchers at FNI have played an important role.

We end this book series by acknowledging an important point. To understand what the Arctic is and what it can be, accurate and reliable analyses are a necessity. We must, more than ever, look at what is actually happening in the region, not just what we hope or fear will happen. Researchers at FNI will continue to base their work on this precept.

BIBLIOGRAPHY

Abbott, Kenneth and Duncan Snidal, 'Hard and soft law in international governance', *International Organization* 54/3 (2000), pp. 421–56.

Abbott, Kenneth, Robert Keohane, Andrew Moravcsik, Anne-Marie Slaughter and Duncan Snidal, 'The concept of legalization', *International Organization* 54/3 (2000), pp. 401–19.

AFoPS (Asian Forum for Polar Sciences), *Who are we?* (Incheon, AfoPS, 2015). Available at http://www.afops.org/m11.php (accessed 29 May 2015).

Agle, Bradley R., Thomas Donaldson, R. Edward Freeman, Michael C. Jensen, Ronald K. Mitchell and Donna J. Wood, 'Dialogue: Toward superior stakeholder theory', *Business Ethics Quarterly* 18 (2008), pp. 153–90.

Aksnes, Dag W., Kristoffer Rørstad and Trude Røsdal, *Norsk polarforskning – forskning på Svalbard. Ressursinnsats og vitenskapelig publisering – indikatorer 2010* [Norwegian Polar Research – research at Svalbard. Resource input and scientific publishing – Indicators 2010], report 3/2012 (Oslo, Nordic Institute for Studies in Innovation, Research and Education, 2012).

Alexeeva, Olga and Frédéric Lasserre, 'China and the Arctic', *Arctic Yearbook* (2012). Available at https://arcticyearbook.com/images/Articles_2012/Alexeeva_and_Lassere.pdf (accessed 4 May 2018).

Alexseev, Mikhail A. and C. Richard Hofstetter, 'Russia, China, and the Immigration Security Dilemma', *Political Science Quarterly* 121 (2006), pp. 1–32.

Allison, Graham, 'Conceptual models and the Cuban Missile Crisis', *American Political Science Review* 63/3 (1969), pp. 689–718.

All-Russian Petroleum Research Institute, *Osnovnye printsipy kompleksnogo osvoenia resursov uglevodorodnogo syria severo-zapadnogo regiona Rossii* (St. Petersburg, VNIGRI, 2005).

AMAP (Arctic Monitoring and Assessment Programme), *Arctic Pollution Issues* (Oslo, AMAP, 1997).

AMAP (Arctic Monitoring and Assessment Programme), *Arctic Pollution Issues: A State of the Arctic Environment Report* (1998). Available at https://www.amap.no/documents/doc/arctic-pollution-issues-a-state-of-the-arctic-environment-report/67 (accessed 23 April 2018).

AMAP (Arctic Monitoring and Assessment Programme), *Arctic Pollution* (2002). Available at http://www.miljodirektoratet.no/old/klif/publikasjoner/2871/ta2871.pdf (accessed 23 April 2018).

AMAP (Arctic Monitoring and Assessment Programme), *Arctic Pollution* (2009). Available at https://www.amap.no/documents/doc/arctic-pollution-2009/88 (accessed 23 April 2018).

AMAP (Arctic Monitoring and Assessment Programme), *AMAP Assessment 2015: Temporal Trends in Persistent Organic Pollutants in the Arctic* (2015). Available at https://www.amap.no/documents/doc/AMAP-Assessment-2015-Temporal-Trends-in-Persistent-Organic-Pollutants-in-the-Arctic/1521 (accessed 23 April 2018).

AMAP (Arctic Monitoring and Assessment Programme), CAFF (Conservation of Arctic Flora and Fauna) and IASC (International Arctic Science Committee), *Arctic Climate Impact Assessment* (Cambridge, Cambridge University Press, 2005).

Andresen, Steinar, 'The role of scientific expertise in multilateral environmental agreements: Influence and effectiveness', in M. Ambrus, K. Arts, E. Hey and H. Raulus (eds), *The Role of 'Experts' in International and European Decision-Making Processes: Advisors, Decision Makers or Irrelevant Actors?* (Cambridge, Cambridge University Press, 2014), 105–25.

Andresen, Steinar, G. Kristin Rosendal and Jon Birger Skjærseth, 'Why negotiate a legally binding mercury treaty', *International Environmental Agreements: Politics, Law and Economics* 13 (2013), pp. 425–40.

Andresen, Steinar, G. Kristin Rosendal and Jon B. Skjærseth, 'Designing knowledge-based, integrated management systems for environmental governance', in A. Dinar (ed.), *Natural Resources and Environmental Policy in the Era of Global Change* (Singapore, World Scientific, 2017), pp. 439–56.

Andresen, Steinar, Jon Birger Skjærseth and Jørgen Wettestad, *Regime, the State and Society: Analyzing the Implementation of International Environmental Commitments*, IIASA Working Paper (1995).

Arctic Council, 'ACIA Policy Document' (2004). Available at http://www.acia.uaf.edu/PDFs/ACIA_Policy_Document.pdf (accessed 14 May 2016).

Arctic Council, *Arctic Council Observer States 2015 National Reports on Enhanced Black Carbon and Methane Emissions Reductions* (2015). Available at https://oaarchive.arctic-council.org/handle/11374/1169 (accessed 7 May 2018).

Arctic Ocean Conference, 'The Ilulissat Declaration' (2008). Available at http://www.oceanlaw.org/downloads/arctic/Ilulissat_Declaration.pdf (accessed 30 May 2018).

Åtland, Kristian, 'Mikhail Gorbachev, the Murmansk Initiative, and the desecuritization of interstate relations in the Arctic', *Cooperation and Conflict* 43 (2008), pp. 289–311.

Baev, Pavel K., 'Bear hug for the Baltic', *The World Today* 54/3 (1998), pp. 78–9.

Balton, David A., 'The Bering Sea Doughnut Hole Convention: Regional solution, global implications', in O. S. Stokke (ed.), *Governing High Seas Fisheries: The Interplay of Global and Regional Regimes* (Oxford, Oxford University Press, 2001), pp. 143–78.

Barents Euro-Arctic Region, 'The Kirkenes Declaration from the Conference of Foreign Ministers on Co-operation in the Barents Euro-Arctic Region', Kirkenes, 11 January 1993.

Bartenstein, Kristin, 'The "Arctic exception" in the Law of the Sea Convention: A contribution to safer navigation in the Northwest Passage?', *Ocean Development and International Law*, 42 (2011), pp. 22–52.

Basel Convention on the Control of Transboundary Movements of Hazardous Wastes and their Disposal. Available at http://www.basel.int/Portals/4/Basel%20Convention/docs/text/BaselConventionText-e.pdf (accessed 23 April 2018).

Beckley, Michael, 'China's Century? Why America's Edge Will Endure', *International Security* 36 (2011/12), pp. 41–78.

Berenskoetter, Felix, 'Friends, there are no friends? An intimate reframing of the international', *Millennium – Journal of International Studies* 35 (2007), pp. 647–76.

Berntsen, Bredo, *Grønne linjer: Natur- og miljøvernets historie i Norge* (Otta, Unipub, 2011).

Berthelsen, Rasmus G., Li Xing and Mette Højris Gregersen, 'Chinese Arctic science diplomacy: An instrument for achieving the Chinese dream?', in E. Conde and S. I. Sánchez (eds), *Global Challenges in the Arctic Region: Sovereignty, Environment and Geopolitical Balance* (New York, Routledge, 2016), pp. 442–60.

Blank, Stephen J. (ed.), 'Russia in the Arctic', *Strategic Studies Institute Monographs* (Carlisle, Strategic Studies Institute, 2011).

Blunden, Margaret, 'Geopolitics and the Northern Sea Route', *International Affairs* 88 (2012), pp. 115–29.

Boele, Otto, *The North in Russian Romantic Literature* (Amsterdam, Rodopi, 1996).

Borgerson, Scott G., 'Arctic meltdown: The economic and security implications of global warming', *Foreign Affairs* 87/2 (2008), pp. 63–77.

Brady, Anne-Marie (ed.), 'China's rise in Antarctica?', *Asian Survey* 50/4 (2010), pp. 759–85.

Brady, Anne-Marie (ed.), *The Emerging Politics of Antarctica* (London, Routledge, 2013).

Brekke, Harald and Philip Symonds, 'The ridge provisions of article 76 of the UN Convention on the Law of the Sea', in M. Nordquist, J. N. Moore and Tomas Heidar (eds), *Legal and Scientific Aspects of Continental Shelf Limits* (Hague, Martinus Nijhoff, 2004).

Browning, Christopher S., *Constructivism, Narrative and Foreign Policy Analysis: A Case Study of Finland* (Bern, Peter Lang, 2008).

Brubaker, R. Douglas and Claes Lykke Ragner, 'A review of the International Northern Sea Route Program (INSROP) – 10 years on', *Polar Geography* 33/1–2 (2010), pp. 15–38.

Buccini, John Anthony, 'The long and winding road to Stockholm: The view from the chair', in D. L. Downie and T. Fenge (eds), *Northern Lights Against POPs: Combatting Toxic Threats in the Arctic* (Montreal, McGill-Queen's University Press, 2003).

Bunik, I., 'Alternative approaches to delimitation of the Arctic Continental Shelf', *International Energy Law Review* 4 (2008), pp. 114–25.

Canadian Government, *Statement on Canada's Arctic Foreign Policy: Exercising Sovereignty and Promoting Canada's Northern Strategy Abroad* (2010). Available at http://www.international.gc.ca/arctic-arctique/assets/pdfs/canada_arctic_foreign_policy-eng.pdf (accessed 23 April 2018).

Carr, David, *Time, Narrative, and History* (Bloomington, Indiana University Press, 1986).

Carson, Rachel, *Silent Spring* (Boston, Houghton Mifflin, 1962).

CAST (China Association for Science and Technology), *China launches polar environmental assessments* (Beijing, CAST, 2012). Available at http://english.cast.org.cn/n1181872/n1182018/n1182078/13722705.html (accessed 2 October 2014).

CAST (China Association for Science and Technology), *China to boost Arctic research* (Beijing, CAST, 2012). Available at http://english.cast.org.cn/n1181872/n1182018/n1182078/13722719.html (accessed 2 October 2014).

CCICED, *A Report to the China Council for International Cooperation on Environment and Development (CCICED). Coordinated Actions for Addressing Climate Change and Air Pollution* (2015). Available at http://www.cciced.net/cciceden/POLICY/rr/prr/2015/201511/P020160810466251190363.pdf (accessed 7 May 2018).

Chasek, Pamela S., David Leonard Downie and Janet Welsh Brown, *Global Environmental Politics* (Boulder, Westview Press, 2017).

Chaturvedi, Sanjay, 'Arctic geopolitics then and now', in M. Nuttall and T. V. Callaghan (eds), *The Arctic: Environment, People, Policy* (Singapore, Harwood Academic Publishers, 2000), pp. 441–58.

Chen, Gang, 'China's emerging Arctic strategy', *The Polar Journal* 2/2 (2012), pp. 358–71.

Chinese Antarctic and Arctic Administration (CAA), *2015 National Annual Report on Polar Programme* (2015). Available at http://www.chinare.gov.cn/caa/userfiles/chinare2015en.pdf (accessed 7 May 2018).

Clark, Roger N., Errol E. Meidinger et al., *Integrating Science and Policy in Natural Resource Management: Lessons and Opportunities from North America*, USDA Forest Service, General Technical Report (1998). Available at https://www.fs.fed.us/pnw/pubs/gtr_441.pdf (accessed 23 April 2018).

Colson, David, 'The delimitation of the outer continental shelf between neighboring states', *American Journal of International Law* 97 (2003), pp. 91–107.

Commission on the Limits of the Continental Shelf (CLCS), 'Scientific and Technical Guidelines', Doc. CLCS/11, 13 May 1999, para. 2.2. Available at http://www.un.org/depts/los/clcs_new/clcs_home.htm (accessed 24 April 2018).

Commission on the Limits of the Continental Shelf (CLCS), 'Internal procedure of the subcommission of the Commission on the Limits on the Continental Shelf', Doc. CLCS/L.12, issued 25 May 2001. Available at http://www.un.org/depts/los/clcs_new/clcs_home.htm (accessed 24 April 2018).

Commission on the Limits of the Continental Shelf (CLCS), 'Statement by the Chairperson of the Commission on the Limits of the Continental Shelf on the Progress of Work in the Commission', Doc. CLCS/32, 12 April 2002. Available at http://www.un.org/depts/los/clcs_new/clcs_home.htm (accessed 24 April 2018).

Commission on the Limits of the Continental Shelf (CLCS), 'Statement by the Chair on the Progress of Work', Doc. CLCS/34, 1 July 2002, para. 33. Available at http://www.un.org/depts/los/clcs_new/clcs_home.htm (accessed 24 April 2018).

Commission on the Limits of the Continental Shelf (CLCS), 'Rules of Procedure of the Commission on the Limits of the Continental Shelf', Doc. CLCS/40/ Rev.1, 17 April 2008. Available at http://www.un.org/depts/los/clcs_new/clcs_home.htm (accessed 24 April 2018).

Commission on the Limits of the Continental Shelf (CLCS), 'Statement by the Chairperson of the Commission on the Limits of the Continental Shelf on the Progress of Work in the Commission', Doc. CLCS/68, 17 September 2010, para. 57. Available at http://www.un.org/depts/los/clcs_new/clcs_home.htm (accessed 24 April 2018).

Commission on the Limits of the Continental Shelf (CLCS), 'Progress of Work of the Commission on the Limits of the Continental Shelf – Statement by the Chairperson',

Doc. CLCS/72, 16 September 2011, para. 49. Available at http://www.un.org/depts/los/clcs_new/clcs_home.htm (accessed 24 April 2018).

Commission on the Limits of the Continental Shelf (CLCS), 'Progress of Work of the Commission on the Limits of the Continental Shelf – Statement by the Chairperson', Doc. CLCS/80, 24 September 2013, para. 38. Available at http://www.un.org/depts/los/clcs_new/clcs_home.htm (accessed 24 April 2018).

Committee for Greenlandic Mineral Resources to the Benefit of Greenland, *To the benefit of Greenland* (Nuuk, University of Greenland and University of Copenhagen, 2014).

Danish Ministry of Foreign Affairs in China, 'Greenland event at embassy on 5th November' (2013).

De Fina, Anna, Deborah Schiffrin and Michael Bamberg 'Introduction', in A. De Fina, D. Schiffrin and M. Bamberg (eds), *Discourse and Identity* (Cambridge, Cambridge University Press, 2006), pp. 1–23.

Delehanty, Will K. and Brent J. Steele, 'Engaging the narrative in ontological (in)security theory: Insights from feminist IR', *Cambridge Review of International Affairs* 22 (2009), pp. 523–40.

Denmark, 'Partial Submission to the Commission on the Limits of the Continental Shelf – The Northern Continental Shelf of Greenland', Executive Summary (2014). Available at http://www.un.org/depts/los/clcs_new/clcs_home.htm (accessed 24 April 2018).

de Pomereu, Jean, *China spreads its polar wings: investigating the infrastructure* (Brussels, International Polar Foundation, 2012). Available at http://www.sciencepoles.org/article/china-spreads-its-polar-wings-investing-in-infrastructure (accessed 2 October 2014).

de Pomereu, Jean, *Korea's polar ambitions* (Brussels, International Polar Foundation, 2012). Available at http://www.sciencepoles.org/interview/koreas-polar-ambitions (accessed 2 October 2014).

Dewailly, Eric and Chris Furgal, 'POPs, the environment, and public health', in D. L. Downie and T. Fenge (eds), *Northern Lights Against POPs: Combatting Toxic Threats in the Arctic* (Montreal, McGill-Queen's University Press, 2003), pp. 3–21.

Dodds, Klaus, 'Flag planting and finger pointing: The Law of the Sea, the Arctic and the political geographies of the outer continental shelf', *Political Geography* 29/2 (2010), pp. 63–73.

Dodds, Klaus and Mark Nuttall, *The Scramble for the Poles: The Geopolitics of the Arctic and Antarctic* (Cambridge, Polity Press, 2016).

Donaldson, Thomas and Lee E. Preston, 'The stakeholder theory of the corporation: Concepts, evidence and implications', *Academy of Management Review* 20 (1995), pp. 65–91.

Downie, David Leonard and Terry Fenge (eds), *Northern Lights Against POPs: Combatting Toxic Threats in the Arctic* (Montreal, McGill-Queen's University Press, 2003).

Duyck, Sébastien, 'Which canary in the coalmine? The Arctic in the international climate change regime', in Timo Koivurova, Gundmundur Alfredsson and Waliul Hasanat (eds), *The Yearbook of Polar Law* (2012). Available at https://papers.ssrn.com/sol3/papers.cfm?abstract_id=2331137 (accessed 29 March 2017).

Economic Council of Greenland, *Grønlands økonomi i 2013* (*Greenland's economy 2013*) (Nuuk, Economic Council of Greenland, 2013).

Eikeland, Sveinung, Larissa Ryabova and Lyudmila Ivanova, 'Northwest Russian fisheries after the disintegration of the USSR: Market structure and spatial impacts', *Polar Geography* 29/3 (2005), pp. 324–36.

Ekspertutvalg for nordområdene, *Mot nord! Utfordringer og muligheter i nordområdene: ekspertutvalg for nordområdene nedsatt av regjeringen 3. mars 2003: avgitt til Utenriksdepartementet 8. desember 2003, Norges offentlige utredninger; NOU 2003:32* (Oslo, Statens forvaltningstjeneste, Informasjonsforvaltning, 2003).

European Parliament, 'Resolution of 9 October 2008 on Arctic Governance', Doc. P6_TA(2008)0474 (2008). Available at http://www.europarl.europa.eu/sides/getDoc.do?type=TA&reference=P6-TA-2008-0474&language=EN (accessed 30 May 2018).

FAO, *The State of World Fisheries and Aquaculture 2013* (Rome, FAO, 2013).

Franck, Thomas M., *The Power of Legitimacy Among Nations* (Oxford, Oxford University Press,1990).

Freeman, R. Edward, *Strategic Management: A stakeholder approach* (Boston, Pitman, 1984).

Friedrich, Jürgen, *International Environmental 'Soft Law': The Functions and Limits of Nonbinding Instruments in International Environmental Governance and Law* (Berlin, Springer, 2013).

Frooman, Jeff, 'Stakeholder influence strategies', *Academy of Management Review* 24 (1999), pp. 191–205.

Gadihoke, Neil, 'Arctic melt: The outlook for India', *Maritime Affairs: Journal of the National Maritime Foundation of India* 8 (2012), pp. 1–12.

Gahr Støre, Jonas, *'Most is north': The High North and the way ahead – international perspective*. Lecture at the University of Tromsø, 29 April 2010. Available at https://www.regjeringen.no/en/aktuelt/Most-is-north/id602113/ (accessed 19 December 2010).

GEUS/BMP, *Minex* (No.15) (1998). Available at http://www.geus.dk/minex/MINEX15.pdf (accessed 20 March 2018).

GEUS/BMP, *Minex* (No.41) (2012). Available at http://www.geus.dk/minex/minex41.pdf (accessed 20 March 2018).

GEUS/MIMR, *The Government of Greenland and London Mining sign mining permit* (Nuuk, Geological Survey of Denmark and Greenland Ministry of Industry and Mineral, 2014). Available at http://www.geus.dk/minex/minex45.pdf (accessed 14 March 2018).

Goff, Patricia and Kevin C. Dunn 'Introduction: In defence of identity', in P. M. Goff and K. C. Dunn (eds), *Identity and Global Politics: Empirical and Theoretical Elaborations* (New York, Palgrave Macmillan, 2004), pp. 1–8.

Gofman, Victoria and Gunn-Britt Retter, *Development of an Arctic Indigenous Marine Use Survey Process* (2011). Available at http://www.pame.is/images/03_Projects/AMSA/Arctic%20Indigenous%20Marine_Use_Survey_Process/Agenda_item_4_AMSA_IIA-Scoping_Paper_Draft_Version_01_15_11.pdf (accessed 6 May 2016).

Government of China, *China issues guidelines on scitech development program* (Beijing, Government of China, 2006). Available at http://www.gov.cn/english/2006–02/09/content_184426.htm (accessed 2 October 2014).

Government of Greenland, *Mineral Strategy 2009. Update of objectives and plans for mineral exploration activities in* Greenland (2009). Available at https://govmin.gl/

images/stories/about_bmp/publications/mineral_strategy_2009.pdf (accessed 20 March 2018).

Government of Greenland, *Høring ved borgermøde vedr. London Minings ansøgning om udnyttelse av jern ved Isua – første møde av 4 høringsmøder* (*Public hearing on London Mining's application for iron exploitation at Isua – first meeting of four hearings*) (2012). Available at http://naalakkersuisut.gl/~/media/Nanoq/Files/Hearings/2012/London%20Mining%20ISUA/Referat%201%20dansk.pdf (accessed 14 March 2018).

Government of Greenland, *Høring ved borgermøde vedr. London Minings ansøgning om udnyttelse av jern ved Isua – tredje møde af 4 høringsmøder* (*Public hearing on London Mining's application for iron exploitation at Isua – third meeting of four hearings*) (2012). Available at http://naalakkersuisut.gl/~/media/Nanoq/Files/Hearings/2012/London%20Mining%20ISUA/Referat%201%20dansk.pdf (accessed 14 March 2018).

Government of Greenland, *Høring ved borgermøde vedr. London Minings ansøgning om udnyttelse af jern ved Isua – fjerde møde af 4 høringsmøder* (*Public hearing on London Mining's application for iron exploration at Isua – fourth meeting of four hearings*) (2012). Available at http://naalakkersuisut.gl/~/media/Nanoq/Files/Hearings/2012/London%20Mining%20ISUA/Referat%204%20dansk.pdf (accessed 14 March 2018).

Government of Greenland, *Udenrigspolitisk Redegørelse 2014* (*Foreign Policy Report 2014*) (2014), p. 50. Available at https://govmin.gl/images/stories/about_bmp/publications/mineral_strategy_2009.pdf (accessed 20 March 2018).

Government of Greenland, *Greenland's oil and mineral strategy 2014–2018* (Report FM 2014/133) (2014). Available at https://govmin.gl/images/stories/about_bmp/publications/mineral_strategy_2009.pdf (accessed 20 March 2018).

Government of Greenland, 'New strong force behind London Mining Greenland' (2015). Available at http://naalakkersuisut.gl/en/Naalakkersuisut/News/2015/01/080115-London-Mining (accessed 27 January 2018).

Government of Norway, *Nye byggesteiner i nord: Neste trinn i Regjeringens nordområdestrategi* (Oslo, Government of Norway, 2009).

Government of Norway and Ministry of Foreign Affairs, *Regjeringens nordområdestrategi* (Oslo, Government of Norway and Ministry of Foreign Affairs, 2006).

Graczyk, Piotr and Timo Koivurova, 'The Arctic Council', in L. C. Jensen and G. Hønneland (eds), *Handbook of the Politics of the Arctic* (Cheltenham, Edward Elgar, 2015), pp. 298–327.

Green, Fergus and Nicholas Stern, 'China's changing economy: Implications for its carbon dioxide emissions', *Climate Policy* 17/4 (2016), pp. 1–15.

Grontmij A/S, *Social Impact Assessment for the ISUA Iron Ore Project for London Mining Greenland A/S. Final* (2013). Available at http://naalakkersuisut.gl/~/media/Nanoq/Files/Attached%20Files/Raastof/Hoeringer/ISUA%202012/SIA%20London%20Mining%20final%20march%202013.pdf (accessed 27 January 2018).

Groven, Kyrre, Hogne Satøen and Carlo Aall, *Regional klimasårbarheitsanalyse for Nord-Norge. Norsk oppfølging av Arctic Climate Impact Assessment (NorACIA)* (2009). Available at https://www.vestforsk.no/sites/default/files/migrate_files/vf-rapport-4-06-noracia.pdf"http://noracia.npolar.no/noracia-prosjekter-2/rapport-vestlandsforskning-2006-regional-sarbarhet.pdf"http://noracia.npolar.no/noracia-prosjekter-2/rapport-vestlandsforskning-2006-regional-sarbarhet.pdf (accessed 14 May 2016).

Haas, Peter M., *Saving the Mediterranean: The Politics of International Environmental Cooperation* (New York, Columbia University Press, 1990).

Hallding, Karl, Guoyl Han and Marie Olsson, 'China's climate and energy security dilemma: Shaping a new path of economic growth', *Journal of Current Chinese Affairs* 38/3 (2009), pp. 119–34.

Hanf, Kenneth, 'The domestic basis of international environmental agreements', in A. Underdal and K. Hanf (eds), *International Environmental Agreements and Domestic Politics - The case of acid rain* (Aldershot, Ashgate, 2000).

Hassol, Susan J., *Impacts of a Warming Arctic. Arctic Climate Impact Assessment* (Cambridge, Cambridge University Press, 2004).

Heggelund Gørild and Han Cheng, 'China's climate policy: Does an Arctic dimension exist?', *Advances in Polar Science* 27/3 (2016), pp. 139–45.

Heggelund, Gørild and Rebecca Nadin, 'Climate change policy and governance', in E. Sternfeld (ed.), *Routledge Handbook of Environmental Policy in China* (Abingdon, Routledge, 2017), pp. 97–112.

Heininen, Lassi, 'Impacts of globalization and the circumpolar North in world politics', *Polar Geography* 29/2 (2005), pp. 91–102.

Hellberg-Hirn, Elena, 'Ambivalent space: Expressions of Russian identity', in J. Smith (ed.), *Beyond the Limits: The Concept of Space in Russian History and Culture* (Helsinki, Finnish Historical Society, 1999), pp. 49–69.

High Representative of the Union for Foreign Affairs and Security Policy, *An integrated European Union policy for the Arctic*, JOIN (2016) 21 final (2016). Available at https://eeas.europa.eu/arctic_region/docs/160427_joint-communication-an-integrated-european-union-policy-for-the-arctic_en.pdf (accessed 30 May 2018).

Hill, Fiona, 'Moscow discovers soft power', *Current History* 105/693 (2006), pp. 341–7.

Hirsch, Francine, 'Toward an empire of nations: Border-making and the formation of Soviet national identities', *Russian Review* 59/2 (2000), pp. 201–26.

Hoel, Alf Håkon, 'Climate change', in O. S. Stokke and G. Hønneland (eds), *International Cooperation and Arctic Governance: Regime Effectiveness and Northern Region Building* (Abingdon, Routledge, 2007), pp. 112–37.

Hong, Nong, 'Emerging interests of non-Arctic countries in the Arctic: A Chinese perspective', *Polar Journal* 4/2 (2014), pp. 271–86.

Hønneland, Geir, 'Compliance in the Fishery Protection Zone around Svalbard', *Ocean Development and International Law* 29 (1998), pp. 339–60.

Hønneland, Geir, *Coercive and Discursive Compliance Mechanisms in the Management of Natural Resources: A Case Study from the Barents Sea Fisheries* (Boston, Springer, 2000).

Hønneland, Geir, *Russia and the West: Environmental Cooperation and Conflict* (New York, Routledge, 2003).

Hønneland, Geir, *Russian Fisheries Management: The Precautionary Approach in Theory and Practice* (Leiden, Martinus Nijhoff, 2004).

Hønneland, Geir, *Making Fishery Agreements Work: Post-Agreement Bargaining in the Barents Sea* (Cheltenham, Edward Elgar, 2012).

Hønneland, Geir, 'Norway's Arctic policy', in R. W. Murray and A. D. Nuttall (eds), *International Relations and the Arctic: Understanding Policy and Governance* (Amherst, Cambria Press, 2014), pp. 235–61.

Hønneland, Geir, 'Delimitation of the Barents Sea', in *Russia and the Arctic: Environment, Identity and Foreign Policy* (London, I.B. Tauris, 2016), pp. 71–102.

Hønneland, Geir and Anne-Kristin Jørgensen, *Implementing International Environmental Agreements in Russia* (Manchester, Manchester University Press, 2003).

Hønneland, Geir and Lars Rowe, 'Western vs. post-Soviet medicine: Fighting tuberculosis and HIV/AIDS in North-West Russia and the Baltic States', *Journal of Communist Studies and Transition Politics* 21 (2005), pp. 395–415.

Hønneland, Geir, Lyudmila Ivanova and Frode Nilssen, 'Russia's Northern Fisheries Basin: Trends in regulation, fleet and industry', *Polar Geography* 27/3 (2003), pp. 225–39.

Hsiung, Christopher Weidacher 'China and Arctic energy: Drivers and limitations', *Polar Journal* 6/2 (2016), pp. 243–58.

Hung, Hayley, Athanasios A. Katsoyiannis, Eva Brorström-Lundén, Kristin Olafsdottir, Wenche Aas, Knut Breivik, Pernilla Bohlin-Nizzetto, Arni Sigurdsson, Hannele Hakola, Rossana Bossi, Henrik Skov, Ed Sverko, Enzo Barresi, Phil Fellin and Simon Wilson, 'Temporal trends of Persistent Organic Pollutants (POPs) in Arctic air: 20 years of monitoring under the Arctic Monitoring and Assessment Programme (AMAP)', *Environmental Pollution* 217 (2016), pp. 52–61.

Huntington, Henry P. and Michelle Sparck, 'POPs in Alaska: Engaging the United States', in D. L. Downie and T. Fenge (eds), *Northern Lights Against POPs. Combatting Toxic Threats in the Arctic* (Montreal, McGill-Queen's University Press, 2003), pp. 214–24.

India, *National Report by India – January 2016. Enhanced Black Carbon and Methane Emissions Reduction – an Arctic Council Framework for Actions* (2016). Available at https://oaarchive.arctic-council.org/bitstream/handle/11374/1169/EDOCS-3137-v1-India_2016_Black_Carbon_Methane_National_Report.PDF?sequence=26&isAllowed=y (accessed 7 May 2018).

Ingimundarson, Valur, 'Framing the national interest: the political uses of the Arctic in Iceland's foreign and domestic policies', *Polar Journal* 5/1 (2015), pp. 82–100.

International Court of Justice, *Maritime Delimitation on the Black Sea (Romania v. Ukraine), Judgement* (International Court of Justice, 2009). Available at http://www.icj-cij.org/files/case-related/132/132-20090203-JUD-01-00-EN.pdf (accessed 21 February 2018).

International Law Association, *Legal Issues of the Outer Continental Shelf*, Second Report (2006), Toronto Conference, pp. 4–7. Available at http://www.ila-hq.org/ (accessed 24 April 2018).

IPCC, 'Working Group II, Final Draft Assessment Report V, Chapter 24' (2013). Available at http://ipcc.ch/pdf/assessment-report/ar5/wg2/drafts/fd/WGIIAR5-Chap24_FGDall.pdf (accessed 7 May 2018).

IPEN, IPEN Press Release, 26 April 2017. Available at https://zerowasteeurope.eu/2017/04/ipen-press-release-at-un-meeting-canada-and-chile-stand-alone-trying-to-legitimize-e-waste-dumping-and-promote-recycling-of-toxic-chemical-into-childrens-products/ (accessed 18 August 2017).

Ivanova, Maria and Are Kristoffer Sydnes, 'Interorganizational coordination in oil spill emergency response: A case study of the Murmansk region of Northwest Russia', *Polar Geography* 33/3–4 (2010), pp. 139–64.

Jakobson, Linda, 'China prepares for an ice-free Arctic', *SIPRI Insights on Peace and Security* 2010/2 (2010), p. 9. Available at https://www.sipri.org/sites/default/files/files/insight/SIPRIInsight1002.pdf (accessed 4 May 2018).

Jakobson Linda and Jingchao Peng, *China's Arctic aspirations*, SIPRI policy paper 34 (Stockholm, Stockholm International Peace Research Institute, 2012).

Japan, 'Japan's Arctic Policy' (Tokyo, Headquarters for Ocean Policy, 2015).

Jensen, Leif Christian, 'From the High North to the Low South: bipolar Norway's Antarctic strategy', *Polar Journal* 6/2 (2016), pp. 273–90.

Jensen, Leif Christian, *International Relations in the Arctic: Norway and the Struggle for Power in the New North* (London, I.B. Tauris, 2016).

Jensen, Leif Christian and Geir Hønneland, 'Framing the High North: Public discourses in Norway after 2000', *Acta Borelia* 8/1 (2011), pp. 37–54.

Jensen, Øystein, 'The Barents Sea: Treaty between Norway and the Russian Federation concerning maritime delimitation and cooperation in the Barents Sea and the Arctic Ocean', *International Journal of Marine and Coastal Law* 26/1 (2011), pp. 151–68.

Jensen, Øystein, *The Commission on the Limits of the Continental Shelf: Law and Legitimacy* (Leiden, Brill/Nijhoff, 2014), pp. 92–152.

Jensen, Øystein, 'Maritime boundary delimitation beyond 200 nautical miles: The international judiciary and the Commission on the Limits of the Continental Shelf', *Nordic Journal of International Law* 84 (2015), pp. 580–604.

Jensen, Øystein, *The Commission on the Limits of the Continental Shelf: Law and Legitimacy* (Leiden, Martinus Nijhoffs, 2014).

Jhun, Jong-Ghap and Eun-Jeong Lee, 'A new East Asian winter monsoon index and associated characteristics of the winter monsoon', *Journal of Climate* 17/4 (2004), pp. 711–26.

Jørgensen, Anne-Kristin, 'Recent developments in the Russian fisheries sector', in E. W. Rowe (ed.), *Russia and the North* (Ottawa, University of Ottawa Press, 2009), pp. 87–106.

Jørgensen, Knud Erik, *International Relations Theory: A New Introduction* (Basingstoke, Palgrave Macmillan, 2010).

Joyner, Chris C., *Governing the Frozen Commons: The Antarctic Regime and Environmental Protection* (South Carolina, University of South Carolina Press, 1998).

Kang, Sung-Ho, Seung Il Nam, Jung Han Yim, Kyung Ho Chung and Jong Kuk Hong, *Cruise report: RV 'Araon' ARA03B, August 1–September 10, 2012. Chukchi borderland and Mendeleyev Ridge* (Incheon, Korea Polar Research Institute, 2012).

Kankaanpää, Paula and Oran R. Young, 'The effectiveness of the Arctic Council', *Polar Research* 31 (2012), pp. 1–14.

Karlaganis, Georg, Renato Marioni, Ivo Sieber and Andreas Weber, 'The elaboration of the Stockholm Convention on Persistent Organic Pollutants (POPs): A negotiation process fraught with obstacles and opportunities', *Environmental Science and Pollution Research* 8 (2001), pp. 216–21.

Keohane, Robert O. and David G. Victor, 'Cooperation and discord in global climate policy', *Nature and Climate Change* 6/6 (2016), pp. 570–5.

Keskitalo, E. Carina H., Timo Koivurova and Nigel Bankes, 'Climate governance in the Arctic: Introduction and theoretical framework', in T. Koivurova, E. C. H. Keskitalo and N. Bankes (eds), *Climate Governance in the Arctic* (Dordrecht, Springer, 2009), pp. 1–26.

Khare, Neloy, 'Indian scientific endeavors in Ny-Ålesund, Arctic', *Antarctic Record* 53/1 (2009), pp. 110–13.

Kim, Jong-Deong, 'Findings and challenges of the North Pacific Arctic Conference', in L. Lunde, J. Yang and I. Stensdal (eds), *Asian Countries and the Arctic Future* (Singapore, World Scientific, 2015).

Kimura, Hiroshi, 'Russia and the CIS in 2004: Putin's offensive and defensive actions', *Asian Survey* 45/1 (2005), pp. 59–66.

Kingdom of Norway and Russian Federation, 'Treaty between the Kingdom of Norway and the Russian Federation concerning Maritime Delimitation and Cooperation in the Barents Sea and the Arctic Ocean' (2010). Available at www.regjeringen.no/upload/UD/Vedlegg/Folkerett/avtale_engelsk.pdf (accessed 19 November 2010).

Koivurova, Timo, 'Alternatives for an Arctic Treaty – evaluation and a new proposal', *Review of European, Comparative & International Environmental Law* 17/1 (2008), pp.14–26.

Koivurova, Timo, 'Implementing guidelines for environmental impact assessment in the Arctic', in C. J. Basmeijer and T. Koivurova (eds), *The Theory and Practice of Transboundary Environmental Impact Assessment* (Leiden, Nijhoff, 2008), pp. 151–74.

Koivurova, Timo, 'Governing Arctic shipping: Finding a role for the Arctic Council', *The Yearbook of Polar Law* 2/1 (2010), pp. 115–38.

Koivurova, Timo, 'Limits and possibilities of the Arctic Council in a rapidly changing scene of governance', *Polar Record* 46/2 (2010), pp. 149–56.

Koivurova, Timo and David VanderZwaag, 'The Arctic Council at 10 years: Retrospect and prospect', *University of British Columbia Law Review* 40/1 (2007), pp. 121–94.

Koivurova, Timo and Erik J. Molenaar, *International Governance and Regulation of the Marine Arctic: Overview and Gap Analysis* (Oslo, WWF, 2009), pp. 1–43.

Koivurova, Timo, Arild Buanes, Larissa Riabova, Vladimir Didyk, Thomas Ejdemo, Gregory Poelzer, Päivi Taavo and Pamela Lesser, '"Social license to operate": a relevant term in Northern European mining?', *Polar Geography* 38 (2015), pp. 194–227.

Kopra, Sanna, 'China's Arctic interests', in *Arctic Yearbook* (2013). Available at https://www.arcticyearbook.com/images/Articles_2013/KOPRA_AY13_FINAL.pdf (accessed 4 May 2018).

KOPRI (Korea Polar Research Institute) *KOPRI annual report 2008* (Incheon, KOPRI, 2009).

Korea, 'Arctic Policy of the Republic of Korea' (Seoul, Korea Maritime Institute, 2013).

Lajeunesse, Adam and P. Whitney Lackenbauer, 'Chinese mining interests and the Arctic', in D. A. Berry, N. Bowles and J. Halbert (eds), *Governing the North American Arctic: Sovereignty, Security, and Institutions* (New York, Palgrave Macmillan, 2016), pp. 74–102.

Lambert, N., C. Rostock, B. Bergfald, L. M. Bjorvik, *Identifying POP candidates for the Stockholm Convention* (2011). Available at http://www.miljodirektoratet.no/old/klif/publikasjoner/2871/ta2871.pdf (accessed 23 April 2018).

Lanteigne, Marc, '"Have you entered the storehouses of the snow?" China as a norm entrepreneur in the Arctic', *Polar Record* 53/2 (2017), pp. 117–30.

Lapenko, M. V., *Rossiya i Kazakhstan na puti sozdaniya voenno-strategicheskovo prostranstva* (Saratov, Voenno-istoricheskie issledovaniya v Povolzhe, 2008), pp. 120–1.

Lapid, Yosef, 'Culture's ship: Returns and departures in international relations theory', in Y. Lapid and F. Kratochwil (eds), *The Return of Culture and Identity in IR Theory* (Boulder, Lynne Rienner Publishers, 1996), pp. 3–20.

Laruelle, Marlene, *Russia's Arctic Strategies and the Future of the Far North* (Armonk, M.E. Sharpe, 2014).

Lasserre, Frédéric, Linyan Huang and Olga V. Alexeeva, 'China's strategy in the Arctic: Threatening or opportunistic?', *Polar Record* 53/1 (2017), pp. 31–42.

Lavrov, S. V., press conference, Russian Ministry of Foreign Affairs, 13 January 2011. Available at http://www.mid.ru. (Accessed 21 January 2011).

Ledovskikh, M. V., 'Geopoliticheskie aspekty razvitiya neftegazovogo kompleksa severo-zapadnogo regiona Rossii', *Mineral'nye resursy Rossii –Ekonomika i upravlenie* 4 (2005), pp. 2–13.

Le Quéré et al., 'Global carbon budget 2014', *Earth System Science Data* 7/1 (2015), pp. 47–85.

Liu, Jiping, Judith A. Curry, Huijun Wang, Mirong Song and Radley M. Horton, 'Impact of declining Arctic sea ice on winter snowfall', *Proceedings of the National Academy of Sciences of the United States of America* 109/11 (2012), pp. 4074–79.

Liu, Zhu, *China's Carbon Emissions Report 2015*, Belfer Center Discussion paper #2015-02 (Cambridge, Harvard Kennedy School of Government, 2015). Available at https://www.belfercenter.org/sites/default/files/legacy/files/carbon-emissions-report-2015-final.pdf (accessed 4 May 2018).

London Mining, *Annual report 2008* (London, London Mining, 2009).

London Mining, *Annual report 2009* (London, London Mining, 2010).

London Mining, *Annual report 2010* (London, London Mining, 2011).

London Mining, *Annual report 2011* (London, London Mining, 2012).

London Mining Greenland, *Isua Iron Ore Project* (2011). Available at https://www.govmin.gl/images/stories/minerals/events/suppliers_seminar_jan_2011/london_mining_eng.pdf (accessed 20 March 2018).

LRTAP, Protocol to the 1979 Convention on Long-range Transboundary Air Pollution on Persistent Organic Pollutants. Available at http://www.unece.org/fileadmin/DAM/env/lrtap/full%20text/1998.POPs.e.pdf (accessed 23 April 2018).

Lukin, Alexander, 'The image of China in Russian border regions', *Asian Survey* 38/9 (1998), pp. 821–35.

Lunde, Leiv, 'Introduction', in I. Stensdal, L. Lunde and J. Yang (eds), *Asian Countries and the Arctic Future* (Singapore, World Scientific Publishing, 2016), pp. 7–11.

Macnab, Ron, 'The outer limits of the continental shelf in the Arctic Ocean', in M. Nordquist, J. N. Moore and Tomas Heidar (eds), *Legal and Scientific Aspects of Continental Shelf Limits* (Hague, Martinus Nijhoff, 2004).

Main, Steven J., 'If spring comes tomorrow … Russia and the Arctic', *Russian Series* (Swindon, Defence Academy of the United Kingdom, 2011).

Magnusson, B. M., 'Outer continental shelf boundary agreements', *International and Comparative Law Quarterly* 62 (2013), pp. 345–72.

Makarychev, Andrey Makarychev, 'Pskov at the crossroads of Russia's trans-border relations with Estonia and Latvia: Between provinciality and marginality', *Europe-Asia Studies* 57/3 (2005), pp. 481–500.

Mankoff, Jeffrey, *Russian Foreign Policy: The Return of Great Power Politics* (Lanham, Rowman & Littlefield, 2012).

March, James G. and Johan P. Olsen, *Rediscovering Institutions: The Organizational Basis of Politics* (New York, Macmillan, 1989).

Martin, Miguel, 'China in Greenland: Mines, Science, and Nods to Independence', *China Brief* 18/43 (Jamestown Foundation, 2018). Available at https://jamestown.org/program/china-greenland-mines-science-nods-independence/ (accessed 15 May 2018).

McDorman, Ted L., 'The outer continental shelf in the Arctic Ocean: Legal framework and recent developments', in D. Vidas (ed.), *Law, Technology and Science for Oceans in Globalisation – IUU Fishing, Oil Pollution, Bioprospecting, Outer Continental Shelf* (Hague, Martinus Nijhoff Publishers, 2010).

McDorman, Ted L. and Clive Schofield, 'Maritime limits and boundaries in the Arctic Ocean: Agreements and disputes', in L. C. Jensen and G. Hønneland (eds.), *Handbook of the Politics of the Arctic* (Cheltenham, Edward Elgar Publishing, 2015), pp. 207–26.

McGrath, Jessica F., 'Evaluating Arctic State Implementation of Ecosystem-Based Management Recommendations Supported by the Arctic Council: Canada Norway, and the US', MA dissertation, University of Washington (2014).

Medvedev, Dmitry, *The foreign policy concept of the Russian Federation* (2010). Available at http://www.mid.ru/ns-sndoc.nsf/0e9272befa34209743256c630042d1aa/cef95560654d4ca5c32574960036cddb (accessed 15 December 2010) (official translation).

Medvedev, Dmitry, 'Vystuplenie na soveshchanii s rossiyskimi poslami i postoyannimi predstavitelyami v mezhdunarodnykh organizatsiyakh' (2010). Available at www.kremlin.ru/transcripts/8325 (accessed 18 December 2010) (our translation).

Medvedev, Dmitry and Jens Stoltenberg, 'Sovmestnaya press-konferentsiya possiysko-norvezhskikh peregovorov' (2010). Available at www.kremlin.ru/transcripts/8924 (accessed 7 December 2010).

Menon, Rajan, 'In the shadow of the bear: Security in post-Soviet Central Asia', *International Security* 20/1 (1995), pp. 149–81.

MID, 'Kommentariy Departamenta informatsii i pechaty MID Rossii v svyazi s podpisaniem rossiysko-norvezhskogo Dogovora o razgranicheniem morskikh prostranstv' (2010). Available at http://www.mid.ru/brp_4.nsf/0/9350CB29FC106130C32577A00027B318 (accessed 2 March 2011).

Mikheev, V., 'Potentsial vrazhdy versus sotrudnichestva', *Pro et Contra* 3/2 (1998), pp. 53–67.

Miles, Edward L., Steinar Andresen, Elaine M. Carlin, Jon B. Skjærseth, Arild Underdal and Jørgen Wettestad, *Environmental Regime Effectiveness: Confronting Theory with Evidence* (Cambridge, MIT Press, 2002).

Mills, William James, *Exploring Polar Frontiers: A Historical Encyclopedia* (Santa Barbara, ABC CLIO, 2003).

Ministry of Foreign Affairs of the Republic of China, Keynote Speech by Vice Foreign Minister Zhang Ming at the China Country Session of the Third Arctic Circle Assembly in October 2015. Available at http://www.fmprc.gov.cn/mfa_eng/wjbxw/t1306858.shtml (accessed 4 May 2018).

Mitchell, Ronald B., 'Sources of transparency: Information systems in international regimes', *International Studies Quarterly* 42/1 (1998), pp.109–30.

Mitchell, Ronald K., Bradley R. Agle and Donna J. Wood, 'Toward a theory of stakeholder identification and salience: Defining the principle of who and what really counts', *Academy of Management Review* 22/4 (1997), pp. 865–9.

Mitchell, Ronald B., William C. Clark, David W. Cash and Nancy M. Dickson (eds), *Global Environmental Assessments: Information and Influence* (Cambridge, MIT Press, 2006).

Moe, Arild, 'Russian and Norwegian petroleum strategies in the Barents Sea', *Arctic Review on Law and Politics* 1/2 (2010), pp. 225–48.

Morales, M., *The Stockholm Convention* (Durham, Duke University, 2014).

Muradyan, E. R., 'Problemy obespecheniya bezopasnosti rossiyskovo gosudarstva', *Vestnik Chelyabinskovo gosudarstvennovo universiteta* 8 (2008), pp. 12–17.

Nadin, Rebecca, Sarah Opitz-Stapleton and Xu Yinlong (eds), *Climate Risk and Resilience in China* (London, Routledge, 2015).

National Research Council, *Scientists, Engineers, and Track-Two Diplomacy: A Half-Century of US–Russian Interacademy Cooperation* (Washington, DC, National Academies Press, 2004).

Nau, Henry R., *At Home Abroad: Identity and Power in American Foreign Policy* (Ithaca, Cornell University Press, 2002).

Nayak, Shailesh, 'Polar research in India', *Indian Journal of Marine Sciences* 37/4 (2008), pp. 352–57.

NCAOR (National Centre for Antarctic and Ocean Research), *Annual report 2012–2013* (Goa, NCAOR, 2013).

NCAOR (National Centre for Antarctic and Ocean Research), *Annual report 2016–2017* (2017), p. 74. Available at http://www.ncaor.gov.in/annualreports (accessed 9 March 2018).

NCAOR (National Centre for Antarctic and Ocean Research), *Delimitation of the outer limits of the continental shelf* (Goa, NCAOR, 2014). Available at http://www.ncaor.gov.in/pages/researchview/8 (accessed 4 November 2014).

NDRC (National Development and Reform Commission), *China's National Climate Change Programme* (2007).

NDRC (National Development and Reform Commission) and MOHURD (Ministry of Housing and Urban-Rural Development), *Action Plan for Climate Change Adaptation in Cities* (in Chinese) (2016). Available at http://bgt.ndrc.gov.cn/zcfb/201602/t20160216_774739.html (accessed 4 May 2018).

Nelson, Rodney, *Iron Ore* (Quarterly Commodity Insights Bulletin March 2013) (2013), p. 1. Available at https://assets.kpmg.com/content/dam/kpmg/pdf/2015/06/iron-ore-q4-2012-march-2013.pdf (accessed 20 March 2018).

Nesterenko, Andrei, Russian MFA Spokesman Andrei Nesterenko response to media question regarding Russian–Norwegian Agreement on Maritime Delimitation in the Barents Sea and the Arctic Ocean (2010). Available at http://www.mid.ru/Brp_4.nsf/arh/28A6508288DACE24C32577140029DBDC?OpenDocument (accessed 2 March 2011).

Nilsson, Annika E., 'A changing Arctic climate: Science and policy in the Arctic Climate Impact Assessment', in T. Koivurova, E. C. H. Keskitalo and N. Bankes (eds), *Climate Governance in the Arctic* (Dordrecht, Springer, 2009) pp. 77–95.

NIPR (National Institute of Polar Research), *Asian forum for polar sciences (AFoPS). Report to XXXII ATCM* (Buenos Aires, Secretariat of the Antarctic Treaty, 2009). Available at www.ats.aq/documents/ATCM32/ip/Atcm32_ip089_e.doc (accessed 4 November 2014).

Nishimura, Kuniyuki, 'Worlds of our remembering: The agent–structure problem as the search for identity', *Cooperation and Conflict* 46 (2011), pp. 96–112.

Norwegian Environmental Agency, *Strategy 2015–2020* (2014). Available at http://www.miljodirektoratet.no/no/Publikasjoner/2014/Desember-2014/Miljodirektoratets-strategi-for-2015-2020/ (accessed 23 April 2018).

Norwegian Government, *Nordkloden. Verdiskaping og ressurser. Klimaendinger og kunnskap. Utviklingen nord på kloden angår oss alle* (Oslo, Norwegian Ministry of Foreign Affairs, 2014). Available at https://www.regjeringen.no/contentassets/23843eabac77454283b0769876148950/nordkloden_rapport-red.pdf (accessed 23 April 2018).

Norwegian Ministries, *Norway's Arctic Strategy – between geopolitics and social development* (Oslo, Norwegian Ministries, 2017).

Norwegian Ministry of Climate and Environment, 'Letter of allocation, the Norwegian Environmental Agency' (2016). Available at https://www.regjeringen.no/contentassets/ab73dcc339ba4a498f8e17df76305bed/miljodirektoratet_tildelingsbrev_2016.pdf (accessed 23 April 2018).

Norwegian Ministry of Environment, *Overenskomst mellom Kongeriket Norges Regjering og Unionen av Sovjetiske Sosialistiske Republikkers Regjering om samarbeid på miljøvernområdet* (Oslo, Norwegian Ministry of the Environment, 1988).

Norwegian Ministry of Environment, *Om norsk politikk mot klimaendringer og utslipp av nitrogenoksider*, St. meld. nr. 41 (1994–95) (Oslo, Norwegian Ministry of Environment, 1995). Available at https://www.stortinget.no/no/Saker-og-publikasjoner/Stortingsforhandlinger/Lesevisning/?p=1994-95&paid=3&wid=d&psid=DIVL516 (accessed 20 May 2016).

Norwegian Ministry of Environment, *Tilleggsmelding til St.meld. nr. 54 (2000–01) Norsk klimapolitikk*, St. meld. nr. 15 (2001–02) (Oslo, Norwegian Ministry of Environment, 2002). Available at https://www.regjeringen.no/contentassets/471533eed2ff47f987699d32b8207043/no/pdfa/stm200120020015000dddpdfa.pdf (accessed 20 May 2016).

Norwegian Ministry of Environment, *Leve med kulturminner*, St.meld.nr. 16 (2004–05) (Oslo, Norwegian Ministry of Environment, 2005).

Norwegian Ministry of Environment, 'Letter of allocation, the Norwegian Environmental Agency' (2009). Available at https://www.regjeringen.no/globalassets/upload/md/vedlegg/brev/tildelingsbrev_2009/sft_etb_2009.pdf (accessed 23 April 2018).

Norwegian Ministry of Environment, 'Tildelingsbrev 2010 til Sjøfartsdirektoratet' (2010). Available at https://www.sjofartsdir.no/Global/Om%20Sdir/Presentasjon%20av%20direktoratet/TIldelingsbrev%20fra%20NHD%20og%20MD/Endelig%20tildelingsbrev%20MD%202010.pdf (accessed 20 April 2016).

Norwegian Ministry of Environment, 'Norwegian implementation plan for the Stockholm Convention on POPs' (Oslo, Norwegian Ministry of the Environment, 2010). Available at http://www.pops.int/documents/implementation/nips/submissions/Norway.pdf (accessed 9 March 2017).

Norwegian Ministry of Environment, 'Tildelingsbrev 2011 til Sjøfartsdirektoratet' (2011). Available at https://www.regjeringen.no/globalassets/upload/md/2011/vedlegg/brev/tildelingsbrev_2011/tildelingsbrev_sjofartdir.pdf (accessed 20 April 2016).

Norwegian Ministry of Environment, 'Endelig tildelingsbrev 2012 for Sjøfartsdirektoratet' (2012). Available at https://www.regjeringen.no/contentassets/7999c83ccc2a4fc39121d776172b7257/sjofartsdirektoratet_2012.pdf (accessed 20 April 2016).

Norwegian Ministry of Environment, 'Endelig tildelingsbrev 2013 for Sjøfartsdirektoratet' (2013). Available at https://www.regjeringen.no/contentassets/eac76c5b603a4ceebfdd7153b5cf5d2f/sjofartsdirekoratet_tildelingsbrev_2013.pdf (accessed 20 April 2016).

Norwegian Ministry of Environment, 'Tildelingsbrev 2014 for Sjøfartsdirektoratet' (2014). Available at https://www.regjeringen.no/globalassets/upload/kld/tildelingsbrev/sjofartsdir_tildelingsbrev_2014.pdf (accessed 20 April 2016).

Norwegian Ministry of Foreign Affairs, 'Avtale mellom Regjeringen i Unionen av Sovjetiske Sosialistiske Republikker og Regjeringen i Kongeriket Norge om samarbeid innen fiskerinæringen', in *Overenskomster med fremmede stater* (Oslo, Norwegian Ministry of Foreign Affairs, 1975), pp. 546–9.

Norwegian Ministry of Foreign Affairs, 'Avtale mellom Norge og Sovjetunionen om en midlertidig praktisk ordning for fisket i et tilstøtende område i Barentshavet med tilhørende protokoll og erklæring', in *Overenskomster med fremmede stater* (Oslo, Norwegian Ministry of Foreign Affairs, 1978), p. 436.

Norwegian Ministry of Foreign Affairs, *Muligheter og utfordringer i nord*, St.meld. nr. 30 (2004–05) (Oslo, Norwegian Ministry of Foreign Affairs, 2005).

Norwegian Ministry of Foreign Affairs, *Norwegian Government's High North Strategy* (Oslo, Norwegian Ministry of Foreign Affairs, 2006).

Norwegian Ministry of Foreign Affairs, *Interesser, ansvar og muligheter: Hovedlinjer in norsk utenrikspolitikk*, St.meld. nr. 15 (2008–09) (Oslo, Norwegian Ministry of Foreign Affairs, 2009).

Norwegian Ministry of Foreign Affairs, *New Building Blocks in the North: The Next Step in the Government's High North Strategy* (Oslo, Norwegian Ministry of Foreign Affairs, 2009). Available at https://www.regjeringen.no/globalassets/upload/ud/vedlegg/nordomradene/new_building_blocks_in_the_north.pdf (accessed 9 May 2016).

Norwegian Ministry of Foreign Affairs, 'Treaty between Norway and the Russian Federation concerning Maritime Delimitation and Cooperation in the Barents Sea and the Arctic Ocean' (Oslo, Norwegian Ministry of Foreign Affairs, 2010).

Norwegian Ministry of Foreign Affairs, *The High North: Visions and Strategies* (Oslo, Norwegian Ministry of Foreign Affairs, 2011). Available at https://www.regjeringen.no/globalassets/upload/ud/vedlegg/nordomradene/ud_nordomrodene_en_web.pdf (accessed 9 May 2016).

Norwegian Ministry of Foreign Affairs, *Nordområdene: Visjon og virkemidler*, Meld.st.7 (2011–12) (Oslo, Norwegian Ministry of Foreign Affairs, 2011).

Norwegian Ministry of Foreign Affairs, *Økt skipsfart i Polhavet – muligheter og utfordringer for Norge* (Oslo, Norwegian Ministry of Foreign Affairs, 2013). Available at https://www.regjeringen.no/globalassets/upload/ud/vedlegg/nordomrc3a5dene/oekt_skipsfart_i_polhavet_rapport.pdf (accessed 29 April 2016).

Norwegian Ministry of Foreign Affairs, *Norwegian interests and policy in the Antarctic*, St. meld. nr. 32 (2014–15) (Oslo, Norwegian Ministry of Foreign Affairs, 2015).

Norwegian Ministry of Justice and Public Security, *Norske interesser og politikk for Bouvetøya*, St. meld. nr. 33 (2014–15) (Oslo, Norwegian Ministry of Justice and Public Security, 2015).

Norwegian Ministry of Labour and Social Inclusion, *Sami Policy*, St. meld. nr. 28 (2007–08) (Oslo, Norwegian Ministry of Labour and Social Inclusion, 2008). Available at https://www.regjeringen.no/contentassets/8e1e26b083304fa394b6495db574a060/no/pdfs/stm200720080028000dddpdfs.pdf (accessed 20 May 2016).

Norwegian Ministry of Trade and Industry, *Between Heaven and Earth: Norwegian space policy for business and public benefit*, St. meld. nr. 32 (2012–13) (Oslo, Norwegian Ministry of Trade and Industry, 2013).

Norwegian Ministry of Trade and Industry, *Regjeringens Maritime Strategi. Stø Kurs 2020* (Oslo, Norwegian Ministry of Trade and Industry, 2013).

Norwegian Ministry of Transportation, *National Transport Plan (2014–23)*, St. meld. nr. 26 (2012–13) (Oslo, Norwegian Ministry of Transportation, 2013). Available at https://www.regjeringen.no/contentassets/e6e7684b5d54473dadeeb7c599ff68b8/en-gb/pdfs/stm201220130026000engpdfs.pdf (accessed 20 May 2016).

Norwegian Polar Institute, *Arctic Climate Impact Assessment. Presentasjoner og oppsummeringer fra fagmøtet Effekter av marine klimaendringer med spesielt fokus på Barentshavet* (2003). Available at https://brage.bibsys.no/xmlui//bitstream/handle/11250/172936/Internrapport14.pdf?sequence=1 (accessed 9 May 2016).

Norwegian Polar Institute, *Klimaendringer i norsk Arktis: Kunnskapsbehov og tilpasningsstrategier for infrastruktur* (2005).

Norwegian Polar Institute, *Klimaendringer og tilpasningsstrategier for samiske næringer* (2005). Available at http://noracia.npolar.no/litteratur/rapport-fagmote-samisk-2005.pdf (accessed 9 May 2016).

Norwegian Polar Institute, *Klimascenarier for norsk Arktis* (2006).

Norwegian Polar Institute, *NorACIA. Norsk Oppfølging av Arktisk Råd-Prosjektet 'Arctic Climate Impact Assessment': Handlingsplan 2006* (2006). Available at http://docplayer.no/6253871-Noracia-norsk-oppfolging-av-arktisk-rad-prosjektet-arctic-climate-impact-assessment-handlingsplan-2006-2009.html (accessed 14 May 2016).

Norwegian Polar Institute, *Klimaendringer i norsk Arktis – ekstremvær og konsekvenser for samfunnet* (2007). Available at http://noracia.npolar.no/fagmoter/foredragene-fra-ekstremverseminaret.html (accessed 9 May 2016).

Nowlan, Linda, 'Arctic legal regime for environmental protection', in *IUCN Environmental Policy and Law Paper* (Cambridge, IUCN, 2001).

Nuttall, Mark, 'The Isukasia iron ore mine controversy: Extracting industries and public consultation in Greenland', *Nordia Geographical Publications* 41/5 (2012), pp. 23–34.

Nuttall, Mark, 'Zero-tolerance, uranium and Greenland's mining future', *Polar Journal* 3/2 (2013), pp. 368–83.

Nuttall, Mark, 'Subsurface politics: Greenlandic discourses on extractive industries', in L. C. Jensen and G. Hønneland (eds), *Handbook of the Politics of the Arctic* (Cheltenham, Edward Elgar, 2015), pp. 105–27.

Nybø, Signe, Karl-Birger Strann, Jarle W. Bjerke, Hans Tømmervik, Dagmar Hagen and Annika Hofgaard, *Tilpasninger til klimaendringer i Nord-Norge og på Svalbard. Vurdering av vernebehovet og terrestriske økosystemers evne til å binde karbon* (2009).

Available at http://www.nina.no/archive/nina/PppBasePdf/rapport/2009/436.pdf (accessed 14 May 2016).

Nye, Joseph S., 'Public diplomacy and soft power', *Annals of the American Academy of Political and Social Science* 616/1 (2008), pp. 94–109.

Offerdal, Kristine, 'Oil gas and the environment', in O. S. Stokke and G. Hønneland (eds), *International Cooperation and Arctic Governance: Regime Effectiveness and Northern Region Building* (Abingdon, Routledge, 2007), pp. 138–64.

Offerdal, Kristine, 'The EU in the Arctic: In pursuit of legitimacy and influence', *International Journal* 66/44 (2011), pp. 861–77.

Ohnishi, Fujio, 'Japan's Arctic policy development: From engagement to a strategy', in L. Lunde, J. Yang and I. Stensdal (eds), *Asian Countries and the Arctic Future* (Singapore, World Scientific, 2015).

Okuyama, Yutaka, 'The dispute over the Kurile Islands between Russia and Japan in the 1990s', *Pacific Affairs* 76/1 (2003), pp. 37–53.

Orttung, Robert W., 'Russia's use of PR as a foreign policy tool', *Russian Analytical Digest* 81 (2010), pp. 7–10.

Østreng, Willy (ed.), *The Natural and Societal Challenges of the Northern Sea Route: A Reference Work* (Dordrecht, Kluwer Academic, 1999).

Øverland, Indra and Hilde Kutschera, 'Pricing pain: Social discontent versus political willpower in Russia's gas sector', *Europe-Asia Studies* 63/2 (2011), pp. 311–29.

Paasche, Øyvind, 'The race for Arctic energy resources', *oilprice.com*, 11 April 2011. Available at https://oilprice.com/Geopolitics/International/The-Race-For-Arctic-Energy-Resources.html (accessed 7 March 2018).

Paasi, Anssi, 'Region and place: Regional identity in question', *Progress in Human Geography* 27 (2003), pp. 475–85.

PAME (Protection of the Arctic Marine Environment), *Program for the Protection of the Arctic Marine Environment PAME* (2005). Available at http://www.pame.is/images/02_Document_Library/Meeting_Reports/PAME%20report%20II-2005.pdf (accessed 18 May 2016).

PAME (Protection of the Arctic Marine Environment), *Program for the Protection of the Arctic Marine Environment PAME* (2006), appendix V–1. Available at http://www.pame.is/images/02_Document_Library/Meeting_Reports/PAME%20report%20I-2006.pdf (accessed 18 May 2016).

PAME (Protection of the Arctic Marine Environment), *Arctic Marine Shipping Assessment 2009 Report* (2009).

PAME (Protection of the Arctic Marine Environment), *PAME Working Group Meeting Report No: PAME I-2009* (2009). Available at https://pame.is/images/02_Document_Library/Meeting_Reports/PAME_I-2009Report._samsett.pdf (accessed 18 May 2016).

PAME (Protection of the Arctic Marine Environment), *PAME Working Group Meeting Report No: PAME I-2009* (2010), annex II. Available at http://www.pame.is/images/02_Document_Library/Meeting_Reports/PAME_I-2009Report._samsett.pdf (accessed 18 May 2016).

PAME (Protection of the Arctic Marine Environment), *Working Group Meeting Report* (2014). Available at http://www.pame.is/images/02_Document_Library/Meeting_Reports/Meeting_Reports/PAME_II_2014_Meeting_Report.pdf (accessed 1 May 2016).

PAME (Protection of the Arctic Marine Environment), *Final draft PAME Work Plan for the SAO Report to Ministers* (2015). Available at https://oaarchive.arctic-council.org/bitstream/handle/11374/1472/PAME_WORKPLAN_Doc2_Final_work_plan_2015-2017_AC_SAO_CA04.pdf?sequence=2&isAllowed=y (accessed 19 May 2016).

PAME (Protection of the Arctic Marine Environment), *Arctic Ship Traffic Data (ASTD) Project Plan* (2016). Available at http://www.pame.is/index.php/projects/arctic-marine-shipping/heavy-fuel-in-the-arctic-phase-i (accessed 1 May 2016).

PAME (Protection of the Arctic Marine Environment), *PAME I-2016 Meeting Report* (2016). Available at http://www.pame.is/images/02_Document_Library/Meeting_Reports/2016/PAME_I_2016_Meeting_Report.pdf (accessed 21 May 2016).

Pan, Min and Henry P. Huntington, 'A precautionary approach to fisheries in the Central Arctic Ocean: Policy, Science, and China', *Marine Policy* 63 (2016), pp. 153–7.

Parkinson, Claire L., 'Recent trend reversals in Arctic Sea ice extents: Possible connections to the North Atlantic Oscillation', *Polar Geography* 31/1–2 (2008), pp. 3–14.

Parliament of Greenland, 'Inatsisartutlov nr. 25 af 18. december 2012 om bygge- og anlægsarbejder ved storskalaprojekter' ('Parliament of Greenland's Act 25 of 18 December 2012 regarding construction of large-scale projects') (2012). Available at http://lovgivning.gl/lov?rid={6D7F52B4-6893-4BDC-A943-601817D309A0(accessed 10 August 2016).

Pedersen, Torbjørn, 'The constrained politics of the Svalbard offshore area', *Marine Policy* 32 (2008), pp. 913–19.

Pedersen, Torbjørn, 'Denmark's policies toward the Svalbard area', *Ocean Development and International Law* 40 (2009), pp. 319–32.

Pedersen, Torbjørn, 'Norway's rule on Svalbard: Tightening the grip on the Arctic islands', *Polar Record* 45 (2009), pp. 147–52.

Pedersen, Torbjørn, 'International law and politics in US policy making: The United States and the Svalbard dispute', *Ocean Development and International Law* 42 (2011), pp. 120–35.

Pendlebury, David A., *White paper: Using bibliometrics in evaluating research* (Sydney, Thomson Reuters, 2008).

Peng, Jingchao and Njord Wegge, 'China's bilateral diplomacy in the Arctic', *Polar Geography* 38/3 (2015), pp. 233–49.

Pharand, Donat, 'The Arctic Waters and the Northwest Passage: A final revisit', *Ocean Development and International Law* 38 (2007), pp. 3–69.

Pielke, Roger, Gwyn Prins, Steve Rayner and Daniel Sarewitz, 'Lifting the taboo on adaptation', *Nature* 445/8 (2007), pp. 597–8.

Poppick, Laura 'Black carbon soot greater in China, India than thought', *Live Science*, 27 January 2014. Available at https://www.livescience.com/42872-black-carbon-exposure.html (accessed 7 May 2018).

Posol'stvo Rossii V Kitae, 'Sovmestnaya Deklaratsiya Rossiyskoy Federatsii i Kitayskoy Narodnoy Respubliki 2004 godu' (2010). Available at http://www.russia.org.cn/rus/2839/31292776.html (accessed 3 January 2011).

Presidential Administration, 'Dogovor o granitse v Barentsevom More ukrepit pravaoy rezhim v Arktike' (2010). Available at http://www.rian.ru/arctic_news/20100915/275973370.html (accessed 2 March 2011).

Presidential Press Service, 'Nachalo vstrechi s premer-ministrom Latvii Aygarsom Kalvitiso' (Presidency of the Russian Federation, 2007). Available at http://archive.kremlin.ru/text/appears/2007/03/121013.shtml (accessed 3 January 2011).

Presidential Press Service, 'Vystuplenie na soveshchanii s rossiyskimi poslami i postoyannimi predstavitelyami v mezhdunarodnykh organizatsiyakh' (2010). Available at www.kremlin.ru/transcripts/8325 (accessed 18 December 2010).

Putin, Vladimir, *Prime Minister Vladimir Putin addresses the international forum 'The Arctic: Territory of Dialogue'* (2010). Available at http://premier.gov.ru/eng/events/news/12304/ (accessed 18 December 2010) (official translation).

Putnam, Robert D., 'Diplomacy and domestic politics: The logic of two-level game', *International Organization* 42/3 (1988), pp. 427–60.

Reiersen, Lars-Otto, Simon J. Wilson and V. Kimstach, 'Circumpolar perspectives on persistent organic pollutants: the Arctic Monitoring and Assessment Programme', in D. L. Downie and T. Fenge (eds), *Northern Lights Against POPs: Combatting Toxic Threats in the Arctic* (Montreal, McGill-Queen's University Press, 2003), pp. 60–86.

RIA Novosti, 'Osvoenie arkticheskogo shelfa mozhet nachatsya lish cherez 12-15 let' (2010). Available at http://www.rosgranitsa.ru/about/international/countries/delimitation (accessed 3 January 2011).

Ringmar, Erik, *Identity, Interest and Action: A Cultural Explanation of Sweden's Intervention in the Thirty Years War* (Cambridge, Cambridge University Press, 1996).

Ringmar, Erik, 'Inter-textual relations: The quarrel over the Iraq War as conflict between narrative types', *Cooperation and Conflict* 41 (2006), pp. 403–21.

Ringmar, Erik, 'The recognition game: Soviet Russia against the west', *Cooperation and Conflict* 37 (2002), pp. 115–36.

Roach, J. Ashley and Robert W. Smith, 'Policy governing the continental shelf of the United States of America', in J. A. Roach and R. W. Smith, *Excessive Maritime Claims* (Hague, Martinus Nijhoff, 2012).

Roache, Shaun K., 'China's impact on world commodity markets (IMF Working Paper no. 12/115) (Washington, DC, IMF, 2012).

ROIS (Research Organization of Information and Systems), *Research Organization of Information and Systems 2011* (Tokyo, ROIS, 2011). Available at http://www.rois.ac.jp/pdf/youran_2011e.pdf (accessed 5 December 2014).

Rosendal, Kristin, 'Norway in UN environmental politics: Ambitions and influence', *International Environmental Agreements: Politics, Law and Economics* 7/4 (2007), pp. 439–55.

Rosendal, Kristin and Peter J. Schei, 'Convention on Biological Diversity: From national conservation to global responsibility', in S. Andresen, E. L. Boasson and G. Hønneland (eds), *International Environmental Agreements: An Introduction* (New York, Routledge, 2011).

Røseth, Tom, 'Russia's China policy in the Arctic', *Strategic Analysis* 38/6 (2014), pp. 841–59.

Rosgranitsa, *Informatsiya o delimitatsii i demarkatsii gosudarstvennoy granitsy Rossiyskoy Federatsii* (Rosgranitsa, 2011). Available at http://www.rosgranitsa.ru/about/international/countries/delimitation (accessed 3 January 2011).

Rottem, Svein Vigeland, 'A note on the Arctic Council agreements', *Ocean Development & International Law* 46/1 (2015), pp. 50–9.

Rotterdam Convention on the Prior Informed Consent Procedure for Certain Hazardous Chemicals and Pesticides in International Trade. Available at http://www.pic.int/TheConvention/Overview/TextoftheConvention/tabid/1048/language/en-US/Default.aspx (accessed 23 April 2018).

Rowe, Elana Wilson and Stina Torjesen, 'Key features of Russian multilateralism', in E. W. Rowe and S. Torjesen (eds), *The Multilateral Dimension in Russian foreign policy* (London, Routledge, 2009), pp. 1–20.

Russian Federation, 'Russian Federation Submission to the Commission on the Limits of the Continental Shelf', Executive Summary (2001). Available at http://www.un.org/depts/los/clcs_new/clcs_home.htm (accessed 24 April 2018).

Russian Federation, 'Revision of the Partial Submission to Commission on the Limits of the Continental Shelf Related to the Sea of Okhotsk', Executive Summary (2013).

Russian Federation, 'Partial Revised Submission of the Russian Federation to the Commission on the Limits of the Continental Shelf in Respect of the Continental Shelf in the Arctic Ocean', Executive Summary (2015). Available at http://www.un.org/depts/los/clcs_new/clcs_home.htm (accessed 24 April 2018).

Russian Federation and Kingdom of Norway, 'Agreement between the Russian Federation and the Kingdom of Norway on the maritime delimitation in the Varangerfjord area' (11 July 2007). Available at http://www.un.org/Depts/los/doalos_publications/LOSBulletins/bulletinpdf/bulletin67e.pdf (accessed 25 January 2011).

Russian Ministry of Foreign Affairs, 'Comment by the Information and Press Department on Russia's application for Arctic shelf expansion', 4 August 2015. Available at http://en.mid.ru/en/%20web/guest/foreign_policy/news//asset_publisher/cKNonkJE02Bw/content/id/1633205 (accessed 24 April 2018).

Sabyrov, A. S., *Obzor pravovoy basy: Natsionalnoe zakonodatelstvo respubliki Kazakhstan* (OSCE Academy, n.d.), pp. 11–12. Available at http://www.osce-academy.org/uploads/files/Republic_of_Kazakhstan.pdf (accessed 3 January 2011).

SaGAA (National Conference on Science and Geopolitics of Arctic and Antarctic), *Brochure* (New Delhi, SaGAA, 2011). Available at http://www.sagaa.co.in/pdf_files/brochure.pdf (accessed 26 October 2012).

Security Council of Russia, 'Osnovy gosudarstvennoy politiki Rossiyskoy Federatsii v Arktike na period do 2020 gode i dal'neyshuyu perspektivu', signed by President Dmitry Medvedev on 18 September 2008. Available at http://www.scrf.gov.ru/documents/15/98.html (accessed 19 December 2010) (our translation).

Selin, Henrik, *Towards International Chemical Safety: Taking Action on Persistent Organic Pollutants (POPs)* (Linköping, Department of Water and Environmental Studies, Linköping University, 2007).

Selin, Henrik, *Global Governance of Hazardous Chemicals. Challenges of Multilevel Management* (Cambridge, MIT Press, 2010).

Selliaas, Andreas, *Russland, Litauen og Kaliningrad – tre enheter, to land, en utfordring?*, FFI report (2002). Available at http://rapporter.ffi.no/rapporter/2002/02023.pdf (accessed 3 January 2011).

Shaffer, Gregory C. and Mark A. Pollack, 'Hard vs. soft law: Alternatives, complements and antagonists in international governance', *Minnesota Law Review* 94/3 (2009), pp. 706–99.

Shearer, Russel and Siu-Ling Han, 'Canadian research and POPs: The Northern Containments Program', in D. L. Downie and T. Fenge (eds), *Northern Lights Against POPs: Combatting Toxic Threats in the Arctic* (Montreal, McGill-Queen's University Press, 2003), pp. 41–60.

Shelton, Dinah (ed.), *Commitment and Compliance: The Role of Non-Binding Norms in the International Legal System* (Oxford, Oxford University Press, 2003).

Shelton, Dinah, 'Introduction: Law, non-law and the problem of "soft law"', in D. Shelton (ed.), *Commitment and Compliance: The Role of Non-Binding Norms in the International Legal System* (Oxford, Oxford University Press, 2003), pp. 1–18.

Shimada, Koji, Takashi Kamoshida, Motoyo Itoh, Shigeto Nishino, Eddy Carmack, Fiona McLaughlin, Sarah Zimmermann and Andrey Proshutinsky, 'Pacific Ocean inflow: Influence on catastrophic reduction of sea ice cover in the Arctic Ocean', *Geophysical Research Letters* 33/8 (2006), pp. 1–4.

Skjærseth, Jon B. (ed.), *International Regimes and Norway's Environmental Policy – Crossfire and Coherence* (Farnham, Ashgate, 2004).

Skjærseth, Jon B., 'International ozone policies: Effective international cooperation', in S. Andresen, E. L. Boasson and G. Hønneland (eds), *International Environmental Agreements: An Introduction* (New York, Routledge, 2012), pp. 38–48.

Slezkine, Yuri, 'Introduction: Siberia as history', in G. Diment and Y. Slezkine (eds), *Between Heaven and Hell: The Myth of Siberia in Russian Culture* (New York, St. Martin's Press, 1993), pp. 1–6.

Smith, Robert W., 'United States–Russia maritime boundary', in G. H. Blake (ed.), *Maritime Boundaries* (New York, Routledge, 1994).

Soltvedt, Ida F., 'Soft law, solid implementation? The influence of precision, monitoring and stakeholder involvement on Norwegian implementation of Arctic Council recommendations', *Arctic Review on Law and Politics* 8 (2017), pp. 73–94.

Somers, Margaret R., 'The narrative constitution of identity: A relational and network approach', *Theory and Society* 23 (1994), pp. 605–49.

Sørensen, Alex Kjær, 'Grønnland' ('Greenland') (2015). Available at http://danmarkshistorien.dk/leksikon-og-kilder/vis/materiale/groenland/ (accessed 11 December 2015).

Srinivas, T. N., S. S. N. Rao, P. V. V. Reddy, M. S. Pratibha, B. Sailaja, B. Kavya, K. H. Kishore, Z. Begum, S. M. Singh and S. Shivaji, 'Bacterial diversity and bioprospecting for cold-active lipases, amylases and proteases, from culturable bacteria of Kongsfjorden and Ny-Alesund, Svalbard, Arctic', *Current Microbiology* 59/5 (2009), pp. 537–47.

State Council, 'China's Arctic Policy' (The State Council Information Office of the People's Republic of China, 26 January 2018). Available at http://english.gov.cn/archive/white_paper/2018/01/26/content_281476026660336.htm (accessed 4 May 2018).

Statistics Greenland, *Statbank* Greenland (dataset) (2016). Available at http://bank.stat.gl/pxweb/en/?rxid=d427561b-fde7-411d-a2c1-191223cb0f83 (accessed 10 August 2016).

Statistics Greenland, *Statistisk årbog 2016* ('Statistical Yearbook 2016') (2016). Available at http://www.stat.gl/sa/saD2016.pdf (accessed 10 August 2016).

Stensdal, Iselin, 'Arctic mining: Asian interests and opportunities', in L. Lunde J. Yang and I. Stensdal (eds), *Asian Countries and the Arctic Future* (Singapore, World Scientific, 2015), pp. 154–67.

Stensdal, Iselin, 'Coming of age? Asian Arctic research, 2004–2013', *Polar Record* 52/2 (2016), pp. 134–43.

Stockholm Convention, 'The New POPs' (2016). Available at http://chm.pops.int/TheConvention/ThePOPs/TheNewPOPs/tabid/2511/Default.aspx (accessed 22 August 2017).

Stockholm Convention, 'Effectiveness evaluation of the Stockholm Convention on Persistent Organic Pollutants pursuant to Article 16' (2017). Available at https://www.informea.org/sites/default/files/imported-documents/UNEP-POPS-COP.8-22.English.pdf (accessed 18 August 2017).

Stokke, Olav S., 'Managing straddling stocks: The interplay of global and regional regimes', *Ocean & Coastal Management* 43/2–3 (2000), pp. 205–34.

Stokke, Olav S., 'A legal regime for the Arctic? Interplay with the Law of the Sea Convention', *Marine Policy* 31/4 (2007), pp. 402–8.

Stokke, Olav S., 'Interplay management, niche selection, and Arctic environmental governance', in S. Oberthür and O. S. Stokke (eds), *Managing Institutional Complexity: Regime Interplay and Global Environmental Change* (Cambridge, MIT Press, 2011), pp. 143–70.

Stokke, Olav S., *Disaggregating International Regimes: A New Approach to Evaluation and Comparison* (London, MIT Press, 2012).

Stokke, Olav S., 'The Law of the Sea', in G. Ritzer (ed.), *Wiley–Blackwell Encyclopedia of Globalization*, vol. 3 (New York, Wiley-Blackwell, 2012), pp. 1280–2.

Stokke, Olav S., 'Regime interplay in Arctic shipping governance: Explaining regional niche selection', *International Environmental Agreements: Politics, Law and Economics* 13 (2013), pp. 65–85.

Stokke, Olav S., 'Asian stakes and arctic governance', *Strategic Analysis* 38/6 (2014), pp. 770–8.

Stokke, Olav S., 'Geopolitics, governance, and Arctic fisheries politics', in E. Conde and S. S. Iglesias (eds), *Global Challenges in the Arctic Region: Sovereignty, the Environment and Geopolitical Balance* (London, Routledge, 2017), pp. 170–96.

Stokke, Olav S. and Davor Vidas (eds), *Governing the Antarctic: The Effectiveness and Legitimacy of the Antarctic Treaty System* (Cambridge, Cambridge University Press, 1996).

Stokke, Olav S. and Geir Hønneland (eds), *International Cooperation and Arctic Governance: Regime Effectiveness and Northern Region Building* (London, Routledge, 2007).

Stokke, Olav S. and Ola Tunander, *The Barents Region: Cooperation in Arctic Europe* (London, Sage, 1994).

Stokke, Olav S., Geir Hønneland and Peter Johan Schei, 'Pollution and Conservation', in O. S. Stokke and G. Hønneland (eds), *International Cooperation and Arctic Governance: Regime Effectiveness and Northern Region Building* (London, Routledge, 2007), pp. 78–111.

Stone, David P., *The Changing Arctic Environment: The Arctic Messenger* (New York, Cambridge University Press, 2015).

Su, Ping and Marc Lanteigne, 'China's developing Arctic policies: Myths and misconceptions', *Journal of China and International Relations* 3/1 (2015).

Synergies among the Basel, Rotterdam and Stockholm conventions. Available at http://www.brsmeas.org/2017COPs/MeetingDocuments/tabid/5385/language/en-US/Default.aspx (accessed23 April 2018).

Szajkowski, Bogdan, 'Will Russia disintegrate into Bantustans?', *The World Today* 49/8–9 (1993), pp. 172–6.

Taagholt, Jørgen and Kent Brooks, 'Mineral riches: A route to Greenland's independence?', *Polar Record* 52/3 (2016), pp. 360–71.

Tamnes, Rolf, *Oljealder 1965–1995 – Norsk utenrikspolitisk historie, bind 6* (Oslo, Universitetsforlaget, 1997).

Third National Assessment of Climate Change Writing Committee, *The Third National Assessment of Climate Change* (in Chinese) (2015).

Third United Nations Conference on the Law of the Sea, Official Records, Vol. VIII, United Nations (1977).

Thürer, Daniel, 'Soft law', in R. Bernhardt (ed.), *Encyclopedia of Public International Law* (Amsterdam, Elsevier, 2000), pp. 452–60.

Timtchenko, Leonid, 'The Russian Arctic sectoral concept: Past and present', *Arctic* 50 (1997), pp. 29–35.

Tonami, Aki, 'The Arctic policy of China and Japan: Multi-layered economic and strategic motivations', *Polar Journal* 4/1 (2014), pp. 105–26.

Tsygankov, Andreo P., 'Russia in the post-western world: The end of the normalization paradigm?', *Post-Soviet Affairs* 25/4 (2009), pp. 347–69.

Uibopuu, Henn-Juri, 'The Caspian Sea: A tangle of legal problems', *The World Today* 51/6 (1995), pp. 119–23.

Ulfstein, Geir, *The Svalbard Treaty: From Terra Nullius to Norwegian Sovereignty* (Oslo, Scandinavian University Press, 1995).

Ulfstein, Geir and Tore Henriksen, 'Maritime delimitation in the Arctic: The Barents Sea Treaty', *Ocean Development & International Law* 42 (2011), pp. 1–21.

Underdal, Arild, 'Science and politics: The anatomy of an uneasy partnership, in S. Andresen, T. Skodvin, A. Underdal and J. Wettestad (eds), *Science and Politics in International Environmental Regimes* (Manchester, Manchester University Press, 2000).

Underdal, Arild, 'Meeting common environmental challenges: The co-evolution of policies and practices', *International Environmental Agreements: Politics, Law and Economics* 13/1 (2013), pp. 15–30.

UN General Assembly, *Fifty-seventh Session, Agenda item 25 (a) Oceans and the law of the sea – Report of the Secretary-General.* Addendum A/57/57/Add.1, 8 October 2002. Available at http://www.un.org/Depts/los/general_assembly/general_assembly_reports.htm (accessed 27 December 2010).

UN General Assembly, 'Report of the UN Secretary-General to the Fifty-Seventh Session of the UN General Assembly under the agenda item "Oceans and the Law of the Sea"', Doc. A/57/57/Add.1, 8 October 2002, para. 41.

United Nations Convention on the Law of the Sea, 10 December 1982, 1833 UNTS.

United States of America and Russian Federation, 'Agreement between the United States and the Soviet Union on the Maritime Boundary', 1 June 1990, in *International Legal Materials*, vol. 29 (1990), p. 941.

Valk, Nathaniel P., *Arctic Council Soft Law: An Effective Analysis* (2012).

VanderZwaag, David, Aldo Chircop, Erik Franckx, Hugh Kindred, Kenneth MacInnis, *Governance of Arctic Marine Shipping* (Halifax, Dalhousie University, 2008). Available at http://arcticportal.org/uploads/bC/JU/bCJUaKAo52XTtHDZ359QNA/5.novAMSA-Governance-of-Arctic-Marine-Shipping-Final-Report-1-Aug.pdf (accessed 20 May 2014).

van Dijk, Pieter, *Iron Ore (Q2, 2015-Q3, 2015)* (Quarterly Commodity Insights Bulletin December 2015) (2015). Available at https://assets.kpmg.com/content/dam/kpmg/pdf/2015/12/iron-ore-2015-Q4.pdf (accessed 20 March 2018).

Victor, David G., *Global Warming Gridlock: Creating More Effective Strategies for Protecting the Planet* (Cambridge, Cambridge University Press, 2011).

Victor, David G., Kal Raustiala and Eugene B. Skolnikoff, *The Implementation and Effectiveness of International Environmental Commitments: Theory and Practice* (Cambridge, MIT Press, 1998).

Vihma, Timo, 'Effects of Arctic sea ice decline on weather and climate: A review', *Surveys in Geophysics* 35/5 (2014).

Virkkunen, Joni, 'Post-socialist borderland: Promoting or challenging the enlarged European Union', *Geographical Annals* 83/3 (2001), pp. 141–51.

Vylegzhanin, A. N. and V. K. Zilanov, *Spitsbergen: Legal Regime of Adjacent Marine Areas* (Utrecht, Eleven International Publishing, 2007).

Wæver, Ole, 'Insecurity, security and asecurity in the West European non-war community', in E. Adleer and M. Barnett (eds), *Security Communities* (Cambridge, Cambridge University Press, 1998), pp. 69–118.

Wang, Xuezhong, Sun Zhaobo and Hu Banghui, 'Relationship between Arctic sea ice thickness distribution and climate of China', *Acta Meteor Sinica* 26/2 (2012), pp. 189–204.

Weiss, Edith B. and Harold Jacobson, *Engaging Countries: Strengthening Compliance with International Environmental Accords* (Cambridge, MIT Press, 1998).

Wendt, Alexander, 'Anarchy is what states make of it: The social construction of power politics', *International Organization* 46 (1992), pp. 391–425.

Wettestad, Jørgen, *Clearing the Air – European Advances in Tackling Acid Rain and Atmospheric Pollution* (Farnham, Ashgate, 2002).

Widdis, Emma, 'Russia as space' in S. Franklin and E. Widdis (eds), *National Identity in Russian Culture: An Introduction* (Cambridge, Cambridge University Press, 2004), pp. 30–49.

Wilson, Andrew and Nicu Popescu, 'Russian and European neighbourhood policies compared', *Southeast European and Black Sea Studies* 9/3 (2009), pp. 317–31.

World Bank, 'World databank' (2014). Available at http://databank.worldbank.org/data/home.aspx (accessed 5 November 2014).

Wright, David Curtis, 'The dragon eyes the top of the world' (Washington DC, US Naval War College, China Maritime Studies Institute, 2011).

Wright, David Curtis, 'The dragon eyes the top of the world – Arctic policy debate and discussion in China', *China Maritime Study* 8/47 (2011). Available at http://www.andrewerickson.com/wp-content/uploads/2017/09/China-Maritime-Study-8_China-Arctic-Policy-Debate_Wright_201108.pdf (accessed 13 March 2018).

Wu, Bingyi, Renhe Zhang, Rosanne D'Arrigo and Junzhi Su, 'On the relationship between winter sea ice and summer atmospheric circulation over Eurasia', *Journal of Climate* 26 (2013), pp. 5523–36.

Wübbeke, Jost, 'China's climate change expert community – principles, mechanisms and influence', *Journal of Contemporary China* 22/82 (2013), pp. 712–31.

Xing, Li and Rasmus Gjedssø Bertelsen, 'The drivers of Chinese Arctic interests: Political stability and energy and transportation security', *Arctic Yearbook* (2013). Available at https://www.arcticyearbook.com/2013-articles/57-the-drivers-of-chinese-arctic-interests-political-stability-and-energy-and-transportation-security (accessed 14 March 2018).

Young, Oran R., *International Governance: Protecting the Environment in a Stateless Society* (Ithaca, Cornell University Press, 1994).

Young, Oran R., 'If an Arctic treaty is not the solution, what is the alternative?', *Polar Record* 47/4 (2011), pp. 327–34.

Zhang, Pei and Yang Jian, 'Changes in the Arctic and China's participation in Arctic governance', in L. Lunde, J. Yang and I. Stensdal (eds), *Asian Countries and the Arctic Future* (Singapore, World Scientific Publishing, 2016).

Zysk, Katarzyna, 'The evolving Arctic security environment: An assessment', in S. Blank (ed.), *Russia in the Arctic* (Carlisle, Strategic Studies Institute of the US Army War College, 2011), pp. 91–138

Zysk, Katarzyna, 'Russia turns north, again: Interests, policies and the search for coherence', in L. C. Jensen and G. Hønneland (eds), *Handbook on the Politics of the Arctic* (Cheltenham, Edward Elgar, 2015), pp. 437–61.

INDEX

Page numbers in *italic* denote figures, those in **bold**, tables.

www.ingramcontent.com/pod-product-compliance
Lightning Source LLC
Chambersburg PA
CBHW070901080426
R18103400001B/R181034PG41932CBX00007B/13
9780755636518